Property Law

Cases and Materials

Volume

2022

Elena Maria Marty-Nelson

Associate Dean Academic Affairs and Professor of Law
Nova Southeastern University College of Law

Eloisa C. Rodriguez-Dod

Associate Dean Academic Affairs and Professor of Law
Florida International University College of Law

Property Law Cases and Materials Open-Source is copyright 2022 by Elena Maria Marty-Nelson and Eloisa C. Rodriguez-Dod. This work may be reused under the terms of the Creative Commons Attribution-NonCommercial-ShareAlike 4.0 International License, https://creativecommons.org/licenses/by-nc-sa/4.0/.

Welcome to property law.

We are excited about this open-source property casebook. We hope that you will enjoy your foray into property law and expect you will find it as fascinating as we do. This volume, Volume One, examines fundamental concepts of property law, including possession, relativity of title, and allocation of property rights. The chapters in this volume include the topics of the rule of capture, found property, bailments, gifts, adverse possession, concurrent ownership, marital interests, homestead, estates in land, future interests, easements, licenses, servitudes, homeowners' associations, condominiums, and cooperatives. Volume Two continues our exploration of property law. The chapters in Volume Two include the topics of zoning, takings, competing sovereigns and treaties, contracts of sale, deeds, recording, chain of title, financing, housing discrimination, landlord and tenant, and an introduction to intellectual property law.

This casebook is designed as a teaching tool. Accordingly, we liberally omit footnotes, internal case citations, headings, and concurring and dissenting opinions without notation. Elisions of substantive text are indicated by ellipses or asterisks. Footnotes that are retained may be renumbered from the original source, but we include Editorial Notes indicating the original footnote number.

A word about the cover art. The depiction is a map of the Florida Everglades. As we both teach in law schools located near the southern Everglades, we often refer to the Everglades when discussing property law concepts.

We are grateful to the H2O team for their help with this open-source casebook and especially thank Catherine Brobston. We also appreciate the work of our research assistant, Kailie Rush. This casebook is enhanced by the spirited discussions we have had with our property law students over our decades of teaching.

Elena Maria Marty-Nelson
Eloisa C. Rodriguez-Dod
January 2022

Table of Contents

1

Chapter 1 · Introduction to Property Law

Studying property law is the beginning of an incredible adventure. This casebook introduces you to the depth and breadth of property law. The concepts discussed in this casebook also serve as the foundation for multiple upper-level courses, including Real Estate Transactions, Intellectual Property, Copyright, Patent, Trademark, Wills and Trusts, Estate Planning, Land Use, and Environmental Law. Even if you do not practice in areas typically associated with property law, such as real estate finance, environmental law, and intellectual property law, you should know that the concepts studied in this course are pervasive in legal practice.

We designed this casebook to encourage you to think about property law issues from various viewpoints, including those of planners and litigators. For that reason, although the concepts are often introduced through appellate law cases, we include numerous questions and problems requiring you to think about drafting or planning around issues for your clients. We want you to think about ways of advocating for your clients outside of litigation. We also include numerous problems asking you to put yourself in the position of advocate for one of the parties in the cases. For example, we might ask you to serve in the role of an attorney for a landlord negotiating a commercial lease with an anchor tenant. You may be asked to advocate on behalf of a party who has lived on land for many years but whose claim to the land is challenged. You may be asked to present arguments on behalf of family members challenging restrictive interpretations of zoning laws.

As you will see, property law is not static. It is developing as society changes. To think about how property law develops, you will also be asked to take on other roles as you go through the course. In some instances, you will be asked to put yourself in the position of a member of the state legislature deciding whether to propose a statute to handle certain property issues. You may also be asked to serve as a judge reviewing the arguments presented by all the parties in a case and making your determination. Finally, there is the important role of the scholar or analyst who will make arguments on how the law should and could develop for a more equitable property law system.

1.1
Introductory Terminology

This chapter begins with some terminology you will encounter at various points in your first-year Property course, in your upper-level property-related courses, and in your practice. A term that is often used to visualize the complex relationships around property is ***bundle of sticks***. Justice Sandra Day O'Connor noted in *United States v. Craft*, an opinion you will be reading in Chapter 7, that a bundle of sticks is a "common idiom" describing "a collection of individual rights which, in certain combinations, constitute property." The term is also referred to as a ***bundle of rights***, which is often described as rights in a tangible or intangible thing enforceable against third parties.

Other terminology may already be familiar. For example, you may recognize the concept of ***relativity of title***. Relativity of title recognizes that a person could have superior title to property relative to one person, but not superior title relative to another. This concept is discussed in more detail in Chapter 3 on finders. Another concept that you will be encountering in these early chapters involves distinctions between real and personal property. The term ***real property*** may be defined as land and the things attached to the land, such as buildings and structures. The term ***personal property*** may be defined simply as any property that is not real property. Note, however, that personal property can be ***tangible*** or ***intangible***. The distinction between tangible and intangible personal property turns on whether the property is subject to physical manifestation. Examples of tangible personal property include vehicles, jewelry, furniture, sports equipment, and machinery. Examples of intangible property include securities, patents, copyrights, trademarks, and goodwill.

1.2
Introductory Questions

The concepts and cases introduced in this casebook often involve myriad economic and social policy issues. As you start your journey through the cases and concepts, ask yourselves several underlying questions about the contours of property rights. How are property rights acquired? When, and why, should society recognize property rights? When two or more persons claim rights in the same property, how should property rights be allocated? What are proper limits to property rights and what obligations do holders of property rights have? How are property rights transferred during life and at death? Can a person transfer some property rights while retaining others? These and other fundamental questions which we will address in the upcoming chapters will guide you as you start exploring property law.

2

Chapter 2 · Rule of Capture

We start our analysis of the rule of capture with the classic wild animal case of *Pierson v. Post*, excerpted below, decided in 1805. We then move forward more than 200 years to the wild animal case of *Madero v. Luffey*, excerpted below, decided in 2020. As you read these cases, ask yourself whether the rule of capture as to wild animals appears to have changed during those two centuries. Also, ask yourself the following questions. When are wild animals deemed property? Should wild animals be deemed property? More broadly, as you read these wild animal cases, consider topics beyond wild animals and ask yourself what role the rule of capture plays or should play in other areas. For example, in *Briggs v. Southwestern Energy Production Company*, excerpted below, the court is asked to address whether the rule of capture applies to oil and gas obtained through hydraulic fracturing. As you read the cases in this chapter, you should also ponder the role that possession plays in allocating property rights.

2.1

Pierson v. Post
3 Cai. R. 175 (N.Y. Sup. 1805)

New York Supreme Court of Judicature

THIS was an action of trespass on the case commenced in a justice's court, by the present defendant against the now plaintiff.

The declaration stated that *Post,* being in possession of certain dogs and hounds under his command, did, "upon a certain wild and uninhabited, unpossessed and waste land, called the beach, find and start one of those noxious beasts called a fox," and whilst there hunting, chasing and pursuing the same with his dogs and hounds, and when in view thereof, *Pierson,* well knowing the fox was so hunted and pursued, did, in the sight of *Post,* to prevent his catching the same, kill and carry it off. A verdict having been rendered for the plaintiff below, the defendant there sued out a *certiorari,* and now assigned for error, that the declaration and the matters therein contained were not sufficient in law to maintain an action.

TOMPKINS, J. delivered the opinion of the court.

This cause comes before us on a return to a *certiorari* directed to one of the justices of *Queens* county.

The question submitted by the counsel in this cause for our determination is, whether *Lodowick Post,* by the pursuit with his hounds in the manner alleged in his declaration, acquired such a right to, or property in, the fox, as will sustain an action against *Pierson* for killing and taking him away?

The cause was argued with much ability by the counsel on both sides, and presents for our decision a novel and nice question. It is admitted that a fox is an animal *feræ naturæ,* and that property in such animals is acquired by occupancy only. These admissions narrow the discussion to the simple question of what acts amount to occupancy, applied to acquiring right to wild animals?

If we have recourse to the ancient writers upon general principles of law, the judgment below is obviously erroneous. *Justinian's Institutes,* lib. 2. tit. 1. s. 13. and *Fleta,* lib. 3. c. 2. p. 175. adopt the principle, that pursuit alone vests no property or right in the huntsman; and that even pursuit, accompanied with wounding, is equally ineffectual for that purpose, unless the animal be actually taken. The same principle is recognised by *Bracton,* lib. 2. c. 1. p. 8.

Puffendorf, lib. 4. c. 6. s. 2. and 10. defines occupancy of beasts *feræ naturæ,* to be the actual corporal possession of them, and *Bynkershoek* is cited as coinciding in this definition. It is indeed with hesitation that *Puffendorf* affirms that a wild beast mortally wounded, or greatly maimed, cannot be fairly intercepted by another, whilst the pursuit of the person inflicting the wound continues. The foregoing authorities are decisive to show that mere pursuit gave *Post* no legal right to the fox, but that he became the property of *Pierson,* who intercepted and killed him.

It therefore only remains to inquire whether there are any contrary principles, or authorities, to be found in other books, which ought to induce a different decision. Most of the cases which have occurred in *England,* relating to property in wild animals, have either been discussed and decided upon the principles of their positive statute regulations, or have arisen between the huntsman and the owner of the land upon which beasts *feræ naturæ* have been apprehended; the former claiming them by title of occupancy, and the latter *ratione soli*. Little satisfactory aid can, therefore, be derived from the *English* reporters.

Barbeyrac, in his notes on *Puffendorf,* does not accede to the definition of occupancy by the latter, but, on the contrary, affirms, that actual bodily seizure is not, in all cases, necessary to constitute possession of wild animals. He does not, however, *describe* the acts which, according to his ideas, will amount to an appropriation of such animals to private use, so as to exclude the claims of all other persons, by title of occupancy, to the same animals; and he is far from averring that pursuit alone is sufficient for that purpose. To a certain extent, and as far as *Barbeyrac* appears to me to go, his objections to *Puffendorf's* definition of occupancy are reasonable and correct. That is to say, that actual bodily seizure is not indispensable to acquire right to, or possession of, wild beasts; but that, on the contrary, the mortal wounding of such beasts, by one not abandoning his pursuit, may, with the utmost propriety, be deemed possession of him; since, thereby, the pursuer manifests an unequivocal intention of appropriating the animal to his individual use, has deprived him of his natural liberty, and brought him within his certain control. So also, encompassing and securing such animals with nets and toils, or otherwise intercepting them in such a manner as to deprive them of their natural liberty, and render escape impossible, may justly be deemed to give possession of them to those persons who, by their industry and labour, have used such means of apprehending them. . . . The case now under consideration is one of mere pursuit, and presents no circumstances or acts which can bring it within the definition of occupancy by *Puffendorf* . . . or the ideas of *Barbeyrac* upon that subject.

The case cited from 11 *Mod.* 74--130. I think clearly distinguishable from the present; inasmuch as there the action was for maliciously hindering and disturbing the plaintiff in the exercise and enjoyment of a private franchise; and in the report of the same case, 3 *Salk.* 9. *Holt,* Ch. J. states, that the ducks were in the plaintiff's decoy pond, and *so in his possession,* from which it is obvious the court laid much stress in their opinion upon the plaintiff's possession of the ducks, *ratione soli.*

We are the more readily inclined to confine possession or occupancy of beasts *feræ naturæ,* within the limits prescribed by the learned authors above cited, for the sake of certainty, and preserving peace and order in society. If the first seeing, starting, or pursuing such animals, without having so wounded, circumvented or ensnared them, so as to deprive them of their natural liberty, and subject them to the control of their pursuer, should afford the basis of actions against others for intercepting and killing them, it would prove a fertile source of quarrels and litigation.

However uncourteous or unkind the conduct of *Pierson* towards *Post,* in this instance, may have been, yet his act was productive of no injury or damage for which a legal remedy can be applied. We are of opinion the judgment below was erroneous, and ought to be reversed.

LIVINGSTON, J.

My opinion differs from that of the court.

Of six exceptions, taken to the proceedings below, all are abandoned except the third, which reduces the controversy to a single question.

Whether a person who, with his own hounds, starts and hunts a fox on waste and uninhabited ground, and is on the point of seizing his prey, acquires such an interest in the animal, as to have a right of action against another, who in view of the huntsman and his dogs in full pursuit, and with knowledge of the chase, shall kill and carry him away?

This is a knotty point, and should have been submitted to the arbitration of sportsmen, without poring over *Justinian, Fleta, Bracton, Puffendorf, Locke, Barbeyrac,* or *Blackstone,* all of whom have been cited; they would have had no difficulty in coming to a prompt and correct conclusion. In a court thus constituted, the skin and carcass of poor *reynard* would have been properly disposed of, and a precedent set, interfering with no usage or custom which the experience of ages has sanctioned, and which must be so well known to every votary of *Diana.* But the parties have referred the question to our judgment, and we must dispose of it as well as we can, from the partial lights we possess, leaving to a higher tribunal, the correction of any mistake which we may be so unfortunate as to make. By the pleadings it is admitted that a fox is a "wild and noxious beast." Both parties have regarded him, as the law of nations does a pirate, "*hostem humani generis,*" and although "*de mortuis nil nisi bonum,*" be a maxim of our profession, the memory of the deceased has not been spared. His depredations on farmers and on barn yards, have not been forgotten; and to put him to death wherever found, is allowed to be meritorious, and of public benefit. Hence it follows, that our decision should have in view the greatest possible encouragement to the destruction of an animal, so cunning and ruthless in his career. But who would keep a pack of hounds; or what gentleman, at the sound of the horn, and at peep of day, would mount his steed, and for hours together, "*sub jove frigido,*" or a vertical sun, pursue the windings of this wily quadruped, if, just as night came on, and his stratagems and strength were nearly exhausted, a saucy intruder, who had not shared in the honours or labours of the chase, were permitted to come in at the death, and bear away in triumph the object of pursuit? Whatever *Justinian* may have thought of the matter, it must be recollected that his code was compiled many hundred years ago, and it would be very hard indeed, at the distance of so many centuries, not to have a right to establish a rule for ourselves. In his day, we read of no order of men who made it a business, in the language of the declaration in this cause, "with hounds and dogs to find, start, pursue, hunt, and chase," these animals, and that, too, without any other motive than the preservation of *Roman* poultry; if this diversion had been then in fashion, the lawyers who composed his institutes, would have taken care not to pass it by, without suitable encouragement. If any thing, therefore, in the digests or pandects shall appear to militate against the defendant in error, who, on this occasion, was the foxhunter, we have only to say *tempora mutantur;* and if men themselves change with the times, why should not laws also undergo an alteration?

It may be expected, however, by the learned counsel, that more particular notice be taken of their authorities. I have examined them all, and feel great difficulty in determining, whether to acquire dominion over a thing, before in common, it be sufficient that we barely see it, or know where it is, or wish for it, or make a declaration of our will respecting it; or whether, in the case of wild beasts, setting a trap, or lying in wait, or starting, or pursuing, be enough; or if an actual wounding, or killing, or bodily tact and occupation be necessary. Writers on general law, who have favoured us with their speculations on these points, differ on them all; but, great as is the diversity of sentiment among them, some conclusion must be adopted on the question immediately before us. After mature deliberation, I embrace that of *Barbeyrac,* as the most rational, and least liable to objection. If at liberty, we might imitate the courtesy of a certain emperor, who, to avoid giving offence to the advocates of any of these different doctrines, adopted a middle course, and by ingenious distinctions, rendered it difficult to say (as often happens after a fierce and angry contest) to whom the palm of victory belonged. He ordained, that if a beast be followed with *large dogs and hounds,* he shall belong to the hunter, not to the chance occupant; and in like manner, if he be killed or wounded with a lance or sword; but if chased with *beagles only,* then he passed to the captor, not to the first pursuer. If slain with a dart, a sling, or a bow, he fell to the hunter, if still in chase, and not to him who might afterwards find and seize him.

Now, as we are without any municipal regulations of our own, and the pursuit here, for aught that appears on the case, being with dogs and hounds of *imperial stature,* we are at liberty to adopt one of the provisions just cited, which comports also with the learned conclusion of *Barbeyrac,* that property in animals *feræ naturæ* may be acquired without bodily touch or manucaption, provided the pursuer be within reach, or have a *reasonable* prospect (which certainly existed here) of taking, what he has *thus* discovered an intention of converting to his own use.

When we reflect also that the interest of our husbandmen, the most useful of men in any community, will be advanced by the destruction of a beast so pernicious and incorrigible, we cannot greatly err, in saying, that a pursuit like the present, through waste and unoccupied lands, and which must inevitably and speedily have terminated in corporal possession, or bodily *seisin,* confers such a right to the object of it, as to make any one a wrongdoer, who shall interfere and shoulder the spoil. The *justice's* judgment ought, therefore, in my opinion, to be affirmed.

Judgment of reversal.

2.2

Madero v. Luffey
439 F. Supp. 3d 493 (W.D. Penn. 2020)

United States District Court, Western District Pennsylvania

STICKMAN IV, J.

Plaintiff, Ronald J. Madero ("Madero"), alleges that he took care of abandoned cats in his neighborhood, giving them food, shelter and occasional medical care. He says that the cats were, in fact, his property. At some point, complaints of neighbors led Pittsburgh Police Officer Christine Luffey ("Officer Luffey") to visit Madero to assess the situation with the cats. Madero claims that Officer Luffey lied about having a warrant in order to secure his consent to search the premises, including an abandoned residence which he could access. The search was conducted by a non-officer volunteer, Mary Kay Gentert ("Gentert"). Madero alleges that Officer Luffey used information from the search to obtain a warrant, which was later executed on his property by Officer Luffey with assistance from Gentert and Tarra Provident ("Provident"), volunteers with Homeless Cat Management Team ("HCMT"). The seized cats were taken to Humane Animal Rescue ("HAR"), a non-profit shelter, where some were euthanized. None of the cats were returned to Madero.

Madero's lengthy Complaint asserts various causes of action under 42 U.S.C. § 1983 and state law arising from an allegedly illegal search and wrongful seizure of the cats. . . .

FACTUAL AND PROCEDURAL HISTORY

Madero is a seventy-eight-year-old man who resides at 5221 ½ Lytle Street in the Hazelwood neighborhood of Pittsburgh with his son, Mark Madero ("Mark"). Mark is the owner of the properties at 5221 ½ and 5223 Lytle Street, which form a duplex. 5223 Lytle Street is not occupied, but it is kept under lock and is accessible by Madero and Mark. Madero stores some of his personal belongings in one of the rooms of 5223.

The properties sit on a dead-end street commonly used to dump abandoned cats and kittens. Madero has attempted to help the abandoned cats by working with Animal

Friends volunteers to conduct mass spay and neuters for cats in the area. He also provided private veterinary care for sick and injured cats and kittens, as well as food and winter shelter for the cats and kittens. Madero claims to have spent thousands of dollars providing veterinary care to the cats and hundreds of dollars for food and winter shelter.

On or about May 23, 2017, a neighbor of Madero contacted Animal Care and Control ("ACC") and complained about kittens abandoned in front of her residence at 5221 Lytle Street. According to Madero, the neighbor has never visited his properties and she did not complain about cats at 5221 ½ or 5223 Lytle Street. Madero states that ACC supervisor David Madden sent an email to Officer Luffey that a complaint was received about cats being kept inside 5221 ½ Lytle Street.

On or about June 15, 2017, Officer Luffey, who was on duty and wearing her uniform, traveled with Gentert to 5221 ½ Lytle Street. Gentert, who is affiliated with HCMT, previously cooperated with Officer Luffey in animal related cases. When the women encountered Madero, Officer Luffey identified herself and identified Gentert as a member of HCMT. Officer Luffey informed Madero that they wanted to inspect the inside of 5223 and 5221 ½ Lytle Street. When he refused, Madero alleges that Officer Luffey claimed to have a search warrant and said she "could bust down his door," and would "call for back up to break the door down and execute the warrant." Madero also alleges that Officer Luffey misrepresented Gentert's presence and purpose, claiming he was led to believe that Gentert was there to help Madero with his "spay and neuter" services for the cats, and it was concealed to him that Gentert was assisting Officer Luffey with an investigation.

Gentert went into 5223 Lytle Street with Madero while Officer Luffey waited outside. Gentert took photographs inside. After Gentert looked inside of 5223 Lytle Street, Officer Luffey told Madero that she and Gentert wanted to see the inside of 5221 ½ Lytle Street. Madero allowed Gentert to enter the property while Officer Luffey waited outside. Afterwards, Officer Luffey obtained a search warrant, which Madero asserts was the result of the information and photographs gathered by Gentert. The warrant identified 5223 Lytle Street as the location to be searched.

On June 29, 2017, Madero took five cats to Animal Friends for veterinary care. He brought five additional cats to Animal Friends the next day, June 30, 2017, and retrieved the first five cats that had surgery. Madero arrived home just after the arrival of Officer Luffey, and other police officers, who were executing the search warrant to seize the cats in 5223 Lytle Street. Gentert, Provident and volunteers from the ACC were present to assist with the cats that were seized.

A total of forty-two cats were seized and transferred to HAR. During the seizure of the cats, Madero contends they "were left for hours on the hot concrete, in the direct sunlight, in 80-degree weather, with no water." Madero further asserts that he was not permitted to assist with placing the cats in carriers, and that "Gentert, Provident, and the ACC used snare catch poles to strangle the cats and force them into carriers or traps [...]."

Once at HAR, Madero posits that the cats received no veterinary treatment for weeks and were kept in small cages in a windowless room. Some of the cats were euthanized. According to Madero, this was done without inquiring into the ownership of the cats, without notice to him, and pursuant to a forged surrender document.

On August 7, 2017, Officer Luffey filed a Criminal Complaint against Madero, accusing him of committing five counts of misdemeanor cruelty to animals and thirty-seven summary counts of cruelty to animals. On August 3, 2018, Madero pled *nolo contendere* to twenty counts of disorderly conduct pursuant to 18 Pa.C.S.A. § 5503(a)(4) at Criminal Docket Number CP-02-CR-0012086-2017 in the Allegheny County Court of Common Pleas of Pennsylvania. He was sentenced to ninety days probation for each count of disorderly conduct, with all twenty sentences to run consecutively.

STANDARD OF REVIEW

A motion to dismiss filed pursuant to Federal Rule of Civil Procedure 12(b)(6) tests the legal sufficiency of the complaint. A plaintiff must allege sufficient facts that, if accepted as true, state a claim for relief that is plausible on its face. A court must accept all well-pleaded factual allegations as true and view them in the light most favorable to the plaintiff.

***

ANALYSIS

***

A. MADERO HAS ADEQUATELY PLED THAT THE CATS WERE HIS PROPERTY.

T.S. Eliot wrote that "the naming of cats is a difficult matter.'"[1] So is, in some circumstances, determining whether someone owns them. Each of the Defendants asserts as a threshold matter that Madero did not own the cats in question and, therefore, cannot maintain many of the statutory and common-law claims that he raises. In other words, they argue that if the cats were not Madero's property, he lacks the standing to assert a claim that they were unconstitutionally seized, or that their seizure will support any of the common law claims that he asserts.

Defendants argue that the Complaint pleads that the cats were merely strays that Madero took care of, rather than his property. Madero rejects this contention. Because a finding that Madero did not have a property interest in the cats would dispose of several of the claims at once, the Court will address this issue first. Determining the ownership of the cats at issue is, as explained below, a "difficult matter."

The Complaint avers that "[t]he 42 cats were property of Mr. Madero." However, "conclusory or bare-bones allegations will no longer survive a motion to dismiss: 'threadbare recitals of the elements of a cause of action, supported by mere conclusory statements, do not suffice.'" *Fowler*, 578 F.3d at 210. Here, the allegations of Madero's Complaint, when viewed as a whole, call into question his conclusory assertions that the cats were his property.

The Complaint asserts that many, if not all, of the cats at issue were strays that Madero cared for in various ways. It states that Madero's residence is on a dead-end street that is "frequently used by people as a dumping ground for unwanted cats and kittens, many of which are abandoned in an unhealthy condition." Madero pleads that he "has done his best to help the cats and kittens abandoned in his neighborhood," "has spent thousands of dollars to provide veterinary care for sick and injured cats and kittens abandoned in his neighborhood," and "spent hundreds of dollars per month on cat food and provided winter shelter for the cats and kittens abandoned in his neighborhood." Further, while Madero lived at 5221 ½ Lytle Street, he had access to an abandoned duplex, located at 5223 Lytle Street, where he permitted several of the cats to stay. Thus, the Complaint makes clear that the cats originated as strays or abandoned cats that Madero acquired, if at all, by providing food, shelter and, occasionally, medical care to them.

Cats have been kept as pets for millennia[2] and are the second-most common pets currently kept in the United States. It may be surprising, then, that the law is unclear as to how one can obtain a property interest in a cat.[3] The cats at issue here were not purchased, adopted or kept as house-cats. If they were, there would be little question that they were Madero's property. Rather, the cats in this case were, as detailed in the Complaint, abandoned in the neighborhood and lived outdoors or in an abandoned structure. There is no specific Pennsylvania authority as to whether and to what extent such cats will be considered a person's property. Indeed, while there have been several state and federal cases which concerned the seizure of cats and other animals, none specifically address the question of whether and by what means a stray cat can be acquired as property.

The nature of cats as pets complicates the question of ownership. While many cats are kept inside, as house pets, many are free to roam around outdoors some or all of the time. Indeed, "[i]t is estimated that over 30% of the approximately 73 million owned cats in the United States are allowed to freely roam outdoors." *See* The Law and Feral Cats, 3 J. Animal L. & Ethics 7, 12 (2009). In addition, "[s]urveys show that approximately 9-25% of households feed one or more 'stray' or 'free-roaming cats.' These cats fall into at least one of the following categories: (1) formerly owned, but intentionally abandoned, domesticated housecats; (2) feral cats[4]; or (3) lost cats that have wandered from homes without identification." *Id.* Madero's Complaint makes clear that some, if not all, of the cats in question were (at least at some point) strays that he provided with some degree of care. It is less clear whether Madero's care was enough to render those cats his property.

There are no Pennsylvania cases or statutes specifically addressing the acquisition of property rights in a stray cat.[5] Cats, like all animals, are considered chattel under Pennsylvania law. *Ferrell v. Trustees of the University of Pennsylvania*, 1994 WL 702869 (E.D.Pa. December 12, 1994). Because cats are not included in the definition of "domestic animal" at 1 Pa.C.S.A. § 1991 they are classified as "wild animals" by the Pennsylvania Game and Wildlife Code. 34 Pa.C.S.A. § 102.[6] The mobile nature of wild animals, including stray or feral cats, makes the determination of whether property rights are acquired more complex than other personal property.

From the dawn of the western legal experience, codes, cases and commentators have recognized the challenge in determining legal possession of a wild animal and have required the exercise of possession, dominion and control over such animal to constitute ownership.

The Institutes of Justinian recognized:

> Wild animals, birds and fish, that is to say all the creatures which the land, the sea, and the sky produce, as soon as they are caught by anyone become at once the property of their captor by the law of nations; for natural reason admits the title of the first occupant to that which previously had no owner...An animal thus caught by you is deemed your property so long as it is completely under your control; but so soon as it has escaped from your control, and recovered its natural liberty, it ceases to be yours, and belongs to the first person who subsequently catches it.

J. INST. 2.1.12. The Roman view espoused by the Institutes was accepted at common law and was described by Blackstone as a qualified property right—wild animals can be the subject of property rights, but only to the extent that they are within the control of their putative owner:

> A qualified property may subsist in animals *ferae naturae*, per industriam hominis: by a man's reclaiming and making them tame by art, industry and education; or by so confining them within his own immediate power, that they cannot escape and use their natural liberty...These are no longer the property of a man, than while they continue in his keeping or actual

possession: but if at any time they regain their natural liberty his property instantly ceases.

2 WILLIAM BLACKSTONE, COMMENTARIES, *391-92. However, Blackstone recognized that some animals, by their nature, tend to return to their "owner" even though they are permitted to roam. He referred to such animals as having an "*animum revertendi*[7], which is only to be known by their usual custom of returning." *Id.* at 392. For such animals:

> The law therefore extends this possession farther than the mere manual occupation; for my tame hawk that is pursuing his quarry in my presence, though he is at liberty to go where he pleases, is nevertheless my property for he hath *animum revertendi*. So are my pigeons, that are flying at a distance from their home (especially those of the carrier kind) and likewise the deer that is chased out of my park or forest, and is instantly pursued by the keeper or forester: all of which remain in my possession, and I still preserve my qualified property in them. But if they stray without my knowledge, and do not return in the usual manner, it is then lawful for any stranger to take them. But if a deer or any wild animal reclaimed, hath a collar or other mark put upon him, and goes and returns at his pleasure, or if a wild swan is taken, and marked and turned loose in the river, the owner's property in him still continues, and it is not lawful for anyone else to take him.

Id.

The principle that wild animals become property only to the extent that they are kept within a person's dominion and control, and that that property interest may be vitiated by the animal's return to nature was adopted by the colonies and, later, the States. For example, in the law-school staple *Pierson v. Post*, 3 Cai.R. 175, 178 (1805), the Supreme Court of New York explored and adopted the jurisprudential history governing acquiring ownership in animals. ("It is admitted that a fox is an animal *ferae naturae*, and that property in such animals is acquired by occupancy only."). The *Pierson* court explained that, to acquire ownership of a wild animal, it is necessary "to deprive them of their natural liberty and subject them to the control of their pursuer." *Id.* at 179.

16

Pennsylvania adopted the common-law view of animal ownership. *See Wallis v. Mease*, 3 Binn. 546 (Pa. 1811) ("Bees are *ferae naturae*. If reclaimed and domesticated as they sometimes are, they are the subject of a qualified property, that is, so long as they remain with the person who hived them."); *Commonwealth v. Agway*, 210 Pa.Super. 150, 232 A.2d 69, 70 (Pa Super. 1967) *Commonwealth v. Agway*, 210 Pa. Super. 150, 232 A.2d 69, 70 (Pa Super. 1967) ("Fish running in the streams of a state or nation are *ferae naturae*. They are not subject of property until they are reduced to possession, and if alive, property in them exists only so long as possession continues."). *See also* Pennsylvania Blackstone, Ch. XXV 9 (quoting 2 WILLIAM BLACKSTONE, COMMENTARIES, above).[8]

Because they are not statutorily classified as domestic animals, cats must be considered wild animals. As such, they became the property of Madero only to the extent that he brought them within his dominion and control. This would conclusively establish that the cats which Madero found, took into his home, provided with food and care and which he considered to be his property were, in fact, his property.

For those cats which were outside of Madero's home, either in the unoccupied side of the duplex or wandering around his property, the analysis is more difficult. The Court holds that the determination of property rights in stray (or, perhaps, formerly stray) cats eludes a bright line definition, but must be determined on a case-by-case basis. Outdoor cats may, in many circumstances, be considered animals with an *animum revertendi*. Indeed, as explained above, it is not uncommon for cats which are considered pets by their owners to be permitted to wander outdoors. Provided that they have a habit of returning to their "home" and their owner considers them to remain his property during their forays into the wild, and the owner acts toward them in a manner which is consistent with ownership, the common law will recognize ongoing property rights in the animal.[9] The application of ancient common law principals will permit a person to claim ownership in a "outside cat" notwithstanding the cat's propensity to wander away from the immediate dominion and control of its owner. In determining whether such cats are the property of a putative owner, a court should consider, *inter alia*, whether the cat is considered to be a pet or owned by the putative owner; whether the cat has been given a name; whether the cat wears a collar and/or tag; the nature, regularity and duration of the relationship; whether the cat is permitted inside the putative owner's residence; whether the owner feeds the cat; and whether the owner provides veterinary care to the cat, and whether the cat exhibits a familiar mannerism with the putative owner. No single factor is dispositive, but rather, the relationship should be viewed as an organic whole.[10]

Madero pled that the cats at issue were abandoned or stray. However, he also pled that they were his property. To support this, he pled that he provided them with food, shelter and occasional veterinary care. Whether he can, ultimately, prove that he owned the cats, Madero has pled sufficient facts to support ownership of the cats to afford him the standing to maintain his claims under Section 1983 and the common law.[11]

B. OFFICER LUFFEY'S MOTION TO DISMISS IS GRANTED IN PART AND DENIED IN PART.

***

2. Madero cannot maintain his common law tort claims against the HAR Defendants.

Madero also asserts claims for conversion (Count XI) and trespass to chattel (Count XII) against the HAR Defendants. Neither of these claims can stand.

Conversion is "the deprivation of another's right of property in, or use or possession of, a chattel or other interference therewith, without the owner's consent and without lawful justification." Stevenson v. Economy Bank of Ambridge, 413 Pa. 442, 197 A.2d 721, 726 (1964). Trespass to chattel consists of dispossessing another of a chattel or using or intermeddling with a chattel in the possession of another. Pestco v. Associated Products, Inc., 880 A.2d 700, 708 (Pa. Super. 2005). The two torts are related and largely coterminous, but "conversion entails a more serious deprivation of the owner's rights such that an award of the full value of the property is appropriate." Rosemont Taxicab Co. v. Philadelphia Parking Authority, 327 F.Supp.3d 803, 828-29 (E.D.Pa. 2018). It can be said that every conversion includes a trespass to chattels, but not every trespass amounts to a conversion.

torts

The HAR Defendants argue that this claim must fail because Madero did not own the cats. Further, they claim that Madero surrendered the cats, never sought their return, and was barred from having so many cats by the Pittsburgh ordinance. As explained above, these arguments do not warrant dismissal at this time because the question of Madero's ownership requires factual development. Rather, the conversion and trespass counts fail for a different reason, the HAR Defendants were justified in receiving the cats under the circumstances of this case.

One of the express elements of the tort of conversion is the interference in possession be "without lawful justification." Conversion and trespass to chattels are so closely related that Pennsylvania caselaw almost always addresses them together. This is reasonable because the difference is not in the nature of the conduct, but rather, only in its duration and extent. The requirement that interference with possession occur "without lawful justification" can reasonably be said to apply to both torts.

***

When the HAR Defendants received the cats from Officer Luffey pursuant to the execution of a warrant issued by a judicial officer of the Commonwealth of Pennsylvania, they were justified to receive them and treat them in a manner consistent with their regular policies and procedures. Animal shelters, like HAR, provide a valuable service by accepting animals that are seized by public officials and providing them with care, unfortunately including euthanasia in certain circumstances. They do not have to make an independent inquiry to authorities as to the circumstances surrounding the animals' seizure and certainly do not have to second guess a warrant or other order of court.

***

There is no question that the HAR Defendants received the cats in question pursuant to search and seizure warrant. They were entitled to rely on that warrant. Moreover, they never received any order, directive or other request requiring them to relinquish custody of the cats to Madero. The HAR Defendants cannot be liable for either conversion or trespass to chattels. Counts XI and XII, as asserted against them, will be dismissed.

D. ALL OF MADERO'S CLAIMS AGAINST PROVIDENT ARE DISMISSED WITH PREJUDICE. HIS CONSPIRACY CLAIMS MAY PROCEED AGAINST HCMT.

***

1. Madero's claims under 42 U.S.C. § 1983 – **Counts I, II, III, IV and V – against HCMT and Provident are dismissed with prejudice.**

Madero has alleged that (a) his Fourth and Fourteenth Amendment rights were violated when the "Execution Team" executed the illegally obtained search warrant on June 30, 2017, and (b) HCMT and Provident were "acting under the color of law" when Provident participated in the seizure of the cats by trapping them. Madero seeks to hold these defendants liable on the theory that it was performing a municipal function on behalf of the City of Pittsburgh. The Court finds that HCMT and Provident are not state actors.

***

Taking care of animals is not a traditional state function. Nor is there any basis for concluding that the services offered by HCMT and its volunteers were ever the exclusive prerogative of the state. No Pennsylvania law requires the City to establish a volunteer animal rescue organization. Moreover, no allegations exist that HCMT or any of its board or individual members, like Provident, were intertwined with the City.

***

CONCLUSION

AND NOW, this 13th day of February 2020, IT IS HEREBY ORDERED that Officer Luffey's Motion to Dismiss is GRANTED IN PART and DENIED IN PART. . . .

IT IS HEREBY ORDERED that the HAR Defendants' Motion to Dismiss is GRANTED. . . .

HCMT's and Provident's Motion to Dismiss is GRANTED IN PART and DENIED IN PART. . . .

1. T.S. ELIOT, The Naming of Cats, in OLD POSSUM'S BOOK OF PRACTICAL CATS (1939). [Editorial Note: This is footnote 3 of the opinion.]

2. Cats were, for example, popular pets in ancient Egypt, where many attained eternal life, or at least preservation, by being mummified along with their owners. See https://carnegiemnh.org/why-were-cats-mummified-in-ancient-egypt/. [Editorial Note: This is footnote 4 of the opinion.]

3. See The Law and Feral Cats, 3 J. Animal L. & Ethics 7 (2009) ("Surprisingly...cats were largely absent from the common law and legislation pertaining to animals until very recently."). [Editorial Note: This is footnote 6 of the opinion.]

4. A feral cat is "the unowned offspring of outdoor cats." Id. at 11 (citing MARGARET R. SLATER, COMMUNITY APPROACHES TO FERAL CATS (Humane Society Press, 2002)). Contrary to strays, feral cats have no experience living with humans and are completely unsocialized. [Editorial Note: This is footnote 7 of the opinion.]

5. While there are no Pennsylvania statutes governing the ownership of cats, the Pennsylvania dog law, 3 P.S. § 459-102 et seq., provides guidance as to the ownership of dogs. . . . While called the "dog law" and generally focused on requirements relating to keeping dogs, some provisions of the dog law apply to cats. . . . Certain requirements for spaying or neutering are also extended to cats. However, the law makes no provision for the ownership of cats and the definition cited above is, by its very terms, limited to dogs. [Editorial Note: This is footnote 8 of the opinion.]

6. The Game and Wildlife Code defines "wild animal" as "[a]ll mammals other than domestic animals as defined in 1 Pa.C.S. § 1991 (relating to definitions). The term shall not include a species or variation of swine, pig or boar, held in captivity." 34 Pa.C.S.A.§ 102. "Domestic Animal" is defined as "[a]ny equine animal, bovine animal, sheep, goat and pig. Dogs are subject to the Pennsylvania Dog Law, 3 P.S. § 459-101, and are, perhaps statutorily carved out of the general definition of "wild animal." No such statute applies to cats. Some older cases refer to dogs and other tame animals as mansuetae naturae, as distinct from ferae naturae. See Andrews v. Smith, 324 Pa. 455, 188 A. 146, 148 (1936). These cases generally address liability for injuries caused by the animal, rather than acquisition of property rights in the same.

In any event, principles of statutory construction require a finding that the limited definition of "domestic animal" renders all others wild animals. [Editorial Note: This is footnote 9 of the opinion.]

7. "Animum revertendi" can be translated as a habit or mind for returning. [Editorial Note: This is footnote 10 of the opinion.]

8. By an interesting extension of common law reasoning, Pennsylvania Courts have deemed oil and gas to be in the nature of ferae naturae, justifying the law of capture. As this Court once observed: Water and oil, and still more strongly gas, may be classed by themselves, if the analogy be not too fanciful, as minerals ferae naturae. In common with animals, and unlike other minerals, they have the power and the tendency to escape without the volition of the owner. Their 'fugitive and wandering existence within the limits of a particular tract is uncertain,' as said by Chief Justice Agnew in Brown v. Vandergrift, 80 Pa. [142] 147, 148 (1875). They belong to the owner of the land, and are part of it, so long as they are on or in it, and are subject to his control; but when they escape, and go into other land, or come under another's control, the title of the former owner is gone. White v. New York State Natural Gas Corp., 190 F.Supp. 342, 346 (W.D.Pa. 1960). [Editorial Note: This is footnote 11 of the opinion.]

9. The Court notes the opinion of a commentator on animal law who proposes a sliding scale analysis for determining whether a person has acquired possession of a cat. Under this regime, if a keeper or caretaker has given a feral cat food and water every day for several years and has provided the animal with periodic veterinary care, that person is more likely to be viewed as an owner—and subject to liability—than a person who has merely fed a feral cat once a day for six months. This type of sliding scale would enable courts to hold feral cat keepers and caretakers responsible when their actions reflect a relatively high degree of ownership. Simultaneously, this system would allow the casual good Samaritan to feed a feral cat without fear of liability. This rule would effectively advance two competing policy goals: (1) encouraging people to care for feral cats; and (2) holding caretakers more responsible when their actions begin to look more like those of an owner than those of a caretaker. David Fry, Detailed Discussion of Feral Cat Legal Issues, MICHIGAN STATE

UNIVERSITY ANIMAL LEGAL AND HISTORICAL CENTER (2010), https://www.animallaw.info/article/detailed-discussion-feral-cat-legal-issues. The Court believes that this sliding scale is consistent with the common law governing wild animals with an animum revertendi, like cats. The key considerations are the habits over time of both the owner and the cat. [Editorial Note: This is footnote 12 of the opinion.]

10. Deuteronomy, from Andrew Lloyd Webber's musical Cats, aptly summarizes some of the factors that should be considered: Before a cat will condescend / To treat you as a trusted friend / Some little token of esteem is needed, like a dish of cream / And you might now and then supply / Some caviar and Strasbourg pie / Some potted grouse or salmon paste / He's sure to have his personal taste / And so in time you reach your aim / And call him by his name. [Editorial Note: This is footnote 13 of the opinion.]

11. Multiple Defendants cite to the City's ordinance limiting residents to five cats to argue that Madero had property rights in only five of the cats. This is not the case. The ordinance can, of course, limit the number of pets that a resident may lawfully keep in his or her residence, but it cannot vitiate the property rights of the owner in supernumerary animals. See e.g., Koorn v. Lacey Tp., 78 Fed.Appx. 199, 207 (3d. Cir. 2003) ("The Ordinance limits the number of dogs that the Koorns can keep at any one dwelling. It does not foreclose them from owning any number of dogs or from owning any particular dwelling."). [Editorial Note: This is footnote 14 of the opinion.]

2.3

Briggs v. Southwestern Energy Production Company
224 A.3d 334 (Pa. 2020)

Supreme Court of Pennsylvania

CHIEF JUSTICE SAYLOR

issue

In this appeal by allowance, we consider whether the rule of capture immunizes an energy developer from liability in trespass, where the developer uses hydraulic fracturing on the property it owns or leases, and such activities allow it to obtain oil or gas that migrates from beneath the surface of another person's land.

I. Background

A. The rule of capture

Oil and gas are minerals, and while in place they are considered part of the land. They differ from coal and other substances with a fixed situs in that they are fugacious in nature – meaning they tend to seep or flow across property lines beneath the surface of the earth. Such underground movement is known as "drainage." Drainage stems from a physical property of fluids in that they naturally move across a pressure gradient from high to low pressure. Indeed, the extraction of oil or gas by drilling is based, at least in part, on creating a low-pressure pathway from the mineral's subterranean location to the earth's surface.

Oil and gas have thus been described as having a "fugitive and wandering existence," *Brown v. Vandergrift*, 80 Pa. 142, 147 (Pa. 1875), and have been compared to wild animals which move about from one property to another. *See Westmoreland & Cambria Nat. Gas Co. v. DeWitt*, 130 Pa. 235, 249, 18 A. 724, 725 (1889) ("In common with animals, and unlike other minerals, [oil, gas, and water] have the power and the tendency to escape without the volition of the owner."). Accordingly, such minerals are subject to the rule of capture, which is

> [a] fundamental principle of oil-and-gas law holding that there is no liability for drainage of oil and gas from under the lands of another so long as there has been no trespass ....

BLACK'S LAW DICTIONARY 1358 (8th ed. 2004)); *accord Brown v. Spilman*, 155 U.S. 665, 669-70, 15 S. Ct. 245, 247, 39 L.Ed. 304 (1895).[1] A corollary to this rule is that an aggrieved property owner's remedy for the loss, through drainage, of subsurface oil or gas has traditionally been to offset the effects of the developer's well by drilling his or her own well, often termed an "offset well." *See Barnard v.*

Monongahela Gas Co., 216 Pa. 362, 365, 65 A. 801, 803 (1907) ("What then can the neighbor do? Nothing; only go and do likewise.").

The reference to "the lands of another" in the above quote does not suggest a developer may invade the subsurface area of a neighboring property by drilling at an angle rather than vertically (referred to as slant drilling or slant wells). . . . This is because the title holder of a parcel of land generally owns everything directly beneath the surface. Rather, and as suggested by the "no trespass" predicate, it refers to the potential for oil and gas to migrate from the plaintiff's property to the developer's land when extracted from a common pool or reservoir spanning both parcels. *See Barnard*, 216 Pa. at 365-66, 65 A. at 803; *Minard Run Oil Co. v. United States Forest Serv.*, 670 F.3d 236, 256 (3d Cir. 2011) ("Under Pennsylvania law, oil and gas resources are subject to the 'rule of capture,' which permits an owner to extract oil and gas even when extraction depletes a single oil or gas reservoir lying beneath adjoining lands."); *Jones v. Forest Oil Co.*, 194 Pa. 379, 383, 44 A. 1074, 1075 (1900) (recognizing that oil and gas belong to the surface property owner while they are in his land, but when they migrate to his neighbor's land they belong to his neighbor).

Finally, the rule of capture applies even where devices such as pumps are used to bring the mineral to the surface and thereby reduce the production of neighboring wells. *See Jones*, 194 Pa. at 384-85, 44 A. at 1075.

B. Hydraulic fracturing

One of the central questions in this matter involves how these principles apply where hydraulic fracturing is used to extract oil or gas from subsurface geological formations. Drillers have enhanced the output of oil and gas wells by fracturing the geological formations for over a century. Initially they used explosives. Hydraulic fracturing was developed in the 1940s, and has been used in Pennsylvania since 1954. . . . According to the federal government, hydraulic fracturing is

> used in "unconventional" gas production. "Unconventional" reservoirs can cost-effectively produce gas only by using a special stimulation technique, like hydraulic fracturing .... This is often because the gas is highly dispersed in the rock, rather than occurring in a concentrated underground location.

United States Environmental Protection Agency (the "EPA"), *The Process of Unconventional Natural Gas Production*, https://www.epa.gov/uog/process-unconventional-natural-gas-production (viewed Oct. 22, 2019). In terms of how the technique works, the EPA continues:

> Fractures are created by pumping large quantities of fluids at high pressure down a wellbore and into the target rock formation. Hydraulic fracturing fluid commonly consists of water, proppant and chemical additives that open and enlarge fractures within the rock formation. These fractures can extend several hundred feet away from the wellbore. The proppants – sand, ceramic pellets or other small incompressible particles – hold open the newly created fractures.

Id.

After injection, fluid is withdrawn from the well while leaving the proppants in place to hold the fissures open. This enhances the drainage of oil or gas into the wellbore where it can be captured.

C. Factual and procedural history of this case

(i) Introduction

This appeal comes to us in a somewhat unusual posture. The parties presently favor essentially the same rule of law: they both, in substance, argue that the traditional rule of capture should apply, subject to the common-law standard for trespass of real property based on physical intrusion onto another's land. *See* RESTATEMENT (SECOND) OF TORTS § 158 & cmt. *i* (1965) (indicating liability follows from the defendant's entry onto the plaintiff's property, and noting this includes throwing, propelling, or placing a thing on the land or above or beneath its surface). Each party, moreover, depicts the other as erroneously suggesting that an exception to this framework should pertain where hydraulic fracturing is used to obtain oil or natural gas. In particular, the plaintiffs suggest that Southwestern wishes to convert the rule of capture into a precept whereby energy developers may physically invade the property of others to capture natural gas so long as they are using hydraulic fracturing. For its part, Southwestern portrays the plaintiffs and the Superior Court decision from which it appeals as positing that the rule of capture simply does not apply when hydraulic fracturing is used for energy development on one's own land.

***

(ii) Undisputed facts

Adam, Paula, Joshua, and Sarah Briggs ("Plaintiffs") own a parcel of real estate consisting of approximately eleven acres in Harford Township, Susquehanna County. During all relevant times, Plaintiffs have not leased their property to any entity for natural gas production. Plaintiffs' property is adjacent to a tract of land leased by Appellant Southwestern Energy Production Company for natural gas extraction (the "Production Parcel"). Southwestern maintains wellbores on the Production Parcel and has used hydraulic fracturing to boost natural gas extraction from the Marcellus Shale formation through those wellbores.

(iii) Proceedings before the Court of Common Pleas

In November 2015, Plaintiffs commenced an action against Southwestern in which they stated two causes of action, trespass and conversion. In terms of factual averments, Plaintiffs alleged that Southwestern "has and continues to extract natural gas from under the land of the Plaintiffs," and that such extraction was "willful[ ], unlawful[ ], outrageous[ ] and in complete conscious disregard of the rights and title of the Plaintiffs in said land and the natural gas thereunder." In Count I (the trespass claim), Plaintiffs averred that Southwestern's actions constituted a trespass which deprived Plaintiffs of the value of the "natural gas extracted from under their land[.]"In Count II (the conversion claim), Plaintiffs alleged that, through its drilling activities, Southwestern had deprived Plaintiffs of their possession and use of the natural gas and converted it to Southwestern's use. Notably, Plaintiffs did not expressly allege that Southwestern's activities had caused a physical intrusion into Plaintiffs' property.

Southwestern filed a responsive pleading denying it had extracted gas from Plaintiffs' land and denying it had trespassed upon Plaintiffs' property or converted their natural gas. Southwestern specifically denied it had drilled underneath Plaintiffs' property and stated, further, that it had "only drilled for oil, gas or minerals from under properties for which [Southwestern] has leases."

***

After the parties engaged in discovery, Southwestern filed a motion for summary judgment and a supporting brief in which it argued that it did not physically invade Plaintiffs' property and, to the extent that it had recovered any gas through drainage from that property to the Production Parcel, again, it was entitled to judgment as a matter of law under the rule of capture. . . . Plaintiffs . . . filed their own motion for partial summary judgment as to liability, asserting that courts should not apply the rule of capture in circumstances where gas has been captured through the use of hydraulic fracturing.

In their supporting brief, Plaintiffs suggested, for the first time, that Southwestern's hydraulic fracturing activities may have caused a disturbance of the subsurface area of their land in the form of rock fractures propagating horizontally from the wellbore, . . .

Plaintiffs also relied on *Young v. Ethyl Corp.*, 521 F.2d 771 (8th Cir. 1975), in which the Eighth Circuit held that the rule of capture did not apply where the developer had injected water beneath the plaintiff's land to force subsurface brine out of its location so that it could be harvested through wells situated on the developer's property. Although, again, Plaintiffs did not contend that Southwestern had done anything similar, their theory was that, just as the brine was non-fugacious and had to be forced out of its place, so natural gas located in shale is non-fugacious and must be "extracted" from its place by hydraulic fracturing. Plaintiffs ultimately concluded that the rule of capture should only apply where oil or gas is obtained from a common underground pool.

By order and opinion, the common pleas court granted Southwestern's motion for summary judgment, [and] denied Plaintiffs' motion for partial summary judgment, . . . The court agreed with Southwestern's position that the rule of capture applied in the circumstances and, as such, Plaintiffs could not recover under theories of trespass or conversion even if some of the gas harvested by Southwestern had drained from under Plaintiffs' property. . . .

Plaintiffs filed a notice of appeal, . . . in which they raised a single issue: whether the trial court erred in determining that the rule of capture precluded liability under theories of trespass and conversion, where Southwestern had used hydraulic fracturing to obtain natural gas which originated under Plaintiffs' land. As with their prior filings, Plaintiffs, again, did not include any suggestion that Southwestern had physically intruded onto their property.

Issue [handwritten in left margin]

***

(iv) Proceedings before the Superior Court

On appeal to the Superior Court, Plaintiffs again focused their advocacy on the concept that the rule of capture should only apply where there is a conventional underground reservoir, and not when hydraulic fracturing is used. . . .

A two-judge panel of the Superior Court reversed in a published decision. . . .

***

[D]rawing support from the *Young* decision (regarding water injected under the plaintiff's property to force subsurface brine toward the operator's well), the panel stated the following: first, that hydraulic fracturing is distinguishable from conventional drilling because it does not involve tapping into reservoirs within which gas flows freely, but instead, extracts gas trapped in a shale formation by using artificial means to stimulate the flow of the resource; second, that the self-help remedy of drilling one's own well is less feasible for small landowners in the hydraulic-fracturing arena than with conventional wells due to the high cost of such operations; and third, that employing the rule of capture would permit a developer to locate a well near the leased property's boundary line and withdraw gas from beneath the adjoining property – which in turn would diminish the developer's incentive to negotiate mineral leases with small property owners.

In light of these conclusions, the panel held that hydraulic fracturing may give rise to liability in trespass, particularly if subsurface fractures, fluid or proppant[s] cross boundary lines, resulting in the extraction of natural gas from beneath an adjoining landowner's property. The court noted, however, that the record did not indicate whether Southwestern's operations had resulted in a subsurface intrusion into

Plaintiffs' property, going so far as to express that "[t]here does not appear to be *any evidence, or even an estimate*, as to how far the subsurface fractures extend from each of the wellbore [sic] on Southwestern's lease." Regardless, the court continued, Plaintiffs' "allegations" were sufficient to preclude summary judgment by "rais[ing] an issue as to whether there has been a trespass." Accordingly, the panel reversed the trial court's order and remanded for additional factual development.

In sum, then, the Superior Court panel's analysis can reasonably be viewed as embodying two distinct, but interrelated, holdings: first, that whenever "artificial means," such as hydraulic fracturing, are used to stimulate the flow of underground resources, the rule of capture does not apply because drainage does not occur through the operation of "natural agencies," and second, that in this particular case summary judgment was premature in light of certain unspecified allegations relating to cross-boundary intrusions into Plaintiffs' land.

(v) Southwestern's request for discretionary review

. . . Southwestern criticized the panel's analysis to the extent it indicated an energy developer may be held liable for damages for trespass if its hydraulic fracturing activities, *conducted on its own property*, captures oil or gas from a neighboring property through drainage. As such, Southwestern framed a single issue for our review, as follows:

> Does the rule of capture apply to oil and gas produced from wells that were completed using hydraulic fracturing and preclude trespass liability for allegedly draining oil or gas from under nearby property, where the well is drilled solely on and beneath the driller's own property *and the hydraulic fracturing fluids are injected solely on or beneath the driller's own property*?

***

II. Preliminary Discussion

A. Trespass

In Pennsylvania, a trespass occurs when a person who is not privileged to do so intrudes upon land in possession of another, whether willfully or by mistake. . . .

Nevertheless, meaningful appellate review at this stage is not straightforward for multiple reasons.

B. Pleading deficiencies, decisional irregularities, and issue limitation

First, Plaintiffs did not assert . . . that Southwestern had effectuated a physical intrusion onto (or into) their property. The Superior Court panel recognized this aspect of Plaintiffs' litigation position, but raised and resolved, *sua sponte*, an issue based on the opposite premise, that Plaintiffs *had* alleged a physical intrusion. Then, stating that there was no record evidence that such an intrusion had taken place, and without referencing any specific aspect of the pleadings, the panel indicated that the Complaint's allegations were alone sufficient to raise a genuine issue of fact so as to preclude summary judgment.

This is in some tension with the governing summary-judgment standard which generally centers on whether the adverse party has produced enough evidence to raise a question of material fact as to each element of the claim. . . .

. . . Southwestern . . . articulated the issue for this Court's consideration in terms of whether the rule of capture should be applied in the same manner it has always been applied: to allow for the capture of oil and gas which merely drains from an adjacent property after the completion of a well using hydraulic fracturing *solely within the developer's property*. This is an issue, again, on which the parties do not presently diverge: they both answer in the affirmative. Their disagreement is limited to whether any physical intrusion has taken place – a question that is not fairly subsumed within the issue framed for our review.

III. Analysis

The issue as stated by Southwestern should nonetheless be resolved for purposes of this dispute – and to provide guidance to the bench and bar – because at least part of the Superior Court's opinion can reasonably be construed as setting forth a *per se* rule foreclosing application of the rule of capture in hydraulic fracturing scenarios, and that rule rests on faulty assumptions. In particular, and most saliently, the panel appears to have indicated that one litmus for whether the rule of capture applies is whether the defendant's gas extraction methodology relies only on the natural drainage of oil or gas within a conventional pool or reservoir, or whether instead those methods utilize some means of artificial stimulation to induce drainage.

The Superior Court's position in this respect logically rests on one of two grounds: (a) the act of artificially stimulating the cross-boundary flow through the use of hydraulic fracturing solely on the developer's property in and of itself renders the rule of capture inapplicable; or (b) as Plaintiffs argue, any time natural gas migrates across property lines resulting, directly or indirectly, from hydraulic fracturing, a physical intrusion into the plaintiff's property must necessarily have taken place.

As to the first proposition, all drilling for subsurface fugacious minerals involves the artificial stimulation of the flow of that substance. The mere act of drilling interferes with nature and stimulates the flow of the minerals toward artificially-created low pressure areas, most notably, the wellbore. This Court has held that the rule of capture applies although the driller uses further artificial means, such as a pump, to enhance production from a source common to it and the plaintiff – so long as no physical invasion of the plaintiff's land occurs. *See Jones*, 194 Pa. at 384, 44 A. at 1075 (indicating that, absent physical intrusion, a developer may use "all the skill and invention of which a man is capable" to appropriate resources from under his own property). There is no reason why this precept should apply any differently to hydraulic fracturing conducted solely within the driller's property.

The Superior Court may have believed it should impose a different rule because of the added expense associated with hydraulic fracturing as compared to conventional drilling. It expressed its concern that drilling an offset well may not be as affordable to an aggrieved landowner today as it was in the era when conventional drilling was still able profitably to produce oil and natural gas. . . .

Hydraulic fracturing may be more expensive than conventional drilling and, as a consequence, the feasibility of drilling an offset well may be diminished for some landowners. The judiciary nonetheless lacks institutional tools necessary to investigate the continuing feasibility of self-help remedies under the myriad of circumstances that may present themselves in the context of a dispute such as this one. The legislative branch is not similarly constrained, and if the General Assembly believes that additional measures are needed in favor of small landowners, it is in a better position to ascertain the need for such measures and to articulate their details.[2] Accordingly, we reject as a matter of law the concept that the rule of capture is inapplicable to drilling and hydraulic fracturing that occurs entirely within the developer's property solely because drainage of natural resources takes place as the direct or indirect result of hydraulic fracturing, or that such drainage stems from less "natural" means than conventional drainage.

The second predicate – that drainage from under a plaintiff's parcel can only occur if the driller first physically invades that property – does not lend itself to a purely legal resolution. By design, hydraulic fracturing creates fissures in rock strata which store hydrocarbons within their porous structure. On the state of the present record, this alone does not establish that a physical intrusion into a neighboring property is necessary for such action to result in drainage from that property. We cannot rule out, for example, that a fissure created through the injection of hydraulic fluid entirely within the developer's property may create a sufficient pressure gradient to induce the drainage of hydrocarbons from the relevant stratum of rock underneath an adjacent parcel even absent physical intrusion. Nor can we discount the possibility that a fissure created within the developer's property may communicate with other, pre-existing fissures that reach across property lines. Whether these, or any other non-invasive means of drainage occasioned by hydraulic fracturing, are physically possible in a given case is a factual question to be established through expert evidence.

The Superior Court panel appears to have assumed, if implicitly, that such occurrences were impossible – but, again, there is no basis in the record for such an assumption. In all events, a plaintiff asserting a cause of action "must be able to prove all the elements of his case by proper evidentiary standards." *Papieves v. Lawrence*, 437 Pa. 373, 379, 263 A.2d 118, 121 (1970). Thus, to the extent this lawsuit goes forward on Plaintiffs' new, physical-intrusion theory, Plaintiffs will bear the burden of demonstrating that such an intrusion took place.

We have not overlooked Southwestern's argument that trespass should not be viewed as occurring miles beneath the surface of the earth. As Southwestern observes, in some jurisdictions traditional concepts of physical trespass have been relaxed where activities take place miles below the surface and the plaintiff is not deprived of the use and enjoyment of the land. Southwestern posits that this is analogous to the principle that trespass does not arise high above the surface. *See Causby*, 328 U.S. at 260-61, 66 S. Ct. at 1065. It emphasizes that other socially useful endeavors – such as carbon sequestration projects, energy storage wells, and waste disposal sites – could be jeopardized if the rule against trespass were to be enforced in an unduly stringent manner where deep subsurface activities are concerned.

Without speaking to the merit of such a claim, we note that this Court is limited to the issue as it was framed in the petition for allowance of appeal, and Southwestern has not articulated any reason an exception should be made in the present dispute. Thus, to the extent Southwestern argues it should be permitted to escape liability even if it is ultimately found to have effectuated a physical intrusion into Plaintiff's subsurface property, its claim in this regard has not been preserved for review by this Court.

This brings us to the question of whether the lawsuit can, indeed, progress on a theory of trespass by physical intrusion, and by extension, to the question of the appropriate mandate from this Court. Ordinarily, and for the reasons explained, we would deem any such contention to be absent from the litigation, as it does not appear to have been mentioned in Plaintiffs' pleadings or argued as a basis to deny Southwestern's motion for summary judgment. The Superior Court, however, evidently believed there was some legitimate basis to dispose of the appeal on the presupposition that Southwestern was alleged to have physically invaded Plaintiffs' subsurface property with hydraulic fracturing liquid and proppants; and, as noted, Southwestern has not challenged the intermediate court's action in this respect.

. . . In these circumstances, . . . we find that the appropriate action at this juncture is to vacate the Superior Court's order and remand for reconsideration in light of the guidance provided in this opinion, and the certified record on appeal.

***

V. Summary and Conclusion

In summary, the parties to the appeal are in agreement — and we concur as well — that the rule of capture remains extant in Pennsylvania, and developers who use hydraulic fracturing may rely on pressure differentials to drain oil and gas from under another's property, at least in the absence of a physical invasion. The Superior Court panel erred to the extent it assumed that either (a) the use of hydraulic fracturing alters this rule, or (b) where hydraulic fracturing is utilized, such physical invasion is a necessary precondition in all cases for drainage to occur from underneath another property. More broadly, insofar as the panel's decision may be construed to suggest that a natural-versus-artificially-induced-flow litmus should be employed to determine whether the rule of capture applies in a given situation, that standard rests on a false distinction and is disapproved.

The order of the Superior Court is vacated and the matter is remanded to that court for further proceedings consistent with this opinion.

CONCURRING AND DISSENTING OPINION

JUSTICE DOUGHERTY

I join the majority's holding that the rule of capture remains effective in Pennsylvania to protect a developer from trespass liability where there has been no physical invasion of another's property. In so holding, the majority correctly recognizes that if there is such a physical invasion the rule of capture will not insulate a developer engaged in hydraulic fracturing from trespass liability. As I agree with both propositions, I also agree the matter should be remanded for further proceedings involving a specific inquiry into a physical invasion. I respectfully dissent, however, from the notion that this question must be determined by the Superior Court on the present record, and would instead remand to the trial court for completion of the discovery that was forestalled by erroneous summary judgment, and for trial, if necessary. *dissent on which court to remand to*

***

Finally, I make the following observations relating to the rule of capture in the context of fracking of non-conventional shale deposits. First, although I recognize natural gas has a "fugacious" nature regardless of whether it lies in an open pool or in a sandstone or shale deposit, it is clear that natural gas trapped in shale drains naturally much more slowly than from a pool or from other materials; indeed, this is the very reason developers engage in fracking, to make shale gas development productive faster, that is, more efficient and economically viable. The practice exploits natural shale fractures and creates new ones, and with present technology, much remains mysterious about precisely what happens so far beneath the surface. . . .

***

1. The term "capture" is also drawn from an analogy to wild animals. At common law, a person could acquire title to such an animal by reducing it to possession.

2. See, e.g., 58 P.S. §§ 401-419 (Oil and Gas Conservation Law of 1961); Hunter Co. v. McHugh, 202 La. 97, 11 So. 2d 495 (1942) (upholding a Louisiana statute aimed at preventing waste and securing equitable apportionment among landowners with subsurface oil or gas), appeal dismissed, 320 U.S. 222, 64 S. Ct. 19, 88 L.Ed. 5 (1943). See generally Frank Sylvester & Robert W. Malmsheimer, Oil & Gas Spacing & Forced Pooling Requirements: How States Balance Energy Development & Landowner Rights, 40 U. DAYTON L. REV. 47 (2015) (describing state-level regulations relating to well spacing and the pooling of interests and profits). . . . [Editorial Note: This is footnote 15 of the opinion.]

2.4
Discussion: Notes, Questions, and Problems

2.4.1
Discussion Note #1. History and analysis of Pierson v. Post

For an in-depth history and analysis of *Pierson v. Post*, see Angela Fernandez, *Pierson v. Post*, The Hunt for the Fox: Law and Professionalization in American Legal Culture (Cambridge University Press 2018).

2.4.2

Discussion Note #2. Feminist perspective of Pierson v. Post

For a feminist perspective of *Pierson v. Post*, excerpted above, see Angela Fernandez, Pierson v. Post—*Rewritten Opinion in* Feminist Judgments: Rewritten Property Opinions (Eloisa C. Rodriguez-Dod & Elena Marty-Nelson eds., Cambridge University Press 2021). For a discussion of Fernandez's revised feminist opinion, see Jill Fraley, *Commentary on* Pierson v. Post—*Rewritten Opinion, in* Feminist Judgments: Rewritten Property Opinions (Eloisa C. Rodriguez-Dod & Elena Marty-Nelson eds., Cambridge University Press 2021).

2.4.3

Discussion Note #3. Regulations affecting rule of capture for oil and gas

While the court in *Briggs v. Southwestern Energy Production Company*, excerpted above, recognized that the rule of capture applies to oil and gas extraction, the court also notes that such extraction is also subject to significant specific laws and regulations. For example, the court cites to *Hunter Co. v. McHugh*, 11 So. 2d 495 (La.1942), which upheld "a Louisiana statute aimed at preventing waste and securing equitable apportionment among landowners with subsurface oil or gas." *Briggs* also noted that spacing regulations play a significant role in oil and gas extraction. For an interesting discussion of the continued viability of the rule of capture and spacing regulations, see Emeka Duruigbo, *Small Tract Owners and Shale Gas Drilling in Texas: Sanctity of Property, Holdout Power or Compulsory Pooling?*, 70 Baylor L. Rev. 527, 530 (2018).

2.4.4

Discussion Question #4. Wild animal regains its natural liberty?

As discussed in *Madero v. Luffey*, excerpted above, the law of wild animals continues to refer to ancient doctrines. For example, *Madero* referenced The Institutes of Justinian, which sets forth the general rule that wild animals as soon as they are caught by anyone become at once the property of their captor. . . . An animal thus caught by . . . is deemed [the captor's] property so long as it is completely under [the captor's] control; but so soon as it has escaped . . . and recovered its natural liberty, it ceases to be [the captor's], and belongs to the first person who subsequently catches it.

Madero also recognized the exception noted by Blackstone in his Commentaries that some animals, by their nature, tend to return to their "owner" even though they are permitted to roam. Blackstone referred to such animals as having an *animum revertendi*. With regard to those animals, "the owner's property in [the animal] still continues, and it is not lawful for anyone else to take him." Can you think of any animals that might have such a custom? Do you agree with the *animum revertendi* exception?

2.4.5

Discussion Problem #5. Rare wild butterfly problem

Assume Albert was trying to capture a rare wild butterfly. Just as Albert spotted the butterfly and was about to swing his large net over it, Bob leapt out from behind a tree where he had been waiting and tossed his net over the butterfly. Bob then ran away with the butterfly in his net. Under the common law, and assuming this all took place on unpossessed and uninhabited land, as between Albert and Bob, who has a superior interest in the butterfly and why? Assume for purposes of this question that, while Bob was running away with the butterfly in his net, he tripped and his net fell open. Assume further that the nimble butterfly escaped Bob's net and flew out of it. If Carl catches the butterfly with his net before Bob recovers his balance, who has a better claim to the butterfly, Bob or Carl and why?

3

Chapter 3 · Found Property

Cases on found property illustrate the concept of relativity of title, introduced in Chapter 1. They also help develop the concept of possession, introduced in Chapter 2.

Occasionally you read in newspapers about people who discover bags with money or jewels or find other items of value. Given the many questions that may arise regarding title to that property, many states have statutes regarding found property. Some states have codified the common law, which classifies found property into four categories: lost, mislaid, abandoned, and treasure trove. The court in *Grande v. Jennings*, excerpted below, helpfully describes the four categories as follows. Property is deemed *lost* when the owner unintentionally parts with it "through either carelessness or neglect." Property is deemed to be *mislaid* when the owner "intentionally places it in a certain place and later forgets about it." Property is deemed *abandoned* when the "property has been thrown away, or was voluntarily forsaken by its owner." Property is deemed *treasure trove* when it is "verifiably antiquated and has been 'concealed [for] so long as to indicate that the owner is probably dead or unknown.'" Courts turn to these classifications to determine competing claims to found property.

Statutes in some jurisdictions change common law rules and abrogate one or more of those classification distinctions. As you read through the found property cases, ask yourself which policy goals are furthered through the common law or statutory rules on found property.

3.1

Benjamin v. Lindner Aviation, Inc.
534 N.W.2d 400 (Iowa 1995)

Iowa Supreme Court

TERNUS, Justice.

Appellant, Heath Benjamin, found over $18,000 in currency inside the wing of an airplane. At the time of this discovery, appellee, State Central Bank, owned the plane and it was being serviced by appellee, Lindner Aviation, Inc. All three parties claimed the money as against the true owner. After a bench trial, the district court held that the currency was mislaid property and belonged to the owner of the plane. The court awarded a finder's fee to Benjamin. Benjamin appealed and Lindner Aviation and State Central Bank cross-appealed. We reverse on the bank's cross-appeal and otherwise affirm the judgment of the district court.

I. *Background Facts and Proceedings.*

In April of 1992, State Central Bank became the owner of an airplane when the bank repossessed it from its prior owner who had defaulted on a loan. In August of that year, the bank took the plane to Lindner Aviation for a routine annual inspection. Benjamin worked for Lindner Aviation and did the inspection.

As part of the inspection, Benjamin removed panels from the underside of the wings. Although these panels were to be removed annually as part of the routine inspection, a couple of the screws holding the panel on the left wing were so rusty that Benjamin had to use a drill to remove them. Benjamin testified that the panel probably had not been removed for several years.

Inside the left wing Benjamin discovered two packets approximately four inches high and wrapped in aluminum foil. He removed the packets from the wing and took off the foil wrapping. Inside the foil was paper currency, tied in string and wrapped in handkerchiefs. The currency was predominately twenty-dollar bills with mint dates before the 1960s, primarily in the 1950s. The money smelled musty.

Benjamin took one packet to his jeep and then reported what he had found to his supervisor, offering to divide the money with him. However, the supervisor reported the discovery to the owner of Lindner Aviation, William Engle. Engle insisted that they contact the authorities and he called the Department of Criminal Investigation. The money was eventually turned over to the Keokuk police department.

Two days later, Benjamin filed an affidavit with the county auditor claiming that he was the finder of the currency under the provisions of Iowa Code chapter 644 (1991).

40

Lindner Aviation and the bank also filed claims to the money. The notices required by chapter 644 were published and posted. *See* Iowa Code § 644.8 (1991). No one came forward within twelve months claiming to be the true owner of the money. *See id.* § 644.11 (if true owner does not claim property within twelve months, the right to the property vests in the finder).

Benjamin filed this declaratory judgment action against Lindner Aviation and the bank to establish his right to the property. The parties tried the case to the court. The district court held that chapter 644 applies only to "lost" property and the money here was mislaid property. The court awarded the money to the bank, holding that it was entitled to possession of the money to the exclusion of all but the true owner. The court also held that Benjamin was a "finder" within the meaning of chapter 644 and awarded him a ten percent finder's fee. *See id.* § 644.13 (a finder of lost property is entitled to ten percent of the value of the lost property as a reward).

Benjamin appealed. He claims that chapter 644 governs the disposition of all found property and any common law distinctions between various types of found property are no longer valid. He asserts alternatively that even under the common law classes of found property, he is entitled to the money he discovered. He claims that the trial court should have found that the property was treasure trove or was lost or abandoned rather than mislaid, thereby entitling the finder to the property.

The bank and Lindner Aviation cross-appealed. Lindner Aviation claims that if the money is mislaid property, it is entitled to the money as the owner of the premises on which the money was found, the hangar where the plane was parked. It argues in the alternative that it is the finder, not Benjamin, because Benjamin discovered the money during his work for Lindner Aviation. The bank asserts in its cross-appeal that it owns the premises where the money was found — the airplane — and that no one is entitled to a finder's fee because chapter 644 does not apply to mislaid property.

II. *Standard of Review.*

***

issue

Whether the money found by Benjamin was treasure trove or was mislaid, abandoned or lost property is a fact question. Therefore, the trial court's finding that the money was mislaid is binding on us if supported by substantial evidence.

III. Does Chapter 644 Supersede the Common Law Classifications of Found Property?

benjamin arg.

Benjamin argues that chapter 644 governs the rights of finders of property and abrogates the common law distinctions between types of found property. As he points out, lost property statutes are intended "to encourage and facilitate the return of property to the true owner, and then to reward a finder for his honesty if the property remains unclaimed." *Paset v. Old Orchard Bank & Trust Co.,* 62 Ill.App.3d 534, 19 Ill.Dec. 389, 393, 378 N.E.2d 1264, 1268 (1978) (interpreting a statute similar to chapter 644). These goals, Benjamin argues, can best be achieved by applying such statutes to all types of found property.

***

Although a few courts have adopted an expansive view of lost property statutes, we think Iowa law is to the contrary. In 1937, we quoted and affirmed a trial court ruling that "the old law of treasure trove is not merged in the statutory law of chapter 515, 1935 Code of Iowa." *Zornes v. Bowen,* 223 Iowa 1141, 1145, 274 N.W. 877, 879 (1937). Chapter 515 of the 1935 Iowa Code was eventually renumbered as chapter 644. The relevant sections of chapter 644 are unchanged since our 1937 decision. As recently as 1991, we stated that "[t]he rights of finders of property vary according to the characterization of the property found." *Ritz v. Selma United Methodist Church,* 467 N.W.2d 266, 268 (Iowa 1991). We went on to define and apply the common law classifications of found property in deciding the rights of the parties. *Id.* at 269. As our prior cases show, we have continued to use the common law distinctions between classes of found property despite the legislature's enactment of chapter 644 and its predecessors.

The legislature has had many opportunities since our decision in *Zornes* to amend the statute so that it clearly applies to all types of found property. However, it has not done so. When the legislature leaves a statute unchanged after the supreme court has interpreted it, we presume the legislature has acquiesced in our interpretation. *State v. Sheffey,* 234 N.W.2d 92, 97 (Iowa 1975). Therefore, we presume here that the legislature approves of our application of chapter 644 to lost property only. Consequently, we hold that chapter 644 does not abrogate the common law classifications of found property. We note this position is consistent with that taken by most jurisdictions. *See, e.g., Bishop v. Ellsworth,* 91 Ill. App.2d 386, 234 N.E.2d 49, 51 (1968) (holding lost property statute does not apply to abandoned or mislaid property); *Foster v. Fidelity Safe Deposit Co.,* 264 Mo. 89, 174 S.W. 376, 379 (1915) (refusing to apply lost property statute to property that would not be considered lost under the common law); *Soven v. Yoran,* 16 Or. 269, 20 P. 100, 105 (1888) (same); *Zech v. Accola,* 253 Wis. 80, 33 N.W.2d 232, 235 (1948) (concluding that if legislature had intended to include treasure trove within lost property statute, it would have specifically mentioned treasure trove).

In summary, chapter 644 applies only if the property discovered can be categorized as "lost" property as that term is defined under the common law. Thus, the trial court correctly looked to the common law classifications of found property to decide who had the right to the money discovered here.

IV. *Classification of Found Property.*

Under the common law, there are four categories of found property: (1) abandoned property, (2) lost property, (3) mislaid property, and (4) treasure trove. *Ritz,* 467 N.W.2d at 269. The rights of a finder of property depend on how the found property is classified. *Id.* at 268-69.

A. *Abandoned property.* Property is abandoned when the owner no longer wants to possess it. Abandonment is shown by *proof* that the owner intends to abandon the property and has voluntarily relinquished all right, title and interest in the property. *Ritz,* 467 N.W.2d at 269. Abandoned property belongs to the finder of the property against all others, including the former owner. *Ritz,* 467 N.W.2d at 269.

B. *Lost property.* "Property is lost when the owner unintentionally and involuntarily parts with its possession and does not know where it is." *Id.* . . . Under chapter 644, lost property becomes the property of the finder once the statutory procedures are followed and the owner makes no claim within twelve months. Iowa Code § 644.11 (1991).

C. *Mislaid property.* Mislaid property is voluntarily put in a certain place by the owner who then overlooks or forgets where the property is. *Ritz,* 467 N.W.2d at 269. It differs from lost property in that the owner voluntarily and intentionally places mislaid property in the location where it is eventually found by another. In contrast, property is not considered lost unless the owner parts with it involuntarily. *Ritz,* 467 N.W.2d at 269; *see Hill v. Schrunk,* 207 Or. 71, 292 P.2d 141, 143 (1956) (carefully concealed currency was mislaid property, not lost property).

The finder of mislaid property acquires no rights to the property. The right of possession of mislaid property belongs to the owner of the premises upon which the property is found, as against all persons other than the true owner. *Ritz,* 467 N.W.2d at 269.

D. *Treasure trove.* Treasure trove consists of coins or currency concealed by the owner. *Id.* It includes an element of antiquity. *Id.* To be classified as treasure trove, the property must have been hidden or concealed for such a length of time that the owner is probably dead or undiscoverable. *Id.* Treasure trove belongs to the finder as against all but the true owner. *Zornes,* 223 Iowa at 1145, 274 N.W. at 879.

V. *Is There Substantial Evidence to Support the Trial Court's Finding That the Money Found by Benjamin Was Mislaid?*

We think there was substantial evidence to find that the currency discovered by Benjamin was mislaid property. In the *Eldridge* case, we examined the location where the money was found as a factor in determining whether the money was lost property. *Eldridge,* 291 N.W.2d at 323; *accord* 1 Am. Jur.2d *Abandoned Property* § 6, at 11-12 ("The place where money or property claimed as lost is found is an important factor in the determination of the question of whether it was lost or only mislaid."). Similarly, in *Ritz,* we considered the manner in which the money had been secreted in deciding that it had not been abandoned. *Ritz,* 467 N.W.2d at 269.

The place where Benjamin found the money and the manner in which it was hidden are also important here. The bills were carefully tied and wrapped and then concealed in a location that was accessible only by removing screws and a panel. These circumstances support an inference that the money was placed there intentionally. This inference supports the conclusion that the money was mislaid. *Jackson v.*

Steinberg, 186 Or. 129, 200 P.2d 376, 378 (1948) (fact that $800 in currency was found concealed beneath the paper lining of a dresser indicates that money was intentionally concealed with intention of reclaiming it; therefore, property was mislaid, not lost); *Schley v. Couch,* 155 Tex. 195, 284 S.W.2d 333, 336 (1955) (holding that money found buried under garage floor was mislaid property as a matter of law because circumstances showed that money was placed there deliberately and court presumed that owner had either forgotten where he hid the money or had died before retrieving it).

The same facts that support the trial court's conclusion that the money was mislaid prevent us from ruling as a matter of law that the property was lost. Property is not considered lost unless considering the place where and the conditions under which the property is found, there is an inference that the property was left there unintentionally. 1 Am.Jur.2d *Abandoned Property* § 6, at 12; *see Sovern,* 20 P. at 105 (holding that coins found in a jar under a wooden floor of a barn were not lost property because the circumstances showed that the money was hidden there intentionally); *see Farrare v. City of Pasco,* 68 Wash.App. 459, 843 P.2d 1082, 1084 (1993) (where currency was deliberately concealed, it cannot be characterized as lost property). Contrary to Benjamin's position the circumstances here do not support a conclusion that the money was placed in the wing of the airplane unintentionally. Additionally, as the trial court concluded, there was no evidence suggesting that the money was placed in the wing by someone other than the owner of the money and that its location was unknown to the owner. For these reasons, we reject Benjamin's argument that the trial court was obligated to find that the currency Benjamin discovered was lost property.

We also reject Benjamin's assertion that as a matter of law this money was abandoned property. Both logic and common sense suggest that it is unlikely someone would voluntarily part with over $18,000 with the intention of terminating his ownership. The location where this money was found is much more consistent with the conclusion that the owner of the property was placing the money there for safekeeping. *See Ritz,* 467 N.W.2d at 269 (property not abandoned where money was buried in jars and tin cans, indicating a desire by the owner to preserve it); *Jackson,*

200 P.2d at 378 (because currency was concealed intentionally and deliberately, the bills could not be regarded as abandoned property); 1 Am. Jur.2d *Abandoned Property* § 13, at 17 (where property is concealed in such a way that the concealment appears intentional and deliberate, there can be no abandonment). We will not presume that an owner has abandoned his property when his conduct is consistent with a continued claim to the property. Therefore, we cannot rule that the district court erred in failing to find that the currency discovered by Benjamin was abandoned property.

Finally, we also conclude that the trial court was not obligated to decide that this money was treasure trove. Based on the dates of the currency, the money was no older than thirty-five years. The mint dates, the musty odor and the rusty condition of a few of the panel screws indicate that the money may have been hidden for some time. However, there was no evidence of the age of the airplane or the date of its last inspection. These facts may have shown that the money was concealed for a much shorter period of time.

Moreover, it is also significant that the airplane had a well-documented ownership history. The record reveals that there were only two owners of the plane prior to the bank. One was the person from whom the bank repossessed the plane; the other was the original purchaser of the plane when it was manufactured. Nevertheless, there is no indication that Benjamin or any other party attempted to locate and notify the prior owners of the plane, which could very possibly have led to the identification of the true owner of the money. Under these circumstances, we cannot say as a matter of law that the money meets the antiquity requirement or that it is probable that the owner of the money is not discoverable.

We think the district court had substantial evidence to support its finding that the money found by Benjamin was mislaid. The circumstances of its concealment and the location where it was found support inferences that the owner intentionally placed the money there and intended to retain ownership. We are bound by this factual finding.

VI. Is the Airplane or the Hangar the "Premises" Where the Money Was Discovered?

Because the money discovered by Benjamin was properly found to be mislaid property, it belongs to the owner of the premises where it was found. Mislaid property is entrusted to the owner of the premises where it is found rather than the finder of the property because it is assumed that the true owner may eventually recall where he has placed his property and return there to reclaim it.

We think that the premises where the money was found is the airplane, not Lindner Aviation's hangar where the airplane happened to be parked when the money was discovered. The policy behind giving ownership of mislaid property to the owner of the premises where the property was mislaid supports this conclusion. If the true owner of the money attempts to locate it, he would initially look for the plane; it is unlikely he would begin his search by contacting businesses where the airplane might have been inspected. Therefore, we affirm the trial court's judgment that the bank, as the owner of the plane, has the right to possession of the property as against all but the true owner.

VII. *Is Benjamin Entitled to a Finder's Fee?*

Benjamin claims that if he is not entitled to the money, he should be paid a ten percent finder's fee under section 644.13. The problem with this claim is that only the finder of *"lost* goods, money, bank notes, and other things" is rewarded with a finder's fee under chapter 644. Iowa Code § 644.13 (1991). Because the property found by Benjamin was mislaid property, not lost property, section 644.13 does not apply here. The trial court erred in awarding Benjamin a finder's fee.

VIII. *Summary.*

We conclude that the district court's finding that the money discovered by Benjamin was mislaid property is supported by substantial evidence. Therefore, we affirm the district court's judgment that the bank has the right to the money as against all but the true owner. This decision makes it unnecessary to decide whether Benjamin or Lindner Aviation was the finder of the property. We reverse the court's decision awarding a finder's fee to Benjamin.

AFFIRMED IN PART; REVERSED IN PART.

SNELL, Justice

(dissenting).

I respectfully dissent.

The life of the law is logic, it has been said. *See Davis v. Aiken,* 111 Ga.App. 505, 142 S.E.2d 112, 119 (1965) (quoting Sir Edward Coke). If so, it should be applied here.

***

After considering the four categories of found money, the majority decides that Benjamin found mislaid money. The result is that the bank gets all the money; Benjamin, the finder, gets nothing. Apart from the obvious unfairness in result, I believe this conclusion fails to come from logical analysis.

Mislaid property is property voluntarily put in a certain place by the owner who then overlooks or forgets where the property is. *Ritz v. Selma United Methodist Church,* 467 N.W.2d 266, 268 (Iowa 1991). The property here consisted of two packets of paper currency totalling $18,910, three to four inches high, wrapped in aluminum foil. Inside the foil, the paper currency, predominantly twenty dollar bills, was tied with string and wrapped in handkerchiefs. Most of the mint dates were in the 1950s with one dated 1934. These packets were found in the left wing of the Mooney airplane after Benjamin removed a panel held in by rusty screws.

These facts satisfy the requirement that the property was voluntarily put in a certain place by the owner. But the second test for determining that property is mislaid is that the owner "overlooks or forgets where the property is." *See Ritz,* 467 N.W.2d at 269. I do not believe that the facts, logic, or common sense lead to a finding that this requirement is met. It is not likely or reasonable to suppose that a person would secrete $18,000 in an airplane wing and then forget where it was.

Cases cited by the majority contrasting "mislaid" property and "lost" property are appropriate for a comparison of these principles but do not foreclose other considerations. After finding the money, Benjamin proceeded to give written notice of finding the property as prescribed in Iowa Code chapter 644 (1993), "Lost Property." As set out in section 556F.8, notices were posted on the courthouse door and in three other public places in the county. In addition, notice was published once each week for three consecutive weeks in a newspaper of general circulation in the county. Also, affidavits of publication were filed with the county auditor who then had them published as part of the board of supervisors' proceedings. Iowa Code § 556F.9. After twelve months, if no person appears to claim and prove ownership of the property, the right to the property rests irrevocably in the finder. Iowa Code § 556F.11.

The purpose of this type of legal notice is to give people the opportunity to assert a claim if they have one. If no claim is made, the law presumes there is none or for whatever reason it is not asserted. Thus, a failure to make a claim after legal notice is given is a bar to a claim made thereafter.

Benjamin followed the law in giving legal notice of finding property. None of the parties dispute this. The suggestion that Benjamin should have initiated a further search for the true owner is not a requirement of the law, is therefore irrelevant, and in no way diminishes Benjamin's rights as finder.

The scenario unfolded in this case convinces me that the money found in the airplane wing was abandoned. Property is abandoned when the owner no longer wants to possess it. *See Ritz*, 467 N.W.2d at 269. The money had been there for years, possibly thirty. No owner had claimed it in that time. No claim was made by the owner after legally prescribed notice was given that it had been found. Thereafter, logic and the law support a finding that the owner has voluntarily relinquished all right, title, and interest in the property. Whether the money was abandoned due to its connection to illegal drug trafficking or is otherwise contraband property is a matter for speculation. In any event, abandonment by the true owner has legally occurred and been established.

I would hold that Benjamin is legally entitled to the entire amount of money that he found in the airplane wing as the owner of abandoned property.

3.2

Grande v. Jennings
278 P.3d 1287 (Ariz. Ct. App. 2012)

Arizona Court of Appeals

PORTLEY, Judge.

This case asks us to resolve who owns the money found in the walls of a Paradise Valley home: the estate of the home's former owner or the couple who owned the home at the time of the discovery. The new homeowners appeal the summary judgment granted to the estate, and claim that the funds were abandoned when the home was sold "as is." For the following reasons, we affirm the judgment.

FACTUAL AND PROCEDURAL BACKGROUND

Robert A. Spann lived in his Paradise Valley home until he passed away in 2001. His daughter, Karen Spann Grande ("Grande"), became the personal representative of his estate. She and her sister, Kim Spann, took charge of the house and, among other things, had some repairs made to the home.[1]

They also looked for valuables their father may have left or hidden. They knew from experience that he had hidden gold, cash, and other valuables in unusual places in other homes. Over the course of seven years, they found stocks and bonds, as well as hundreds of military-style green ammunition cans hidden throughout the house, some of which contained gold or cash.

The house was sold "as is" to Sarina Jennings and Clinton McCallum ("Jennings/McCallum") in September 2008. They hired Randy Bueghly and his company, Trinidad Builders, Inc., to remodel the dilapidated home. Shortly after the work began, Rafael Cuen, a Trinidad employee, discovered two ammunition cans full of cash in the kitchen wall, went looking, and found two more cash-filled ammo cans inside the framing of an upstairs bathroom.

After Cuen reported the find to his boss, Bueghly took the four ammo cans but did not tell the new owners about the find, and tried to secret the cans. Cuen, however, eventually told the new owners about the discovery and the police were called. The police ultimately took control of $500,000, which Bueghly had kept in a floor safe in his home.

Jennings/McCallum sued Bueghly for fraudulent misrepresentation, conversion, and a declaration that Bueghly had no right to the money, and Bueghly later filed a counterclaim for a declaration that he was entitled to the found funds. In the meantime, Grande filed a petition in probate court on behalf of the estate to recover the *money*. The two cases were consolidated in June 2009.

The estate filed a motion for summary judgment and argued that Jennings/McCallum had no claim to the money found in the home. After briefing, the motion was granted. The trial court found that there were "no questions of material fact as to whether Robert A. Spann abandoned or mislaid the currency found in the house purchased by [Jennings/McCallum]" and that the estate did not waive its rights because "[the personal representative] claimed the property as soon as she became aware of it." Final judgment pursuant to Arizona Rule of Civil Procedure 54(b) was entered on January 12, 2011, leading to this appeal.

DISCUSSION

Jennings/McCallum argue that summary judgment was inappropriate because there was a genuine issue of material fact as to whether the estate had abandoned its rights to the found money. Specifically, they assert that a jury could have found that Grande "consciously ignored" the possibility that additional large sums of money could be hidden in the home because she did not locate all of the cash that her father had withdrawn from the bank and did not systematically search all potential hiding spots; therefore, the estate abandoned any rights it had when the house was sold. As a result, Jennings/McCallum argue, they are entitled to the discovered funds.

A.

We review a summary judgment de novo to determine "whether any genuine issues of material fact exist and whether the trial court properly applied the law." *Brookover v. Roberts Enters., Inc.,* 215 Ariz. 52, 55, ¶ 8, 156 P.3d 1157, 1160 (App.2007). And, we view the facts "in the light most favorable to [Jennings/McCallum], the party against whom summary judgment was entered."

B.

Although elementary school children like to say "finders keepers," the common law generally categorizes found property in one of four ways.[2] *E.g., Benjamin v. Lindner Aviation, Inc.,* 534 N.W.2d 400, 406 (Iowa 1995) (citing *Ritz v. Selma United Methodist Church,* 467 N.W.2d 266, 269 (Iowa 1991)). Found property can be mislaid, lost, abandoned, or treasure trove. *Id.* (citing *Ritz,* 467 N.W.2d at 269. Property is "mislaid" if the owner intentionally places it in a certain place and later forgets about it. *Terry v. Lock,* 343 Ark. 452, 37 S.W.3d 202, 207 (2001). "Lost" property includes property the owner unintentionally parts with through either carelessness or neglect. *Id.* at 206. "Abandoned" property has been thrown away, or was voluntarily forsaken by its owner. *Id.* (citations omitted). Property is considered "treasure trove" if it is verifiably antiquated and has been "concealed [for] so long as to indicate that the owner is probably dead or unknown." 1 Am.Jur.2d *Abandoned, Lost, and Unclaimed Property* § 16 (2012).

A finder's rights depend on how a court classifies the found property. *Terry,* 37 S.W.3d at 206 (citation omitted); *Ritz,* 467 N.W.2d at 268-69; *Hill v. Schrunk,* 207 Or. 71, 292 P.2d 141, 142 (1956). In characterizing the property, a court should consider all of the particular facts and circumstances of the case. *Terry,* 37 S.W.3d at 206 (citing *Schley v. Couch,* 155 Tex. 195, 284 S.W.2d 333, 336 (1955)); *Corliss,* 34 P.3d at 1103 (citing 1 Am.Jur.2d *Abandoned, Lost, and Unclaimed Property* §§ 1-14 (1994)) (distinctions between categories of found property are determined by "an analysis of the facts and circumstances in an effort to divine the intent of the true owner at the time he or she parted with the property"). Under the common law, "the finder of lost or abandoned property and treasure trove acquires a right to possess the property against the entire world but the rightful owner regardless of the place of finding." *Corliss,* 34 P.3d at 1104 (citing *Terry,* 37 S.W.3d at 206). A finder of mislaid property, however, must turn the property over to the premises owner, "who has the duty to safeguard the property for the true owner." *Id.* (citing *Terry,* 37 S.W.3d at 206); *see also Benjamin,* 534 N.W.2d at 406 (citing *Ritz,* 467 N.W.2d at 269) ("The right of possession of mislaid property belongs to the owner of the premises upon which the property is found, as against all persons other than the true owner.").

Significantly, among the various categories of found property, "only lost property necessarily involves an element of involuntariness." *Corliss,* 34 P.3d at 1104 (citation omitted). The remaining categories entail intentional and voluntary acts by the rightful owner in depositing property in a place where someone else eventually discovers it. *Id.* For example, the Iowa Supreme Court has stated that "[m]islaid property is voluntarily put in a certain place by the owner who then overlooks or forgets where the property is," and that one who finds mislaid property does not necessarily attain any rights to it because possession "belongs to the owner of the premises upon which the property is found," absent a claim by the true owner. *Benjamin,* 534 N.W.2d at 406 (citation omitted). In *Benjamin,* the court determined that packets of money found in a sealed panel of a wing during an inspection of a repossessed airplane were mislaid property because the money was intentionally placed there by one of the two prior owners. *Id.* at 403, 407-08.

Arizona follows the common law. In *Strawberry Water Co. v. Paulsen,* we stated that in order to abandon personal property, one must voluntarily and intentionally give up a known right. 220 Ariz. 401, 408, ¶ 16, 207 P.3d 654, 661 (App.2008) (citation omitted); *see also* 1 Am.Jur.2d *Abandoned, lost, and Unclaimed Property* § 3 (2012) ("Abandonment ... is the owner's relinquishment of a right with the intention to forsake and desert it."). Abandonment is "a virtual throwing away [of property] without regard as to who may take over or carry on." 1 Am.Jur.2d *Abandoned, Lost, and Unclaimed Property* § 3 (footnote omitted). In fact:

> While personal property of all kinds may be abandoned, the property must be of such a character as to make it clear that it was voluntarily abandoned by the owner. In this connection, it has been said that people do not normally abandon their money; and, accordingly, that found money will not be considered as abandoned, but as lost or mislaid property.

25 Am. Jur.2d *Abandonment of Tangible Personal Property* § 2 (1981).

C.

Here, it is undisputed that Spann placed the cash in the ammunition cans and then hid those cans in the recesses of the house. He did not, however, tell his daughters where he had hidden the cans before he passed away. His daughters looked for and found many of the ammo cans, but not the last four. In fact, it was not until the wall-mounted toaster oven and bathroom drywall were removed that Cuen found the remaining cash-filled cans. As a result, and as the trial court found, the funds are, as a matter of law, mislaid funds that belong to the true owner, Spann's estate.

Other state courts have also characterized found money as mislaid funds. For example, in *Hill v. Schrunk,* the Oregon Supreme Court held that cash, which was wrapped in oiled paper, placed in waterproof containers, and found lodged in the bottom of a natural water pool on the decedent's property, belonged to him at his death, and was mislaid rather than abandoned, lost, or treasure trove property. 292 P.2d at 142-43. Similarly, the Arkansas Supreme Court affirmed the trial court's finding that a dusty cardboard box containing about $38,000 and found in the ceiling of a motel room during renovation was mislaid property because " 'the money ... was intentionally placed where it was found for its security, in order to shield it from unwelcome eyes....' " *Terry,* 37 S.W.3d at 203-04, 208. As a result, the court affirmed the determination that the motel owner's rights to the funds were superior to those of the whole world except the true owner. *Id.* at 209.

D.

Jennings/McCallum assert, however, that the mislaid funds were abandoned because Grande consciously ignored the fact that neither she nor her sister had found all of the money that their father had withdrawn from his bank account, and did not do more to find it. We disagree.

First, evidence of the decedent's cash withdrawals from the bank was not presented to the trial court as part of the summary judgment motion. Second, the fact that the trial court correctly determined that the funds were mislaid precludes the funds from being considered abandoned. *See Terry,* 37 S.W.3d at 207-09 (citations omitted) (A finder of lost or abandoned property acquires ownership rights inferior only to those of the true owner; in contrast, " '[t]he finder of mislaid property must turn it over to the owner or occupier of the premises where it is found ..., [who then has a] duty to keep mislaid property for the [true] owner, and ... must use the care required of a gratuitous bailee for its safekeeping until the true owner calls for it.' ").

Moreover, abandonment is generally not presumed, but must be proven. Here, the facts are undisputed that the estate did not know that the money was mislaid, and did not intend to abandon the funds. In fact, the evidence is to the contrary; once Grande learned of the discovery, she filed a probate petition to recover the property.

Her action as the personal representative undermines the argument that the sisters abandoned the money through "conscious ignorance."

***

Based on the evidence before the trial court, there were no facts from which we could begin to infer that the estate intended to relinquish any valuable items that may have been secreted within the home. *See Benjamin*, 534 N.W.2d at 407 (rejecting the assertion that money found in airplane panel was abandoned because "[b]oth logic and common sense suggest that it is unlikely someone would voluntarily part with over $18,000 with the intention of terminating his ownership"). In fact, the evidence is to the contrary. Accordingly, summary judgment was appropriately granted.

CONCLUSION

Based on the foregoing, we affirm the summary judgment.

1. Robert Spann had allowed the home to fall into disrepair over the years.

2. At least one court has recognized a fifth category — "embedded property" — which is property that becomes part of the earth. Generally, embedded property "belongs to the owner of the soil" unless the true owner claims the property. See Klein v. Unidentified Wrecked & Abandoned Sailing Vessel, 758 F.2d 1511, 1514 (11th Cir.1985); see also 1 Am.Jur.2d Abandoned, Lost, and Unclaimed Property § 17 (2012) (footnote and citations omitted) (" 'Property embedded in the earth' includes anything other than gold or silver which is so buried, and is distinguished, in this respect, from 'treasure trove.' "). [Editorial Note: This is footnote 4 of the opinion.]

3.3

Favorite v. Miller
407 A.2d 974 (Conn. 1978)

Connecticut Supreme Court

Bogdanski, J.

On July 9, 1776, a band of patriots, hearing news of the Declaration of Independence, toppled the equestrian statue of King George III, which was located in Bowling Green Park in lower Manhattan, New York. The statue, of gilded lead, was then hacked apart and the pieces ferried over Long Island Sound and loaded onto wagons at Norwalk, Connecticut, to be hauled some fifty miles northward to Oliver Wolcott's bullet-molding foundry in Litchfield, there to be cast into bullets. On the journey to Litchfield, the wagoners halted at Wilton, Connecticut, and while the patriots were imbibing, the loyalists managed to steal back pieces of the statue. The wagonload of the pieces lifted by the Tories was scattered about in the area of the Davis swamp in Wilton and fragments of the statue have continued to turn up in that area since that time.1

Although the above events have been dramatized in the intervening years, the unquestioned historical facts are: (1) the destruction of the statue; (2) cartage of the pieces to the Wolcott foundry; (3) the pause at Wilton where part of the load was scattered over the Wilton area by loyalists; and (4) repeated discoveries of fragments over the last century.

In 1972, the defendant, Louis Miller, determined that a part of the statue might be located within property owned by the plaintiffs. On October 16 he entered the area of the Davis Swamp owned by the plaintiffs although he knew it to be private property. With the aid of a metal detector, he discovered a statuary fragment fifteen inches square and weighing twenty pounds which was embedded ten inches below the soil. He dug up this fragment and removed it from the plaintiffs' property. The plaintiffs did not learn that a piece of the statue of King George III had been found on their property until they read about it in the newspaper, long after it had been removed.

In due course, the piece of the statue made its way back to New York City, where the defendant agreed to sell it to the Museum of the City of New York for $5500. The museum continues to hold it pending resolution of this controversy.

In March of 1973, the plaintiffs instituted this action to have the fragment returned to them and the case was submitted to the court on a stipulation of facts. The trial court found the issues for the plaintiffs, from which judgment the defendant appealed to this court. The sole issue presented on appeal is whether the claim of the defendant, as finder, is superior to that of the plaintiffs, as owners of the land upon which the historic fragment was discovered.

Issue

Traditionally, when questions have arisen concerning the rights of the finder as against the person upon whose land the property was found, the resolution has turned upon the characterization given the property. Typically, if the property was found to be "lost" or "abandoned," the finder would prevail, whereas if the property was characterized as "mislaid," the owner or occupier of the land would prevail.

Lost property has traditionally been defined as involving an involuntary parting, i.e., where there is no intent on the part of the loser to part with the ownership of the property. Abandonment, in turn, has been defined as the voluntary relinquishment of ownership of property without reference to any particular person or purpose; i.e., a "throwing away" of the property concerned; *Foulke* v. *New York Consolidated R. Co.,* 228 N.Y. 269, 273, 127 N.E. 237 (1920); while mislaid property is defined as that which is intentionally placed by the owner where he can obtain custody of it, but afterwards forgotten. *Foster* v. *Fidelity Safe Deposit Co.,* supra; *Loucks* v. *Gallogly,*[1] Misc. 22, 23 N.Y.S. 126 (1892).

It should be noted that the classification of property as "lost," "abandoned," or "mislaid" requires that a court determine the intent or mental state of the unknown party who at some time in the past parted with the ownership or control of the property.

PP

The trial court in this case applied the traditional approach and ruled in favor of the landowners on the ground that the piece of the statue found by Miller was "mislaid." The factual basis for that conclusion is set out in the finding, where the court found that "the loyalists did not wish to have the pieces [in their possession] during the turmoil surrounding the Revolutionary War and hid them in a place where they could resort to them [after the war], but forgot where they put them."

def. arg.

The defendant contends that the finding was made without evidence and that the court's conclusion "is legally impossible now after 200 years with no living claimants to the fragment and the secret of its burial having died with them." While we cannot agree that the court's conclusion was legally impossible, we do agree that any conclusion as to the mental state of persons engaged in events which occurred over two hundred years ago would be of a conjectural nature and as such does not furnish an adequate basis for determining rights of twentieth century claimants.

The defendant argues further that his rights in the statue are superior to those of anyone except the true owner (i.e., the British government). He presses this claim on the ground that the law has traditionally favored the finder as against all but the true owner, and that because his efforts brought the statue to light, he should be allowed to reap the benefits of his discovery. In his brief, he asserts: "As with archeologists forever probing and unearthing the past, to guide man for the betterment of those to follow, explorers like Miller deserve encouragement, and reward, in their selfless pursuit of the hidden, the unknown."

There are, however, some difficulties with the defendant's position. The first concerns the defendant's characterization of himself as a selfless seeker after knowledge. The facts in the record do not support such a conclusion. The defendant admitted that he was in the business of selling metal detectors and that he has used his success in finding the statue as advertising to boost his sales of such metal detectors, and that the advertising has been financially rewarding. Further, there is the fact that he signed a contract with the City Museum of New York for the sale of the statuary piece and that he stands to profit thereby.

Moreover, even if we assume his motive to be that of historical research alone, that fact will not justify his entering upon the property of another without permission. It is unquestioned that in today's world even archeologists must obtain permission from owners of property and the government of the country involved before they can conduct their explorations. Similarly, mountaineers must apply for permits, sometimes years in advance of their proposed expeditions. On a more familiar level, backpackers and hikers must often obtain permits before being allowed access to certain of our national parks and forests, even though that land is public and not private. Similarly, hunters and fishermen wishing to enter upon private property must first obtain the permission of the owner before they embark upon their respective pursuits.

Although few cases are to be found in this area of the law, one line of cases which have dealt with this issue has held that except where the trespass is trivial or merely technical, the fact that the finder is trespassing is sufficient to deprive him of his normal preference over the owner of the place where the property was found. The basis for the rule is that a wrongdoer should not be allowed to profit by his wrongdoing. Another line of cases holds that property, other than treasure trove,[2] which is found embedded in the earth is the property of the owner of the locus in quo. *Allred* v. *Biegel,* 240 Mo. App. 818, 219 S.W.2d 665 (1949) (prehistoric Indian canoe); *Ferguson* v. *Ray,* 44 Or. 557, 77 P. 600 (1904); *Schley* v. *Couch,* 155 Tex. 195, 284 S.W.2d 333 (1955); *South Staffordshire Water Co.* v. *Sharman,* 2 Q.B. 44 (1896); *Elwes* v. *Brigg Gas Co.,* 33 Ch. 562 (1886) (prehistoric boat); . . . The presumption in such cases is that possession of the article found is in the owner of the land and that the finder acquires no rights to the article found.

The defendant, by his own admission, knew that he was trespassing when he entered upon the property of the plaintiffs. He admitted that he was told by Gertrude Merwyn, the librarian of the Wilton Historical Society, *before* he went into the Davis Swamp area, that the land was privately owned and that Mrs. Merwyn recommended that he call the owners, whom she named, and obtain permission before he began his explorations. He also admitted that when he later told Mrs. Merwyn about his discovery, she again suggested that he contact the owners of the property, but that he failed to do so.

In the stipulation of facts submitted to the court, the defendant admitted entering the Davis Swamp property "with the belief that part of the 'King George Statue' . . . might be located within said property and with the intention of removing [the] same if located." The defendant has also admitted that the piece of the statue which he found was embedded in the ground ten inches below the surface and that it was necessary for him to excavate in order to take possession of his find.

In light of those undisputed facts the defendant's trespass was neither technical nor trivial. We conclude that the fact that the property found was embedded in the earth and the fact that the defendant was a trespasser are sufficient to defeat any claim to the property which the defendant might otherwise have had as a finder.

Where the trial court reaches a correct decision but on mistaken grounds, this court has repeatedly sustained the trial court's action if proper grounds exist to support it. The present case falls within the ambit of that principle of law and we affirm the decision of the court below.

There is no error.

1. The fascinating story of the journey which these pieces of lead took following the revolution is fully narrated in the New York Times of February 4, 1973; Nooks and Corners of Old New York (American Heritage series, Charles Scribner's 1899); Andrist, "Alas, Poor George, Where Is Your Head?" Smithsonian, September, 1974, and in numerous books familiar to students of American history.

2. Treasure trove has traditionally been strictly and narrowly defined as "any gold or silver in coin, plate, or bullion found concealed in the earth or in a house or other private place." 1 Am. Jur. 2d 6, Abandoned, Lost, and Unclaimed Property § 4. This strict definition is well established in American law. Danielson v. Roberts, 44 Or. 108, 74 P. 913 (1904) (gold coin); Zech v. Accola, 253 Wis. 80, 33 N.W.2d 232(1948) (paper certificates). Since the fragment of the statue recovered by the defendant was of gilded lead, he makes no claim that the fragment constituted treasure trove.

3.4
Discussion: Notes, Questions, and Problems

3.4.1
Discussion Note #1. Overriding issues

Where overriding issues appear, such as trespass or embedded property, some courts will not award found property to the finder despite the applicability of the common law categories. *See Favorite v. Miller*, excerpted above, and footnote 2 of *Grande v. Jennings*, excerpted above.

3.4.2

Discussion Question #2. Mislaid property to owner of locus?

Do you agree that mislaid property should generally go to the owner of the locus?

3.4.3

Discussion Question #3. Treasure trove to finder?

When, if ever, should treasure trove go to the owner of the locus rather than the finder?

3.4.4

Discussion Problem #4. Fitting room problem

Assume a customer was shopping in a clothing store. When the customer went to the fitting room to try on some clothing, the customer noticed a package on the chair of the fitting room. The package contained valuable electronic merchandise, but nothing to identify the owner of the merchandise. In a dispute between the customer and the clothing store owner, who would have a better claim to the merchandise and why?

4

Chapter 4 · Bailments

Although you may not be familiar with the term bailment, you are likely very familiar with the concept of a bailment. A **bailment** is the transfer of possession of goods to another with the understanding, express or implied, that the goods will be returned. Common examples include transferring possession of a car to a valet for valet parking, dropping off a suit with a dry cleaner, or more casually allowing a friend to borrow a book. All of these are typical examples of bailments. As you review the cases be sure to distinguish bailment relationships from other arrangements such as trusts. Note that the bailee has possession during the period of the bailment but not title to the property. Disputes in this area often arise when the bailed goods were damaged, stolen, or misdelivered during the duration of the bailment. Ask yourself what standard of care may apply. Be sure to properly categorize the parties. Note that the **bailor** transfers the property to the **bailee**.

4.1

Allen v. Hyatt Regency-Nashville Hotel 668 S.W.2d 286 (Tenn. 1984)

Tennessee Supreme Court

HARBISON, Justice.

In this case the Court is asked to consider the nature and extent of the liability of the operator of a commercial parking garage for theft of a vehicle during the absence of the owner. Both courts below, on the basis of prior decisions from this state, held that a bailment was created when the owner parked and locked his vehicle in a modern, indoor, multi-story garage operated by appellant in conjunction with a large hotel in downtown Nashville. We affirm.

There is almost no dispute as to the relevant facts. Appellant is the owner and operator of a modern high-rise hotel in Nashville fronting on the south side of Union Street. Immediately to the rear, or south, of the main hotel building there is a multi-story parking garage with a single entrance and a single exit to the west, on Seventh Avenue, North. As one enters the parking garage at the street level, there is a large sign reading "Welcome to Hyatt Regency-Nashville." There is another Hyatt Regency sign inside the garage at street level, together with a sign marked "Parking." The garage is available for parking by members of the general public as well as guests of the hotel, and the public are invited to utilize it.

On the morning of February 12, 1981, appellee's husband, Edwin Allen, accompanied by two passengers, drove appellee's new 1981 automobile into the parking garage. Neither Mr. Allen nor his passengers intended to register at the hotel as a guest. Mr. Allen had parked in this particular garage on several occasions, however, testifying that he felt that the vehicle would be safer in an attended garage than in an unattended outside lot on the street.

The single entrance was controlled by a ticket machine. The single exit was controlled by an attendant in a booth just opposite to the entrance and in full view thereof. Appellee's husband entered the garage at the street level and took a ticket which was automatically dispensed by the machine. The machine activated a barrier gate which rose and permitted Mr. Allen to enter the garage. He drove to the fourth floor level, parked the vehicle, locked it, retained the ignition key, descended by elevator to the street level and left the garage. When he returned several hours later, the car was gone, and it has never been recovered. Mr. Allen reported the theft to the attendant at the exit booth, who stated, "Well, it didn't come out here." The attendant did not testify at the trial.

Mr. Allen then reported the theft to security personnel employed by appellant, and subsequently reported the loss to the police. Appellant regularly employed a number of security guards, who were dressed in a distinctive uniform, two of whom were on duty most of the time. These guards patrolled the hotel grounds and building as well as the garage and were instructed to make rounds through the garage, although not necessarily at specified intervals. One of the security guards told appellee's husband that earlier in the day he had received the following report:

"He said, 'It's a funny thing here. On my report here a lady called me somewhere around nine-thirty or after and said that there was someone messing with a car.' "

The guard told Mr. Allen that he closed his office and went up into the garage to investigate, but reported that he did not find anything unusual or out of the ordinary.

Customers such as Mr. Allen, upon entering the garage, received a ticket from the dispensing machine. On one side of this ticket are instructions to overnight guests to present the ticket to the front desk of the hotel. The other side contains instructions to the parker to keep the ticket and that the ticket must be presented to the cashier upon leaving the parking area. The ticket states that charges are made for the use of parking space only and that appellant assumes no responsibility for loss through fire, theft, collision or otherwise to the car or its contents. The ticket states that cars are parked at the risk of the owner, and parkers are instructed to lock their vehicles.[1] The record indicates that these tickets are given solely for the purpose of measuring the time during which a vehicle is parked in order that the attendant may collect the proper charge, and that they are not given for the purpose of identifying particular vehicles.

The question of the legal relationship between the operator of a vehicle which is being parked and the operator of parking establishments has been the subject of frequent litigation in this state and elsewhere. The authorities are in conflict, and the results of the cases are varied.

It is legally and theoretically possible, of course, for various legal relationships to be created by the parties, ranging from the traditional concepts of lessor-lessee, licensor-licensee, bailor-bailee, to that described in some jurisdictions as a "deposit." Several courts have found difficulty with the traditional criteria of bailment in analyzing park-and-lock cases. One of the leading cases is McGlynn v. Parking Authority of City of Newark, 86 N.J. 551, 432 A.2d 99 (1981). There the Supreme Court of New Jersey reviewed numerous decisions from within its own state and from other jurisdictions, and it concluded that it was more "useful and straightforward" to consider the possession and control elements in defining the duty of care of a garage operator to its customers than to consider them in the context of bailment. That Court concluded that the "realities" of the relationship between the parties gave rise to a duty of reasonable care on the part of operators of parking garages and parking lots. It further found that a garage owner is usually better situated to protect a parked car and to distribute the cost of protection through parking fees. It also emphasized that owners usually expect to receive their vehicles back in the same condition in which they left them and that the imposition of a duty to protect parked vehicles and their contents was consistent with that expectation. The Court went further and stated that since the owner is ordinarily absent when theft or damage occurs, the obligation to come forward with affirmative evidence of negligence could impose a difficult, if not insurmountable, burden upon him. After considering various policy considerations, which it acknowledged be the same as those recognized by courts holding that a bailment is created, the New Jersey Court indulged or authorized a presumption of negligence from proof of damage to a car parked in an enclosed garage. 432 A.2d at 105.[2]

Although the New Jersey Court concluded that a more flexible and comprehensive approach could be achieved outside of traditional property concepts, Tennessee courts generally have analyzed cases such as' this in terms of sufficiency of the evidence to create a bailment for hire by implication. We believe that this continues to be the majority view and the most satisfactory and realistic approach to the problem, unless the parties clearly by their conduct or by express contract create some other relationship.

The subject has been discussed in numerous previous decisions in this state. One of the leading cases is Dispeker v. New Southern Hotel Co., 213 Tenn. 378, 373 S.W.2d 904 (1963). In that case the guest at a hotel delivered his vehicle to a bellboy who took possession of it and parked it in a lot adjoining the hotel building. The owner kept the keys, but the car apparently was capable of being started without the ignition key. The owner apparently had told the attendant how to so operate it. Later the employee took the vehicle for his own' purposes and damaged it. Under these circumstances the Court held that a bailment for hire had been created and that upon proof of misdelivery of the vehicle the bailee was liable to the customer.

In the subsequent case of Scruggs v. Dennis, 222 Tenn. 714, 440 S.W.2d 20 (1969), upon facts practically identical to those of the instant case, the Court again held that an implied bailment contract had been created between a customer who parked and locked his vehicle in a garage. Upon entry he received a ticket dispensed by a machine, drove his automobile to the underground third level of the garage and parked. He retained his ignition key, but when he returned to retrieve the automobile in the afternoon it had disappeared. It was recovered more than two weeks later and returned to the owner in a damaged condition.

In that case the operator of the garage had several attendants on duty, but the attendants did not ordinarily operate the parked vehicles, as in the instant case.

Although the Court recognized that there were some factual differences between the Scruggs case and that of Dispeker v. New Southern Hotel Co., supra, it concluded that a bailment had been created when the owner parked his vehicle for custody and safe keeping in the parking garage, where there was limited access and where the patron had to present a ticket to an attendant upon leaving the premises.

***

On the contrary, in the case of Rhodes v. Pioneer Parking Lot, Inc., 501 S.W.2d 569 (Tenn.1973), a bailment was found not to exist when the owner left his vehicle in an open parking lot which was wholly unattended and where he simply inserted coins into a meter, received a ticket, then parked the vehicle himself and locked it.

Denying recovery, the Court said:

> "In the case at bar, however, we find no evidence to justify a finding that the plaintiff delivered his car into the custody of the defendant, nor do we find any act or conduct upon the defendant's part which would justify a reasonable person believing that an obligation of bailment had been assumed by the defendant." 501 S.W.2d at 571.

In the instant case, appellee's vehicle was not driven into an unattended or open parking area. Rather it was driven into an enclosed, indoor, attended commercial garage which not only had an attendant controlling the exit but regular security personnel to patrol the premises for safety.

Under these facts we are of the opinion that the courts below correctly concluded that a bailment for hire had been created, and that upon proof of nondelivery appellee was entitled to the statutory presumption of negligence provided in T.C.A. § 24-5-111.

We recognize that there is always a question as to whether there has been sufficient delivery of possession and control to create a bailment when the owner locks a vehicle and keeps the keys. Nevertheless, the realities of the situation are that the operator of the garage is, in circumstances like those shown in this record, expected to provide attendants and protection. In practicality the operator does assume control and custody of the vehicles parked, limiting access thereto and requiring the presentation of a ticket upon exit. As stated previously, the attendant employed by appellant did not testify, but he told appellee's husband that the vehicle did not come out of the garage through the exit which he controlled. This testimony was not amplified, but the attendant obviously must have been in error or else must have been inattentive or away from his station. The record clearly shows that there was no other exit from which the vehicle could have been driven.

Appellant made no effort to rebut the presumption created by statute in this state (which is similar to presumptions indulged by courts in some other jurisdictions not having such statutes). While the plaintiff did not prove positive acts of negligence on the part of appellant, the record does show that some improper activity or tampering with vehicles had been called to the attention of security personnel earlier in the day of the theft in question, and that appellee's new vehicle had been removed from the garage by some person or persons unknown, either driving past an inattentive attendant or one who had absented himself from his post, there being simply, no other way in which the vehicle could have been driven out of the garage.

Under the facts and circumstances of this case, we are not inclined to depart from prior decisions or to place the risk of loss upon the consuming public as against the operators of commercial parking establishments such as that conducted by appellant. We recognize that park-and-lock situations arise under many and varied factual circumstances. It is difficult to lay down one rule of law which will apply to all cases. The expectations of the parties and their conduct can cause differing legal relationships to arise, with consequent different legal results. We do not find the facts of the present case, however, to be at variance with the legal requirements of the traditional concept of a bailment for hire. In our opinion it amounted to more than a mere license or hiring of a space to park a vehicle, unaccompanied by any expectation of protection or other obligation upon the operator of the establishment.

The judgment of the courts below is affirmed at the cost of appellant. The cause will be remanded to the trial court for any further proceedings which may be necessary.

DROWOTA, Justice,

dissenting.

In this case we are asked to consider the nature and extent of liability of the operator of a commercial "park and lock" parking garage. In making this determination, we must look to the legal relationship between the operator of the vehicle and the operator of the parking facility. The majority opinion holds that a bailment contract has been created, and upon proof of non-delivery Plaintiff is entitled to the statutory presumption of negligence provided in T.C.A. § 24-5-111. I disagree, for I find no bailment existed and therefore the Plaintiff does not receive the benefit of the presumption. Consequently, the Plaintiff had the duty to prove affirmatively the negligence of the operator of the parking facility and this Plaintiff failed to do.

***

The majority opinion states: "[W]e do not find the facts of the present case to be at variance with the legal requirements of the concept of a bailment for hire." I must disagree, for I feel the facts of the present case are clearly at variance with what I consider to be the legal requirements of the traditional concept of a bailment for hire.

***

From its earliest origins, the most distinguishing factor identifying a bailment has been delivery. Our earliest decisions also recognize acceptance as a necessary factor, requiring that possession and control of the property pass from bailor to bailee, to the exclusion of control by others. The test thus becomes whether the operator of the vehicle has made such a delivery to the operator of the parking facility as to amount to a relinquishment of his exclusive possession, control, and dominion over the vehicle so that the latter can exclude it from the possession of all others. If so, a bailment has been created.

***

The Scruggs opinion was recently cited in a dissenting opinion in Kentucky where the plaintiff entered a six-story, self-parking garage in downtown Louisville. The only employee on duty was the attendant who collected the money from the driver upon exiting. The garage was patrolled three times daily by garage personnel. The Kentucky Supreme Court chose not to follow the Scruggs rationale and held "when a person parks his automobile in a garage by receiving a ticket from an automated machine, choosing his own space and taking his keys with him, the garage is not a bailee and is not liable in the absence of negligence on its part." Central Parking System v. Miller, 586 S.W.2d 262, 263 (Ky.1979).

The difficulty in these types of cases seems to arise when the traditional elements of bailment are missing and courts must determine whether there is an implied bailment created by implication from the surrounding circumstances and the conduct of the parties. In Jackson v. Metropolitan Government of Nashville, 483 S.W.2d 92 (Tenn.1972), the Court based its opinion on the finding that the Defendants, by their conduct, "impliedly promised to use ordinary and reasonable care to preserve the property during the term of the bailment and to return the bail property to complainant on demand or to his order." Id., at 95.

The majority opinion "recognize[s] that there is always a question as to whether there has been sufficient delivery of possession and control to create a bailment when the owner locks a vehicle and keeps the keys." The majority finds that "in practicality the operator does assume control and custody of the vehicles parked, limiting access thereto and requiring the presentation of a ticket upon exit." The majority opinion, as did the Scruggs court, finds custody and control implied because of the limited access and because "the presentation of a ticket upon exit" is required. I cannot agree with this analysis as creating a bailment situation. I do not believe that based upon the fact that a ticket was required to be presented upon leaving, that this factor created a proper basis upon which to find a bailment relationship. The ticket did not identify the vehicle or the operator of the vehicle, as do most bailment receipts. The cashier was not performing the traditional bailee role or identifying and returning a particular article, but instead was merely computing the amount owed and accepting payment due for use of a parking space. I do not believe the Defendant exercised such possession and control over Plaintiff's automobile as is necessary in an implied bailment.

As recently stated in Merritt v. Nationwide Warehouse Co., Ltd., 605 S.W.2d 250, 253 (Tenn.App.1980), "Such full delivery must be made as will entitle the bailee to exclude the possession of all other persons and put him in sole custody and control." The full transfer of possession and control, necessary to constitute delivery, should not be found to exist simply by the presentation of a ticket upon exit. In the case at bar, I find no such delivery and relinquishment of exclusive possession and control as to create a bailment. Plaintiff parked his car, locked it and retained the key. Certainly Defendant cannot be said to have sole custody of Plaintiff's vehicle, for Defendant could not move it, did not know to whom it belonged, and did not know when it would be reclaimed or by whom. Anyone who manually obtained a ticket from the dispenser could drive out with any vehicle he was capable of operating. Also, a cashier was not always on duty. When on duty, so long as the parking fee was paid— by what means could the Defendant reasonably exercise control? The necessary delivery and relinquishment of control by the Plaintiff, the very basis upon which the bailment theory was developed, is missing.

We should realize that the circumstances upon which the principles of bailment law were established and developed are not always applicable to the operation of the modern day automated parking facility. The element of delivery, of sole custody and control are lacking in this case.

1. It is not insisted that the language of the ticket is sufficient to exonerate appellant, since the customer is not shown to have read it or to have had it called to his attention. See Savoy Hotel Corp. v. Sparks, 57 Tenn.App. 537, 421 S.W.2d 98 (1967).

2. Other courts, declining to find a bailment, have onerated the customer with proving negligence. E.g., Central Parking System v. Miller, 586 S.W.2d 262 (Ky.1979). [Editorial Note: This is footnote 4 of the opinion.]

Shamrock Hilton Hotel v. Caranas
488 S.W.2d 151 (Tex. Ct. App. 1972)

Texas Court of Civil Appeals

BARRON, Justice.

This is an appeal in an alleged bailment case from a judgment non obstante veredicto in favor of plaintiffs below.

Plaintiffs, husband and wife, were lodging as paying guests at the Shamrock Hilton Hotel in Houston on the evening of September 4, 1966, when they took their dinner in the hotel restaurant. After completing the meal, Mr. and Mrs. Caranas, plaintiffs, departed the dining area leaving her purse behind. The purse was found by the hotel bus boy who, pursuant to the instructions of the hotel, dutifully delivered the forgotten item to the restaurant cashier, a Mrs. Luster. The testimony indicates that some short time thereafter the cashier gave the purse to a man other than Mr. Caranas who came to claim it. There is no testimony on the question of whether identification was sought by the cashier. The purse allegedly contained $5.00 in cash, some credit cards, and ten pieces of jewelry said to be worth $13,062. The misplacement of the purse was realized the following morning, at which time plaintiffs notified the hotel authorities of the loss.

Plaintiffs filed suit alleging negligent delivery of the purse to an unknown person and seeking a recovery for the value of the purse and its contents.

The trial was to a jury which found that the cashier was negligent in delivering the purse to someone other than plaintiffs, and that this negligence was a proximate cause of the loss of the purse. The jury further found that plaintiffs were negligent in leaving the purse containing the jewelry in the hotel dining room, and that this negligence was a proximate cause of the loss.

A motion for judgment n. o. v. and to disregard findings with respect to the findings that plaintiffs' negligence was a proximate cause of the loss of the purse and its contents was granted, and judgment was entered by the trial court for plaintiffs in the amount of $11,252.00 plus interest and costs. Shamrock Hilton Hotel and Hilton Hotels Corporation have perfected this appeal.

We find after a full review of the record that there is sufficient evidence to warrant the submission of appellees' issues complained of and to support the jury findings on the special issues to the effect that the misdelivery was negligence and a proximate cause of the loss to appellees. . . .

Contrary to appellants' contention, we find that there was indeed a constructive bailment of the purse. The delivery and acceptance were evidenced in the acts of Mrs. Caranas' unintentionally leaving her purse behind in the hotel restaurant and the bus boy, a hotel employee, picking it up and taking it to the cashier who accepted the purse as a lost or misplaced item. The delivery need not be a knowingly intended act on the part of Mrs. Caranas if it is apparent that were she, the quasi or constructive bailor, aware of the circumstances (here the chattel's being misplaced) she would have desired the person finding the article to have kept it safely for its subsequent return to her.

As stated above, the evidence conclusively showed facts from which there was established a bailment with the Caranases as bailors and the hotel as bailee. The evidence also showed that the hotel, as bailee, had received Mrs. Caranas' purse and had not returned it on demand. Such evidence raised a presumption that the hotel had failed to exercise ordinary care in protecting the appellees' property. When the hotel failed to come forward with any evidence to the effect that it had exercised ordinary care, that the property had been stolen, or that the property had been lost, damaged or destroyed by fire or by an act of God, the appellees' proof ripened into proof by which the hotel's primary liability was established as a matter of law.

***

Further, this bailment was one for the mutual benefit of both parties. Appellees were paying guests in the hotel and in its dining room. Appellant hotel's practice' of keeping patrons' lost personal items until they could be returned to their rightful owners, as reflected in the testimony, is certainly evidence of its being incidental to its business, as we would think it would be for almost any commercial enterprise which caters to the general public. Though no direct charge is made for this service there is indirect benefit to be had in the continued patronage of the hotel by customers who have lost chattels and who have been able to claim them from the management.

Having found this to have been a bailment for the mutual benefit of the parties, we hold that the appellants owed the appellees the duty of reasonable care in the return of the purse and jewelry, and the hotel is therefore liable for its ordinary negligence.

Appellants urge that if a bailment is found it existed only as to "the purse and the usual petty cash or credit cards found therein" and not to the jewelry of which the hotel had no actual notice. This exact question so far as we can determine has never been squarely put before the Texas Courts, but as appellants concede, the general rule in other jurisdictions is that a bailee is liable not only for lost property of which he has actual knowledge but also the property he could reasonably expect to find contained within the bailed property. . . .

We believe appellants' contention raises the question of whether or not it was foreseeable that such jewelry might be found in a woman's purse in a restaurant of a hotel such as the Shamrock Hilton under these circumstances.

Although the burden may rest with the appellees to prove that the jewelry was a part of the total bailment and the issue of whether it was reasonably foreseeable that such jewelry might be contained within the lost purse ordinarily should have been submitted by appellees, it remains for the hotel to object to the omission of the issue if it wishes to avoid the possibility of deemed findings by the Court. We cannot say as a matter of law that there is no evidence upon which a jury could reasonably find that it was foreseeable that such jewelry might be found in a purse under such circumstances as here presented. It is known that people who are guests in hotels such as the Shamrock Hilton, a well-known Houston hotel, not infrequently bring such expensive jewelry with them, and it does not impress us as unreasonable under the circumstances that one person might have her jewelry in her purse either awaiting a present occasion to wear it or following reclaiming it from the hotel safe in anticipation of leaving the hotel.

We find that the question of whether it is reasonably foreseeable that a woman, under the circumstances of this case, might keep jewelry in a purse which is determinative of whether there was a bailment of jewelry and whether the negligence in losing the purse was a proximate cause of losing the jewelry, is an omitted issue in the grounds of recovery to which the submitted issues are reasonably or necessarily referable. Appellants were on notice that recovery was sought primarily for the value of the jewelry and that the only ground for recovery was the hotel's negligence with respect to the bailment, purse and contents. This is reflected in appellants' second amended original answer where they allege that there was no bailment as to the jewelry within the purse.

The record reflects no timely objection to the issues submitted or to the omitting of a special issue, and therefore in support of the judgment . . . , we deem it to be found that one might reasonably expect to find valuable jewelry within a purse under the circumstances of this case in support of the judgment below. It follows that the findings of negligence and proximate cause of the loss of the purse apply to the jewelry as well, which is deemed to be a part of the bailment. There was no error in the judgment insofar as it was complained that there was no bailment of the jewelry and that there was no connection between the findings of negligence and proximate cause as regards the purse and the jewelry.

Appellant's final point of error complains of the trial court's granting of appellees' motion for judgment notwithstanding the verdict and disregarding the jury's findings on special issues that appellees' leaving the purse was negligence and a proximate cause of the loss of the jewelry. In support of this contention appellants cite Southwestern Hotel Co. v. Rogers, 183 S.W.2d 751 (Tex.Civ.App.—El Paso 1944), aff'd 143 Tex. 343, 184 S.W.2d 835 (1945) and Driskill Hotel Co. v. Anderson, 19 S.W.2d 216 (Tex.Civ.App.—Austin 1929, no writ), for the proposition that contributory negligence of a guest of a hotel is an absolute defense to a claim for jewelry or money lost in the hotel. Both cases, however, are distinguishable on the facts in that here the loss occurred *after* appellees had relinquished possession of the purse and its contents, and the hotel alone had assumed responsibility for the items.
. . .

***

The bus boy and cashier assumed possession and control of the purse per instructions of the hotel with respect to articles misplaced or lost by customers. . . . In each instance, once the bailee assumed possession he alone had the duty to safeguard the bailed article. We find therefore under these facts that the negligence of Mrs. Caranas was not a cause " . . . which in a natural and continuous sequence produces an event . . ."of this nature.

***

The judgment of the trial court is affirmed.

SAM D. JOHNSON

(dissenting).

If, as found by the majority, the evidence conclusively showed facts from which there was established a bailment, it is well to examine the relationship of the parties. Mrs. Caranas is characterized as a quasi or constructive bailor. The bailment is characterized as a mutual benefit and as a constructive bailment. If a bailment was created it was certainly unintentional. Mrs. Caranas had no intention of creating a bailment. The hotel had no such intention. Neither, in fact, for a considerable period of time knew of its existence.

This, for two reasons forming the basis of this dissent, is at least true of the jewelry allegedly contained in the purse. First, it seems to be conceded that the hotel had no actual notice of the existence of the jewelry in the purse .and there is no authority in this state for the proposition that a bailee is liable for property he could reasonably expect to find contained in the bailed property. Secondly, even if the foregoing were true it does not occur to this writer that it is reasonable to expect a purse, inadvertently left under a chair in a hotel's restaurant and not even missed by the owner until the next day, might contain ten pieces of jewelry valued at $13,062.00.

This dissent is therefore most respectfully submitted.

4.3

Ziva Jewelry, Inc. v. Car Wash Headquarters, Inc.
897 So. 2d 1011 (Ala. 2004)

Alabama Supreme Court

STUART, Justice.

Ziva Jewelry, Inc., appeals from a summary judgment in favor of Car Wash Headquarters, Inc. ("CWH"). We affirm.

Background

Ziva Jewelry, Inc., is a jewelry wholesaler. Stewart Smith was employed by Ziva Jewelry as a traveling sales representative. In connection with that employment, Smith drove his own vehicle to meet with potential customers and traveled with samples of expensive jewelry furnished to him by Ziva Jewelry. Smith testified by deposition that he knew that sales representatives in the jewelry business constantly faced the risk of robbery. Smith stated in his deposition that he was aware that a gang of thieves preyed upon traveling jewelry sales representatives. According to Smith, these thieves are aware of where and when jewelry trade shows are held, and they will follow a jewelry sales representative to and from a jewelry trade show, waiting for an opportunity to steal the jewelry. He testified that he knew that thieves were most likely to strike when the jewelry or the sales representative's car was left unattended.[1]

Smith's practice was to keep the jewelry in the trunk of his vehicle while he was traveling on business.[2] He kept the trunk padlocked, and he kept the only key to the padlock on the key ring with his ignition key.

On August 10, 2000, Smith was returning from a jewelry trade show; his wife had accompanied him to the trade show. He and his wife stopped at a restaurant in Cullman to eat. While they were in the restaurant, they noticed an unidentified person peeking in the window of the restaurant.[3] After eating, the Smiths returned to their vehicle and drove to Vestavia. While in Vestavia, Smith's wife went into a store to shop and Smith went to get his car washed at Rain Tunnel Car Wash. CWH owns and operates Rain Tunnel. At Rain Tunnel, the driver leaves his vehicle with employees of the car wash, and the vehicle is sent through a wash "tunnel." Upon completion of the wash cycle, an employee drives the vehicle to another area of the car-wash premises to be hand-dried. Once the vehicle is dried, the driver is signaled to retrieve his vehicle.

Smith left his car and his keys with a car-wash employee. The jewelry was locked in the trunk. He did not advise any of the employees of the car wash of the presence of the jewelry. Smith testified that he watched the car as it went through the car-wash tunnel. He watched as the employees dried the vehicle. As he was standing at the counter waiting to pay the cashier, he saw the employee wave a flag, indicating that his car was ready for Smith. Smith then saw the employee walk away from his vehicle. While Smith was standing at the cashier counter waiting to pay, someone jumped into Smith's vehicle and sped off the car-wash premises. The police were telephoned and Smith's car was recovered 15 minutes later; it was undamaged. However, the jewelry was missing from the trunk. The value of the missing jewelry was $851,935; it was never recovered.

Ziva arg.

Ziva Jewelry sued CWH, alleging that CWH, as bailee, took possession of Smith's vehicle and of the jewelry in the vehicle, but failed to exercise due care to safeguard and to return the bailed vehicle and its contents to Smith. Ziva Jewelry also alleged that CWH breached an oral contract it entered into with Smith to safeguard, to exercise due care in regard to, and to return Smith's vehicle, including the jewelry in the vehicle, to Smith. Finally, Ziva Jewelry alleged that CWH was negligent in otherwise failing to act reasonably and prudently.

CWH arg.

CWH moved for a summary judgment on all counts, asserting that no bailment existed as to the jewelry, that Smith had been contributorily negligent, and that CWH could not be held liable for the criminal acts of a third party. Ziva Jewelry opposed that summary-judgment motion. Ziva Jewelry argued that CWH is liable for failing to properly safeguard Smith's vehicle and that CWH failed to return Smith's vehicle in the same condition in which it received it. Ziva Jewelry also offered the deposition testimony of Chris Finley, a Rain Tunnel employee. Finley testified that, on the day of the incident, he had noticed an unidentified male on the premises of the car wash. Finley testified that he knew that this unidentified male was not an employee of Rain Tunnel and that the male did not appear to be a customer. Ziva Jewelry argued that Finley failed to report this unidentified male as a "suspicious person" and, therefore, failed to follow the procedures set forth in CWH's "manual." Ziva Jewelry also argued that Finley had acted negligently in leaving Smith's car unattended with the keys in the ignition. Finally, Ziva Jewelry offered the testimony of criminologist John Lombardi, who testified that the theft of a vehicle from the premises was foreseeable and that CWH did not comply with generally accepted principles of security and crime prevention for businesses.

Ziva Jewelry argued that because CWH took custody and control of Smith's vehicle, CWH necessarily took custody and control of the contents of Smith's vehicle. Ziva Jewelry argued that its doing so constituted a bailment of the jewelry. Ziva Jewelry also argued that Smith had entrusted his vehicle, including the jewelry, to CWH and that CWH had breached its contract to safeguard that property and to return it in the same condition in which CWH had received it.

The trial court rejected those arguments and entered a summary judgment for CWH. The trial court concluded that no bailment of the jewelry had been created. Without a bailment of the jewelry, Ziva could not establish its claims of negligent failure to safeguard the jewelry and breach of a contract to safeguard the jewelry. Ziva Jewelry appeals.

Standard of Review

We review a summary judgment de novo. . . .

Discussion

"A bailment is defined as the delivery of personal property by one person to another for a specific purpose, with a contract, express or implied, that the trust shall be faithfully executed, and the property returned or duly accounted for when the special purpose is accomplished, or kept until the bailor reclaims it. In order for a bailment to exist the bailee must have voluntarily assumed the custody and possession of the property for another."

S/M Indus., Inc. v. Hapag-Lloyd A.G., 586 So.2d 876, 881-82 (Ala.1991). We agree with the trial court that Smith's vehicle was the subject of a bailment. Smith delivered his vehicle to CWH for the specific purpose of having the car washed. He paid a fee for that service. As a result, CWH owed Smith a duty to use reasonable or ordinary care with regard to Smith's vehicle.

However, the above-quoted statement of the law on bailment does not answer the question whether a bailment was created as to the contents of the trunk of Smith's vehicle. The trial court correctly noted that no Alabama cases have directly addressed the issue whether a bailee is liable for the loss of contents hidden inside a bailed item. However, the trial court cited other jurisdictions that have addressed this issue. See *Davidson v. Ramsby,* 133 Ga.App. 128, 210 S.E.2d 245 (1974) (a bailee is not liable for the loss of the contents of a bailed vehicle when the bailee did not have actual or implied knowledge of the contents of the vehicle); *Jack Boles Servs., Inc. v. Stavely,* 906 S.W.2d 185 (Tex.Ct.App.1995) (a bailee is liable for lost property of which it has actual knowledge as well as property it could reasonably expect to find inside a bailed item).

The facts of this case are strikingly similar to those of *Jack Boles Services,* supra. In *Jack Boles Services,* the Texas Court of Appeals addressed whether a valet-parking service was liable for a valuable painting taken when the vehicle it was in was stolen from the parking lot of a country club. The painting was hidden in the trunk of the stolen vehicle. The Texas Court of Appeals held that the valet service had no duty of care in regard to the undisclosed painting in the vehicle. That court stated:

> "The general rule in other jurisdictions is that a bailee is liable for lost property of which it has actual knowledge as well as property it could reasonably expect to find contained inside a bailed item of which it has express knowledge.... In Texas, similarly, a bailee is liable for the contents of a bailed vehicle if the contents were (1) in plain view when the vehicle was bailed or (2) constitute the usual, ordinary equipment of a car, such as articles contained in a trunk, which are reasonably anticipated to be there."

Jack Boles Servs., 906 S.W.2d at 188. . . .

In *Jack Boles,* when the parking-service employees accepted responsibility for the vehicle, they had no knowledge that a valuable painting was in the trunk. The court noted that the parking-service employees had no reason to expect that an expensive painting would be in the trunk of the vehicle. For those reasons, the court concluded that the valet-parking service could not be charged with accepting responsibility for the painting merely by accepting responsibility for the vehicle.

We agree with and adopt the reasoning of *Jack Boles.* In this case, Ziva Jewelry cannot establish that CWH expressly or impliedly agreed to take responsibility for the jewelry hidden inside Smith's trunk. Ziva Jewelry acknowledges that the jewelry was not plainly visible; that its presence was not made known to the car-wash employees; and that there was no reason that the employees should have expected expensive jewelry to be in the trunk of Smith's vehicle. Thus, Ziva Jewelry cannot claim that CWH knew or that it should have reasonably foreseen or expected that it was taking responsibility for over $850,000 worth of jewelry when it accepted Smith's vehicle for the purpose of washing it.

Thus, there is no evidence indicating that CWH expressly or impliedly accepted responsibility for the jewelry in the trunk of Smith's vehicle. Without express or implied acceptance by the purported bailee, a bailment cannot arise. We agree with the trial court that the breach-of-contract claims asserted by Ziva Jewelry fail as a matter of law.

***

[W]e cannot impose upon CWH a duty for the criminal act of the thief in this case. We cannot say that the particular criminal conduct at issue in this case — the theft of valuable jewelry from Smith's vehicle — was foreseeable to CWH, or that CWH possessed any specialized knowledge of the criminal activity at issue or that the theft of the jewels from the vehicle was a probability. There is no evidence indicating that other similar crimes had occurred at Rain Tunnel or in the vicinity of the Rain Tunnel car wash. Additionally, CWH was unaware that the jewelry was even on its premises; consequently, it could not have foreseen the theft and it could not have had specialized knowledge of the risk of the theft. . . .

***

CWH had no duty to protect Ziva Jewelry from the specific criminal act at issue in this case — the theft by a third person of the jewelry belonging to Ziva Jewelry from Smith's vehicle. For these reasons, CWH cannot be liable under a negligence theory for the theft of that jewelry. We affirm the trial court's summary judgment in favor of CWH.

AFFIRMED.

1. In fact, Smith testified that he had been robbed while working for a previous employer. On that occasion, he had left the jewelry unattended in his car while he ate in a restaurant. He testified that a traveling jewelry sales representative was "petrified constantly." [Editorial Note: This is footnote 2 of the opinion.]

2. The jewelry furnished to Smith was covered under Ziva's insurance policy. However, in order for Ziva's insurance policy to be effective while the jewelry was in the sales representative's possession and in his or her car, the sales representative must be "in or upon the vehicle." Ziva described this as "either on [the representative's] person, with him in the car, or [with him] touching the car." Ziva required its sales representatives to follow this procedure at all times. [Editorial Note: This is footnote 3 of the opinion.]

3. Smith testified that because of the constant risk of robbery or theft he followed specific procedures when he was traveling on business. He testified that he and his wife would eat only at restaurants where they could park their vehicle right in front of a window and where they could sit within view of the vehicle. [Editorial Note: This is footnote 4 of the opinion.]

Discussion: Notes, Questions, and Problems

Discussion Question #1. Strict liability or negligence?

Should the hotel in Shamrock Hilton Hotel v. Caranas have been strictly liable for misdelivery?

Discussion Question #2. Procedural difference when bailment?

What procedural advantage may exist for the bailor if the court finds that the relationship between the parties as to the property is a bailment?

5

Chapter 5 · Gifts

A gift is generally defined as a gratuitous transfer of property from a **donor** to a **donee**. Both an **inter vivos** gift and a gift **causa mortis** are made during the donor's lifetime and require the following elements: present donative **intent**, **delivery** such as to divest the donor of dominion and control, and **acceptance** by the donee. For a gift to be deemed causa mortis, however, the donor must have made the gift under apprehension of death.

An **inter vivos** gift is irrevocable with only two very limited exceptions. One exception is for engagement rings, which could be deemed conditional gifts. The other exception is for gifts **causa mortis**. A gift causa mortis is revocable by (1) express revocation by the donor, (2) the donor's recovery from peril or illness, or (3) the death of the donee prior to the donor.

As you read the cases excerpted below, ask yourself whether the elements for a gift were met and what evidence the courts rely on for determining whether a gift was made.

5.1

Gruen v. Gruen
496 N.E.2d 869 (N.Y. 1986)

New York Court of Appeals

Simons, J.

Plaintiff commenced this action seeking a declaration that he is the rightful owner of a painting which he alleges his father, now deceased, gave to him. He concedes that he has never had possession of the painting but asserts that his father made a valid gift of the title in 1963 reserving a life estate for himself. His father retained possession of the painting until he died in 1980. Defendant, plaintiff's stepmother, has the painting now and has refused plaintiff's requests that she turn it over to him. She contends that the purported gift was testamentary in nature and invalid insofar as the formalities of a will were not met or, alternatively, that a donor may not make a valid inter vivos gift of a chattel and retain a life estate with a complete right of possession. Following a seven-day nonjury trial, Special Term found that plaintiff had failed to establish any of the elements of an inter vivos gift and that in any event an attempt by a donor to retain a present possessory life estate in a chattel invalidated a purported gift of it. The Appellate Division held that a valid gift may be made reserving a life estate and, finding the elements of a gift established in this case, it reversed and remitted the matter for a determination of value (104 AD2d 171). That determination has now been made and defendant appeals directly to this court, pursuant to CPLR 5601 (d), from the subsequent final judgment entered in Supreme Court awarding plaintiff $2,500,000 in damages representing the value of the painting, plus interest. We now affirm.

The subject of the dispute is a work entitled "Schloss Kammer am Attersee II" painted by a noted Austrian modernist, Gustav Klimt. It was purchased by plaintiffs father, Victor Gruen, in 1959 for $8,000. On April 1, 1963 the elder Gruen, a successful architect with offices and residences in both New York City and Los Angeles during most of the time involved in this action, wrote a letter to plaintiff, then an undergraduate student at Harvard, stating that he was giving him the Klimt painting for his birthday but that he wished to retain the possession of it for his lifetime. This letter is not in evidence, apparently because plaintiff destroyed it on instructions from his father. Two other letters were received, however, one dated May 22, 1963 and the other April 1, 1963. Both had been dictated by Victor Gruen and sent together to plaintiff on or about May 22, 1963. The letter dated May 22, 1963 reads as follows:

"Dear Michael:

"I wrote you at the time of your birthday about the gift of the painting by Klimt.

"Now my lawyer tells me that because of the existing tax laws, it was wrong to mention in that letter that I want to use the painting as long as I live. Though I still want to use it, this should not appear in the letter. I am enclosing, therefore, a new letter and I ask you to send the old one back to me so that it can be destroyed.

"I know this is all very silly, but the lawyer and our accountant insist that they must have in their possession copies of a letter which will serve the purpose of making it possible for you, once I die, to get this picture without having to pay inheritance taxes on it.

"Love,

"s/Victor".

Enclosed with this letter was a substitute gift letter, dated April 1, 1963, which stated:

"Dear Michael:

"The 21st birthday, being an important event in life, should be celebrated accordingly. I therefore wish to give you as a present the oil painting by Gustav Klimt of Schloss Kammer which now hangs in the New York living room. You know that Lazette and I bought it some 5 or 6 years ago, and you always told us how much you liked it.

"Happy birthday again.

"Love,

"s/Victor".

Plaintiff never took possession of the painting nor did he seek to do so. Except for a brief period between 1964 and 1965 when it was on loan to art exhibits and when restoration work was performed on it, the painting remained in his father's possession, moving with him from New York City to Beverly Hills and finally to Vienna, Austria, where Victor Gruen died on February 14, 1980. Following Victor's death plaintiff requested possession of the Klimt painting and when defendant refused, he commenced this action.

The issues framed for appeal are whether a valid inter vivos gift of a chattel may be made where the donor has reserved a life estate in the chattel and the donee never has had physical possession of it before the donor's death and, if it may, which factual findings on the elements of a valid inter vivos gift more nearly comport with the weight of the evidence in this case, those of Special Term or those of the Appellate Division. Resolution of the latter issue requires application of two general rules. First, to make a valid inter vivos gift there must exist the intent on the part of the donor to make a present transfer; delivery of the gift, either actual or constructive to the donee; and acceptance by the done (Matter of Szabo, 10 NY2d 94, 98). Second, the proponent of a gift has the burden of proving each of these elements by clear and convincing evidence.

two rules

Donative Intent

There is an important distinction between the intent with which an inter vivos gift is made and the intent to make a gift by will. An inter vivos gift requires that the donor intend to make an irrevocable present transfer of ownership; if the intention is to make a testamentary disposition effective only after death, the gift is invalid unless made by will.

Defendant contends that the trial court was correct in finding that Victor did not intend to transfer any present interest in the painting to plaintiff in 1963 but only expressed an intention that plaintiff was to get the painting upon his death. The evidence is all but conclusive, however, that Victor intended to transfer ownership of the painting to plaintiff in 1963 but to retain a life estate in it and that he did, therefore, effectively transfer a remainder interest in the painting to plaintiff at that time. Although the original letter was not in evidence, testimony of its contents was received along with the substitute gift letter and its covering letter dated May 22, 1963. The three letters should be considered together as a single instrument and when they are they unambiguously establish that Victor Gruen intended to make a present gift of title to the painting at that time. But there was other evidence for after 1963 Victor made several statements orally and in writing indicating that he had previously given plaintiff the painting and that plaintiff owned it. Victor Gruen retained possession of the property, insured it, allowed others to exhibit it and made necessary repairs to it but those acts are not inconsistent with his retention of a life estate. Furthermore, whatever probative value could be attached to his statement that he had bequeathed the painting to his heirs, made 16 years later when he prepared an export license application so that he could take the painting out of

Austria, is negated by the overwhelming evidence that he intended a present transfer of title in 1963. Victor's failure to file a gift tax return on the transaction was partially explained by allegedly erroneous legal advice he received, and while that omission sometimes may indicate that the donor had no intention of making a present gift, it does not necessarily do so and it is not dispositive in this case.

Defendant contends that even if a present gift was intended, Victor's reservation of a lifetime interest in the painting defeated it. She relies on a statement from Young v Young (80 NY 422) that " '[a]ny gift of chattels which expressly reserves the use of the property to the donor for a certain period, or * * * as long as the donor shall live, is ineffectual' " (id., at p 436, quoting 2 Schouler, Personal Property, at 118). The statement was dictum, however, and the holding of the court was limited to a determination that an attempted gift of bonds in which the donor reserved the interest for life failed because there had been no delivery of the gift, either actual or constructive (see, id., at p 434; see also, Speelman v Pascal, 10 NY2d 313, 319-320). The court expressly left undecided the question "whether a remainder in a chattel may be created and given by a donor by carving out a life estate for himself and transferring the remainder" (Young v Young, supra, at p 440). We answered part of that question in Matter of Brandreth (169 NY 437, 441-442, supra) when we held that "[in] this state a life estate and remainder can be created in a chattel or a fund the same as in real property". The case did not require us to decide whether there could be a valid gift of the remainder.

Defendant recognizes that a valid inter vivos gift of a remainder interest can be made not only of real property but also of such intangibles as stocks and bonds. Indeed, several of the cases she cites so hold. That being so, it is difficult to perceive any legal basis for the distinction she urges which would permit gifts of remainder interests in those properties but not of remainder interests in chattels such as the Klimt painting here. The only reason suggested is that the gift of a chattel must include a present right to possession. The application of Brandreth to permit a gift of the remainder in this case, however, is consistent with the distinction, well recognized in the law of gifts as well as in real property law, between ownership and possession or enjoyment. Insofar as some of our cases purport to require that the donor intend to transfer both title and possession immediately to have a valid inter vivos gift, they state the rule too broadly and confuse the effectiveness of a gift with the transfer of the possession of the subject of that gift. The correct test is " 'whether the maker intended the [gift] to have no effect until after the maker's death, or whether he intended it to transfer some present interest' " (McCarthy v Pieret, 281 NY 407, 409, supra [emphasis added]. As long as the evidence establishes an intent to make a present and irrevocable transfer of title or the right of ownership, there is a present transfer of some interest and the gift is effective immediately. Thus, in Speelman v Pascal (supra), we held valid a gift of a percentage of the future royalties to the play "My Fair Lady" before the play even existed. There, as in this case, the donee received title or the right of ownership to some property immediately upon the making of the gift but possession or enjoyment of the subject of the gift was postponed to some future time.

Defendant suggests that allowing a donor to make a present gift of a remainder with the reservation of a life estate will lead courts to effectuate otherwise invalid testamentary dispositions of property. The two have entirely different characteristics, however, which make them distinguishable. Once the gift is made it is irrevocable and the donor is limited to the rights of a life tenant not an owner. Moreover, with the gift of a remainder title vests immediately in the donee and any possession is postponed until the donor's death whereas under a will neither title nor possession vests immediately. Finally, the postponement of enjoyment of the gift is produced by the express terms of the gift not by the nature of the instrument as it is with a will.

Delivery

In order to have a valid inter vivos gift, there must be a delivery of the gift, either by a physical delivery of the subject of the gift or a constructive or symbolic delivery such as by an instrument of gift, sufficient to divest the donor of dominion and control over the property. As the statement of the rule suggests, the requirement of delivery is not rigid or inflexible, but is to be applied in light of its purpose to avoid mistakes by donors and fraudulent claims by donees. Accordingly, what is sufficient to constitute delivery "must be tailored to suit the circumstances of the case" (Matter of Szabo, supra, at p 98). The rule requires that " '[t]he delivery necessary to consummate a gift must be as perfect as the nature of the property and the circumstances and surroundings of the parties will reasonably permit' " (id).

Defendant contends that when a tangible piece of personal property such as a painting is the subject of a gift, physical delivery of the painting itself is the best form of delivery and should be required. Here, of course, we have only delivery of Victor Gruen's letters which serve as instruments of gift. Defendant's statement of the rule as applied may be generally true, but it ignores the fact that what Victor Gruen gave plaintiff was not all rights to the Klimt painting, but only title to it with no right of possession until his death. Under these circumstances, it would be illogical for the law to require the donor to part with possession of the painting when that is exactly what he intends to retain.

Nor is there any reason to require a donor making a gift of a remainder interest in a chattel to physically deliver the chattel into the donee's hands only to have the donee redeliver it to the donor. As the facts of this case demonstrate, such a requirement could impose practical burdens on the parties to the gift while serving the delivery requirement poorly. Thus, in order to accomplish this type of delivery the parties would have been required to travel to New York for the symbolic transfer and redelivery of the Klimt painting which was hanging on the wall of Victor Gruen's Manhattan apartment. Defendant suggests that such a requirement would be stronger evidence of a completed gift, but in the absence of witnesses to the event or any written confirmation of the gift it would provide less protection against fraudulent claims than have the written instruments of gift delivered in this case.

Acceptance

Acceptance by the donee is essential to the validity of an inter vivos gift, but when a gift is of value to the donee, as it is here, the law will presume an acceptance on his part. Plaintiff did not rely on this presumption alone but also presented clear and convincing proof of his acceptance of a remainder interest in the Klimt painting by evidence that he had made several contemporaneous statements acknowledging the gift to his friends and associates, even showing some of them his father's gift letter, and that he had retained both letters for over 17 years to verify the gift after his father died. Defendant relied exclusively on affidavits filed by plaintiff in a matrimonial action with his former wife, in which plaintiff failed to list his interest in the painting as an asset. These affidavits were made over 10 years after acceptance was complete and they do not even approach the evidence in Matter of Kelly (285 NY 139, 148-149) where the donee, immediately upon delivery of a diamond ring, rejected it as "too flashy". We agree with the Appellate Division that interpretation of the affidavit was too speculative to support a finding of rejection and overcome the substantial showing of acceptance by plaintiff.

Accordingly, the judgment appealed from and the order of the Appellate Division brought up for review should be affirmed, with costs.

5.2

Koerner v. Nielsen
8 N.E.3d 161 (Ill. App. Ct. 2014)

Appellate Court of Illinois, 1st District, 1st Division

Justice CUNNINGHAM delivered the judgment of the court, with opinion.

Plaintiff-appellant, Jennifer Koerner (Koerner), appeals from an order of the circuit court of Cook County which found that she had given the dog at issue (the Stig) to defendant-appellee, Kent Nielsen (Nielsen), as a gift and that he was thus its rightful owner. On appeal, Koerner contends that the trial court erred in finding that: (1) an *inter vivos* gift had occurred; (2) she had not revoked the gift prior to delivery; and (3) the burden of disproving a completed *inter vivos* gift lies with the party challenging the gift. She thus requests that this court reverse the trial court's judgment and enter an order stating that she is the Stig's rightful owner. . . . For the following reasons, we affirm the judgment of the circuit court of Cook County.

BACKGROUND

The record shows that on November 5, 2010, Koerner adopted the Stig from the Anti–Cruelty Society in Chicago, Illinois, and used her credit card to pay the $95 fee. On or about December 25, 2010, Koerner wrote a poem in which she expressed her intent to give the Stig to Nielsen, her then live-in boyfriend, as a gift. A copy of the poem is not included in the record on appeal.

The record further shows that Koerner and Nielsen ended their relationship in early February 2012. Nielsen permanently left their shared residence on February 6, 2012, taking the Stig with him, and, that same day, Koerner filed a police report in relation to the incident. The record further shows that throughout February and March 2012, Koerner and Nielsen exchanged emails relating to the logistics of their separation. In those emails, Koerner repeatedly stated that she and Jessie, her dog, missed the Stig and asked Nielsen to bring the Stig "home." Nielsen repeatedly responded that the Stig belonged to him, but that he would allow the Stig to visit Koerner and Jessie, so long as Koerner confirmed in writing that he had "total ownership" of the Stig. On April 20, 2012, Koerner filed a complaint against Nielsen in the circuit court of Cook County, alleging that she is the Stig's rightful owner and seeking his return.

On August 21, 2012, a bench trial commenced in this case and was continued to September 11, 2012. No court reporter was present on either day, so Koerner prepared and filed an affidavit bystander's report (Bystander's Report) pursuant to Illinois Supreme Court Rule 323 (eff. Dec. 13, 2005). Although Nielsen did not take part in creating the Bystander's Report, Koerner represented in her motion to certify that he was served with the proposed report and did not oppose it or submit any proposed amendments. The Bystander's Report was certified by the trial court on March 11, 2013, and entered as a supplement to the record on appeal.

The Bystander's Report reflects that at trial, Koerner maintained that she is the true owner of the Stig because the donative intent she expressed in the poem was subsequently revoked both verbally and in writing in February 2012, and that delivery never occurred. In support of that contention, Koerner noted that she never conveyed title or executed documents transferring ownership of the Stig to Nielsen. Koerner testified that the Stig's city registration, microchip identification, and veterinary insurance were always in her name and that she paid the majority of costs related to his care. Koerner acknowledged that she had given up "exclusive dominion and control" of the Stig, but argued that delivery requires giving up complete dominion and control of the object of the gift.

Nielsen maintained he is the true owner of the Stig because Koerner gave the dog to him upon writing the poem, that delivery occurred when she gave up exclusive dominion and control of the Stig, and that acceptance is assumed. When asked if he had attempted to change the microchip identification ownership information into his name, Nielsen responded that he had but could not do so without written authorization from the current owner or a court order and, further, that he started a new veterinary policy for the Stig in his own name after February 6, 2012.

On September 11, 2012, the trial court entered a written order finding that Nielsen had established that the Stig was a gift from Koerner and that she had failed to establish that the gift had been revoked. The court ordered that judgment was entered in favor of Nielsen and that he shall continue to be the Stig's rightful owner.

***

ANALYSIS

On appeal, Koerner contends that the trial court erred in finding that a valid *inter vivos* gift had occurred and in imposing the burden of proof on her regarding the gift. The facts of this case are uncontested. As such, we are presented with a mixed question of law and fact, which we review under the clearly erroneous standard of review.

Initially, we observe that Koerner filed an action in replevin. The primary purpose of this statutory proceeding is to test the right of possession of personal property and to place the successful party in possession of that property. A plaintiff commences such an action by filing a verified complaint describing the property at issue, stating that she is lawfully entitled to its possession, and stating that the property is being wrongfully detained by defendant. After holding a hearing on the matter, the court shall issue an order of replevin if plaintiff establishes a *prima facie* case to a superior right of possession of the property and if plaintiff also demonstrates to the court the probability that she will ultimately prevail on the underlying claim of the right to possession.

Accordingly, in a replevin action, plaintiff bears the burden of establishing that she is lawfully entitled to possession of the property at issue and that defendant wrongfully detained the property and refuses to deliver possession of the property to plaintiff. *Id.* If plaintiff makes such a *prima facie* showing, the burden then shifts to defendant to establish the elements of a valid gift by clear, convincing and unequivocal evidence.

In this case, Nielsen claims that Koerner gave him the Stig for Christmas in 2010, and Koerner acknowledged that she expressed this sentiment in the poem she wrote and presented to him on December 25, 2010. The record shows that Koerner and Nielsen continued living together and remained romantically involved for the next 13 months, before ending their relationship in February 2012. At that time, Nielsen and the Stig moved out of Koerner's home.

As noted above, the poem has not been included in the record on appeal, and thus any doubts arising from this incompleteness will be resolved against plaintiff. That said, there is no evidence in the record that the poem included language indicating that the gift was in any way conditional, such as on a continuation of the romantic relationship. Nor does the record indicate that Koerner and Nielsen were engaged at any point in time, and thus, there is no presumption that the Stig was a gift in contemplation of marriage. *Hofferkamp v. Brehm,* 273 Ill.App.3d 263, 272, 210 Ill.Dec. 405, 652 N.E.2d 1381 (1995); *cf. Carroll,* 392 Ill.App.3d at 514, 332 Ill.Dec. 86, 912 N.E.2d 272 (noting that an engagement ring given in contemplation of marriage is a conditional gift). Under these circumstances, we find that Koerner did not establish a *prima facie* case to a superior right of possession of the Stig . . . .

In reaching that conclusion, we disagree with Koerner's contention that in announcing its finding at the close of evidence and argument, the trial court was solely referring to the burden of disproving a completed *inter vivos* gift when it referred to Koerner's "burden." Koerner overlooks the fact that she filed the action in replevin contesting Nielsen's continued possession of the Stig. Koerner also overlooks that in its written order, the court specifically found that Nielsen "shall continue to be the rightful owner of" the Stig, indicating that Koerner had not met her burden of establishing a *prima facie* case of ownership. The court also stated in its written order that Nielsen had established that the Stig was a gift from Koerner and that she failed to establish that the gift had been revoked. Thus, Koerner's argument that the trial court erroneously imposed the burden related to the existence of a valid *inter vivos* gift on her also fails.

Notwithstanding Koerner's argument, we observe that on review, we consider the correctness of the circuit court's ruling without regard to the validity of its rationale. Accordingly, we may affirm for any reason that the record warrants without regard to the reasons relied upon by the trial court.

Where defendant claims ownership as a gift, he is required to prove, by clear and convincing evidence, donative intent, the donor's parting with exclusive dominion and control over the subject of the gift, and delivery to the donee. Here, Koerner does not contest Nielsen's assertion that the poem she wrote and gave to him on December 25, 2010, demonstrated her donative intent to give the Stig to him as a gift. She maintains, however, that she revoked her donative intent 13 months later, as evidenced by the emails she sent to Nielsen in February and March 2012.

Donative intent is determined at the time of the alleged transfer of property, and is controlled by what the parties said or did at the time of the transaction, and not what is said at a later time. As noted above, there is no evidence in this record that the gift of the dog in this case was conditional. Accordingly, we find that Koerner's statements 13 months after her demonstration of unconditional donative intent do not impact the validity of the donative intent she acknowledged that she expressed in the poem at the time she made the gift. As such, we find that Koerner's donative intent to give the Stig to Nielsen as a gift on December 25, 2010, was established at that time.

Koerner further maintains that delivery never occurred because she did not part with complete dominion and control over the Stig, and she never conveyed title of the Stig to Nielsen, as reflected by her name being listed on the Stig's registration papers, his insurance policy, and his microchip identification. We observe that "[m]ere documentary title is not conclusive of ownership", and that a donor need only part with exclusive dominion or control of a gift.

Here, Koerner acknowledged at trial that she had given up exclusive dominion and control of the Stig during the period of cohabitation. Given the fact that she and Nielsen lived in the same residence at the time she gifted him the Stig, the need for a physical delivery of the dog was obviated. Moreover, given the romantic nature of the relationship between Koerner and Nielsen and their joint living situation, it stands to reason that both parties would be involved in the Stig's day-to-day care, even after she gave him to Nielsen as a gift. Given this shared living situation, Nielsen may not have felt compelled to add his name to all of the Stig's pertinent paperwork, as he attempted to do after the relationship ended. We thus find by clear and convincing evidence that Nielsen established that the Stig was a gift from Koerner and affirm the judgment of the circuit court of Cook County, which ordered that Nielsen continue to be the Stig's rightful owner.

For the foregoing reasons, the judgment of the circuit court of Cook County is affirmed.

Affirmed.

5.3

Braun v. Brown
94 P.2d 348 (Cal. 1939)

Supreme Court of California

PULLEN, J., *pro* tem.

***

The action was brought against the administrator of the estate of Julius H. Schmidt, deceased, to establish a gift *causa mortis* by deceased to plaintiff of certain personal property, and to quiet title thereto. This personal property, consisting of stocks, bonds, promissory notes, a diamond ring and bank deposit books during his lifetime belonged to Schmidt, and was kept in a safe deposit box in a bank in the city of Los Angeles. After the death of Schmidt, plaintiff attempted to take over the box and its contents, but upon refusal of the bank to surrender possession to her, she turned the key to the box over to defendant, who had previously obtained letters of administration in the estate of Schmidt, and upon the refusal of the administrator to recognize her claim to the property brought this action to secure the same or its value.

The underlying facts as revealed by the record briefly are that some time in 1922 Schmidt met Teresa A. Braun, the plaintiff, at a church bazaar in Chicago. He was then a man about 52 years of age and unmarried. In 1924 plaintiff, then a young woman, came to California with her parents, who established their home in Los Angeles. The following year Schmidt, who had retired from business, also came to Los Angeles, and from that time until his last illness spent several hours almost every day in the company of plaintiff, either in her home or accompanying her to and from her place of employment or escorting her to church and places of entertainment. During that time she received from him notes and Easter cards addressed to her in terms of friendship and endearment, and on more than one occasion he proposed marriage, which proposals were neither accepted nor encouraged by plaintiff. In 1925 he attempted to make her a gift of a diamond engagement ring, which she refused, and in 1926 he purchased and offered her an automobile, which she also refused to accept. The relationship between the two, however, continued very friendly and apparently did not abate.

On January 6, 1937, Schmidt complained to the sexton of his church that he did not feel well, and later in the day he suffered a slight paralytic stroke. The next day he was confined to his room and a doctor was called to attend him. A few days later Mr. Assmann, a brother-in-law, came over from Long Beach, where he was spending the winter, and remained with him almost continuously until Schmidt was taken to a hospital on January 26th, where he remained until his death on February 11, 1937.

After Schmidt was confined to his room by reason of illness, Miss Braun called upon him almost daily. On January 21st she called as usual. After some conversation about what had occurred that day at her place of employment Schmidt asked his brother-in-law, who was present, to bring to him his purse. He thereupon took from this purse a safe deposit key which he handed to plaintiff, saying, "Teresa, every thing in the box belongs to you," and, turning to Assmann, said, "Bernard, you hear, I want Teresa to have every thing in the box." He also told her that there was more than enough money in the box for her to live on and that she would not have to work any more. A day or so later Schmidt gave plaintiff a check for $175, drawn from funds other than those in the safe deposit box, and gave it to plaintiff in order that she might pay his hotel and hospital bills. Plaintiff then took the key and kept it among her effects at her home until after the death of Schmidt, when, as stated above, she gave it to the administrator and, upon his refusal to redeliver the key, this action was commenced.

The trial court confirmed the gift to plaintiff and ordered that the property be delivered to her or, in the alternative, the value thereof. It is from that judgment that this appeal is taken.

Certain preliminary motions . . . have already been before this court and disposed of, leaving for consideration the basic question in controversy, that is, did Schmidt on the 21st day of January, 1937, entertain and express the specific intention then and there to give to plaintiff the property in the safe deposit box; and did he then and there effectuate that intention by the delivery of that property to her, divesting himself of dominion thereover, and was he actuated therein by the thought of death, and did plaintiff accept the same?

Section 1149 of the Civil Code defines a gift in view of death "as one, which is made in contemplation, fear or peril of death, and with intent that it shall take effect only in case of the death of the giver", and by section 1150 of the Civil Code a gift is presumed to be in view of death when made during the last illness of the giver or under circumstances which would naturally impress him with an expectation of speedy death.

The court found it to be true that on the, 21st day of January, 1937, Julius H. Schmidt was the sole owner and in the exclusive possession of all the property here involved; that the same was kept in a certain safe deposit box, and the sole means of access thereto and the contents thereof was by one key kept in possession of Schmidt; that during his last illness he transferred, delivered and handed over to plaintiff this key and at the same time told her he was thereby making to her a gift of all the contents of said box; that by such delivery of the key and his statement he thereby made a gift and transfer *causa mortis* to plaintiff; and that plaintiff accepted said gift and delivery and that such gift was unrevoked and remained valid and binding at his death.

Appellant contends that the failure of the court to specifically find that Schmidt acted in contemplation of death is reversible error. The finding recited that by the delivery of the key Schmidt gave to plaintiff, *causa mortis,* all his interest in the property. By the adverbial use of the words *"causa mortis"* there is embodied in the finding all the elements as to the influence of the thought of death connoted by such words, making the finding adequate.

The evidence fairly establishes that the gift was made by Schmidt during his last illness, and there can be little doubt from the evidence that the circumstances surrounding such illness impressed him with the expectation of death, and, by the delivery of the key and his statement to plaintiff he intended to set over to plaintiff all his interest in the property.

At the time of the making of the gift Schmidt was ill in bed in his hotel room; he had suffered a stroke and had told certain friends that he was not feeling well. He was arranging to go to a hospital and had made provision for plain-, tiff to pay his hotel and hospital bills. His brother-in-law, realizing the seriousness of his condition, had left his place of abode in Long Beach and had a cot moved into the room of Schmidt, so he could be near him all night; he was at times delirious; a doctor had examined him and advised hospital care. He was then about 67 years of age and had never theretofore been sick. He left the hotel January 26th and died 15 days later. Such circumstances could not but have caused even the most optimistic of men to contemplate to some degree at least the fact of death. Realizing, however, that under such circumstances any reference to or discussion of death is universally avoided by the patient, his friends and the doctor, section 1150 of the Civil Code declares that a gift made during the last illness or under circumstances which would naturally impress one with an expectation of speedy death is presumed to be a gift in view of death. This presumption is evidence and is sufficient to establish the fact unless rebutted.

But the fear of impending death is not a sole essential element of a gift *causa mortis.* The code predicates such a gift on either contemplation of death or peril of death; and as pointed out in *Donovan* v. *Hibernia Sav. & Loan Soc.,* 90 Cal. App. 489 [265 Pac. 995], while one may make general statements to the effect that he is feeling fine, yet his condition may be known to him to be critical. One may realize himself to be in peril of death and yet not expect to die. He may still believe his chances to live are greater than his chances to die, yet prudently take steps to adjust his affairs in case of death. In *Knight* v. *Tripp,* 121 Cal. 674 [54 Pac. 267], Mrs. Cook was about to undergo an operation. She sent for her friend, the defendant, and by an instrument in writing attempted to convey to him various personal property. In considering whether there was a gift *causa mortis,* the court said:

> "Mrs. Cook was an invalid, 54 years of age, and it must be assumed that she had at best a hope that she would come safely out of the surgical operation that she was about to undergo and that her life, would be prolonged thereby. . . . Her disposition of her property was evidently made in contemplation of her death under the surgical operation but' it was not necessary for her to state that fact as one of its terms. If the circumstances under which it was made were such as to authorize such conclusion it will be treated the same as if it had been so stated by her."

Both the circumstantial evidence and the presumption raised by the provisions of the code are sufficient to support the finding that the gift by Schmidt to respondent was made by him in contemplation of death and was a gift *causa mortis.*

It is next urged by appellant that there is no substantial evidence in the record to support the finding that Schmidt had the specific intent then and there to give to plaintiff the contents of the safe deposit box, or did anything to effectuate delivery, or that plaintiff accepted the same.

As to the intent, we find that when Schmidt handed the key to plaintiff he said, "Every thing in the box belongs to you," and also said to plaintiff that she wouldn't have to work any more, there would be enough money there for her to live on, and, calling upon his brother-in-law as a witness, said, "Bernard, you hear, I want Teresa to have every thing in the box." Here are words of present donation, accompanied by the delivery into her hands of the means of access to the property in the presence of a witness particularly enjoined to act as such.

The mother of plaintiff in her broken English testified as to a conversation with Schmidt some five or six days after the delivery of the key, wherein Schmidt, according to her, said, "Yes, every thing what I have in the box belongs to Teresa; I told her that all the time," and also testified that at that time Schmidt "asked Bernard to make a paper out for that he want to sign it that every thing belongs to Teresa", to which Bernard replied, "We go to the hospital, then you can make out all the papers what you want. ' ' She also said Schmidt said, "Every thing was in the box— give to her."

Appellant, analyzing this testimony, claims to find no express or direct words of gift or giving, nor any clear expression of intent that what had theretofore been the property of Schmidt then and there passed from him into the sole ownership of plaintiff. It cannot be fairly required that words spoken by one during one's last illness or in fear of death shall be as grammatically correct or as comprehensive as would be language used under different circumstances, nor should the words of one to whom the use of English is obviously an effort outweigh other circumstances in the case. All that is required is that appropriate words of gift be used, and such words are here found. Nor, as said in *Mellor* v. *Bank of Willows,* 173 Cal. 454 [160 Pac. 567], need the intention to give be manifested solely by the particular words employed by the donor.

"It is a question of fact to be determined like other questions of fact upon all the evidence in the case—the situation of the parties, their relationship, the circumstances surrounding the transaction, the apparent purpose in making the gift, the words spoken at the time, and the like. (Citing cases.) If the words accompanying the delivery of the thing can be said to be expressive of a gift and, in the light of the circumstances, consistent with the intention to give, the execution of a gift is established."

Appellant stresses the fact that on more than one occasion after saying to plaintiff, "Every thing in the box belongs to you," he repeated to others, among them the mother, "Every thing what I have in the box belongs to Teresa," as indicating some future contingency. With this we cannot agree. Schmidt knew that he had not actually handed to plaintiff the physical possession of the contents of the box. He knew that at some future time she would actually possess herself of them. It was, therefore, of that future event and not the gift itself upon which his mind dwelt. So, also, the desire of Schmidt to sign a paper of some kind to confirm the fact that he had made a gift to respondent in no way affects the validity of the gift. . . .

Assuming, as appellant does, that the language used by Schmidt was ambiguous, and that some extrinsic evidence was necessary to clarify his intention, such is found in the relationship of plaintiff and the deceased; the proposals of marriage, the declaration of affection by donor, statements that he intended to give her his property and that she would not have to work, the absence of an immediate family or close relatives of Schmidt who might otherwise be natural objects of his bounty, his illness, all have force in explaining the acts of the donor, even if his words could be considered ambiguous. Furthermore, the intent with which an act is done is a question of fact to be determined from all the evidence in the case and a finding thereon by the trial court will not be disturbed. So, also, do we find some support for the claim of plaintiff that it was the intention of Schmidt then to make an immediate gift of the contents of the deposit box to her in the fact that at that time he did not direct her to pay his hotel and hospital bills out of any funds in the box, but had a clerk from a different bank call and make out a check for the $175 necessary to care for his expenses.

Appellant contends that plaintiff has failed to establish delivery. We are here dealing with personal property locked in a deposit box. The box was not capable of manual delivery, therefore, the well-recognized rule that a valid gift may be made under such circumstances by the transfer of the key thereto is applicable. Nor can any rule or regulation of the depository affect the validity of the gift to plaintiff. The court found that the sole means of access to the deposit box was one key which was in the possession of Schmidt; that during his last illness he handed over to plaintiff this key and at the time stated to her that he was thereby making a gift to her of all the contents of the box. With the evidence in the record supporting the finding, there can be no question as to the divestiture of dominion. Appellant makes some point of a second key. This key, however, was locked in the box and was accessible to the one alone who had control of the Schmidt key. This second key may, therefore, be dismissed from consideration.

Lastly, appellant claims that because plaintiff did not exercise her authority by using the key and taking possession of the property before the death of Schmidt the gift never became effective and failed for lack of acceptance. In *Wilson* v. *Crocker First*

Nat. Bank, 12 Cal. App. (2d) 627 [55 Pac. (2d) 1208], it was contended but unsuccessfully that because a donee had not assumed dominion and withdrawn money from the bank prior to the death of the donor the gift was incomplete. In *Paddock* v. *Fonner,* 84 Cal. App. 652 [258 Pac. 423], although the gift failed because of lack of donative intent, the court held that the acceptance was sufficient if the donee received the bank book and order and took into his possession the means of obtaining the funds on deposit; and that he later offered to turn over to the administratrix of the estate the bank book for the purpose of adjudication of a dispute did not affect the validity of the gift as far as acceptance was concerned. To the same effect was the holding in *Estate of Elliott,* 312 Pa. 493 [167 Atl. 289, 90 A. L. R. 360], where the donee turned over the keys of the deposit box to the administratrix prior to suit.

This cause has been very fully and diligently presented. All the points presented by appellant have not been commented upon, as what we have said makes further discussion unnecessary. The motion to recall the writ of *supersedeas,* having now become *functus officio,* is dismissed. The judgment should be affirmed and it is so ordered.

Rehearing denied.

5.4

McGrath v. Dockendorf
793 S.E.2d 336 (Va. 2016)

Supreme Court of Virginia

OPINION BY JUSTICE STEPHEN R. McCULLOUGH

We resolve in this appeal whether the "heart balm" statute, Code § 8.01-220, bars an action in detinue for recovery of an engagement ring following the breakoff of the engagement. We conclude that the heart balm statute does not bar such an action, and, therefore, we affirm.

BACKGROUND

On August 25, 2012, Ethan L. Dockendorf proposed to Julia V. McGrath. She accepted. He offered her a two-carat engagement ring worth approximately $26,000. In September 2013, after the relationship deteriorated, he broke off the engagement. The parties never married. Love yielded to litigation, and Dockendorf filed an action in detinue seeking, among other things, the return of the ring. In response, McGrath demurred to Dockendorf's complaint, arguing that it was barred by Code § 8.01-220. Following a hearing, the trial court agreed with Dockendorf. The court found that the ring was a conditional gift. It also held that Code § 8.01-220 did not bar the action in detinue for recovery of the ring. The court ordered McGrath to either return the ring within 30 days or it would enter judgment in the amount of $26,000 for Dockendorf. This appeal followed.

ANALYSIS

The issue before us is one of statutory construction, which we review de novo.

Virginia previously recognized suits for breach of a promise to marry. Such suits allowed an aggrieved fiancée to recover damages for improper breach of an engagement. *See Grubb v. Sult*, 73 Va. 203, 207 (1879). Because it was "impossible to fix any rule or measure of damages," the factfinder could "take into consideration all the circumstances of the case, the loss of comfort, the injury to the feelings, affections and wounded pride of the plaintiff." *Id.* at 209. The plaintiff could seek "expectation damages to place [him or] her in the financial and social position [he or] she would have attained had the marriage taken place (very much akin to the rights of a divorced spouse)." Alan Grant & Emily Grant, *The Bride, the Groom, and the Court: A One-Ring Circus*, 35 Cap. U. L. Rev. 743, 745 (2007). The plaintiff could also ask for "traditional tort damages to recover for the emotional anguish and humiliation of the broken engagement." *Id.* Finally, the plaintiff could seek "reliance damages including the lost economic security, opportunity costs of a foregone alternative such as employment, and also the impaired prospects of marrying another due to the [plaintiff's] status now as 'damaged goods.'" *Id.*

"By the late nineteenth century, breach of promise to marry suits were more popular in America than they were in England." *Id.* at 746. Such "trials had become 'social phenomen[a]'-entertainment for the entire town and fodder for sensationalistic tabloid media." *Id.* Over time, such actions were severely "criticized as being anachronistic, contrary to modern notions of justice, and subject to abuse by blackmail." Note: *Heartbalm Statutes and Deceit Actions* , 83 Mich. L. Rev. 1770, 1770 (1985). Breach of promise to marry actions were criticized for excessive verdicts, fueled by "[l]ax evidentiary standards [that] allowed for private and sensational details to be admitted and often skewed the outcome of the case in favor of the plaintiff." Grant & Grant, 35 Cap. U. L. Rev. at 746.

In response, beginning in the 1930's, states began to enact "statutes colloquially called 'heart balm' acts that abolished actions for breach of promise to marry and often abolished the related common law actions for alienation of affections, criminal conversation, and seduction as well." *Heartbalm Statutes and Deceit Actions* , 83 Mich. L. Rev. at 1771. *See also Matthew v. Herman* , 56 V.I. 674, 682-84 (V.I. 2012) (discussing reasons underlying legislative and judicial abrogation of amatory torts of alienation of affection and criminal conversation, as well as cause of action for breach of promise to marry). In 1968, the Virginia General Assembly enacted Code § 8.01-220, which currently provides in subsection (A):

> Notwithstanding any other provision of law to the contrary, no civil action shall lie or be maintained in this Commonwealth for alienation of affection, breach of promise to marry, or criminal conversation upon which a cause of action arose or occurred on or after June 28, 1968.

In addition to an action for breach of promise to marry, Virginia law also recognized a separate right to seek the return of an engagement ring when the engagement is broken off. This right of action is rooted in the common law of conditional gifts. We held in *Pretlow v. Pretlow* , 177 Va. 524, 555, 14 S.E.2d 381, 388 (1941), that when a prospective husband makes a present to his intended wife "and the inducement for the gift is the fact of her promise to marry him, if she break off the marriage, he may recover from her the value of such present."

McGrath argues that the text of the statute forecloses Dockendorf's action. She notes that an action to recover an engagement ring is, in effect, an action for breach of promise to marry because without a breached promise to marry there would be no action to recover the ring. Dockendorf responds that the text and purpose of the statute evince a legislative intent to abolish a specific type of common law action not at issue in this case. We agree with Dockendorf.

"The primary objective in statutory construction is to determine and give effect to the intent of the legislature as expressed in the language of the statute." *Appalachian Power Co. v. State Corp. Comm'n*, 284 Va. 695, 706, 733 S.E.2d 250, 256 (2012). As a textual matter, Code § 8.01-220(A) bars three specific civil actions: (1) alienation of affection; (2) breach of promise to marry, and (3) criminal conversation. The statute says nothing about the law of conditional gifts. Dockendorf did not file a civil action seeking damages based upon McGrath's breach of a promise to marry. Instead, he filed an action in detinue seeking the recovery of the ring or its monetary value on a theory of conditional gift. *See Pavlicic v. Vogtsberger*, 390 Pa. 502, 136 A.2d 127, 131 (1957) (in seeking to recover an engagement ring, the plaintiff is "not asking for damages because of a broken heart or a mortified spirit[; rather, h]e is asking for the return of things which he bestowed with an attached condition precedent, a condition which was never met").

Detinue differs from an action for breach of a promise to marry in significant ways. Breach of promise to marry suits were intended to broadly compensate a plaintiff for the loss and humiliation of a broken engagement. In contrast, "[t]he object of a detinue action is to recover specific personal property and damages for its detention." *Broad Street Auto Sales, Inc. v. Baxter*, 230 Va. 1, 2, 334 S.E.2d 293, 294 (1985). "The action is employed to recover a chattel from one in possession who unlawfully detains it from either the true owner or one lawfully entitled to its possession." *Id.* To succeed in a detinue action, a plaintiff must establish the following:

> (1) The plaintiff must have property in the thing sought to be recovered; (2) he must have the right to its immediate possession; (3) it must be capable of identification; (4) the property must be of some value, and (5) the defendant must have had possession at some time prior to the institution of the action.

Vicars v. Atlantic Discount Co., 205 Va. 934, 938, 140 S.E.2d 667, 670 (1965). Damages are limited. "If the specific property cannot be returned, judgment is rendered for its value." *Broad Street Auto Sales, Inc.*, 230 Va. at 2, 334 S.E.2d at 294. Simply put, due to its limited scope and the limited relief afforded by it, a detinue action rooted in a theory of conditional gift is not and does not resemble an action for breach of a promise to marry.

We note that a majority of other courts have, consistent with our interpretation of Virginia's statute, rejected the argument that their state's heart balm statute foreclosed an action for recovery of a ring or other property. *See In re Marriage of Heinzman*, 198 Colo. 36, 596 P.2d 61, 63 (1979); *Piccininni v. Hajus*, 180 Conn. 369, 429 A.2d 886, 888 (1980) ; *Gill v. Shively*, 320 So.2d 415, 416-17 (Fla. Dist. Ct. App. 1975); *De Cicco v. Barker*, 339 Mass. 457, 159 N.E.2d 534, 535 (1959) ; *Gikas v. Nicholis* , 96 N.H. 177, 71 A.2d 785, 786 (1950) ; *Beberman v. Segal* , 6 N.J.Super. 472, 69 A.2d 587, 587 (Ct. Law Div. 1949); *Pavlicic*, 136 A.2d at 131; *Bryan v. Lincoln* , 168 W.Va. 556, 285 S.E.2d 152, 153-55 (1981). *Albinger v. Harris* , 310 Mont. 27, 48 P.3d 711 (2002), upon which McGrath relies, does not support her position. The court in that case concluded that Montana's heart balm statute did not foreclose an action for recovery of property exchanged in contemplation of marriage and that such claims "are still determined by existing law and common-law principles." *Id* . at 716.[1] That is the view we take.

An additional consideration bolsters the conclusion we draw from the plain language of the statute. The General Assembly is presumed to be aware of the decisions of this Court when enacting legislation. *Dodson v. Potomac Mack Sales & Serv., Inc.*, 241 Va. 89, 94, 400 S.E.2d 178, 180-81 (1991). The *Pretlow* case had been decided several decades prior to the enactment of Code § 8.01-220. Therefore, we presume the General Assembly was aware of this separate avenue for recovery of property or its value. Had the General Assembly wished to bar actions in detinue for the recovery of engagement rings, it would have chosen a vehicle that unequivocally does so.

***

McGrath also seeks to analogize the present cause of action to *McDermott v. Reynolds* , 260 Va. 98, 530 S.E.2d 902 (2000). In *McDermott* , the plaintiff relied on a theory of intentional infliction of emotional distress to recover damages stemming from an adulterous relationship the defendant maintained with the plaintiff's wife. We held that Code § 8.01-220 barred this action. We reasoned that "when the General

Assembly enacted Code § 8.01-220, it manifested its intent to abolish common law actions seeking damages for a particular type of conduct, regardless of the name that a plaintiff assigns to that conduct." *Id.* at 101, 530 S.E.2d at 903. Because the plaintiff's complaint was based on conduct that would have supported a civil action for alienation of affection, Code § 8.01-220 barred the suit. Our stated objective was to "effectuate [legislative] intent and foreclose a revival of the abolished tort of alienation of affection asserted in the guise of an action for intentional infliction of emotional distress." *Id.* at 103, 530 S.E.2d at 904. Unlike the plaintiff in *McDermott* , Dockendorf is not trying to pour old wine into new wineskins. Dockendorf simply seeks to recover property given as a conditional gift when the condition that formed the basis for the gift did not occur.

***

CONCLUSION

The heart balm statute, Code § 8.01-220, does not bar a detinue action to recover conditional gifts, such as an engagement ring, that were given in contemplation of marriage. The trial court found as fact that the ring was given as a conditional gift in contemplation of marriage. The marriage did not occur. Consequently, we will affirm the judgment of the trial court.

Affirmed.

1. We acknowledge the existence of a split of authority with respect to whether fault is a relevant consideration in actions to recover an engagement ring. Compare Fowler v. Perry, 830 N.E.2d 97, 105-06 (Ind. Ct. App. 2005) (noting split and citing cases) with Clippard v. Pfefferkorn, 168 S.W.3d 616, 619-20 (Mo. Ct. App. 2005) (employing a fault based approach). We need not resolve the question in this case, however, because the sole assignment of error before us is whether "the Trial Court erred in failing to apply the Heart Balm Statute to an action for the return of an engagement ring when the wedding never occurs." The question of fault may (or may not) bear upon the viability of a detinue action, but it is not relevant to our construction of the heart balm statute. [Editorial Note: This is footnote 3 of the opinion.]

5.5

Discussion: Notes, Questions, and Problems

5.5.1

Discussion Note #1. Be alert to social media posts on engagements

In *Luce v. Fleck*, 75 N.Y.S.3d 822 (N.Y. Sup. Ct. 2018), the parties disputed whether a ring was an engagement ring and, thus, a conditional gift or was just a ring. According to the plaintiff, the ring was given "to celebrate our romantic and intimate relationship. At the time of the delivery of the gift of said ring, he did not propose marriage and he did not state or imply that the gift of the ring was conditional, qualified or temporary." *Id.* at 825.

In response to that claim, the defendant submitted affidavits from two mutual friends of the couple and attached as exhibits screenshots from the plaintiff's Facebook page. The court in *Luce* noted that in one of the screenshots from her Facebook page, the plaintiff posted that "Robert Fleck proposed to me with my Grandparents and Aunt Barbara and Uncle John and I said yes." Accompanying that post is a picture of the ring. The court also noted that in another post on her Facebook page one week later, the plaintiff says "[w]ell as you all must know by now Robert Fleck and I are engaged. I have put in for a transfer to New York." *Id.* at 826.

The court found that the plaintiff's "Facebook posts constitute documentary evidence of Plaintiff's admissions to being given the ring as an engagement ring, upon her acceptance of Defendant's proposal of marriage. Indeed, they are not just admissions, but proclamations to the world of her engagement." *Id.*

5.5.2

Discussion Problem #2. Aunt Lola's bracelet problem

While Aunt Lola and her 13-year-old niece, Miranda, were having their weekly lunch, Miranda told Aunt Lola how much she admired Aunt Lola's jewel encrusted bracelet.

Aunt Lola took the bracelet off her own wrist and placed it on Miranda's and said, "it looks lovely on you, when you are older, I will give it to you." Aunt Lola then took the bracelet off of Miranda's wrist and put it back on her own. Aunt Lola died six years later. Aunt Lola had a validly executed Last Will and Testament leaving all of her property to her new husband, Brad. Miranda makes a claim for the bracelet stating that she had acquired the bracelet by gift. Brad does not want Miranda to get it. What is the best argument for Brad?

5.5.3

Discussion Problem #3. Sky diving problem

Doris was about to go sky diving for her 70th birthday and, although excited, she was in sincere apprehension of death. Doris called her granddaughter, Gloria, into her house and, in front of her good friends, Doris said "since I may not make it back from the jump in one piece, I want you, Gloria, to have my valuable watch." Doris then gave the watch to Gloria. Gloria immediately put on the watch. Doris made it back from her adventure and wants her watch back. What is Doris's best argument?

6

Chapter 6 · Adverse Possession

Adverse possession allows a person to obtain title to real property owned by another despite the owner's intent. Generally, adverse possession claims are justified because adverse possession encourages the productive use and development of land that is otherwise not being possessed. These claims are justified as protecting against stale claims and encouraging true owners to bring ejectment or trespass actions in a timely manner. Another justification is that adverse possession claims provide a mechanism to quiet title and settle property rights.

Are these policy justifications convincing? Those concerned with the environment and overdevelopment may not be persuaded. In *Meyer v. Law*, 287 So. 2d 37, 41 (Fla. 1973), the Florida Supreme Court critiqued the "development" justification for adverse possession, stating as follows:

> The concept of adverse possession is an ancient and, perhaps, somewhat outdated one. It stems from a time when an ever-increasing use of land was to be, and was, encouraged. Today, however, faced, as we are, with problems of unchecked over-development, depletion of precious natural resources, and pollution of our environment, the policy reasons that once supported the idea of adverse possession may well be succumbing to new priorities. A man who owns some virgin land, who refrains from despoiling that land, even to the extent of erecting a fence to mark its boundaries, and who makes no greater use of that land than an occasional rejuvenating walk in the woods, can hardly be faulted in today's increasingly 'modern' world.

Despite such critiques, adverse possession appears to continue in full strength.

6.1

Elements

To bring a successful claim for adverse possession, the possessor must meet the elements established for adverse possession for the required time period in the jurisdiction where the real property is located. Jurisdictions vary considerably as to the required time period. For example, while 10, 15, or 20 year time periods are fairly common, some jurisdictions require as few as 5 years and others require as many as 30 years. In many jurisdictions, the time period is shortened if the adverse possession claim is made under color of title, that is, when the claim is based in part on a defective deed or instrument.

elements

Generally, the elements that a claimant would need to prove for a successful adverse possession claim may be listed as follows: actual possession, claim of right, open and notorious, continuous, required time, adverse/hostile, and exclusive. Some jurisdictions may use slightly different phrasing for the elements. For example, in *City of Philadelphia v. Galdo*, excerpted below, the Supreme Court of Pennsylvania explained that a claimant by adverse possession in Pennsylvania "must prove actual, continuous, exclusive, visible, notorious, distinct, and hostile possession of the land for [the required] period," which in Pennsylvania is twenty-one years. However, differing terms are basically semantics. Also note that lists with fewer elements generally combine related elements. Nonetheless, as the Supreme Court of Indiana in *Marengo Cave Co. v. Ross*, excerpted below, aptly stated,

> "the authorities agree that before the owner of the legal title can be deprived of his land by another's possession, through the operation of the statute of limitation, the possession must have been actual, visible, notorious, exclusive, under claim of ownership and hostile to the owner of the legal title and to the world at large (except only the government) and continuous for the full period prescribed by the statute. The rule is not always stated in exactly the same words in the many cases dealing with the subject of adverse possession, yet the rule is so thoroughly settled that there is no doubt as to what elements are essential to establish a title by adverse possession."

Some jurisdictions have additional statutory requirements for adverse possession claims. For example, some jurisdictions require that the adverse possession claimant have paid the real property taxes on the claimed property during the time period. See, for example, Fla Sta. § 95.18. Also, for color of title claims, some jurisdictions require that the defective instrument for the property have been recorded. See, for example, Fla Sta. § 95.16. Both of these Florida statutes are excerpted in Discussion Note #1 below.

6.1.1

City of Philadelphia v. Galdo
217 A.3d 811 (Pa. 2019)

Supreme Court of Pennsylvania

JUSTICE BAER

This appeal involves an ejectment action commenced by the City of Philadelphia ("City") against Francis Galdo and a counterclaim to quiet title filed by Galdo, claiming ownership of the property at issue by adverse possession. The trial court ruled in favor of the City, holding that it was immune from suit because a claim of adverse possession cannot lie against a municipality. The Commonwealth Court vacated the trial court's order and remanded for trial on the adverse possession claim. The court held that the adverse possession claim could proceed against the City because the property was not devoted to a public use during the twenty-one-year prescriptive period, as required for immunity to apply. For the reasons set forth herein, we agree that the City is not immune from a claim of adverse possession under the facts presented and affirm the order of the Commonwealth Court.

I. Background

The record establishes that the property at issue in this appeal is a rectangular lot of undeveloped land located at 1101-1119 N. Front Street in Philadelphia (hereinafter, "the Parcel"). To understand the origin of the City's ownership of the Parcel, we begin by observing that on May 31, 1956, the City passed an ordinance granting consent to the Department of Highways of the Commonwealth of Pennsylvania to establish and occupy rights of way and certain traffic interchanges for the construction of the Delaware Expressway between the Walt Whitman Bridge and Poquessing Creek in Philadelphia. The City entered into an agreement with the Commonwealth on July 30, 1962, to assist in the construction of the various state highways. . . .

***

On January 19, 1976, the Commonwealth filed a notice of condemnation against several of the City's lots, indicating that the Commonwealth would permanently retain the land in the I-95 right-of-way, and that the Commonwealth would have a temporary easement on other condemned properties, including the Parcel condemned by the City, during the period that the Elevated Frankford train line was rerouted to allow for construction of I-95. Germane to this appeal, the parties agree that the City has not physically occupied the Parcel since completion of the work connected to the rerouting of the Elevated Frankford train line in the 1970s.[1] Further, it is undisputed that the City has not performed any maintenance, grass-cutting, grading, or landscaping on the Parcel. Instead, after the highway construction was completed, the City viewed the Parcel as "surplus property" that was not actively being used.

At least a decade after construction of I-95 had been completed, in September of 1989, Galdo purchased a two-story dwelling on 1115 N. Lee Street, Philadelphia, which is located directly across the street from the Parcel. At that time, the Parcel was not being maintained and was purportedly home to "prostitutes" and "derelicts". In early 1990, Galdo cleared the Parcel of weeds and trash, poured a concrete slab, and parked his vehicles there. He also used the Parcel to discard debris from the remodeling of his home. By 1992, Galdo poured another concrete slab on the Parcel for storing materials and enclosed that area with a fence. In 1994, he installed on the Parcel a fire pit and a picnic table affixed to the ground.

In 1997, a nearby factory burned down and Galdo created a driveway on the Parcel with materials collected from the remains of the factory. He also planted two maple trees and built a carport with metal poles, which was later replaced with a wooden pavilion. Additionally in 1997, Galdo converted the fire pit on the Parcel into a brick barbeque, installed two oversized trailers to store gardening tools and the like, and installed a sand volleyball court and horseshoe pit. Between 1998 and 2001, Galdo planted grass seed on a portion of the Parcel, and he planted a willow tree in 2010. From 2010 through 2014, he built a tree-house deck on the Parcel. Although Galdo regularly obtained permits to work on properties that he owns in connection with his business, he has never obtained any permits to make improvements to the Parcel, did not pay property taxes for the Parcel, and did not provide evidence that he insured the Parcel. Further, it is undisputed that the City never gave Galdo permission to possess the land at issue.

In the meantime, in 2008, the City entered into an agreement to sell the Parcel to Tower Properties, but that sale was never finalized. On or about February 4, 2013, the City posted a public notice on the Parcel, directing all individuals to remove personal property from the site within thirty days of the notice. Galdo refused to comply. On April 24, 2014, the City filed an ejectment action against Galdo. Galdo responded by filing a counterclaim to quiet title, claiming ownership of the property by adverse possession. In his counterclaim, Galdo contended that he had been in continuous and exclusive possession of the Parcel without the City's consent or authorization since September of 1989. He further asserted that the Parcel had not constituted a public use since 1976. . . .

* * *

In its opinion dated June 27, 2016, the trial court explained that it was unnecessary to examine the elements of adverse possession because one "cannot adversely possess a property owned by the City of Philadelphia." Citing the Commonwealth Court's decision in *Lysicki v. Montour School District*, 701 A.2d 630, 631-32 (Pa. Cmwlth. 1997), the trial court reasoned that adverse possession could never be established against the Commonwealth or its agents; thus, the City was immune as a Commonwealth agent because it condemned the Parcel "at the behest of the Commonwealth to facilitate the Commonwealth's construction of a highway." Notably, in addition to finding immunity based on an agency theory, the trial court further held that the City was immune because the Parcel was devoted to a public use, as the City obtained the Parcel through its eminent domain power.

* * *

The Commonwealth Court . . . remanded the matter for trial on Galdo's adverse possession claim. The intermediate appellate court viewed the primary issue as "whether a claim of adverse possession can lie against the City, a municipality, when the City's only use of the [Parcel] during the statutory period was to hold the [Parcel] for possible future sale." The court began its analysis by acknowledging the well-established proposition that "political subdivisions, such as counties, townships, municipalities, and boroughs, are not immune from claims of adverse possession, although the Commonwealth is." It explained, however, that claims alleging title by adverse possession cannot be made against any entity, including a municipality, where the property at issue is devoted to a public use.

***

Significantly, the Commonwealth Court further discounted the trial court's alternative holding that the City was immune from Galdo's claim of adverse possession because it held the Parcel for a public use. The court agreed that immunity arises when the property in question is devoted to a public use, but concluded there was no public use here. In reaching this conclusion, the Commonwealth Court examined *Torch v. Constantino*, 227 Pa.Super. 427, 323 A.2d 278 (1974), which held that the twenty-one-year prescriptive period for adverse possession tolled during the years that the county held the property for tax sale for the nonpayment of taxes. The intermediate appellate court reasoned that, in *Torch*, it was the legislative mandate, requiring counties to act as trustee and hold property for tax sale for the nonpayment of taxes, which served as the basis for finding that the property was devoted to a public use.

* * *

This Court subsequently granted the City's petition for allowance of appeal to address whether the Parcel was devoted to a public use where the property was acquired by condemnation to assist the Commonwealth with the construction of I-95 and was held by the City for subsequent resale. The determination of whether the Parcel was devoted to a public use is a question of law over which our standard of review is *de novo* and our scope of review is plenary.

II. The Parties' Arguments

The City, as appellant, contends that it is immune from Galdo's adverse possession claim because the Parcel was devoted to a public use. [T]he City contends that a public use was established because the Parcel was condemned by the City to assist the Commonwealth with the construction of I-95, and the City had always planned to resell the property after the construction was completed to return the property to taxable status. The City relies upon the Superior Court's decision in *Torch*, which it interprets as holding that a municipality's acquisition of property at a tax sale, followed by the municipality's subsequent holding of the property for future resale, constitutes a public use, even if the future resale does not occur for decades and the land lies fallow in the interim. The City posits that there are sound reasons for this holding, including eliminating impediments placed on tax titles that drive purchasers away from tax sales, affording municipalities the opportunity to sell the property at a time when they would receive a considerable profit, and restoring properties to tax assessment lists.

City args

The City maintains that there is no reason to distinguish the public use in *Torch* (obtaining ownership of an individual's property in consideration for delinquent taxes and thereafter holding the property for future resale) from the public purpose here (acquiring the Parcel by condemnation to assist the Commonwealth with construction of I-95 and thereafter holding it for future resale). In both cases, it contends, the government initially acquired the properties with the intent of ultimately reselling it for the public purpose of offsetting government expenses with economic efficiency.

* * *

The City further argues that neither the length of time a property is left idle nor the municipality's lack of vigilance in reselling the property should negate its immunity. This is so, it asserts, because the government does not have the same incentives as private property owners to monitor its properties and because effective monitoring is burdensome, considering there are tens of thousands of vacant properties spread across Philadelphia. According to the City, it makes no sense to lose municipal land due to oversight, indifference, or mistake of government employees.[2]

Finally, the City deems unfounded the Commonwealth Court's concern that a ruling in its favor would render every municipal acquisition of private property by condemnation a public use. Notably, it concedes that a municipality's acquisition of private property would not be protected by immunity where it continues to hold the property long after the stated public use has lapsed or has been abandoned or where the City acquires property in its proprietary capacity by contract. Here, the City contends, it did not abandon the public use because the record demonstrates that it had intended at the time of condemnation to sell the Parcel after the construction of I-95 had been completed. The City maintains that it should be afforded the opportunity to sell the property when the market best supports its disposition. It clarifies that it is not suggesting that a municipality's taking of property for resale, in and of itself, devotes the property to a public use. Rather, the essence of the City's contention is that when a municipality acquires property for a public use with the intent to resell it after that use is completed, the public use continues into perpetuity until the property is sold.

Galdo responds that the Commonwealth Court was correct in holding that the City does not have immunity from his claim of adverse possession under the facts presented. He asserts that the parties agree that the Commonwealth is immune from all claims of adverse possession, and that political subdivisions are generally not immune unless the property at issue is devoted to a public use. Galdo maintains that a public use is established where there is actual occupation of the property to benefit the public, such as a public park, or where there is a legal obligation requiring the municipality to hold the property for a public use. He contends that neither occurred here because the City never physically occupied the Parcel during the twenty-one-year prescriptive period, and the City's holding of the Parcel for decades after the initial public use had lapsed was voluntary and not legislatively required. Accordingly, Galdo concludes that his claim for adverse possession should proceed against the City.

* * *

Galdo argues that *Torch* did not declare that a political subdivision's voluntary holding of property for eventual resale constitutes a public use. Rather, he submits, *Torch* stands for the proposition that absent a political subdivision's physical occupation of the property for a public use, a public use may still exist if the political subdivision is holding the property pursuant to a legal obligation imposed by the legislature as herein described. Unlike in *Torch*, Galdo maintains, there was no legal obligation in the instant case requiring the City to hold the Parcel from the late 1970s, after the public use had lapsed because the construction of I-95 was completed, until 2014, when Galdo asserted title by adverse possession. He finds no precedent supporting the City's position that once property is condemned for a public use, the political subdivision is forever immune from adverse possession claims, regardless of whether the public use continues.

Moreover, Galdo contends, if this Court were to adopt the City's position, political subdivisions would be immunized from all adverse possession claims by simply contending in each case that it intended to sell the condemned property at a later time. In this regard, he submits, the Commonwealth Court correctly observed that municipalities could institute a taking of private property for a land bank, keeping the property indefinitely until the market provides for a formidable profit upon its resale. Galdo asserts that any suggestion of public use simply because a municipality acquires title by condemnation is not the law of Pennsylvania.

* * *

III. Analysis

Adverse possession is an extraordinary doctrine that permits one to achieve ownership of another's real property by operation of law. *Weible v. Wells*, 156 A.3d 1220, 1224 (Pa. Super. 2017). The doctrine is dependent upon an individual's possession of another's property for an enumerated period of time authorized by statute. *Id.; see also* 68 P.S §§ 81-88 (governing claims by adverse possession); and 42 Pa.C.S. § 5530 (setting forth twenty-one year limitations period in actions for the possession of real property).[3] . . . An individual who claims title by adverse possession in Pennsylvania must prove actual, continuous, exclusive, visible, notorious, distinct, and hostile possession of the land for a period of twenty-one years.

As alluded to *supra*, it is well-established that a claim of title by adverse possession does not lie against Commonwealth property. *Commonwealth v. J.W. Bishop & Co.*, 497 Pa. 58, 439 A.2d 101, 103 (1981); *see also* 68 P.S. § 88 (entitled "Act not to apply to claims adverse to the Commonwealth).[4] The basis for this rule of immunity emanates from the doctrine *nullum tempus occurrit regi*, meaning "[t]ime does not run against the king," which has its roots in the prerogative of the Crown. *J.W. Bishop & Co.*, 439

A.2d at 103 (citing 1 Blackstone, Commentaries at 247-4872 P.S. §
5860.101).[5] Underlying the doctrine of *nullum tempus* is the vindication of public rights
and the protection of public policy.

For well over a century, it has been the law of Pennsylvania that the doctrine of
nullum tempus is reserved exclusively for the Commonwealth. *Evans v. Erie County*, 66
Pa. at 228. In *Evans*, this Court held that a claim for title by adverse possession could
proceed against Erie County as it was not protected by the doctrine of *nullum tempus*.
This Court explained that the running of the statute of limitations "against a county
or other municipal corporation ... cannot be doubted," as the "prerogative is that of
the sovereign alone." *Id.* We held that grantees of the sovereign, "though artificial
bodies created by her, are in the same category as natural persons." *Id.* Accordingly,
as a general rule, political subdivisions in this Commonwealth may be subject to
claims of adverse possession.

An exception to this general rule exposing political subdivisions to claims of adverse
possession exists where the property owned by the political subdivision is devoted
to a public use.[6] A determination of whether property is devoted to a public use is
dependent upon the individualized facts of each case.

Here, it is undisputed that the City condemned the Parcel in 1974 for transit purposes
to assist in the construction of I-95. Thus, we conclude, without hesitation, that the
Parcel was acquired for the public use of the construction of a state highway. It is
also undisputed that the transit purposes underlying the condemnation lapsed in the
late 1970s when the work relating to the rerouting of the Elevated Frankford line
was completed to assist in the construction of I-95. The parties agree that the City
has not physically occupied the Parcel for a public use during the nearly forty-year
period since that time. Indeed, the City viewed the Parcel as "surplus property" that
was not actively being used.

Further, the City concedes as a matter of law that a public use can lapse or be
abandoned. The Eminent Domain Code supports this view as it contemplates the
abandonment of the purpose for which property has been condemned. *See* 26 Pa.C.S.
§ 310(a) (setting forth the means of disposition of condemned property where the
condemnor abandons the purpose for which the property has been condemned).

The crux of the City's argument in this appeal is its narrow assertion that there was no abandonment of the public use under the facts presented because the ultimate disposition of condemned property through its sale constitutes an extension of the original public use that supported the condemnation. Thus, the City's defense of immunity against Galdo's claim of adverse possession relies exclusively on its declaration in 1974 that it intended to dispose of the Parcel after the highway construction concluded. On a more global scale, it is the City's view that once it acquires property for a public use, it can retain that property in perpetuity without being subject to adverse possession claims so long as it does so for the putative purpose of resale, without any obligation to maintain such property and regardless of whether the land continues to function in its dedicated capacity.

We find the City's position to be unsupported by legal precedent and antithetical to the policies underlying the doctrine of adverse possession, particularly the promotion of the active and efficient use of land. The City cites no authority, and we have found none, to support the proposition that holding condemned property formerly devoted to a public use for resale constitutes a public use. The reason necessitating the sale of the property is because the public use no longer exists. Absent the public use, a municipality's holding of abandoned property, here for decades, offers no benefit to the public. Under such circumstances, the public is not occupying the property in any way, no tax dollars are being received from the property, and the neighborhoods in which the dormant properties are located risk the threat of becoming blighted. This scenario constitutes the opposite of devoting property to a public use as the indefinite holding of abandoned municipal property is detrimental to those tax payers who own property nearby and to the community at large.

While we acknowledge the vast number of condemned properties that the City oversees, we emphasize the high burden that adverse possessors must satisfy to obtain title under the doctrine and observe that the City need only intervene to prevent adverse possessors on each municipal property at some point prior to the end of the twenty-first year after the purpose of the condemnation has lapsed. Encumbering municipalities with the limited responsibility to monitor their properties at some point during the twenty-one-year prescriptive period or face claims of adverse possession will promote the goals of municipal efficiency and the active and efficient use of the land by motivating municipalities to either use the retained property for the public benefit or sell it to private individuals so that it may be taxed for the municipality's and the public's financial benefit.

* * *

We agree with Galdo that *Torch* does not stand for the broad proposition that a political subdivision's holding of municipal property for eventual resale constitutes a public use. Critically, as the Commonwealth Court cogently observed below, the finding of a public use in *Torch* was based upon Erie County's legal obligation to acquire and hold tax delinquent property for tax sale purposes pursuant to the Real Estate Tax Sale Law. The decision in no way suggested that a municipality who acquired property by other means, such as condemnation, could hold that property indefinitely after the public purpose for the condemnation had lapsed, without being subject to claims of adverse possession. Rather, the county's method of acquisition of the property to carry out its legal obligation of tax collection, coupled with the subsequent holding of the property for that same purpose, created the public use. . . .

Unlike the instant case, the public use in *Torch* was never extinguished or abandoned because the public use derived from the legal obligation to hold the property. The same cannot be said for the condemned property at issue here. As established at length *supra*, the public purpose for condemnation of the Parcel lapsed in the late 1970s, approximately ten years before the alleged period of adverse possession began in 1989. After the construction of I-95 ceased, the City retained the Parcel and left it idle for nearly forty years, during which it had no legal obligation to hold the property and failed to otherwise occupy the property for a public use.

In summary, we hold that, generally, political subdivisions in this Commonwealth may be subject to claims of adverse possession. An exception to this general rule is where the property is devoted to a public use. A public use may lapse or be abandoned. Here, the public use of the Parcel to assist in the construction of a state highway lapsed in the late 1970s and the only purported public use proffered by the City thereafter was the holding of the Parcel for resale. For the reasons set forth *supra*, we hold that condemned property that is held for eventual resale by a political subdivision after the original public purpose for the condemnation has lapsed does not constitute a public use of the property that affords a municipality immunity from adverse possession claims.

Because the trial court deemed the City immune from adverse possession, there has been no factual determination of whether Galdo has satisfied the requisites thereof. Accordingly, we affirm the order of the Commonwealth Court, which vacated the trial court's order finding immunity, and remanded to the trial court for further proceedings on Galdo's adverse possession claim.

1. Other than a general reference to the 1970s, the record is unclear as to precisely when construction of I-95 was completed or when occupation of the Parcel ceased. This lack of specificity does not affect our resolution of this appeal as Galdo claims that his period of prescriptive possession did not begin until 1989.

2. The City observes that some states apply similar public policy rationales to grant absolute immunity to municipalities from claims of adverse possession, regardless of whether the property was acquired and maintained as a public use. Significantly, however, the City does not advocate that we adopt such an approach and, instead, recognizes that in Pennsylvania "municipalities have partial immunity from adverse possession - - where the property is devoted to public use." Moreover, the City acknowledges expressly that it never argued below that municipalities are always immune from claims alleging title by adverse possession. Accordingly, we need not reexamine the well-established case law, set forth infra, permitting claims of title by adverse possession to proceed against municipal property, unless the property is devoted to a public use. [Editorial Note: This is footnote 6 of the opinion.]

3. Upon expiration of the twenty-one-year statute of limitations governing actions for the possession of real property, the property owner's right to bring an ejectment action against the adverse possessor is precluded. [Editorial Note: This is footnote 8 of the opinion.]

4. Section 88 provides that "[n]othing contained in this act shall be construed to give any title to any lands by a claim of title adverse to that of the Commonwealth of Pennsylvania, and no claim of title adverse to the Commonwealth of Pennsylvania

shall be made or recorded under the provisions of this act." 68 P.S. § 88. [Editorial Note: This is footnote 9 of the opinion.]

5. This maxim is sometimes expressed as nullum tempus occurrit republicae ("time does not run against the state"). J.W. Bishop & Co., 439 A.2d at 102 n.2. [Editorial Note: This is footnote 10 of the opinion.]

6. Another exception to the general rule arises where the political subdivision is acting as an agent of the Commonwealth. See Lysicki, 701 A.2d at 632 (holding that because school districts are agents of the Commonwealth, they are protected by the Commonwealth's immunity from claims of adverse possession). As noted supra, the City has abandoned its agency argument in this appeal. [Editorial Note: This is footnote 12 of the opinion.]

6.1.2

Romero v. Garcia
546 P.2d 66 (N.M. 1976)

Supreme Court of New Mexico

SOSA, Justice.

Plaintiff-appellee Ida Romero, formerly Garcia, filed suit to quiet title against defendants-appellants Mr. and Mrs. Antonio Garcia, who are her former father-in-law and mother-in-law. The suit to quiet title was based upon adverse possession for more than ten years under color of title and payment of taxes. From judgment for the plaintiff, defendants appeal. We affirm the trial court.

On appeal the defendants urge for reversal: (1) the trial court erred by rejecting the applicable law that plaintiff, whose claim to quiet title was based on adverse possession, must recover, if at all, on the strength of her own title and must establish adverse possession by clear and convincing evidence; (2) the deed that plaintiff relied on did not constitute color of title because the description did not furnish means of identifying any ascertainable tract of land, and because it was "void and of no effect" under New Mexico community property law because the mother-in-law failed to sign the deed; (3) the land was not adequately assessed and taxes were not continuously paid as required by statute.

The facts are the following: In 1947 plaintiff Ida Garcia Romero and her deceased husband Octaviano Garcia, son of the defendants, purchased the 13 acres in dispute for $290 from Octaviano's father, Antonio Garcia. Mrs. Antonio Garcia failed to join in the conveyance. The 13 acres were carved out of 165 acres Antonio Garcia had purchased in 1923. The plaintiff and her deceased husband entered into possession in 1947 and built a home on the land with the help of both defendants. The deed was recorded in May, 1950. Ida and Octaviano lived in their home until 1962, when he died, whereupon she moved to Colorado and subsequently remarried.

appellant arg.

The main thrust of the appellants' argument concerns the deed. Appellants argue that (1) the void deed was inadequate for color of title and (2) the deed's description was inadequate for adverse possession because it failed to describe a specific piece of property. The first argument is clearly erroneous. A deed is sufficient for the purpose of color of title even though it is void because it lacks the signature of a member of the community.

issue

We move to the question of whether the deed was insufficient for adverse possession because it failed to describe adequately a parcel of land which can be ascertained on the ground. Since the deed in question was in Spanish, the court and the parties relied on the following English translation of the description:

> A piece of land containing 13 acres more or less, within the following description: NE 1/4 SE 1/4, S 1/2 SE 1/4 NE 1/4, Section 32, NW 1/4 SW 1/4, S 1/2 SW 1/4 NW 1/4, Section 33, Township 32 N. Range 7E N.M.P.M., said 13 acres are bounded as follows: East and South bounded by property of Antonio Garcia; on the North by the National Forest and on the West by property of Alfonso Marquez. The said 13 acres are in the NW corner of the ranch above described.

Not translated but part of the deed to the appellee's husband are the following words in Spanish: "Con derecho de agua del Sublet del Rio de Los Pinos," which translated mean "with water rights assigned from the Sublet [creek] of the Los Pinos river."

The description in the deed specified that the land is bounded on the north by the National Forest and on the west by Alfonso Marquez and on the south and east by the grantor. The deed also specified that there shall be water rights to the land from the Los Pinos River. The Los Pinos River is generally to the south of this property and at one point only some twenty feet from the alleged southern boundary. In *Richardson v.* Duggar, 86 N.M. 494, 497, 525 P.2d 854, 857 (1974) we held that the deed is not void for want of proper description if, with the deed and with extrinsic evidence on the ground, a surveyor can ascertain the boundaries. Justice Oman quoted the following:

> The purpose of a description of the land, which is the subject matter of a deed of conveyance, is to identify such subject matter; and it may be laid down as a broad general principle that a deed will not be declared void for uncertainty in description if it is possible by any reasonable rules of construction to ascertain from the description, aided by extrinsic evidence, which property is intended to be conveyed. It is sufficient if the description in the deed or conveyance furnishes a means of identification of the land or by which the property conveyed can be located. . . . So, if a surveyor with the deed before him can, with the aid of extrinsic evidence if necessary, locate the land and establish its boundaries, the description therein is sufficient. 16 Am.Jur. (Deeds) § 262.

In the case at bar we had testimony from the grantor that the fence line along the entire northern boundary had been there for over fifty years, and the fence line on the western boundary of the property which he conveyed to his son had also been there for more than fifty years. We therefore see that the northwest corner was adequately established as being the intersection of these two fence lines. The surveyor testified that the plaintiff showed him generally where the land was and pointed to the house that was built by the plaintiff and the defendants. The surveyor walked down the western boundary line and found a pipe in position; he established that pipe as the southwest corner. He shot an angle parallel to the northern boundary line and found a pile of rocks which he established as the southeastern corner. He then closed the parallelogram by shooting a line to the northern boundary parallel to the western fence. This parallelogram measured 12.95 acres; the deed granted "13 acres more or less." Thus, the land is in the shape of a parallelogram and is bounded by the National Forest on the north, by Alfonso Marquez (now lands of Mr. L. C. White) on the west, and on the south and east by the grantor. This parallelogram is also in close proximity to the river from which water could be used in accordance with the assignment of the water rights.

Mrs. Romero consistently identified this land as the property she and her deceased husband had purchased and which she thereafter possessed and from which she sold the hay for several years. Defendant failed to object to this testimony. Defendant Antonio Garcia recognized that his son owned property, and, although he did not explicitly identify the property that he sold to his son, it can be reasonably inferred from his testimony that it was the above described property.

The trial court made the following findings of fact:

> The land described in the complaint of the plaintiff herein, by virtue of the description of the said deed itself and' the actions and understandings of the parties as to the boundaries of said land, is capable of determination as to the exact location of the boundaries of said land conveyed to Plaintiff's deceased husband.

> The Northwest corner of the land conveyed is established by the intersection of a fence line extending along the entire northern boundary of said property from east to west, and the point where an existing fence line along the westerly boundary of said property intersected; the Southwest corner of said lands of the Plaintiff was marked by an iron pipe found in place by a surveyor, and the Southeast corner of said property conveyed was marked by a pile of rocks, and the Northeast corner of said tract was marked by an existing fence extending from East to West along the entire northerly boundary of said tract of land.

boundaries

The court feels that when the evidence, with all reasonable inferences deducible therefrom, is viewed in the light most favorable in support of the findings, there was substantial evidence to support these findings of fact and others relevant to this issue. The Supreme Court will not disturb findings, weigh evidence, resolve conflicts or substitute its judgment as to the credibility of witnesses where evidence substantially supports findings of fact and conclusions of law of the trial court.

The court in *Garcia v. Garcia,* 86 N.M. 503, 505, 525 P.2d 863, 865 (1974) stated that " . . .an indefinite and uncertain description may be clarified by subsequent acts of the parties [citing cases]", and found that:

> The evidence here is clear that subsequent acts of the parties in going upon and generally pointing out the boundaries of the lands to the surveyor, aided by other extrinsic evidence, enabled the surveyor to prepare the plat relied upon by all the parties. In fact, if it were not for the extrinsic evidence by which the surveyor was able to locate the lands, the 1968 deed from Nazario to plaintiffs would fail for lack of means by which to identify any lands.

In the case at bar the subsequent acts of the parties in erecting a house and pointing to the land were sufficient to ascertain the boundaries.

Finally, appellants argue that appellee failed to pay the tax continuously, for appellee had been in arrears several times, ranging from 1½ to almost 4 years. However, appellee did pay the taxes in each case before a tax deed was issued to the state. Thus, we hold that appellee complied substantially with the continuous payment of taxes requirement of adverse possession under § 23-1-22 N.M.S.A.1953 (Supp.1975).

6.1.3

Marengo Cave Co. v. Ross
10 N.E.2d 917 (Ind. 1937)

Supreme Court of Indiana

Roll, J.

Appellee and appellant were the owners of adjoining land in Crawford County, Indiana. On appellant's land was located the opening to a subterranean cavity known as "Marengo Cave." This cave extended under a considerable portion of appellant's land and the southeastern portion thereof extended under lands owned by appellee. This action arose out of a dispute as to the ownership of that part of the cave that extended under appellee's land. Appellant was claiming title to all the cave and cavities including that portion underlying appellee's land. Appellee instituted this action to quiet his title as against appellant's claim. Appellant answered by a general denial and filed a cross-complaint wherein he sought to quiet its title to all the cave including that portion underlying appellee's land. There was a trial by jury which returned a verdict for the appellee. Appellant filed its motion for a new trial which was overruled by the court, and this is the only error assigned on appeal. Appellant assigns as grounds for a new trial that the verdict of the jury is not sustained by sufficient evidence, and is contrary to law. These are the only grounds urged for a reversal of this cause.

The facts as shown by the record are substantially as follows: In 1883 one Stewart owned the real estate now owned by appellant, and in September of that year some young people who were upon that land discovered what afterwards proved to be the entrance to the cavern since known as Marengo Cave, this entrance being approximately 700 feet from the boundary line between the lands now owned by appellant and appellee, and the only entrance to said cave. Within a week after discovery of the cave, it was explored, and the fact of its existence received wide publicity through newspaper articles and otherwise. Shortly thereafter the then owner of the real estate upon which the entrance was located, took complete possession of the entire cave as now occupied by appellant and used for exhibition purposes, and began to charge an admission fee to those who desired to enter and view the cave, and to exclude therefrom those who were unwilling to' pay for admission. This practice continued from 1883, except in some few instances when persons were permitted by the persons claiming to own said cave to enter same without payment of the usual required fee, and during the following years the successive owners of the land upon which the entrance to the cave was located, advertised the existence of said cave through newspapers, magazines, posters, and otherwise, in order to attract visitors thereto; also made improvements within the cave, including the building of concrete walks, and concrete steps where there was a difference in elevation of said cavern, widened and heightened portions of passageways; had available and furnished guides, all in order to make the cave more easily accessible to visitors desiring to view the same; and continuously, during all this time, without asking or obtaining consent from anyone, but claiming a right so to do, held and possessed said subterranean passages constituting said cave, excluding therefrom the "whole world" except such persons as entered after paying admission for the privilege of so doing, or by permission.

Appellee has lived in the vicinity of said cave since 1903, and purchased the real estate which he now owns in 1908. He first visited the cave in 1895, paying an admission fee for the privilege, and has visited said cave several times since. He has never, at any time, occupied or been in possession of any of the subterranean passages or cavities of which the cave consists, and the possession and use of the cave by those who have done so has never interfered with his use and enjoyment of the lands owned by him. For a period of approximately twenty-five years prior to the time appellee purchased his land, and for a period of twenty-one years afterwards, exclusive possession of the cave has been held by appellant, its immediate and remote grantors.

The cave, as such, has never been listed for taxation separately from the real estate wherein it is located, and the owners of the respective tracts of land have paid the taxes assessed against said tracts.

A part of said cave at the time of its discovery and exploration extended beneath real estate now owned by appellee, but this fact was not ascertained until the year 1932, when the boundary line between the respective tracts through the cave was established by means of a survey made by a civil engineer pursuant to an order of court entered in this cause. Previous to this survey neither of the parties to this appeal, nor any of their predecessors in title, knew that any part of the cave was in fact beneath the surface of a portion of the land now owned by appellee. Possession of the cave was taken and held by appellant's remote and immediate grantors, improvements made, and control exercised, with the belief on the part of such grantors that the entire cave as it was explored and held, was under the surface of lands owned by them. There is no evidence of the dispute as to ownership of the cave, or any portion thereof, prior to the time when in 1929 appellee requested a survey, which was approximately forty-six years after discovery of the cave and the exercise of complete dominion thereover by appellant and its predecessors in title.

It is appellant's contention that it has a fee simple title to all of the cave. That it owns that part underlying appellee's land by adverse possession. Section 2-602 Burns Rev. St. 1933, §61 Baldwin's 1934, provides as follows:

"'The following actions shall be commenced within the periods herein prescribed after the cause of action has accrued, and not afterward: . . . Sixth. Upon contracts in writing other than those for the payment of money, on judgments of courts of record, and for the recovery of the possession of real estate, within twenty (20) years.'"

It will be noted that appellee nor his predecessors in title had never effected a severance of the cave from the surface estate. Therefore the title of the appellee extends from the surface to the center, but actual possession is confined to the surface. Appellee and his immediate and remote grantors have been .in possession of the land and estate here in question at all times, unless it can be said that the possession of the cave by appellant as shown by the evidence above set out, has met all the requirements of the law relating to the acquisition of land by adverse possession. A record title may be defeated by adverse possession. All the authorities agree that before the owner of the legal title can be deprived of his land by another's possession, through the operation of the statute of limitation, the possession must have been actual, visible, notorious, exclusive, under claim of ownership and hostile to the owner of the legal title and to the world at large (except only the government) and continuous for the full period prescribed by the statute. The rule is not always stated in exactly the same words in the many cases dealing with the subject of adverse possession, yet the rule is so thoroughly settled that there is no doubt as to what elements are essential to establish a title by adverse possession. Let us examine the various elements that are essential to establish title by adverse possession and apply them to the facts that are established by the undisputed facts in this case.

(1) The possession must be actual. It must be conceded that appellant, in the operation of the "Marengo Cave," used not only the cavern under its own land but also that part of the cavern that under-laid appellee's land, and assumed dominion over all of it. Yet it must also be conceded that during all of the time appellee was in constructive possession, as the only constructive possession known to the law is that

130

which inheres in the legal title and with which the owner of that title is always endowed. Whether the possession was actual under the peculiar facts in this case we need not decide.

(2) The possession must be visible. The owner of land who, having notice of the fact that it is occupied by another who is claiming dominion over it, nevertheless stands by during the entire statutory period and makes no effort to eject the claimant or otherwise protect his title, ought not to be permitted, for reasons of public policy, thereafter to maintain an action for the recovery of his land. But, the authorities assert, in order that the possession of the occupying claimant may constitute notice in law, it must be visible and open to the common observer so that the owner or his agent on visiting the premises might readily see that the owner's rights are being invaded. What constitutes open and visible possession has been stated in general terms, thus: it is necessary and sufficient if its nature and character is such as is calculated to apprise the world that the land is occupied and who the occupant is; and such an appropriation of the land by claimant as to appraise, or convey visible' notice to the community or neighborhood in which it is situated that it is in his exclusive use and enjoyment. It has been declared that the disseisor "must unfurl his flag" on the land, and "keep it flying," so that the owner may see, if he will, that an enemy has invaded his domains, and. planted the standard of conquest. *Robin* v. *Brown* (1932), 308 Pa. 123, 162 Atl. 161, 168.

(3) The possession must be open and notorious. The mere possession of the land is not enough. It is knowledge, either actual or imputed, of the possession of his lands by another, claiming to own them bona fide and openly, that affects the legal owner thereof. Where there has been no actual notice, it is necessary to show that the possession of the disseisor was so open, notorious and visible as to warrant the inference that the owner must, or should have known of it. *In Philbin v. Carr* (1921), 75 Ind. App. 560, 584, 129 N. E. 19, it was said:

"However, in order that the possession of the occupying claimant may constitute notice, it must be visible and open to the common observer so that the owner or his agent on visiting the premises might readily see the owner's rights are being invaded.

In accordance with the general .rule applicable to the subject of constructive notice, before possession can operate as such notice it must be clear and unequivocal."

Holcroft v. *Hunter* (1832), 3 Blackf. 147; *Towle* v. *Quante, supra*. And again, the possession must be notorious. It must be so conspicuous that it is generally known and talked of by the public. "It must be manifest to the community." Thus, the Appellate Court said in *Philbin* v. *Carr, supra,* that (p. 584) :

"Where the persons who have passed frequently over and along the premises have been unable to see any evidence of occupancy, evidently the possession has not been of the character required by the rule. The purpose of this requirement is to support the principle that a legal title will not be extinguished on flimsy and uncertain evidence. Hence, where there has been no actual notice, the possession must have been so notorious as to warrant the inference that the owner ought to have known that a stranger was asserting dominion over his land. Insidious, desultory, and fugitive acts will not serve that purpose. To have that effect the possession should be clear and satisfactory, not doubtful and equivocal." See cases there cited on p. 585.

(4) The possession must be exclusive. It is evident that two or more persons cannot hold one tract of land adversely to each other at the same time. "It is essential that the possession of one who claims adversely must be of such an exclusive character that it will operate as an ouster of the owner of the legal title; because, in the absence of ouster the legal title draws to itself the constructive possession of the land. A possession which does not amount to an ouster or disseisor is not sufficient." *Philbin* v. *Carr, supra.* See cases cited on p. 585.

The facts as set out above show that appellee and his predecessors in title have been in actual and continuous possession of his real estate since the cave was discovered in 1883. At no time were they aware that anyone was trespassing upon their land. No one was claiming to be in possession of appellee's land. It is true that appellant was asserting possession of the "Marengo Cave." There would seem to be quite a difference in making claim to the "Marengo Cave," and making claim to a portion of appellee's land, even though a portion of the cave extended under appellee's land, when this latter fact was unknown to anyone. The evidence on both sides of this case is to the effect that the "Marengo Cave" was thought to be altogether under the land owned by appellant, and this erroneous supposition was not revealed until a survey was made at the request of appellee and ordered by the court in this case. It seems to us that the following excerpt from *Lewey* v. *H. C. Fricke Coke Co.* (1895), 166 Pa. 536, 31 Atl. 261, is peculiarly applicable to the situation here presented, inasmuch as we are dealing with an underground cavity. It was stated in the above case (pp. 545-547):

"The title of the plaintiff extends from the surface to the center, but actual possession is confined to the surface. Upon the surface he must be held to know all that the most careful observation by himself and his employees could reveal, unless his ignorance is induced by the fraudulent conduct of the wrongdoer. But in the coal veins deep down in the earth he cannot see. Neither in person nor by his servants nor employees can he explore their recesses in search for an intruder. If an adjoining owner goes beyond his own boundaries in the course of his mining operations the owner on whom he enters has no means of knowledge within his reach. Nothing short of an accurate survey of the interior of his neighbor's mines would enable him to ascertain the fact. This would require the services of a competent mining engineer and his assistants, inside the mines of another, which he would have no right to insist upon. To require an owner under such circumstances to take notice of a trespass upon his underlying coal at the time it takes place is to require an impossibility; and to hold that the statute begins to run at the date of the trespass is in most cases to take away the remedy of the injured party before he can know that an injury has been done him. A result so absurd and so unjust ought not to be possible. . . .

"The reason for the distinction exists in the nature of things. The owner of land may be present by himself or his servants on the surface of his possessions no matter how extensive they may be. He is for this reason held to be constructively present wherever his title extends. He cannot be present in the interior of the earth. No amount of vigilance will enable him to detect the approach of a trespasser who may be working his way through the coal seams underlying adjoining lands. His senses cannot inform him of the encroachment by such trespasser upon the coal that is hidden in the rocks under his feet. He cannot reasonably be held to be constructively present where his presence is in the nature of things impossible. He must learn of such a trespass by other means than such as are within his own control, and until these come within his reach he is necessarily ignorant of his loss. He cannot reasonably be required to act until knowledge that action is needed is possible to him."

We are not persuaded that this case falls within the rule of mistaken boundary as announced in *Rennert* v. *Shirk* (1904), 163 Ind. 542, 551, 72 N. E. 546, wherein this court said:

"Appellant insists, however, that if one takes and holds possession of real estate under a mistake as to where the true boundary line is, such possession can not ripen into a title. In this State, when an owner of land, by mistake as to the boundary line of his land, takes actual, visible, and exclusive possession of another's land and holds it as his own continuously for. the statutory period of twenty years, he thereby acquires the title as against the real owner. The possession is regarded as adverse, without reference to the fact that it is based on mistake; it being *prima facie* sufficient that actual, visible, and exclusive possession is taken under a claim of right."

The reason for the above rule is obvious. Under such circumstances appellant was in possession of the necessary means of ascertaining the true boundary line, and to hold that a mere misapprehension on the part of appellant as to the true boundary line would nullify the well established law on adverse possession. In that case appellee had actual, visible, notorious and exclusive possession. The facts in the present case are far different. Here the possession of appellant was not visible. No one could see below the earth's surface and determine that appellant was trespassing upon appellee's lands. This fact could not be determined by going into the cave. Only by a survey could this fact be made known. The same undisputed facts clearly show that appellant's possession, was not notorious. Not even appellant itself nor any of its remote grantors knew that any part of the "Marengo Cave" extended beyond its own boundaries, and they at no time, even down to the time appellee instituted this action, made any claim to appellee's lands. Appellee and his predecessors in title at all times have been in possession of the land which he is now claiming. No severance by deed or written instrument was ever made to the cave, from the surface. In the absence of a separate estate could appellant be in the exclusive possession of the cave that underlies appellee's land?

"If there is no severance an entry upon the surface will extend downward and draw to it a title to the underlying minerals; so that he who disseizes another and acquires title by the statute of limitation will succeed to the estate of him upon whose possession he has entered." *Pres. & Mgrs. of the Delaware & Hudson Canal Company* v. *Hughes et al.* (1897), 183 Pa. St. 66, 73, 38 Atl. 568, 63 Am. St. Rep. 743.

Even though it could be said that appellant's possession has been actual, exclusive and continuous all these years, we would still be of the opinion, that appellee has not lost his land. It has been the uniform rule in equity that the statute of limitation does not begin to run until the injured party discovers, or with reasonable diligence might have discovered, the facts constituting the injury and cause of action. Until then the owner cannot know that his possession has been invaded. Until he has knowledge, or ought to have such knowledge, he is not called upon to act, for he does not know that action in the premises is necessary and the law does not require absurd or impossible things of anyone.

***

So in the case at bar, appellant pretended to use the "Marengo Cave" as his property and all the time he was committing a trespass upon appellee's land. After twenty years of secret user, he now urges the statute of limitation, Section 2-602 Burns St. 1933, §61 Baldwin's 1934, as a bar to appellee's action. Appellee did not know of the trespass of appellant, and had no reasonable means of discovering the fact. It is true that appellant took no active measures to prevent the discovery, except to deny appellee the right to enter the cave for the purpose of making a survey, and disclaiming any use of appellee's lands, but nature furnished the concealment, or where the wrong conceals itself. It amounts to the taking of another's property without his knowledge of the fact that it is really being taken from him. In most cases the ignorance is produced by artifice. But in this case nature has supplied the situation which gives the trespasser the opportunity to occupy the recesses on appellee's land and caused the ignorance of appellee which he now seeks to avail himself. We cannot assent to the doctrine that would enable one to trespass upon another's property through a subterranean passage and under such circumstances that the owner does not know, or by the exercise of reasonable care could not know, of such secret occupancy, for twenty years or more and by so doing obtained a fee simple title as against the holder of the legal title. The fact that appellee had knowledge that appellant was claiming to be the owner of the "Marengo Cave," and advertised it to the general public, was no knowledge to him that it was in possession of appellee's land or any part of it. We are of the opinion that appellant's possession for twenty years or more of that part of "Marengo Cave," underlying appellee's land, was not open, notorious, or exclusive, as required by the law applicable to obtaining title to land by adverse possession.

We cannot say that the evidence is not sufficient to support the verdict or that the verdict is contrary to law.

Judgment affirmed.

6.1.4

Nome 2000 v. Fagerstrom
799 P.2d 304 (Alaska 1990)

Alaska Supreme Court

MATTHEWS, Chief Justice.

This appeal involves a dispute over a tract of land measuring approximately seven and one-half acres, overlooking the Nome River (hereinafter the disputed parcel). Record title to a tract of land known as mineral survey 1161, which includes the disputed parcel, is held by Nome 2000.

On July 24, 1987, Nome 2000 filed suit to eject Charles and Peggy Fagerstrom from the disputed parcel. The Fagerstroms counterclaimed that through their use of the parcel they had acquired title by adverse possession.

A jury trial ensued and, at the close of the Fagerstroms' case, Nome 2000 moved for a directed verdict on two grounds. First, it maintained that the Fagerstroms' evidence of use of the disputed parcel did not meet the requirements of the doctrine of adverse possession. Alternatively, Nome 2000 maintained that the requirements for adverse possession were met only as to the northerly section of the parcel and, therefore, the Fagerstroms could not have acquired title to the remainder. The trial court denied the motion. After Nome 2000 presented its case, the jury found that the Fagerstroms had adversely possessed the entire parcel. The court then entered judgment in favor of the Fagerstroms.

On appeal, Nome 2000 contests the trial court's denial of its motion for a directed verdict and the sufficiency of the evidence in support of the jury verdict. It also challenges two evidentiary rulings made by the trial court and the trial court's award of attorney's fees to the Fagerstroms.

I. FACTUAL BACKGROUND

The disputed parcel is located in a rural area known as Osborn. During the warmer seasons, property in Osborn is suitable for homesites and subsistence and recreational activities. During the colder seasons, little or no use is made of Osborn property.

Charles Fagerstrom's earliest recollection of the disputed parcel is his family's use of it around 1944 or 1945. At that time, he and his family used an abandoned boy scout cabin present on the parcel as a subsistence base camp during summer months. Around 1947 or 1948, they moved their summer campsite to an area south of the disputed parcel. However, Charles and his family continued to make seasonal use of the disputed parcel for subsistence and recreation.

In 1963, Charles and Peggy Fagerstrom were married and, in 1966, they brought a small quantity of building materials to the north end of the disputed parcel. They intended to build a cabin.

In 1970 or 1971, the Fagerstroms used four cornerposts to stake off a twelve acre, rectangular parcel for purposes of a Native Allotment application. The northeast and southeast stakes were located on or very near mineral survey 1161. The northwest and southwest stakes were located well to the west of mineral survey 1161. The overlap constitutes the disputed parcel. The southeast stake disappeared at an unknown time.

Also around 1970, the Fagerstroms built a picnic area on the north end of the disputed parcel. The area included a gravel pit, beachwood blocks as chairs, firewood and a 50-gallon barrel for use as a stove.

About mid-July 1974, the Fagerstroms placed a camper trailer on the north end of the disputed parcel. The trailer was leveled on blocks and remained in place through late September. Thereafter, until 1978, the Fagerstroms parked their camper trailer on the north end of the disputed parcel from early June through September. The camper was equipped with food, bedding, a stove and other household items.

About the same time that the Fagerstroms began parking the trailer on the disputed parcel, they built an outhouse and a fish rack on the north end of the parcel. Both fixtures remained through the time of trial in their original locations. The Fagerstroms also planted some spruce trees, not indigenous to the Osborn area, in 1975-76.

During the summer of 1977, the Fagerstroms built a reindeer shelter on the north end of the disputed parcel. The shelter was about 8x8 feet wide, and tall enough for Charles Fagerstrom to stand in. Around the shelter, the Fagerstroms constructed a pen which was 75 feet in diameter and 5 feet high. The shelter and pen housed a reindeer for about six weeks and the pen remained in place until the summer of 1978.

During their testimony, the Fagerstroms estimated that they were personally present on the disputed parcel from 1974 through 1978, "every other weekend or so" and "[a] couple times during the week ... if the weather was good." When present they used the north end of the parcel as a base camp while using the entire parcel for subsistence and recreational purposes. Their activities included gathering berries, catching and drying fish and picnicking. Their children played on the parcel. The Fagerstroms also kept the property clean, picking up litter left by others.

While so using the disputed parcel, the Fagerstroms walked along various paths which traverse the entire parcel. The paths were present prior to the Fagerstroms' use of the parcel and, according to Peggy Fagerstrom, were free for use by others in connection with picking berries and fishing. On one occasion, however, Charles Fagerstrom excluded campers from the land. They were burning the Fagerstroms' firewood.

Nome 2000 placed into evidence the deposition testimony of Dr. Steven McNabb, an expert in anthropology, who stated that the Fagerstroms' use of the disputed parcel was consistent with the traditional Native Alaskan system of land use. According to McNabb, unlike the non-Native system, the traditional Native system does not recognize exclusive ownership of land. Instead, customary use of land, such as the Fagerstroms' use of the disputed parcel, establishes only a first priority claim to the land's resources. The claim is not exclusive and is not a matter of ownership, but is more in the nature of a stewardship. That is, other members of the claimant's social group may share in the resources of the land without obtaining permission, so long as the resources are not abused or destroyed. McNabb explained that Charles' exclusion of the campers from the land was a response to the campers' use of the Fagerstroms' personal property (their firewood), not a response to an invasion of a perceived real property interest.[1]

Nevertheless, several persons from the community testified that the Fagerstroms' use of the property from 1974 through 1977 was consistent with that of an owner of the property. For example, one Nome resident testified that since 1974 "[the Fagerstroms] cared for [the disputed parcel] as if they owned it. They made improvements on it as if they owned it. It was my belief that they did own it."

During the summer of 1978, the Fagerstroms put a cabin on the north end of the disputed parcel. Nome 2000 admits that from the time that the cabin was so placed until the time that Nome 2000 filed this suit, the Fagerstroms adversely possessed the north end of the disputed parcel. Nome 2000 filed its complaint on July 24, 1987.

II. DISCUSSION

A.

The Fagerstroms' claim of title by adverse possession is governed by AS 09.-10.030, which provides for a ten-year limitations period for actions to recover real property.[2] Thus, if the Fagerstroms adversely possessed the disputed parcel, or any portion thereof, for ten consecutive years, then they have acquired title to that property. *See Hubbard v. Curtiss,* 684 P.2d 842, 849 (Alaska 1984) ("[T]itle automatically vests in the adverse possessor at the end of the statutory period."). Because the Fagerstroms' use of the parcel increased over the years, and because

Nome 2000 filed its complaint on July 24, 1987, the relevant period is July 24, 1977 through July 24, 1987.

We recently described the elements of adverse possession as follows: "In order to acquire title by adverse possession, the claimant must prove, by clear and convincing evidence, ... that for the statutory period 'his use of the land was continuous, open and notorious, exclusive and hostile to the true owner.' " *Smith v. Krebs,* 768 P.2d 124, 125 (Alaska 1989) (citations omitted). The first three conditions — continuity, notoriety and exclusivity — describe the physical requirements of the doctrine. The fourth condition, hostility, is often imprecisely described as the "intent" requirement.

On appeal, Nome 2000 argues that as a matter of law the physical requirements are not met absent "significant physical improvements" or "substantial activity" on the land. Thus, according to Nome 2000, only when the Fagerstroms placed a cabin on the disputed parcel in the summer of 1978 did their possession become adverse. For the prior year, so the argument goes, the Fagerstroms' physical use of the property was insufficient because they did not construct "significant structure[s]" and their use was only seasonal. Nome 2000 also argues that the Fagerstroms' use of the disputed parcel was not exclusive because "[o]thers were free to pick the berries, use the paths and fish in the area." We reject these arguments.

Whether a claimant's physical acts upon the land are sufficiently continuous, notorious and exclusive does not necessarily depend on the existence of significant improvements, substantial activity or absolute exclusivity. Indeed, this area of law is not susceptible to fixed standards because the quality and quantity of acts required for adverse possession depend on the *character* of the land in question. Thus, the conditions of continuity and exclusivity require only that the land be used for the statutory period as an average owner of similar property would use it. *Alaska National Bank v. Linck,* 559 P.2d 1049, 1052 (Alaska 1977) (One test for determining continuity of possession is to ask whether the land was used as an average owner would use it.); *Peters v. Juneau-Douglas Girl Scout Council,* 519 P.2d 826, 831 (Alaska 1974) ("[Possession need not be absolutely exclusive; it need only be a type of possession which would characterize an owner's use."). Where, as in the present case, the land is rural, a lesser exercise of dominion and control may be reasonable. *See*

Linck, 559 P.2d at 1052 (citing *Cooper v. Carter Oil Co.,* 7 Utah 2d 9, 316 P.2d 320 (1957) for the proposition that "pasturing of sheep for three weeks a year is sufficient where land is suitable only for grazing"), 1053 (citing *Monroe v. Rawlings,* 331 Mich. 49, 49 N.W.2d 55, 56 (1951) for the proposition that "6 visits per year to hunting cabin plus some timber cutting found sufficient where land was wild and undeveloped"); *Peters,* 519 P.2d at 831 (citing *Pulcifer v. Bishop,* 246 Mich. 579, 225 N.W. 3 (1929) for the proposition that exclusivity is not destroyed as to beach property commonly used by others).

The character of the land in question is also relevant to the notoriety requirement. Use consistent with ownership which gives visible evidence of the claimant's possession, such that the reasonably diligent owner "could see that a hostile flag was being flown over his property," is sufficient. *Shilts v. Young,* 567 P.2d 769, 776 (Alaska 1977). Where physical visibility is established, community repute is also relevant evidence that the true owner was put on notice.

Applying the foregoing principles to this case, we hold that the jury could reasonably conclude that the Fagerstroms established, by clear and convincing evidence, continuous, notorious and exclusive possession for ten years prior to the date Nome 2000 filed suit. We point out that we are concerned only with the first year, the summer of 1977 through the summer of 1978, as Nome 2000 admits that the requirements of adverse possession were met from the summer of 1978 through the summer of 1987.

The disputed parcel is located in a rural area suitable as a seasonal homesite for subsistence and recreational activities. This is exactly how the Fagerstroms used it during the year in question. On the premises throughout the entire year were an outhouse, a fish rack, a large reindeer pen (which, for six weeks, housed a reindeer), a picnic area, a small quantity of building materials and some trees not indigenous to the area. During the warmer season, for about 13 weeks, the Fagerstroms also placed a camper trailer on blocks on the disputed parcel. The Fagerstroms and their children visited the property several times during the warmer season to fish, gather berries, clean the premises, and play. In total, their conduct and improvements went well beyond "mere casual and occasional trespasses" and instead "evince[d] a purpose to exercise exclusive dominion over the property." *See Peters,* 519 P.2d at 830. That others were free to pick berries and fish is consistent with the conduct of a hospitable landowner, and undermines neither the continuity nor exclusivity of their possession. *See id.* at 831 (claimant "merely acting as any other hospitable landowner might" in allowing strangers to come on land to dig clams).

With respect to the notoriety requirement, a quick investigation of the premises, especially during the season which it was best suited for use, would have been sufficient to place a reasonably diligent landowner on notice that someone may have been exercising dominion and control over at least the northern portion of the property. Upon such notice, further inquiry would indicate that members of the community regarded the Fagerstroms as the owners. Continuous, exclusive, and notorious possession were thus established.

Nome 2000 also argues that the Fagerstroms did not establish hostility. It claims that "the Fagerstroms were required to prove that they intended to claim the property as their own." According to Nome 2000, this intent was lacking as the Fagerstroms thought of themselves not as owners but as stewards pursuant to the traditional system of Native Alaskan land usage. We reject this argument and hold that all of the elements of adverse possession were met.

What the Fagerstroms believed or intended has nothing to do with the question whether their possession was hostile. *See Peters,* 519 P.2d at 832 (with respect to the requirement of hostility, the possessor's "beliefs as to the true legal ownership of the land, his good faith or bad faith in entering into possession ... are all irrelevant."); *The Law of Property* at 761 (citing, *inter alia, Peters* for the view "of most decisions and of nearly all scholars, that what the possessor believes or intends should have nothing to do with [hostility]"). Hostility is instead determined by application of an *objective* test which simply asks whether the possessor "acted toward the land as if he owned it," without the permission of one with legal authority to give possession. *Hubbard,* 684 P.2d at 848 (citing *Peters,* 519 P.2d at 832). As indicated, the Fagerstroms' actions toward the property were consistent with ownership of it, and Nome 2000 offers no proof that the Fagerstroms so acted with anyone's permission. That the Fagerstroms' objective manifestations of ownership may have been accompanied by what was described as a traditional Native Alaskan mind-set is irrelevant. To hold otherwise would be inconsistent with precedent and patently unfair.

Having concluded that the Fagerstroms established the elements of adverse possession, we turn to the question whether they were entitled to the entire disputed parcel. Specifically, the question presented is whether the jury could reasonably conclude that the Fagerstroms adversely possessed the southerly portion of the disputed parcel.

Absent color of title,[3] only property actually possessed may be acquired by adverse possession. *Bentley Family Trust v. Lynx Enterprises, Inc.,* 658 P.2d 761, 768 (Alaska 1983) and *Linck,* 559 P.2d at 1052-53 n. 8. *See also Krebs,* 768 P.2d at 126 and n. 7 (recognizing the possibility that the requirements of adverse possession may be met only as to a portion of a disputed parcel). Here, from the summer of 1977 through the summer of 1978, the Fagerstroms' only activity on the southerly portion of the land included use of the pre-existing trails in connection with subsistence and recreational activities, and picking up litter. They claim that these activities, together with their placement of the cornerposts, constituted actual possession of the southerly portion of the parcel. Nome 2000 argues that this activity did not constitute actual possession and, at most, entitled the Fagerstroms to an easement by prescription across the southerly portion of the disputed parcel.

Nome 2000 is correct. The Fagerstroms' use of the trails and picking up of litter, although perhaps indicative of adverse use, would not provide the reasonably diligent owner with visible evidence of another's exercise of dominion and control. To this, the cornerposts add virtually nothing. Two of the four posts are located well to the west of the disputed parcel. Of the two that were allegedly placed on the parcel in 1970, the one located on the southerly portion of the parcel disappeared at an unknown time. The Fagerstroms maintain that because the disappearing stake was securely in place in 1970, we should infer that it remained for a "significant period." Even if we draw this inference, we fail to see how two posts on a rectangular parcel of property can, as the Fagerstroms put it, constitute "[t]he objective act of taking physical possession" of the parcel. The two posts simply do not serve to mark off the boundaries of the disputed parcel and, therefore, do not evince an exercise of dominion and control over the entire parcel. Thus, we conclude that the superior court erred in its denial of Nome 2000's motion for a directed verdict as to the southerly portion. This case is remanded to the trial court, with instructions to determine the extent of the Fagerstroms' acquisition in a manner consistent with this opinion.

***

Affirmed in part, reversed in part, and remanded.

1. However, Charles Fagerstrom testified that when he excluded the campers he felt that they were "on our property." He also testified that during the mid to late 70's he would have "frowned" upon people camping on "my property." [Editorial Note: This is footnote 5 of the opinion.]

2. A seven-year period is provided for by AS 09.25.050 when possession is under "color and claim of title." The Fagerstroms do not maintain that their possession was under color of title. [Editorial Note: This is footnote 6 of the opinion.]

3. "Color of title exists only by virtue of a written instrument which purports to pass title to the claimant, but which is ineffective because of a defect in the means of conveyance or because the grantor did not actually own the land he sought to convey." Hubbard, 684 P.2d at 847. As noted above, see n. 6, the Fagerstroms do not claim the disputed parcel by virtue of a written instrument. [Editorial Note: This is footnote 10 of the opinion.]

6.1.5

Discussion: Notes, Questions, and Problems

6.1.5.1

Discussion Note #1. Examples of statutes with tax payments or other requirements

For an example of a jurisdiction that has additional statutory requirements for both color of title and claim of right adverse possession claims, see Fla. Stat. § 95.16 and Fla. Stat. § 95.18, excerpted below.

> **95.16 Real property actions; adverse possession under color of title.—**
>
> (1) When the occupant, or those under whom the occupant claims, entered into possession of real property under a claim of title exclusive of any other right, founding the claim on a written instrument as being a conveyance of the property, or on a decree or judgment, and has for 7 years been in continued possession of the property included in the instrument, decree, or judgment, the property is held adversely. If the property is divided into lots, the possession of one lot shall not be deemed a possession of any other lot of the same tract. Adverse possession . . . shall not be deemed adverse possession under color of title until the instrument upon which the claim of title is founded is recorded in the office of the clerk of the circuit court of the county where the property is located.
>
> (2) For the purpose of this section, property is deemed possessed in any of the following cases:
>
> (a) When it has been usually cultivated or improved.
>
> (b) When it has been protected by a substantial enclosure. All land protected by the enclosure must be included within the description of the property in the written instrument, judgment, or decree. If only a portion of the land protected by the enclosure is included

within the description of the property in the written instrument, judgment, or decree, only that portion is deemed possessed.

(c)   When, although not enclosed, it has been used for the supply of fuel or fencing timber for husbandry or for the ordinary use of the occupant.

(d)   When a known lot or single farm has been partly improved, the part that has not been cleared or enclosed according to the usual custom of the county is to be considered as occupied for the same length of time as the part improved or cultivated.

95.18   Real property actions; adverse possession without color of title.—

(1)   When the possessor has been in actual continued possession of real property for 7 years under a claim of title exclusive of any other right, but not founded on a written instrument, judgment, or decree, or when those under whom the possessor claims meet these criteria, the property actually possessed is held adversely if the person claiming adverse possession:

(a)   Paid . . . all outstanding taxes and matured installments of special improvement liens levied against the property by the state, county, and municipality within 1 year after entering into possession;

(b)   Made a return, as required under subsection (3), of the property by proper legal description to the property appraiser of the county where it is located within 30 days after complying with paragraph (a); and

(c)   Has subsequently paid . . . all taxes and matured installments of special improvement liens levied against the property by the state, county, and municipality for all remaining years necessary to establish a claim of adverse possession.

(2)   For the purpose of this section, property is deemed to be possessed if the property has been:

    (a)   Protected by substantial enclosure; or

    (b)   Cultivated, maintained, or improved in a usual manner.

(3)   A person claiming adverse possession under this section must make a return of the property by providing to the property appraiser a uniform return on a form provided by the Department of Revenue. . . .

***

6.1.5.2

Discussion Question #2. How would you draft statute?

Put yourself in the role of a state legislature proposing a statute on adverse possession. Would you draft the statute to include a particular state of mind for the claimant and, if so, which one? Would you require the claimant to have paid property taxes? Would you make it more, or less, difficult for an adverse possessor to obtain title than is currently the law in the state where your law school is located and why?

6.1.5.3

Discussion Question #3. Preference for color of title claims?

Should there be a distinction between color of title and claim of right?

6.1.5.4

Discussion Question #4. Best practices for record owners and prospective purchasers?

What should owners of real property do to protect themselves from adverse possessors?

6.2

Tacking

The required time for possession could be met under the concept of tacking. Tacking combines the period of possession of a prior possessor with that of a subsequent possessor. Although tacking does not require a formal conveyance from one possessor to another, it requires privity of possession. Thus, it does not apply when one possessor physically removes another, such as by ouster. Tacking also would not apply when a prior possessor abandons the property and a subsequent possessor commences possession of the property. The excerpt below from *Shelton v. Strickland* illustrates the concept of tacking.

6.2.1

Shelton v. Strickland
21 P.3d 1179 (Wash. App. Div. 2001)

Washington Court of Appeals

Grosse, J.

Adverse possession is ultimately a doctrine of repose. Its purpose is to make legal boundaries conform to boundaries that are long maintained on the ground even if it means depriving an owner of title. Here, title of an approximate 3 x 10 foot strip of land passed to Mabel Hitching and/or her estate long before John E. Shelton acquired his interest in the land. The decision of the trial court is affirmed.

FACTS

The parties to this case, John E. Shelton and Edward and Margaret Strickland, are owners of adjoining waterfront properties in Friday Harbor, Washington.

Mabel Hitching acquired title to the land now owned by Edward and Margaret Strickland from her parents in November 1933. The Hitching lot was improved with a single-family residence. A shed/cottage was also constructed on the property. Cement work for the shed had a number "59" inscribed in it. The structure was shown to encroach upon the Shelton parcel in a survey of record in April of 1975.

The structure was used by Hitching as a potting shed and painting studio during her life, and was built by her companion Arthur Hedman.

Hitching died in 1982. Through her will she provided Mr. Hedman with a life estate in the premises, and he continued to reside on the property until his death in 1985. Jack Ridley, Hitching's nephew and personal representative, filed Hitching's will in San Juan County in September 1986, and recorded a conveyance from the estate to himself. Ridley resided in California and never used or occupied the house. In 1993 he sold the property to the Stricklands.

Peter and Jenny Wangoe owned the Shelton lot from 1978 through 1985. Mr. Wangoe was aware of the shed/cottage as he had observed it over the years despite his infrequent visits to the property. He was not aware that the structure necessarily extended over the property line onto his property. The structure is visible from the street.

Shelton purchased his property in February 1993. When purchased by Shelton, the property was overgrown and unimproved. Although aware of the existence of the shed/ cottage structure, he was not aware that it encroached onto his property until he obtained a survey before constructing his home.

The encroaching shed was used as an office during construction of the Stricklands' home. The Stricklands made some repairs to the structure but did not alter its location. They continue to use the shed. There was no evidence presented to suggest that anyone other than the predecessors of the Stricklands have ever used the encroaching structure.

Shelton filed a complaint to quiet title to the property on which the shed stood and moved for summary judgment on that claim. The Stricklands answered and filed a cross motion for summary judgment alleging adverse possession of the area encumbered by the structure, which they admit essentially straddles the boundary line.

The trial court heard argument on the cross motions and granted the Stricklands' motion, awarding title to approximately 40 square feet of the Shelton lot, along with an exclusive easement of 2 feet around the perimeter of the structure for maintenance purposes.

Shelton arg

On appeal, Shelton alleges the trial court erred in determining that title had been held by adverse possession for 10 years and had ripened into original title prior to its transfer to Jack Ridley from the estate of Mabel Hitching. Further, he asserts that there was no privity in the chain of title from Mabel Hitching through Jack Ridley to the Stricklands. Finally, Shelton asserts that the trial court erred in determining that the Stricklands acquired the disputed property through the conveyance from Ridley.

DISCUSSION

The usual standard of review for summary judgment applies. In reviewing a grant of summary judgment, this court engages in the same inquiry as the trial court. Here the parties submitted cross motions for summary judgment, essentially conceding that there were no issues of material fact. "Where the facts in an adverse possession case are not in dispute, whether the facts constitute adverse possession is for the court to determine as a matter of law." Thus the question is whether the legal conclusions of the court are correct.

Shelton asserts there is insufficient evidence in the record that Mabel Hitching adversely possessed the disputed area for the requisite period of time. Additionally, he claims there is insufficient evidence that the use of the shed was "notorious."

To establish ownership of a piece of property through adverse possession, a claimant must prove that his or her possession of the property was: (1) open and notorious, (2) actual and uninterrupted, (3) exclusive, (4) hostile and under a claim of right, (5) for a period of 10 years. "As the presumption of possession is in the holder of legal title, the party claiming to have adversely possessed the property has the burden of establishing the existence of each element." Possession is established if it is of such a character as a true owner would exhibit considering the nature and location of the land in question.

The claim of right element of adverse possession requires only that the claimant or successors treated the land as his or her own as against the world throughout the statutory period. The nature of the possession will be determined on the basis of the manner in which the possessor treats the property. Subjective beliefs regarding a true interest in the land and any intent to dispossess or not dispossess another are irrelevant to the determination.

A reasonable inference from the evidence led the trial court to believe that the structure was built in 1959. Evidence in the form of a survey clearly shows that the structure existed in early 1975. Hitching and her estate (life estate in Mr. Hedman) continued to occupy the disputed area until her personal representative conveyed the property to himself in May of 1987. At the very least, Mr. Hedman continued to live on the property until his death in 1985. This certainly meets the 10-year requirement of adverse possession.

On urban property, the placement of structures on another's land, or encroaching partially on another's land, amounts to possession not only of the land covered by the structure but of a reasonable amount of the surrounding territory. In addition, the construction and maintenance of a structure on, or partially on the land of another, almost necessarily is exclusive, actual and uninterrupted, open and notorious, hostile and made under a claim of right.

Shelton claims that the "minor encroachment" of the shed was not "notorious." The open and notorious element of adverse possession requires proof that (1) the true owner has actual notice of the adverse use throughout the statutory period, *or* (2) the claimant (and/or predecessors) uses the land in a way that any reasonable person would assume that person to be the owner. Although there may be insufficient evidence that all of the previous owners of Shelton's land had "actual notice" of Hitching's adverse possession, there were certainly acts of ownership sufficient to prove that any reasonable person would assume that she was the owner. There is sufficient evidence to support the determination that the possession was open and notorious. The trial court did not err in determining that Hitching and her estate, through Mr. Hedman, adversely possessed the area at issue.

Shelton claims that even if there were adverse possession, title to the encroaching area must be conveyed with the land and that the legal description here failed in that regard. Further, he asserts there was no privity of title. As stated by Professor Stoebuck:

To understand tacking, it is useful to recall the concept of "inchoate title," .... Before the statute has run, an adverse possessor has something which, though it is wrongful and cannot stand up against the true owner, is rightful and good against everyone else. This "shadow title," ... is founded in possession; so, it makes sense that it can be transferred by transferring possession. There must be a relationship between the successive adverse possessors, one in which, at a minimum, the prior possessor willingly turns over possession to the succeeding one. This relationship the courts usually call "privity," though, to avoid confusion with the several other meanings of that word, the word "nexus" is better.

The "privity" or "nexus" required to permit tacking of the adverse use of successive occupants of real property does not have to be more than such a reasonable connection between the successive occupants as will raise their claim of right above the status of wrongdoer or trespasser. A formal conveyance between the parties describing some or all of the property is not essential to establish such connection. "The requirement of privity had its roots in the notion that a succession of trespasses, even though there was no appreciable interval between them, should not, in equity, be allowed to defeat the record title." However, there is a substantial difference between the squatter or trespasser and a property purchaser. "The deed running between the parties purporting to transfer the land possessed traditionally furnishes the privity of estate which connects the possession of the successive occupants."

Just as the intent of the adverse possessor is irrelevant to a determination of the element of hostility, it does not bar the application of privity to successors through documentary conveyances. "This is particularly true in light of the rule allowing tacking when an adversely possessed strip [of land] is physically 'turned over' in connection with the conveyance of adjoining land the possessor owns." Where, as in this case, the successive inheritor and purchasers received record title to what was a mistaken belief as to the boundary line, but where possession of the area was open and notorious for over 10 years, there is sufficient privity of estate to permit tacking and thus establish adverse possession as a matter of law.

Shelton has not shown any abandonment or an intervening occupation of the disputed land by any titleholder sufficient to stop the running of the 10-year statute of limitation required for adverse possession. Title passed to Mabel Hitching and/or her estate long before Shelton acquired an interest in the property.

The decision of the trial court is affirmed.

6.2.2
Discussion: Notes, Questions, and Problems

6.2.2.1
Discussion Problem #5. Owen's vacation cabin problem

In 1995, Owen, a wealthy art dealer, who lived primarily in the city, purchased a vacation cabin four hours away in a rural area of the state. For several years after Owen purchased the cabin, Owen would regularly visit the cabin, especially in the summers. Owen stopped visiting the cabin in 1999 because he preferred vacationing in other places. In 2000, Albert noticed the empty cabin and started living in the cabin. In 2005, Owen was going over his finances with his accountant and they both decided that Owen should sell the cabin. Accordingly, in 2005, Owen sold the cabin to Bernardo for valuable consideration and delivered to Bernardo a properly executed deed. Bernardo did not inspect the cabin before buying it from Owen. In 2010, Albert was fishing in the woods near the cabin and came across Alice who was canoeing. Albert and Alice became friends. In 2011, Alice moved into the cabin with Albert. In 2011, Albert told Alice that he was restless and was off to explore the world. Albert also told Alice that he was done with the cabin and that she could have it. Alice has been living in the cabin since 2011. In 2022, Bernardo discovered that Alice is living in the cabin. Bernardo brings an action for ejectment. Assume the jurisdiction has a 20-year period for adverse possession. As between Bernardo and Alice, who has the better claim and why?

6.2.2.2

Discussion Problem #6. Alex's goats and chickens problem

When grandmother Grace died in the year 2000, her only son, Sam, obtained a life estate in what had been Grace's farm and her granddaughter, Nina, obtained the remainder. Assume that neither Sam nor Nina lived near the farm, and they did not visit the farm after grandmother Grace's death. In 2005, Alex entered the farm and started living there. In fact, Alex brought goats and chickens to the farm and started selling eggs from the farm. Assume that Alex complies with all the elements of adverse possession in a jurisdiction with a 15-year period. In 2020, what has Alex obtained assuming that both Sam and Nina are alive? What would have to happen for Alex to obtain full title?

6.3

Entry and Disability

Even if the adverse possessor otherwise complies with the elements for adverse possession, there are certain conditions that could impede an adverse possessor's successful claim to the real property. One such condition is if the adverse possessor enters the property at a time when the property is owned by someone who holds a future interest in the property. In that case, the future interest holder does not presently have the right to possession. Since an action for ejectment can generally only be brought by a party with the right to possession, the statute of limitations would not run against the future interest holder.

Similarly, if the adverse possession claimant enters the property while the property was subject to a mortgage, the statute of limitations does not run against the mortgagee because, in most states, the mortgagee would not be able to bring an action for ejectment until the mortgagee had the right of possession, which would generally be only through foreclosure. Another condition that could impede an adverse possessor's claim is if the true owner is under a disability (e.g., infancy) protected by the disability statute in the jurisdiction.

Battle v. Battle
70 S.E.2d 492 (N.C. 1952)

Supreme Court of North Carolina

Devin, O. J.

This was an action to determine the title to certain lots in the city of Rocky Mount on West Thomas Street. It was established by the verdict of the jury that the plaintiffs James H. Boddie and Julia Boddie Galloway were the owners of the lot known and designated as No. 817, and that the plaintiffs and defendants as heirs of Arcenia Hopkins were tenants in common in the other adjoining lots described in the pleadings. The bone of contention was the title to lot No. 817. There was no controversy as to the title to the other lots.

These several lots had been originally conveyed to Arcenia Hopkins in 1902. The plaintiffs' evidence tended to show that in 1908 Arcenia Hopkins placed her daughter Arcenia Boddie and her husband Julius Boddie in possession of lot No. 817, and that Arcenia Hopkins joined with them in building a house thereon in which the daughter and husband made their home and reared their children. In 1919 Arcenia Hopkins made a deed to Arcenia and Julius Boddie intending to convey this lot to them, but by some mistake, not discovered at the time, the particular description of the lot did not include No. 817. Arcenia and Julius Boddie continued in the exclusive and undisturbed occupancy of this house and lot claiming it as their own, paying taxes, making additions, and holding adversely to Arcenia Hopkins and all others until the death of Arcenia Hopkins which occurred in 1925. Thereafter Arcenia and Julius Boddie continued in the exclusive possession of this house and lot, holding adversely to the heirs of Arcenia Hopkins, until the death of Arcenia Boddie in 1941. Julius Boddie had predeceased her. Thereafter plaintiffs James H. Boddie and Julia Boddie Galloway, the only children and heirs of Arcenia and Julius Boddie, continued in possession of the house and lot, either occupying it or renting it, and have continued to do so up to the present time. This suit to clarify the title was instituted 5 May, 1950.

***

Plaintiffs' claim of title was based on adverse possession for 20 years, under known and visible lines and boundaries. The court properly submitted to the jury the question of whether the possession and occupancy of the house and lot by plaintiffs and those under whom they claim was permissive or adverse, and, if so, whether it was continually and exclusively maintained for the statutory period.

The evidence of the investiture of Arcenia Boddie and her husband in possession of this lot and of the execution of a deed intended by the-owner to convey it to them, was properly submitted to the jury to be-considered with the other evidence of continuous and exclusive occupancy in the support of plaintiffs' contention that possession thereafter by them and those to whom their right descended was adverse, and that it was maintained with intent to claim against the former owner and all other persons.

This was not a case of mistaken boundary, but on the contrary plaintiffs' evidence tended to show claim of title as owners of a particular lot. ascertained under known and visible lines and boundaries. The court correctly instructed the jury as to the elements necessary to constitute adverse possession under the facts here in evidence, and properly submitted to them the question whether plaintiffs' possession was by permission of the owner or owners, or was adverse to them and to all other persons.

But the plaintiffs in making out their case were unable to show adverse possession for a sufficient length of time to ripen title before the death of Arcenia Hopkins in 1925, and could not in law under the circumstances of this case, tack that inadequate period to their subsequently continued possession after her death, for the reason that their title to the house and lot not having ripened, upon the death of Arcenia Hopkins, in whom the title still remained, Arcenia and Julius Boddie became tenants in common with the other children of Arcenia Hopkins.

Thereupon the possession of lot No. 817 by Arcenia and Julius Boddie and their successors by descent became in law the possession also of their cotenants, and it required 20 years adverse possession thereafter to constitute an ouster.

However, we think there was evidence as found by the jury tending to show possession by Arcenia and Julius Boddie and by the plaintiffs James H. Boddie and Julia Boddie Galloway, their successors by descent, adverse to their cotenants and all others for more than 20 years, sufficient to ripen title against those who were not under disability at the time the statute began to run.

. . . It may be noted that a majority of the heirs of Arcenia Hopkins have joined with James H. Boddie and Julia Boddie Galloway as parties plaintiff and are asking that these two be declared sole owners of Lot No. 817.

All the defendants are of full age except the four children of Dorsey Battle who was a son of Arcenia Hopkins. These are represented by a guardian *ad litem,* who, after investigation, has admitted the facts alleged in the complaint. None of the children of Arcenia Hopkins were under disability [of minority] at the time the statute of limitations began to run against them. There is a well recognized rule that when the statute of limitations has begun to run no subsequent disability will interfere with it. "Where the statute of limitations begins to run in favor of one in adverse possession against an owner who dies leaving heirs who are minors, their disability of infancy does not affect the operation of the statute, since the disability is subsequent to the commencement of the running of the statute." 1 Am. Jur. 803, 43 A.L.R. 943 (note). However, this rule does not apply to Henderson Battle, a son of Arcenia Hopkins, who was and has been since infancy *non compos mentis.* The statute of limitations would not bar his right to an undivided interest in lot No. 817, nor would adverse possession ripen plaintiffs' title as against him. It is apparent, therefore, that Henderson Battle's one-ninth interest in this lot has not been divested. Though his guardian *ad litem* admitted the facts alleged in the complaint, this would not adversely affect rights which the admitted facts disclose. It follows that plaintiffs James H. Boddie and Julia Boddie Galloway have acquired title to eight-ninths undivided interest in lot No. 817, and are tenants in common therein with Henderson Battle who is entitled to a one-ninth undivided interest in the fee thereof. The judgment must be modified accordingly.

***

Modified and affirmed.

6.3.2

Discussion: Notes, Questions, and Problems

6.3.2.1

Discussion Question #7. Tolling the time period?

Does your jurisdiction have a statute tolling the time period for adverse possession if the owner is under a disability? If so, which conditions qualify as a disability?

6.3.2.2

Discussion Question #8. Leasing by claimants?

In *Battle*, excerpted above, the court noted that, during their period of adverse possession, the claimants "continued in possession of the house and lot, either occupying it or renting it, and have continued to do so up to the present time." Is there a risk when an adverse possessor leases the property to a third party during the time required to obtain title by adverse possession? Fla. Stat. § 95.18(10) provides that a "person who occupies or attempts to occupy a residential structure solely by claim of adverse possession under this section and offers the property for lease to another commits theft under § 812.014." If a similar statute had been in effect in North Carolina in *Battle*, do you think the adverse possession claimants would have been found to have committed theft for renting the property?

7

Chapter 7 · Concurrent Ownership, Marital Interests, and Homestead

The term ***concurrent ownership*** applies when two or more persons have interests in the same property at the same time. A typical example of concurrent ownership is when spouses co-own their residence. Currently, there are three different types of concurrent estates: tenancy in common, joint tenancy, and tenancy by the entirety. See the U.S. Supreme Court's opinion in *United States v. Craft*, excerpted below, describing some of the history behind and the characteristics of the three concurrent estates.

7.1

Creation, Types, and Unities

Before differentiating among the three types of concurrent estates, you should understand the common law concept of the ***unities***, which are analyzed for both creating and maintaining the particular type of concurrent estate. There are five possible unities: time, title, interest, possession, and person. ***Tenancy in common*** only requires one unity – the unity of possession. Traditionally, a ***joint tenancy*** requires the four unities of time, title, interest, and possession. A ***tenancy by the entirety*** requires all five unities, including the unity of person, which is found when the cotenants are married. You should note that even though a tenancy in common only requires one unity – the unity of possession – a tenancy in common could include any or all of the remaining unities. Similarly, although a joint tenancy requires only the unities of time, title, interest, and possession, it could also include the unity of person.

To determine which type of concurrent estate was created, we look to the language used in the granting instrument. At very early common law, if the language in the instrument was ambiguous as to the type of concurrent estate intended among cotenants and if the unities of time, title, interest, and possession were present, the grant was presumed to create a joint tenancy. Currently, jurisdictions have reversed that presumption, usually by statute. The modern presumption is that a conveyance to two or more persons creates a tenancy in common, not a joint tenancy. If, however, the cotenants are married and the grant is ambiguous, the jurisdictions are split as to which type of concurrent estate arises. Some jurisdictions presume that an ambiguous grant to married persons creates a tenancy by the entirety and other jurisdictions follow the modern presumption of a tenancy in common.

A major distinction among the three types of concurrent estates is whether the estate includes the ***right of survivorship***. The right of survivorship determines the effect of the death of a cotenant on the concurrent estate. When the right of survivorship applies, upon the death of a cotenant, the deceased cotenant ceases to be part of the owning group and the surviving cotenant(s) owns the portion of the share of the deceased cotenant. A tenancy in common does not include the feature of right of survivorship. By contrast, both the joint tenancy and the tenancy by the entirety include the feature of right of survivorship.

7.1.1

Michael Estate
218 A.2d 338 (Pa. 1966)

Supreme Court of Pennsylvania

Mr. Justice Jones,

This is an appeal from a decree of the Orphans' Court of Lycoming County entered in a proceeding brought under the Uniform Declaratory Judgments Act. The purpose of the proceeding was to obtain an interpretation and construction of a deed to determine whether the decedent, Bertha W. Michael, died owning any interest in realty located in Wolf and Moreland Townships, Lycoming County, known as "King Farm."

On February 24, 1947, Joyce E. King deeded certain real estate in Lycoming County, known as "King Farm", to Harry L. Michael and Bertha M. Michael, his wife, and Ford W. Michael (son of Bertha and Harry L. Michael) and Helen M. Michael, his wife. The pertinent provisions of the lawyer-drawn deed are as follows:

"This Indenture Made the 24th day of February in the year of our Lord one thousand nine hundred forty-seven (1947).

"Between Joyce E. King, widow, of Milton, Northumberland County, State of Pennsylvania, party of the first part, Harry L. Michael and Bertha M. Michael, his wife, tenants by the entireties and Ford W. Michael and Helen M. Michael, his wife, as tenants by the entireties, *with right of survivorship*, of Hughesville, Lycoming Comity, Pennsylvania, parties of the second part." (Emphasis supplied).

. . have granted, bargained, sold, aliened, enfeoffed, released, conveyed and confirmed and by these presents does grant, bargain, sell, alien, enfeoff, release, convey and confirm unto the said parties of the second part, their heirs and assigns.

"To Have and To Hold the said hereditaments and premises hereby granted or mentioned and intended so to be with the appurtenances unto the said parties of the second part, their heirs and assigns to and for the only proper use and behoof of the said parties of the second part, their heirs and assigns forever."

Harry L. Michael died prior to February 20, 1962 leaving to survive him his wife, Bertha W. Michael and two sons, Ford W. Michael, one of the grantees, and Robert C. Michael, the appellant.

Bertha W. Michael died testate, November 26, 1963, leaving to survive her two sons, Ford W. and Robert C. Michael. By her will dated February 20, 1962, she provided, inter alia, as follows:

"Second. It is my sincere wish and I hereby direct that my Executors settle my estate in such way that my sons Ford W. Michael and Robert C. Michael each receive an equal share of the same. Because of the fact that a good portion of my estate may be in the form of real estate, my Executors shall use their own discretion in the matter of the method to be used to make the division. The following, however, are my desires in this matter and these desires follow closely the wishes of their father, namely: .. . (d) That my interest in the "King Farm" situate partly in Wolf and partly in Moreland Townships go to Robert C. Michael and the sum of $1,000.00, be paid to Ford W. Michael to balance this gift."

The two sons were appointed executors of their mother's estate. Soon thereafter a dispute arose as to what, *if any,* interest Bertha W. Michael had in the real estate known as "King Farm." The answer to this question turns on the construction of the language, above-quoted, contained in the deed of 1947. The court below held that the deed created a joint tenancy with right of survivorship between the two sets of husbands and wives.

appellant arg The appellant urges that the deed created a tenancy in common as between the two married couples, each couple holding its undivided one-half interest as tenants by the entireties.[12] *appellees arg.* The appellees, conceding that the respective one-half interests were held by husband and wife as tenants by the entireties, contend, however, that *as to each other* the couples held as joint tenants with a right of survivorship. The lower court, predicating its decision on the use in the deed of the phrase "with right of survivorship", held that there was a clear expression of an intended right of survivorship between the two couples. To further support its decision, the court found it significant that the phrase was not used twice in modification of each husband-wife-grantee designation, but rather was utilized after both couples had been named and had been designated severally as tenants by the entireties.

At common law, joint tenancies were favored, and the doctrine of survivorship was a recognized incident to a joint estate. The courts of the United States have generally been opposed to the creation of such estates, the presumption being that all tenants hold jointly as tenants in common, unless a clear intention to the contrary is shown.

In Pennsylvania, by the Act of 1812, the incident of survivorship in joint tenancies was eliminated unless the instrument creating the estate expressly provided that such incident should exist. The Act of 1812 has been repeatedly held to be a statute of construction; it does not *forbid* creation of a joint tenancy if the language creating it *clearly* expresses that intent. Whereas before the Act, a conveyance or devise to two or more persons (not husband and wife or trustees) was presumed to create a joint tenancy with the right of survivorship unless otherwise clearly stated, the presumption is reversed by the Act, with the result that now such a conveyance or devise carries with it no right of survivorship unless clearly expressed, and in effect it creates, not a joint tenancy, but a tenancy in common.

Since passage of the Act of 1812, the question of survivorship has become a matter of intent and, in order to engraft the right of survivorship - on a co-tenancy which might otherwise be a tenancy in common, the intent to do so must be expressed with sufficient clarity to overcome the statutory presumption that survivorship is not intended. Whether or not survivorship was intended is to be gathered from the instrument and its language, but no particular form of words is required to manifest such intention. The incident of survivorship may be expressly provided for in a deed or a will or it may arise by necessary implication.

Applying the above-stated principles to the instant facts, we fail to find a sufficiently *clear* expression of intent to create a right of survivorship, as required by the case law, to overcome the presumption against such a right arising from the Act of 1812. Neither the research of the parties involved nor our own has yielded any case involving language or involving facts similar to that in the present litigation.

The lower court found that the use in the deed of the phrase "with right of survivorship" and the location of that phrase in such deed (see quoted provision of deed, supra) constituted a clear expression of an intended right of survivorship. The inherent difficulty with such an interpretation is that it is purely conjectural and finds certainty in a totally ambiguous phrase.

The phrase, "with right of survivorship", is capable, as appellant properly urges, of at least three possible interpretations: (1) explanatory of the one of the incidents of the estate, known as tenancy by the entirety; (2) explanatory of the one tenancy by the entirety, the creation of which it follows or (3), as the appellee and the lower court contend, indicative of the creation of a right of survivorship as between the two sets of spouses. Anyone of these interpretations is a *possibility* but deciding which was intended by the parties would involve nothing but a mere guess. Such ambiguous terminology falls far short of the *clear* expression of intent required to overcome the statutory presumption.

Nowhere in the deed is the term "joint tenants" employed. To create a right of survivorship the *normal* procedure is to employ the phrase "joint tenants, with a right of survivorship, and not as tenants in common" in describing the manner in which the grantees are to take or hold the property being conveyed or transferred.

The deed herein involved also uses the term *"their* heirs and assigns forever." (emphasis supplied). The use of the plural would tend to indicate a tenancy in common. If *"his* or *her"* heirs and assigns had been used a strong argument could be made that the grantor intended a right of survivorship and that the survivor of the four named grantees would have an absolute undivided fee in the property.

Both the Act of 1812 and our case law clearly dictate that joint tenancies with the incident right of survivorship are not to be deemed favorites of the law. We cannot find within the four corners of this deed a *clearly* expressed intention to create a joint tenancy with the right of survivorship. Having failed to find a *clear* intention to overcome the statutory presumption against such estates, the Act of 1812 compels us to find that the deed of 1947 created a tenancy in common as between the two sets of married couples, each couple holding its undivided one-half interest as tenants by the entireties.

Decree reversed. Each party to bear own costs.

1. Appellant, in urging the creation of a tenancy in common, points to decedent's will (above-quoted in part) wherein she indicated that she expected her interest in the property to pass under her will. From this appellant argues that the interest was considered by the parties to be one of tenancy in common rather than joint tenancy. Such an argument is insufficient to establish the intention of the parties. The question must be answered solely by reference to the language employed in the conveying instrument. [Editorial Note: This is footnote 2 of the opinion.]

7.1.2

Beal Bank, SSB v. Almand & Associates
780 So. 2d 45 (Fla. 2001)

Florida Supreme Court

PARIENTE, J.

We have for review the decision of the Fifth District Court of Appeal in *Beal Bank, SSB v. Almand & Associates*, 710 So.2d 608 (Fla. 5th DCA 1998), certifying two questions as ones of great public importance. We have jurisdiction. The certified questions arise from the central issue in this case: whether bank accounts titled in the name of both spouses were held as tenancies by the entireties and, therefore, not subject to execution by a creditor of only one of the spouses. . . .

I. FACTUAL BACKGROUND

Petitioner Beal Bank obtained judgments against respondents, Amos F. Almand, Jr. (Almand, Jr.), and his son, Amos F. Almand, III (Almand, III), based on obligations that arose in connection with the Almands' businesses. Among other attempts to collect on these judgments, Beal Bank, as creditor, sought to garnish several bank accounts held by the Almands and their wives. It is undisputed that the Almands' wives were neither parties to the judgments nor personally liable for the obligations. The subject bank accounts that we discuss were held in three banks: multiple accounts in Compass Bank, one account in SouthTrust Bank, and one account in Barnett Bank.

With regard to the accounts held in Compass Bank that the Almands jointly owned, the signature cards list the account owners as follows: (1) "Amos F. Almand III, Sue C. Almand"; (2) "Amos F. Almand or Sue C. Almand"; (3) "Almand, Doris W. or Almand, Amos"; and (4) "Amos F. Almand, Jr. and Doris J. Almand." None of these signature cards specify a particular form of joint ownership such as "tenants in common," "joint tenancy with right of survivorship," or "tenancy by the entireties."

As for the account held in SouthTrust Bank, the signature card signed by Almand, Jr. lists the "account legal title" as owned by "Amos F. Almand, Jr. or Doris J. Almand, JT TEN." According to the signature card, the depositors own the account "as joint tenants with right of survivorship, unless another manner of ownership is specifically set forth in connection with the account legal title on this card."

The signature card for the Barnett Bank account specifies that the account is owned by "Amos F. Almand Jr. or Doris J. Almand Jt. Tenants with Rights of Survivorship."

According to the signature card, persons signing the card "acknowledge(s) receipt of and agree(s) to the Rules and Regulations of the Bank for the account ... not limited to ... Barnett Bank's Welcome Brochure." The multi-page Welcome Brochure provides that it "contains the rules and regulations governing" the Barnett Bank account. Paragraph 16 of the Welcome Brochure is entitled "Ownership of Account and Transfer of Ownership," and states:

> 16. Ownership of Account and Transfer of Ownership: If the account is designated a JOINT account, or if the names of two or more owners are joined by the word "or" or "and" on the signature card or in the title of the account, the Customer agrees that all sums now or hereafter deposited in the account are and shall be joint property owned by the Customer and any co-owners of the account as joint tenants with the right of survivorship and not as tenants in common or as tenants by the entireties.... Even if the Bank at the Customer's request titles the Customer's account as "Tenants by the Entireties" or receives oral or written notice that the Customer intends to treat the funds as being held as such, the Customer agrees that as between the Customer and the Bank, the Bank may treat the account like any other joint account and subject to all the terms and provisions set forth above.

After the trial court issued writs of garnishment against the Compass Bank, SouthTrust Bank, and Barnett Bank accounts, the Almands and their wives filed motions to dissolve the writs, and the court held an evidentiary hearing on the motions. At the hearing, both father and son testified regarding their intent in opening the joint accounts held with their wives.

According to the son, Almand III, he and his wife Sue C. Almand had been married for over twenty-one years at the time of the hearing. Almand III testified that he and his wife were joint owners of the accounts, which belonged to them both as a whole, with each of them possessing the accounts equally. Either one could write checks on the account, as they both had "equal access" to it. Almand III stated that his intent in opening the accounts was:

> [T]o open this account where the monies would belong to the two of us and that either party could sign for any or all of the monies. I still don't think I

have a clear enough understanding of the difference between joint tenants, tenants with rights of survivorship, tenants without, or tenants by the entireties, to really know what I was asking for in legal terms, you know, but my intent was to have the monies belong to both parties and have equal access to that money.

father almad Jr.

The father, Almand, Jr., also testified regarding the accounts he held with his wife. At the time of the hearing, he and his wife Doris Almand had been married for almost 52 years. Almand, Jr. testified that none of the monies in any of the accounts had been derived from property owned solely in his name, at least during the two years preceding the hearing. He also testified that he and his wife opened each of the accounts with the intent that "everything that we put into the bank was ours;" that he and his wife both controlled their money; that they were both entitled to the funds; that they owned the property "together;" and that they both had the same interest in the funds. In addition, Almand, Jr. testified that they used the funds to pay marital expenses, but he admitted that when they opened the accounts, he had never heard of a "tenancy by the entirety account." After the evidentiary hearing, the trial court entered an order dissolving the writs of garnishment directed to all of these accounts. *trial court decision*

II. THE FIFTH DISTRICT'S OPINION

In a split decision, the Fifth District reversed the trial court as to some accounts, but affirmed the trial court as to the remainder of the accounts and certified the questions for our review. The decision includes a short per curiam majority opinion. In addition, Judges Cobb and Harris both wrote opinions concurring in part and dissenting in part, and Judge Sharp concurred in result only with a separate opinion.

With regard to the accounts at issue here, the per curiam majority opinion held that the Compass Bank accounts were not subject to execution, but that the Barnett Bank and SouthTrust Bank accounts held in the names of Almand III and his wife were subject to execution. The majority opinion did not explain the basis for this result, so we must derive the rationale from the separate opinions of the individual judges.

According to Judge Cobb's concurring in part, dissenting in part opinion, the Almands had not demonstrated that they held any of the bank accounts as tenancies by the entireties or that the accounts were exempt from the creditors of one of the spouses. In addition to the wording of the actual bank documents, Judge Cobb focused on the husbands' testimony that in each marriage either spouse, acting alone and without the knowledge of the other, could withdraw the funds in any accounts for any purpose. Judge Cobb further deemed it important that the Almands testified that they themselves did not know the legal significance of a tenancy by the entireties account at the time they created the accounts. *See Beal Bank,* 710 So.2d at 611. Based on the Almands' testimony and their wives' failure to testify, Judge Cobb reasoned that "there was no evidence, much less clear and convincing evidence, that the various accounts were created with the intent of the parties that they were to be held as tenancies by the entireties."

In contrast, Judge Harris concluded that the Almands held all of the accounts at issue as tenancies by the entireties and, therefore, the trial court's findings as to these accounts should have been affirmed. *See id.* at 617 (Harris, J., concurring in part and dissenting in part). In making this determination, Judge Harris found that "regardless of the depositors' relationship with the bank, as between third parties, the question remains as to whether the depositors intended that each own all of the account." In Judge Harris's opinion, the Almands satisfied their burden of proof by their testimony. Judge Harris concluded that a party need not have a clear understanding of the legal definition of a tenancy by the entireties in order to benefit from that form of ownership. Moreover, Judge Harris opined that even without the testimony from the wives, the husbands' testimony established "the intent that each spouse owns the entire account and not a divisible portion thereof," which was sufficient to establish their intent to form a tenancy by the entirety.

Judge Sharp, in her separate opinion, agreed with Judge Harris that there was sufficient evidence in the record to sustain the trial court's determination that the Almands held the Compass Bank accounts as tenancies by the entireties. *See id.* at 615 (Sharp, J., concurring in result only). However, Judge Sharp concluded that the Almands did not hold the Barnett Bank and SouthTrust Bank accounts as tenancies by the entireties. In Judge Sharp's view, "because of the express language contained in the account documents," the Barnett Bank and SouthTrust Bank accounts, were "truly joint accounts and not tenancies by the entireties." Accordingly, she would not have permitted the parties to "resort to extrinsic, parol evidence of intent" to support the creation of a tenancy by the entirety because Judge Sharp reasoned that the account documents for these two accounts clearly stated an intent to form a joint tenancy with right of survivorship.

III. ANALYSIS

A. TENANCIES BY THE ENTIRETIES

To understand the key legal issues in this case, we start with an overview of the different forms of legal ownership of property in the State of Florida. Property held as a tenancy by the entireties possesses six characteristics: (1) unity of possession (joint ownership and control); (2) unity of interest (the interests in the account must be identical); (3) unity of title (the interests must have originated in the same instrument); (4) unity of time (the interests must have commenced simultaneously); (5) survivorship; and (6) unity of marriage (the parties must be married at the time the property became titled in their joint names). Because of the sixth characteristic—unity of marriage—a tenancy by the entireties is a form of ownership unique to married couples.

Although only a married couple is legally entitled to hold property as a tenancy by the entireties, a married couple may also hold property jointly as tenants in common or as joint tenants with right of survivorship. Tenancies in common, joint tenancies, and tenancies by the entireties all share the characteristic of unity of possession. Joint tenancies and tenancies by the entireties share the characteristic of survivorship and three additional unities of interest, title, and time. In other words, for both joint tenancies and tenancies by the entireties, the owners' interests in the property must be identical, the interests must have originated in the identical conveyance, and the interests must have commenced simultaneously.

Although a tenancy by the entireties and joint tenancy with right of survivorship share all of the same characteristics of form, there are significant differences in the legal consequences between the forms of ownership when creditors of one spouse seek to garnish these assets, when one spouse declares bankruptcy, or when one spouse attempts to recover monies transferred without his or her permission. When a married couple holds property as a tenancy by the entireties, each spouse is said to hold it "per tout," meaning that each spouse holds the "whole or the entirety, and not a share, moiety, or divisible part." *Bailey v. Smith,* 89 Fla. 303, 103 So. 833, 834 (1926). Thus, property held by husband and wife as tenants by the entireties belongs to neither spouse individually, but each spouse is seized of the whole. In a joint tenancy with right of survivorship, each person has only his or her own separate share ("per my"), which share is presumed to be equal for purposes of alienation; whereas, for purposes of survivorship, each joint tenant owns the whole ("per tout"), so that upon death the remainder of the estate passes to the survivor.

Because of this distinction between each spouse owning the whole versus each owning a share, if property is held as a joint tenancy with right of survivorship, a creditor of one of the joint tenants may attach the joint tenant's portion of the property to recover that joint tenant's individual debt. However, when property is held as a tenancy by the entireties, only the creditors of both the husband and wife, jointly, may attach the tenancy by the entireties property; the property is not divisible on behalf of one spouse alone, and therefore it cannot be reached to satisfy the obligation of only one spouse.

Early this century, this Court adopted the common law rule that a tenancy by the entireties may exist in both real property and personal property. *See Bailey,* 103 So. at 834. In the years following *Bailey,* this Court has continued to adhere to its holding that a tenancy by the entireties in personal property constitutes a legally recognized form of ownership.

Despite the fact that this Court has recognized the tenancy by the entireties form of ownership in both real property and personal property, this Court has adopted different standards of proof for each. Where real property is acquired specifically in the name of a husband and wife, it is considered to be a "rule of construction that a tenancy by the entireties is created, although fraud may be proven." *Hector Supply Co.,* 254 So.2d at 780. As explained in *Hector Supply Co.,* when we reaffirmed the vitality of the tenancy by the entireties form of ownership in both real property and personal property:

> Though the modern tendency is to regard the creation of an estate by the entireties as resting, not upon a rule of law arising from the supposed incapacity of husband and wife to hold in moities, but upon a rule of construction based on the presumption of intention, it may be laid down as a general proposition that, where land [and also personalty] is conveyed to both husband and wife, they *become* seized *of* the estate thus granted *per tout et non per my,* and not as joint tenants or tenants in common. The estate thus created is, however, essentially a joint tenancy, modified by the common-law doctrine that the husband and wife are one person.

Hector Supply Co., 254 So.2d at 780 (quoting *English v. English,* 66 Fla. 427, 63 So. 822, 823 (1913).

In the case of ownership of real property by husband and wife, the ownership in the name of both spouses vests title in them as tenants by the entireties. Thus, "[a] conveyance to spouses as husband and wife creates an estate by the entirety in the absence of express language showing a contrary intent." *In re Estate of Suggs,* 405 So.2d 1360, 1361 (Fla. 5th DCA 1981) (citing *Losey v. Losey,* 221 So.2d 417 (Fla.1969).

Unlike real property titled in the name of both spouses that is presumptively considered to be a tenancy by the entireties as long as the other unities are established, our jurisprudence has treated bank accounts and other personal property differently. In determining whether personal property is held as a tenancy by the entireties, we have applied "a different standard" by requiring that "not only must the form of the estate be consistent with entirety requirements, but the intention of the parties must be proven." *Hector Supply Co.,* 254 So.2d at 780. In contrast, in real property, intent to hold the property as a tenancy by the entireties is presumed. *See Losey,* 221 So.2d at 418; *Hector Supply Co.,* 254 So.2d at 780. In *Hector Supply Co.,* we explained our reasoning for having applied a different standard for personal property:

> Realty matters are matters of record which occur infrequently, and which generally involve formal transactions necessarily requiring consent of both spouses. Personalty, on the other hand, is generally not under mandate of record; it may easily be passed by either spouse without mutual consent or

without knowledge of the other spouse; finally, it may change hands with great frequency, as in the case of the checking account.

Id. at 780 (citing *In re Estate of Lyons,* 90 So.2d at 42).

B. PROBLEMS ARISING FROM THE DIFFERENT STANDARD

Once this Court determined that personal property could be held as a tenancy by the entireties, but also determined that no presumption of a tenancy by the entireties would arise when a husband and wife acquired and held personal property jointly, there were bound to be difficulties in how to prove the intent to own the personal property as a tenancy by the entireties versus a joint tenancy with right of survivorship. It was for this precise reason that Justice Boyd's concurring in part, dissenting in part opinion in *Hector Supply Co.* urged the Court to accord the same presumption to the ownership of personal property by husband and wife as was recognized in the case of real property. 254 So.2d at 783. In his opinion:

> [A contrary rule requiring proof of intent] creates, in effect, a presumption against the creation of estates by the entireties in personalty. This is contrary to the common experience of men [and women] as we know it and will require litigation in almost every instance, where, as is often true, the parties have not expressly provided in writing for a tenancy by the entireties.
>
> ***
>
> ... [T]he presumption favoring creation of tenancies by the entireties in personal property ... will generally eliminate the necessity for litigation concerning the intent of the parties.

Id. at 782-83.

In addition to the litigation necessary to establish intent, the problems in proof are compounded by a lack of uniform documentation to assist the inquiry into what form of tenancy the married couple had intended to establish. Neither the law nor "banking practices ... require account holders to expressly delineate the form of ownership they are creating in the jointly, held monies." *Sitomer,* 660 So.2d at 1113. Indeed, over forty years ago, Justice Thornal, writing for this Court in *Winters,* pointed out that much litigation involving the legal status of bank accounts could be avoided if, when the account is established, banks and depositors "would add language to the signature card stating clearly whether it is or is not intended to create a tenancy by the entirety." 91 So.2d at 652. Beal Bank also acknowledges that much of the confusion in this area could be avoided if banks offered signature cards that include a designation allowing the account holders to affirmatively select tenancy by the entireties accounts. Unfortunately, this suggestion has not been heeded either by financial institutions or through legislative enactment.

A final reason for the difficulty in proving whether personal property is held as a tenancy by the entireties or as a joint tenancy with right of survivorship is that the characteristics and unities of a joint tenancy held by a married couple and a tenancy by the entireties are identical. Although both forms of ownership share identical *characteristics* when held by a married couple, the types of ownership have legally distinguishable *consequences*. For example, one legally distinguishable consequence of ownership as a tenancy by the entireties is the inability of one spouse to alienate a portion of the estate without the consent of the other. However, this Court in *Hector Supply Co*. found that the ability of either spouse to alienate the account individually was not dispositive proof that a tenancy by the entireties did not exist so long as the account "contains a statement of permission for one spouse to act for the other." 254 So.2d at 781. Accordingly, the ability of a spouse to alienate a portion of the account unilaterally would not serve to differentiate these two forms of ownership as long as there is evidence that each spouse had permission to act for the other.

C. SHOULD A PRESUMPTION OF A TENANCY BY THE ENTIRETIES ARISE IN PERSONAL PROPERTY?

As the Almands point out, many financial institutions do not provide married couples with the opportunity to declare their intent to establish a tenancy by the entireties, and some financial institutions even affirmatively attempt to limit the ability of a married couple to establish a tenancy by the entireties. The Almands also assert that most consumers have no training in the complexities of property law, but simply may have the reasonable expectation that the legal consequences of an account jointly held by them as a married couple is no different than a home owned by them as a married couple.

Over the past fifty years, Florida jurisprudence has continued to struggle with the application of common law real property ownership concepts to modern banking relationships. In that time, consumers have not been provided with informed choices on the signature card with regard to the various forms of legal ownership, which could minimize the necessity for litigation.

As Judge Harris noted, "the *Hector* court did not intend to set up an obstacle course for married couples to run in order to set up a tenancy by the entireties account." *Beal Bank,* 710 So.2d at 617 (Harris, J., concurring in part, dissenting in part). Unfortunately, the effect of our decisions not to recognize a presumption in favor of a tenancy by the entireties when a bank account is jointly held by husband and wife was to set up both an obstacle course for litigation and a trap for the unwary — and to contribute to confusion in the law. Recent commentators have observed:

> Because most Florida banks do not include TBE language on the depositors' signature card, or fail to recognize the account ownership status entirely, the intent requirement has generated much post-judgment and bankruptcy litigation. The proofs required by various Florida courts are amorphous and inconsistent. Borrowers, lenders, and lower courts are in need of intervention by the Florida Supreme Court or the Florida Legislature so that everyone will more readily discern what accounts may be subject to reach of creditors.

Henry T. Sorenson II & Philip V. Martino, *Marital Bank Accounts as Entireties Property: What is the Current State of Florida Law?,* Fla. B.J., Apr. 1999, at 60, 60. Indeed, jurists and legal commentators have labeled the law regarding tenancies by the entireties in personal property to be "relatively conflicting and confusing" and "a state of morass." The fact that the Fifth District's review of this case produced three separate opinions from three distinguished jurists resulting in questions certified to this Court lends support to the accuracy of these observations.

Although we understand the considerations that originally led to this Court's decision not to adopt a presumption of a tenancy by the entireties in personal property similar to that in real property, we conclude that stronger policy considerations favor allowing the presumption in favor of a tenancy by the entireties when a married couple jointly owns personal property. In fact, other jurisdictions apply a presumption in favor of a tenancy by the entireties to both real property and personal property. As the authors of a recent article have reasoned: "because of the stringent and conflicting proofs needed by some Florida courts to demonstrate the depositors' intent to create the account, a rebuttable presumption that a marital account is held as [tenancy by the entireties] property in the absence of express language otherwise would conserve judicial resources and solidify the legitimate expectations of borrowers and lenders." Sorenson & Martino, *supra*, at 62 (footnote omitted).

We agree that the legitimate expectations of the parties regarding an account jointly held by them as a married couple should be no different than a home jointly owned by them as a married couple. The time has come for us to recognize that more confusion and less predictability in the law exists because of our Court's failure to recognize a presumption in favor of a tenancy by the entireties arising from joint ownership of bank accounts by husband and wife. Because this issue involves one arising from this State's common law and because the refusal to extend a presumption to personal property was a product of this Court's jurisprudence, we conclude that it is appropriate for us to recede from our prior case law. As we recently have reiterated:

> "[A]ll rules of the common law are designed for application to new conditions and circumstances," and we "exercise a 'broad discretion' taking 'into account the changes in our social and economic customs arid present day. conceptions of right and justice.' " *Hoffman v. Jones,* 280 So.2d 431, 435-36 (Fla.1973) (quoting *Duval v. Thomas,* 114 So.2d 791, 795 (Fla.1959)). "[Contemporary conditions must be met with contemporary standards which are realistic and better calculated to obtain justice among all the parties involved." *Id.* at 436. Therefore, the common law " 'must keep pace with changes in our society,'" and to that end "may be altered when the reason for the rule of law ceases to exist, or when change is demanded by public necessity or required to vindicate fundamental rights."

Stone v. Wall, 734 So.2d 1038, 1043 (Fla.1999).

Accordingly, we hold that as between the debtor and a third-party creditor (other than the financial institution into which the deposits have been made), if the signature card of the account does not expressly disclaim the tenancy by the entireties form of ownership, a presumption arises that a bank account titled in the names of both spouses is held as a tenancy by the entireties as long as the account is established by husband and wife in accordance with the unities of possession, interest, title, and time and with right of survivorship. The presumption we adopt is a presumption affecting the burden of proof pursuant to section 90.304, Florida Statutes (2000), thus shifting the burden to the creditor to prove by a preponderance of evidence that a tenancy by the entireties was not created. . . .

holding

***

Moreover, today's decision in no way limits creditors' ability to protect their interests against debtors who seek to shield assets from creditors.[1] Concerns such as preventing fraud on creditors or fraudulent transfers, however, are more properly addressed by those statutes that prevent fraudulent transfers; for example, the Uniform Fraudulent Transfer Act, found in chapter 726 of the Florida Statutes. *See* §§ 726.101-.201, Fla. Stat. (2000).[2] In these instances, the standard of proof and burden of proof are those set forth by the applicable case law and statutes.

D. EFFECT OF EXPRESS STATEMENTS AND EXPRESS DISCLAIMERS ON SIGNATURE CARD ON PRESUMPTION

We next address the effect on the presumption of language on the signature card that expressly states that the account is held as a tenancy by the entireties and the effect of language on the signature card that expressly states that it is not held as a tenancy by the entireties. Although we recede from *Hector Supply Co.*, we agree with the statement in *Hector Supply Co.* that an express designation on the signature card that the account is held as a tenancy by the entireties ends the inquiry as to the form of ownership. *Hector Supply Co.*, 254 So.2d at 781. Following *Hector Supply Co.*, other courts have excluded extrinsic evidence where the account documents clearly indicated the legal form of ownership.

In addition, just as a signature card can contain an express statement that a tenancy by the entireties was intended, so too can _ a signature card contain an express disclaimer that a tenancy by the entireties was not intended. An express disclaimer can take the form of an express statement signed by the depositor that a tenancy by the entireties was not intended, coupled with an express designation of another form of legal ownership. Alternatively, an express disclaimer of an intent not to hold the account as a tenancy by the entireties arises if the financial institution affirmatively provides the depositors with the option on the signature card to select a tenancy by the entireties among other options, and the depositors expressly select another form of ownership option of either a joint tenancy with right of survivorship or a tenancy in common.

In contrast, a statement on the signature card that the bank account titled in the name of a husband and wife is held as a joint tenancy with right of survivorship does not alone constitute an express disclaimer that the account is *not* held as a tenancy by the entireties. This is because a tenancy by the entireties is "essentially a joint tenancy, modified by the common-law doctrine that the husband and wife are one person." *Hector Supply Co.*, 254 So.2d at 780.

Thus, if a signature card does not expressly disclaim a tenancy by the entireties form of ownership, a rebuttable presumption arises that a tenancy by the entireties exists provided that all the other unities necessary for a tenancy by the entireties are established. However, if a signature card expressly states that the account is not held as a tenancy by the entireties and another form of legal ownership is expressly designated, no presumption of a tenancy by the entireties arises. Absent evidence of fraud, this express disclaimer would end the inquiry as to whether a tenancy by the entireties was intended. However, if the debtor establishes that the financial institution did not offer a tenancy by the entireties form of account ownership or expressly precluded that form of ownership, then the debtor may prove by other evidence an intent that the debtor and his or her spouse held the account as a tenancy by the entireties. In this circumstance, no presumption arises and the debtor has the burden of establishing a tenancy by the entireties by a preponderance of the evidence.

. . .

E. THIS CASE

Having articulated the applicable law to utilize, we now turn to analyze the accounts in this case. As an initial matter, we hold that none of the accounts at issue contained an express disclaimer negating ownership as a tenancy by the entireties. In the Compass Bank accounts, no form of ownership was specified on the signature card and both spouses were listed as account owners. In the case of the South-Trust Bank account, the signature card provided that it was owned as "Almos F. Almand, Jr. or Doris J. Almand, JT TEN" and the signature card contained the form language that the depositors own the account "as joint tenants with right of survivorship, unless another manner of ownership is specifically set forth in connection with the account legal title on this card." To the extent Judge Sharp concluded that the language on the SouthTrust bank account cards expressly disclaimed it was held as a tenancy by the entireties, *see Beal Bank,* 710 So.2d at 615, we respectfully disagree that a statement that an account is held as a joint tenancy with right of survivorship constitutes an express disclaimer that it is not held as a tenancy by the entireties. As we have explained, a tenancy by the entireties is "essentially a joint tenancy modified by the common-law doctrine that the husband and wife are one person." *Hector Supply Co.,* 254 So.2d at 780. Because there was no express statement of an intent not to hold the accounts as a tenancy by the entireties and no provision of alternative options on the signature card, there was no express disclaimer as to any of the accounts.

In the case of the Barnett Bank account, all the unities necessary for a tenancy by the entireties were established. However, the signature card specified that the account was held as "Almos F. Almand Jr. or Doris J. Almand, Jt. Tenants with Right of Survivorship." This is essentially the same designation as the SouthTrust signature card. In a document separate from the signature card, Barnett Bank attempted through its rules and regulations contained in its Welcome Brochure to preclude its depositors from establishing a tenancy by the entireties. That agreement would be binding as between the depositor and Barnett Bank. However, because the signature card did not contain an express disclaimer that the account was not held as a tenancy by the entireties, the reference in the Welcome Brochure alone would not be sufficient to eliminate the presumption in favor of tenancy by the entireties as between the depositor and a third party creditor.

Accordingly, a presumption arose that the Almands and their spouses held the Compass, SouthTrust and Barnett Bank accounts as tenancies by the entireties. As to the legal status of these accounts, Beal Bank urges that we should find dispositive the fact that the Almands testified that either they or their wives had the ability to withdraw funds from the accounts at their own discretion without the other spouse's approval and for purposes unrelated to the marital unit. Thus, Beal Bank argues the accounts could not be considered tenancy by the entireties accounts because the essential distinguishing characteristic of a tenancy by the entireties is the inalienability of the estate by one spouse. However, as we have explained, the ability of one spouse to make an individual withdrawal from the account does not defeat the unity of possession so long as the account agreement contains a statement giving each spouse permission to act for the other. *See Hector Supply Co.*, 254 So.2d at 781. Thus, we agree with Judge Harris's explanation in his concurring in part, dissenting in part opinion, "the inability of one spouse to unilaterally dispose of the property (money in the account) is not an 'element' of the estate, it is the legal consequence of it." *Beal Bank*, 710 So.2d at 617.

Likewise, we do not find the statement in the Compass Bank signature card for these accounts that "multiple-party accounts" are owned "in proportion to net contributions unless there is clear and convincing evidence of a different intent" to be conclusive of the form of ownership. Although the creditor could use this statement to argue that the depositors did not intend to own the accounts as a tenancies by the entireties, the trial court considered that evidence in this case and concluded to the contrary.

We point out that even without application of the presumption in this case, there was competent substantial evidence in the form of the testimony of the Almands to support the trial court's findings that each of these accounts constituted a tenancy by the entireties as explained by the separate opinion of Judge Harris. Accordingly, the trial court's findings that a tenancy by the entireties existed were in conformity with the holding that we announce today.

IV. CONCLUSION

We have endeavored to shed light on what has been termed a morass in the common law. In receding from *Hector,* we do so based on the common law of this State that has always recognized presumptions in favor of a tenancy by the entireties in real property owned by a married couple. We hope to bring greater predictability and uniformity to the common law governing accounts held at financial institutions and to eliminate the confusion that has arisen from our prior decisions in this area as exemplified by the Fifth District's splintered decision and its certification to this Court of questions of great public importance.

Although we recognize that we cannot mandate that financial institutions provide affirmative choices to select each form of ownership on the signature cards, with an explanation of each type of ownership, we strongly encourage this practice.[3] Such a practice of affirmative selection would minimize the likelihood of litigation and would put third persons on notice of the manner in which the account is held.

Based on our analysis in this case, we . . . approve in part and quash in part the per curiam decision of the Fifth District and remand for proceedings consistent with this opinion.

It is so ordered.

WELLS, C.J.,

dissenting.

I dissent as to the decision and opinion of the majority. I would affirm the decisions of the district court majorities.

Obviously, this Court's majority opinion is a reversal of the existing law in receding from *Hector* Supply. I cannot agree with the creation of a presumption which has heretofore not existed and its application to an existing case. I have even more concern about judicially creating a disclaimer and still more about applying that disclaimer to an existing case.

I certainly understand that the various forms of personalty ownership are confusing, and I agree that it would be beneficial to all concerned that there be clarification. However, such clarification is better a legislative task. There are many consequences of such changes — some known and, in all probability, many unknown and likely unintended. Contracts and other business arrangements are made on the basis of existing commercial laws, and to suddenly judicially change those laws and place new legal requirements on those contracts and business arrangements appears to me to create a myriad of legal, constitutional, and fairness issues.

1. Notably, Beal Bank does not assert that in this case there was any intent to defraud creditors in the creation or maintenance of the Almands' joint bank accounts with their wives. [Editorial Note: This is footnote 21 of the opinion.]

2. Section 726.105(l)(a), Florida Statutes (2000), prohibits any transfer made with "actual intent to hinder, delay or defraud" any creditor. See also § 726.108, Fla. Stat. (2000) (providing remedies for fraudulent transfers). [Editorial Note: This is footnote 22 of the opinion.]

3. We urge the Legislature to enact such a requirement. For example, section 655.79(1), Florida Statutes (2000), provides that when two people open an account at a financial institution a presumption arises that they intended to create a survivorship account, unless the contract, agreement, or signature card provides otherwise. This presumption can only be overcome by proof of fraud, undue influence, or clear and convincing evidence of a contrary intent. See § 655.79(2). For all other personal property, the Florida statutes provide that the doctrine of right of survivorship shall not apply to personal property held by joint tenants "unless the instrument creating the estate shall expressly provide for the right of survivorship." § 689.15, Fla. Stat. (2000). [This is footnote 24 of the opinion.]

7.1.3

Discussion: Notes, Questions, and Problems

7.1.3.1

Discussion Question #1. Presumptions when cotenants?

In footnote 24 of *Beal Bank*, excerpted above, the Florida Supreme Court referenced Fla. Stat. § 655.79 and Fla. Stat. § 689.15 regarding presumptions when there are cotenants.

Fla. Stat. § 689.15 provides as follows:

> **689.15 Estates by survivorship.**—The doctrine of the right of survivorship in cases of real estate and personal property held by joint tenants shall not prevail in this state; that is to say, except in cases of estates by entirety, a devise, transfer or conveyance heretofore or hereafter made to two or more shall create a tenancy in common, unless the instrument creating the estate shall expressly provide for the right of survivorship; and in cases of estates by entirety, the tenants, upon dissolution of marriage, shall become tenants in common.

Contrast Fla. Stat. § 689.15 with Fla. Stat. § 655.79, which applies to deposits and accounts. Fla. Stat. § 655.79, amended after *Beal Bank*, provides as follows:

> **655.79 Deposits and accounts in two or more names; presumption as to vesting on death.**—
>
> (1) Unless otherwise expressly provided in a contract, agreement, or signature card executed in connection with the opening or maintenance of an account, including a certificate of deposit, a deposit account in the names of two or more persons shall be presumed to have been intended by such persons to provide that, upon the death of any one of them, all rights, title, interest, and claim in, to, and in respect of such deposit account, less all proper setoffs and charges in favor of the institution, vest in the surviving

person or persons. Any deposit or account made in the name of two persons who are husband and wife shall be considered a tenancy by the entirety unless otherwise specified in writing.

(2)   The presumption created in this section may be overcome only by proof of fraud or undue influence or clear and convincing proof of a contrary intent. . . .

How do the presumptions differ between these two statutes?

Notice that Fla. Stat. § 689.15 does not expressly provide for a presumption for a conveyance to a married couple. What presumption applies for a conveyance to married couples? *See Losey v. Losey*, 221 So. 2d 417 (Fla. 1969); Fla. Stat. § 689.11.

7.1.3.2
Discussion Problem #2. Four brothers problem

Four brothers, Andrew, Bob, Charles, and Dan, owned Blackacre as joint tenants. Andrew died. Andrew's will left his entire estate to the American Red Cross. What interest, if any, does the American Red Cross have in Blackacre?

7.1.3.3
Discussion Problem #3. Four sisters problem

Four sisters, Ana, Belinda, Carmen, and Dolores, owned Greenacre as joint tenants. During her lifetime, Ana conveyed her interest in Greencare to her friend Felicia for $100,000 (an amount that is the fair market value of ¼ of Greenacre). Which type of concurrent interest, if any, does Felicia have in Greenacre after the conveyance?

7.2
Rights and Obligations Among Co-tenants

What rights and obligations do cotenants have with regard to each other? Allocation of rights and obligations can be a source of significant tensions among cotenants, even when the cotenants are each in possession of the property. These tensions can rise exponentially when one cotenant is in possession of the property, but the others are not. For example, if only one cotenant is in possession of the property and the others are not, does the cotenant in sole possession have to compensate the others for the tenant's sole use? Should compensation turn on the reason why the other cotenants are not in possession? Note that cotenants may voluntarily decide not to be in possession. For example, a cotenant may obtain a job in another city and move out of the co-owned property. What if, however, a cotenant did not leave voluntarily but, rather, was ousted by the other cotenant? In that case, would the tenant in sole possession have to compensate the ousted cotenant?

Other rights and obligations are also important to analyze. Should upkeep expenses be allocated proportionally among cotenants based on each cotenant's fractional interest? What about costs of improvements to the property? What if the property generates income, how should such income be allocated?

Best practices suggest that cotenants discuss and negotiate these issues before they arise and enter into a contract expressly delineating their agreed upon rights and obligations. Property law concepts step into the breach when there is no contract or when the contract does not address the particular issues. As you read the cases below, ask yourselves several questions. What is the effect of an ouster? What remedies might be available for cotenants who have not received their share of income generated from the property? What remedies are available for a cotenant who has paid upkeep expenses and has not been reimbursed by the other cotenants? What if one cotenant pays to build a structure on the property that the other cotenants do not want, must the other cotenants pay part of the costs of the structure? What is the difference between a contribution action and a partition action?

7.2.1

Graham v. Inlow
790 S.W.2d 428 (Ark. 1990)

Arkansas Supreme Court

Tom Glaze, Justice.

This second appeal stems from our earlier reversal and remand of this partition suit case wherein we held valid a deed from Robert Inlow to his second wife, Freda, and his three children. Robert had two children, Charles and Carol, by his wife Freda, and he had another child, Patricia Graham, by his first wife. In remanding this case, the trial court was placed in the position of reconsidering Graham's request for partitioning the parties' one-fourth respective interest in the 287 acre farm. The chancellor found the property could not be partitioned in kind and ordered the sale of the farm. The chancellor further held that Graham was entitled to certain rental income and timber sale proceeds after her commencement of the suit as well as attorney fees and costs in connection with prosecuting this partition action. He also awarded Freda the sum of $70,000 for improvements she made on the disputed property. Graham appeals and the Inlows cross appeal from the awards made by the chancellor.

In the first point, the appellant argues that the chancellor erred in awarding reimbursement for improvements made on the property for two reasons: (1) Freda did not show that the improvements were made in good faith and . . . 2) Freda failed to present any testimony to show the improvement's enhanced value to the land. Because we agree with appellant's . . . argument on this point, we reverse and remand.

***

It is well settled that a tenant in common has the right to make improvements on the land without the consent of his cotenants; and, although he has no lien on the land for the value of his improvements, he will be indemnified for them, in a proceeding in equity to partition the land between himself and cotenants, either by having the part upon which the improvements are located allotted to him or by having compensation for them, if thrown into the common mass. The improvements must be made in good faith and have benefit to the premises. Thompson, *Real Property,* § 5295 (1957).

Here, the record reflects that the appellee Freda made improvements which benefited the land beginning in 1979. The majority of those improvements were in the form of repairs and renovations to already existing buildings such as barns. There is no showing that these benefits were not made in good faith. However, because tenants in common might be improved out of their property, the cotenant can only receive the enhancement value of the improvement to the property. . . . The proper measurement is the difference between the value of the land without the improvements and the value of the land with the improvements in their then condition.

Appellee Freda attempted to prove this value through the testimony of a real estate appraiser, Mr. Hinshaw. Hinshaw testified about improvements made to each separate itemized item and the enhanced value of those improvements on each item. He then explained that this value was not the cost value but the contributory value. Hinshaw explained that the contributory value was determined by comparing a similar piece of property without a building, like the building improved on the land in question, to the value of the land in question with the building. In addition, Hinshaw gave testimony about the difference in value of raw land and the value of the land in question with buildings on it.

expert testimony

Hinshaw's testimony showed the court the following things: (1) the difference in ① value between raw land and land with buildings; (2) the contributory value of a barn, ② for instance, to the land, which is figured by knowing the selling price of a similar piece of land without a barn, and (3) the difference in value or enhancement of the ③ building before and after the improvement. However, as shown by the following exchange on cross-examination, Hinshaw did not testify as to the difference in value of property without improvements and the value of property after improvements.

> Q So you're not prepared to tell me and this Court how much these improvements that you made reference to here . . . actually enhanced the value of the entire property? What you're saying is what they enhanced each individual building or item; is that correct?
>
> A Well, yes, but they in total affected the property also. I'm saying you were trying to get me to compare it with the value of the property before anything was done to 'em and I can't do that without some special work. I can do it. . . . But I don't have the figures here to do it.

Even though Hinshaw later stated that he thought that the values he testified to showed both the enhancement of the individual items that were improved and the value of those improvements to the property as a whole, we do not agree. From our review of Hinshaw's testimony, we cannot find any testimony to support this measure of recovery. Thus, in awarding Freda $70,000 for the improvements as a result of Hinshaw's testimony, we hold that the chancellor erred in determining the proper amount to be allowed for the improvements, and we remand the case with directions to proceed in a manner not inconsistent with this opinion.

In the second issue, the appellant argues that the chancellor erred in holding that she could only recover rents after the commencement of her partition suit. On this same issue, the appellees in their cross appeal argue that the chancellor erred in awarding any rents to the appellant. We find no error in the chancellor's holding on this point.

One of the characteristics of tenancy in common is that each tenant has the right to occupy the premises, and neither tenant can lawfully exclude the other. The occupation of one tenant in common is deemed possession by all. For the possession of one tenant in common to be adverse to that of his cotenants, knowledge of his adverse claim must be brought home to them directly or by such acts that notice may be presumed. We have stated that the dispossession of a cotenant is a question of fact, and we will not reverse the chancellor's determination absent a showing it was clearly erroneous.

Under the property laws of common tenancy, until the appellant asserted her right for common enjoyment of the farm, the other tenants in common were not obligated to stay out. A tenant in possession who does not exclude his cotenants is not liable for rent. *Lawrence* v. *Lawrence,* 231 Ark. 324, 329 S.W.2d 416 (1969).

From our review of the record, we cannot say that the chancellor's finding that the appellant did not assert her right for common enjoyment until the filing of her partition suit is clearly erroneous. In so ruling, we note that the appellant lived on part of the farm and there is ample evidence, albeit conflicting, to reflect she had reasonable access to all the property. While we would agree that there seems to be bad blood between the appellant and her stepmother Freda, we cannot conclude that the appellees excluded the appellant prior to her commencement of the partition suit.

***

For the reasons above, we affirm in part and reverse and remand in part. We affirm on cross appeal.

7.2.2

Coggan v. Coggan
239 So. 2d 17 (Fla. 1970)

Florida Supreme Court

MOODY, Circuit Judge.

This cause is before this court on petition for writ of certiorari to review the decision of the District Court of Appeals, Second District, in the case of Coggan v. Coggan, 230 So.2d 34.

Petitioner, husband, defendant in the trial court, owned an office building jointly with his wife, plaintiff below, which he occupied as his medical office. In 1963 the parties were divorced and they thereby became tenants in common of the property. No provision was made in the decree, or by agreement, as to its use and possession. The defendant continued in possession, paying the taxes, making necessary repairs, and otherwise exercising complete control. In 1967 the former wife filed a partition suit praying for an accounting of one-half the rental value of the office building from the date of the final decree of divorce. The defendant counterclaimed for partition of the plaintiff's home which, by the terms of the final decree, was purchased as a tenancy in common with the exclusive possession granted to the plaintiff. The trial court ordered a partition sale of the office building and an accounting in favor of the plaintiff for one-half the rental value of the premises since the date of the divorce. The counterclaim was denied.

***

On the question of the accounting, the District Court also affirmed the lower court and in its opinion correctly stated the governing law as follows:

> " * * * when one cotenant has exclusive possession of lands owned as tenant in common with another and uses those lands for his own benefit and does not receive rents or profits therefrom, such cotenant is not liable or

accountable to his cotenant out of possession *unless* such cotenant in exclusive possession holds adversely or as the result of ouster or the equivalent thereof. This was the rule of common law, as modified by the Statute of Anne and as it was expressly adopted as the law of Florida in 1875 by our Supreme Court in Bird v. Bird (Fla.1875), 15 Fla. 424. The rule has persisted unchanged and has heretofore been recognized by this court. *See,* Taylor v. Taylor (Fla.App.2d 1960), 119 So.2d 811, 813. Thus it appears that appellant's point is well taken unless the case falls within one of the exceptions to the rule; i. e., unless it is shown that appellant held exclusive possession of his professional office adversely to appellee, or as the result of ouster *or the equivalent thereof. See,* 51 A.L.R.2d 388, 437, § 13."

It then found, based on the undisputed facts, that the defendant's actions were "the equivalent of ouster." The facts being undisputed, it becomes a question of law as to whether or not the tenant in possession held the property adversely or as a result of ouster or the equivalent thereof.

The possession of a tenant in common is presumed to be the possession of all cotenants until the one in possession brings home to the other the knowledge that he claims the exclusive right or title. What is called "exclusive possession" may amount merely to sole possession without actual exclusion of a co-tenant or denial, or invasion of the rights of such cotenant.

There can be no holding adversely or ouster or its equivalent, by one cotenant unless such holding is manifested or communicated to the other. Where a tenant out of possession claims an accounting of a tenant in possession, he must show that the tenant in possession is holding the exclusive possession of the property adversely or holding the exclusive possession as a result of ouster or the equivalent thereof. This possession must be attended with such circumstances as to evince a claim of the exclusive right or title by the tenant in possession imparted to the tenant out of possession.

In the case of Stokely et al. v. Conner (1915) 69 Fla. 412, 68 So. 452, this court stated:

> "But a tenant in common, to show an ouster of his cotenant, must show acts of possession inconsistent with, and exclusive of, the rights of such

cotenant, and such as would amount to an ouster between landlord and tenant, and knowledge on the part of his cotenant of his claim of exclusive ownership. He has the right to assume that the possession of his cotenant in his possession, until informed to the contrary, either by express notice, or by acts and declarations that may be equivalent to notice."

See also Gracy v. Fielding (1916) 71 Fla. 1, 70 So. 625 and Cook et al. v. Rochford (Fla.1952) 60 So.2d 531.

In the case at Bar, although the defendant continued in sole possession of the property after the divorce decree, the record is devoid of any evidence that, prior to the filing of the partition suit, he advised the plaintiff he was claiming adversely to her, or that he had taken any action adverse to her interest or title, or that he had taken any steps to actually or constructively oust her from possession, or that she knew or should have known he was claiming any right of title adverse to her.

The claim of the defendant was manifested for the first time in his unsworn answer to the complaint for partition wherein he denied the existence of any cotenancy. This pleading cannot be considered as evidence. It was not an admission in a pleading eliminating the necessity of proof, but was a general denial of plaintiff's claim or a conclusion of law upon which evidence would be necessary for determination. The District Court based its decisions upon the denial in the pleading and the defendant's testimony at the trial that he had always considered himself to be the sole owner of the property and that his former wife had no rights therein. However, as previously noted, there was no evidence that he had expressed this attitude or belief to her, or that she was otherwise cognizant of this claim.

In consideration of the foregoing, the decision of the District Court is quashed to the extent set forth herein with directions that the case be remanded to the trial court for further proceedings not inconsistent herewith.

BOYD, Justice

(dissenting).

I must dissent. The trial court and the District Court of Appeal correctly concluded that the evidence showed a consistent denial by petitioner that a cotenancy of any

190

kind ever existed between the respondent and the petitioner in the subject office building. The record here supports the holding of the courts below that petitioner is liable to account to respondent for respondent's share of the rental value of the premises.

I would affirm the decision of the District Court.

7.2.3
Discussion: Notes, Questions, and Problems

7.2.3.1
Discussion Note #4. Feminist perspective of Coggan v. Coggan

For a feminist perspective of *Coggan v. Coggan*, excerpted above, see Phyliss Craig-Taylor, Coggan v. Coggan—*Rewritten Opinion in* Feminist Judgments: Rewritten Property Opinions (Eloisa C. Rodriguez-Dod & Elena Marty-Nelson eds., Cambridge University Press 2021). For a discussion of Craig-Taylor's revised feminist opinion, see Natasha N. Varyani & Stevie Leahy, *Commentary on* Coggan v. Coggan—*Rewritten Opinion, in* Feminist Judgments: Rewritten Property Opinions (Eloisa C. Rodriguez-Dod & Elena Marty-Nelson eds., Cambridge University Press 2021).

7.2.3.2
Discussion Question #5. Accounting for cotenant's sole possession?

Absent an ouster, does a tenant in possession need to account to the non-occupying cotenants for the value the occupying tenant derives from possession of the whole of the property and why?

7.2.3.3

Discussion Question #6. Can cotenant seek partition?

Can a tenant in common who wishes to terminate the concurrent estate bring an action for partition? Can a joint tenant who wishes to terminate the concurrent estate bring an action for partition?

7.3

Rights of Creditors of Cotenants

When can creditors of a debtor cotenant reach the debtor cotenant's interest in concurrently owned property? Generally, a creditor can reach anything that a debtor alone can voluntarily alienate. Read carefully *Sawada v. Endo* and *United States v. Craft*, both excerpted below, as you think through these issues.

7.3.1

Sawada v. Endo
561 P.2d 1291 (Haw. 1977)

Supreme Court of the State of Hawaii

MENOR, J.

This is a civil action brought by the plaintiffs-appellants, Masako Sawada and Helen Sawada, in aid of execution of money judgments in their favor, seeking to set aside a conveyance of real property from judgment debtor Kokichi Endo to Samuel H. Endo and Toru Endo, defendants-appellees herein, on the ground that the conveyance as to the Sawadas was fraudulent.

On November 30, 1968, the Sawadas were injured when struck by a motor vehicle operated by Kokichi Endo. On June 17, 1969, Helen Sawada filed her complaint for damages against Kokichi Endo. Masako Sawada filed her suit against him on August 13,1969. The complaint and summons in each case was served on Kokichi Endo on October 29, 1969.

On the date of the accident, Kokichi Endo was the owner, as a tenant by the entirety with his wife, Ume Endo, of a parcel of real property situate at Wahiawa, Oahu, Hawaii. By deed, dated July 26, 1969, Kokichi Endo and his wife conveyed the property to their sons, Samuel H. Endo and Toru Endo. This document was recorded in the Bureau of Conveyances on December 17, 1969. No consideration was paid by the grantees for the conveyance. Both were aware at the time of the conveyance that their father had been involved in an accident, and that he carried no liability insurance. Kokichi Endo and Ume Endo, while reserving no life interests therein, continued to reside on the premises.

On January 19, 1971, after a consolidated trial on the merits, judgment was entered in favor of Helen Sawada and against Kokichi Endo in the sum of $8,846.46. At the same time, Masako Sawada was awarded judgment on her complaint in the amount of $16,199.28. Ume Endo, wife of Kokichi Endo, died on January 29, 1971. She was survived by her husband, Kokichi. Subsequently, after being frustrated in their attempts to obtain satisfaction of judgment from the personal property of Kokichi Endo, the Sawadas brought suit to set aside the conveyance which is the subject matter of this controversy. The trial court refused to set aside the conveyance, and *PP* the Sawadas appeal.

I

The determinative question in this case is, whether the interest of one spouse in real property, held in tenancy by the entireties, is subject to levy and execution by his or her individual creditors. This issue is one of first impression in this jurisdiction.

A brief review of the present state of the tenancy by the entirety might be helpful. Dean Phipps, writing in 1951, pointed out that only nineteen states and the District of Columbia continued to recognize it as a valid and subsisting institution in the field of property law. Phipps divided these jurisdictions into four groups. He made no mention of Alaska and Hawaii, both of which were then territories of the United States.

In the Group I states (Massachusetts, Michigan, and North Carolina) the estate is essentially the common law tenancy by the entireties, unaffected by the Married Women's Property Acts. As at common law, the possession and profits of the estate are subject to the husband's exclusive dominion and control. In all three states, as at common law, the *husband* may convey the entire estate subject only to the possibility that the wife may become entitled to the whole estate upon surviving him. As at common law, the obverse as to the wife does not hold true. Only in Massachusetts, however, is the estate in its entirety subject to levy by the husband's creditors. In both Michigan and North Carolina, the use and income from the estate is not subject to levy during the marriage for the separate debts of either *spouse*.

In the Group II states (Alaska, Arkansas, New Jersey, New York, and Oregon) the interest of the debtor spouse in the estate may be sold or levied upon for his or her separate debts, subject to the other spouse's contingent right of survivorship. Alaska, which has been added to this group, has provided by statute that the interest of a debtor spouse in any type of estate, except a homestead as defined and held in tenancy by the entirety, shall be subject to his or her separate debts.

In the Group III jurisdictions (Delaware, District of Columbia, Florida, Indiana, Maryland, Missouri, Pennsylvania, Rhode Island, Vermont, Virginia, and Wyoming) an attempted conveyance by either spouse is wholly void, and the estate may not be subjected to the separate debts of one spouse only.

In Group IV, the two states of Kentucky and Tennessee hold that the contingent right of survivorship appertaining to either spouse is separately alienable by him and attachable by his creditors during the marriage. [The use and profits, however, may neither be alienated nor attached during coverture.

It appears, therefore, that Hawaii is the only jurisdiction still to be heard from on the question. Today we join that group of states and the District of Columbia which hold that under the Married Women's Property Acts the interest of a husband or a wife in an estate by the entireties is not subject to the claims of his or her individual creditors during the joint lives of the spouses. In so doing, we are placing our stamp of approval upon what is apparently the prevailing view of the lower courts of this jurisdiction.

Hawaii has long recognized and continues to recognize the tenancy in common, the joint tenancy, and the tenancy by the entirety, as separate and distinct estates. *See Paahana v. Bila,* 3 Haw. 725 (1876). That the Married Women's Property Act of 1888

194

was not intended to abolish the tenancy by the entirety was made clear by the language of Act 19 of the Session Laws of Hawaii, 1903 (now HRS § 509-1). The tenancy by the entirety is predicated upon the legal unity of husband and wife, and the estate is held by them in single ownership. They do not take by moieties, but both and each are seized of the whole estate. *Lang v. Commissioner,* 289 U.S. 109 (1933).

A joint tenant has a specific, albeit undivided, interest in the property, and if he survives his cotenant he becomes the owner of a larger interest than he had prior to the death of the other joint tenant. But tenants by the entirety are each deemed to be seized of the entirety from the time of the creation of the estate. At common law, this taking of the "whole estate" did not have the real significance that it does today, insofar as the rights of the wife in the property were concerned. For all practical purposes, the wife had no right during coverture to the use and enjoyment and exercise of ownership in the marital estate. All she possessed was her contingent right of survivorship.

The effect of the Married Women's Property Acts was to abrogate the husband's common law dominance over the marital estate and to place the wife on a level of equality with him as regards the exercise of ownership over the whole estate. The tenancy was and still is predicated upon the legal unity of husband and wife, but the Acts converted it into a unity of equals and not of unequals as at common law. No longer could the husband convey, lease, mortgage or otherwise encumber the property without her consent. The Acts confirmed her right to the use and enjoyment of the whole estate, and all the privileges that ownership of property confers, including the right to convey the property in its entirety, jointly with her husband, during the marriage relation. *Jordan v. Reynolds,* 105 Md. 288, 66 A. 37 (1907); *Hurd v. Hughes,* 12 Del. Ch. 188, 109 A. 418 (1920); *Vasilion v. Vasilion, supra; Frost v. Frost,* 200 Mo. 474, 98 S.W. 527 (1906). They also had the effect of insulating the wife's interest in the estate from the separate debts of her husband. *Jordan v. Reynolds, supra.*

Neither husband nor wife has a separate divisible interest in the property held by the entirety that can be conveyed or reached by execution. *Fairclaw v. Forrest,* 130 F.2d

829 (D.C.Cir. 1942). A joint tenancy may be destroyed by voluntary alienation, or by levy and execution, or by compulsory partition, but a tenancy by the entirety may not. The indivisibility of the estate, except by joint action of the spouses, is an indispensable feature of the tenancy by the entirety.

In *Jordan v. Reynolds, supra,* the Maryland court held that no lien could attach against entirety property for the separate debts of the husband, for that would be in derogation of the entirety of title in the spouses and would be tantamount to a conversion of the tenancy into a joint tenancy or tenancy in common. In holding that the spouses could jointly convey the property, free of any judgment liens against the husband, the court said:

> "To hold the judgment to be a lien at all against this property, and the right of execution suspended during the life of the wife, and to be enforced on the death of the wife, would, we think, likewise encumber her estate, and be in contravention of the constitutional provision heretofore mentioned, protecting the wife's property from the husband's debts.
>
> It is clear, we think, if the judgment here is declared a lien, but suspended during the life of the wife, and not enforceable until her death, if the husband should survive the wife, it will defeat the sale here made by the husband and wife to the purchaser, and thereby make the wife's property liable for the debts of her husband. " 105 Md. at 295, 296, 66 A. at 39.

In *Hurd v. Hughes, supra,* the Delaware court, recognizing the peculiar nature of an estate by the entirety, in that the husband and wife are the owners, not merely of equal interests but of the whole estate, stated:

> "The estate [by the entireties] can be acquired or held only by a man and woman while married. Each spouse owns the whole while both live; neither can sell any interest except with the other's consent, and by their joint act and at the death of either the other continues to own the whole, and does not acquire any new interest from the other. There can be no partition between them. From this is deduced the indivisibility and unseverability of the estate into two interests, and hence that the creditors of either spouse cannot during their joint lives reach by execution any interest which the

debtor had in land so held. . . . One may have doubts as to whether the holding of land by entireties is advisable or in harmony with the spirit of the legislation in favor of married women; but when such an estate is created due effect must be given to its peculiar characteristics." 12 Del. Ch. at 190, 109 A. at 419.

In *Frost v. Frost, supra,* the Missouri court said:

"Under the facts of the case at bar it is not necessary for us to decide whether or not under our married women's statutes the husband has been shorn of the exclusive right to the possession and control of the property held as an estate in entirety; it is sufficient to say, as we do say, that the title in such an estate is as it was at common law; neither husband nor wife has an interest in the property, to the exclusion of the other. Each owns the whole while both live and at the death of either the other continues to own the whole, freed from the claim of any one claiming under or through the deceased. " 200 Mo. at 483, 98 S.W. at 528, 529.

We are not persuaded by the argument that it would be unfair to the creditors of either spouse to hold that the estate by the entirety may not, without the consent of both spouses, be levied upon for the separate debts of either spouse. No unfairness to the creditor is involved here. We agree with the court in *Hurd v. Hughes, supra:*

"But creditors are not entitled to special consideration. If the debt arose prior to the creation of the estate, the property was not the basis of credit, and if the debt arose subsequently the creditor presumably had notice of the characteristics of the estate which limited his right to reach the property." 12 Del. Ch. at 193, 109 A. at 420.

We might also add that there is obviously nothing to prevent the creditor from insisting upon the subjection of property held in tenancy by the entirety as a condition precedent to the extension of credit. Further, the creation of a tenancy by the entirety may not be used as a device to defraud existing creditors. *In re Estate of Wall,* 440 F.2d 215 (D.C. Cir. 1971).

Were we to view the matter strictly from the standpoint of public policy, we would still be constrained to hold as we have done here today. In *Fairclaw v. Forrest, supra,* the court makes this observation:

> "The interest in family solidarity retains some influence upon the institution [of tenancy by the entirety]. It is available only to husband and wife. It is a convenient mode of protecting a surviving spouse from inconvenient administration of the decedent's estate and from the other's improvident debts. It is in that protection the estate finds its peculiar and justifiable function." 130 F.2d at 833.

It is a matter of common knowledge that the demand for single-family residential lots has increased rapidly in recent years, and the magnitude of the problem is emphasized by the concentration of the bulk of fee simple land in the hands of a few. The shortage of single-family residential fee simple property is critical and government has seen fit to attempt to alleviate the problem through legislation. When a family can afford to own real property, it becomes their single most important asset. Encumbered as it usually is by a first mortgage, the fact remains that so long as it remains whole during the joint lives of the spouses, it is always available in its entirety for the benefit and use of the entire family. Loans for education and other emergency expenses, for example, may be obtained on the security of the marital estate. This would not be possible where a third party has become a tenant in common or a joint tenant with one of the spouses, or where the ownership of the contingent right of survivorship of one of the spouses in a third party has cast a cloud upon the title of the marital estate, making it virtually impossible to utilize the estate for these purposes.

If we were to select between a public policy favoring the creditors of one of the spouses and one favoring the interests of the family unit, we would not hesitate to choose the latter. But we need not make this choice for, as we pointed out earlier, by the very nature of the estate by the entirety as we view it, and as other courts of our sister jurisdictions have viewed it, "[a] unilaterally indestructible right of survivorship, an inability of one spouse to alienate his interest, and importantly for this case,

a broad immunity from claims of separate creditors remain among its vital incidents."
In re Estate of Wall, supra, 440 F.2d at 218.

Having determined that an estate by the entirety is not subject to the claims of the creditors of one of the spouses during their joint lives, we now hold that the conveyance of the marital property by Kokichi Endo and Ume Endo, husband and wife, to their sons, Samuel H. Endo and Toru Endo, was not in fraud of Kokichi Endo's judgment creditors. *Cf. Jordan v. Reynolds, supra.*

Affirmed.

DISSENTING OPINION OF

KIDWELL, J.

***

The majority reaches its conclusion by holding that the effect of the Married Women's Act was to equalize the positions of the spouses by taking from the husband his common law right to transfer his interest, rather than by elevating the wife's right of alienation of her interest to place it on a position of equality with the husband's. I disagree. I believe that a better interpretation of the Married Women's Acts is that offered by the Supreme Court of New Jersey in *King v. Greene,* 30 N.J. 395, 412, 153 A.2d 49, 60 (1959):

It is clear that the Married Women's Act created an equality between the spouses in New Jersey, insofar as tenancies by the entirety are concerned. If, as we have previously concluded, the husband could alienate his right of survivorship at common law, the wife, by virtue of the act, can alienate her right of survivorship. And it follows that if the wife takes equal rights with the husband she must take equal disabilities. Such are the dictates of common equality. Thus the judgment creditors of either spouse may levy and execute on their separate rights of survivorship.

One may speculate whether the courts which first chose the path to equality now followed by the majority might have felt an unexpressed aversion to entrusting a wife with as much control over her interest as had previously been granted to the husband with respect to his interest. Whatever may be the historical explanation for these decisions, I feel that the resultant restriction upon the freedom of the spouses to deal independently with their respective interests is both illogical and unnecessarily at odds with present policy trends. Accordingly, I would hold that the separate interest of the husband in entireties property, at least to the extent of his right of survivorship, is alienable by him and subject to attachment by his separate creditors, so that a voluntary conveyance of the husband's interest should be set aside where it is fraudulent as to such creditors, under applicable principles of the law of fraudulent conveyances.

7.3.2

United States v. Craft
535 U.S. 274 (2002)

Supreme Court of the United States

Justice O'Connor

delivered the opinion of the Court.

This case raises the question whether a tenant by the entirety possesses "property" or "rights to property" to which a federal tax lien may attach. 26 U. S. C. §6321. Relying on the state law fiction that a tenant by the entirety has no separate interest in entireties property, the United States Court of Appeals for the Sixth Circuit held that such property is exempt from the tax lien. We conclude that, despite the fiction, each tenant possesses individual rights in the estate sufficient to constitute "property" or "rights to property" for the purposes of the lien, and reverse the judgment of the Court of Appeals.

I

In 1988, the Internal Revenue Service (IRS) assessed $482,446 in unpaid income tax liabilities against Don Craft, the husband of respondent Sandra L. Craft, for failure to file federal income tax returns for the years 1979 through 1986. When he failed to pay, a federal tax lien attached to "all property and rights to property, whether real or personal, belonging to" him. 26 U. S. C. §6321.

At the time the lien attached, respondent and her husband owned a piece of real property in Grand Rapids, Michigan, as tenants by the entirety. After notice of the lien was filed, they jointly executed a quitclaim deed purporting to transfer the husband's interest in the property to respondent for one dollar. When respondent attempted to sell the property a few years later, a title search revealed the lien. The IRS agreed to release the lien and allow the sale with the stipulation that half of the net proceeds be held in escrow pending determination of the Government's interest in the property.

Respondent brought this action to quiet title to the escrowed proceeds. The Government claimed that its lien had attached to the husband's interest in the tenancy by the entirety. It further asserted that the transfer of the property to respondent was invalid as a fraud on creditors. . . .

. . . The Sixth Circuit held that the tax lien did not attach to the property because under Michigan state law, the husband had no separate interest in property held as a tenant by the entirety. It remanded to the District Court to consider the Government's alternative claim that the conveyance should be set aside as fraudulent.

On remand, the District Court concluded that where, as here, state law makes property exempt from the claims of creditors, no fraudulent conveyance can occur. It found, however, that respondent's husband's use of nonexempt funds to pay the mortgage on the entireties property, which placed them beyond the reach of creditors, constituted a fraudulent act under state law, and the court awarded the IRS a share of the proceeds of the sale of the property equal to that amount.

Both parties appealed the District Court's decision, the Government again claiming that its lien attached to the husband's interest in the entireties property. The Court of Appeals held that the prior panel's opinion was law of the case on that issue. It also affirmed the District Court's determination that the husband's mortgage payments were fraudulent.

We granted certiorari to consider the Government's claim that respondent's husband had a separate interest in the entireties property to which the federal tax lien attached.

II

Whether the interests of respondent's husband in the property he held as a tenant by the entirety constitutes "property and rights to property" for the purposes of the federal tax lien statute, 26 U. S. C. § 6321, is ultimately a question of federal law. The answer to this federal question, however, largely depends upon state law. The federal tax lien statute itself "creates no property rights but merely attaches consequences, federally defined, to rights created under state law." United States v. Bess, 357 U. S. 51, 55 (1958); see also United States v. National Bank of Commerce, 472 U. S. 713, 722 (1985). Accordingly, "[w]e look initially to state law to determine what rights the taxpayer has in the property the Government seeks to reach, then to federal law to determine whether the taxpayer's state-delineated rights qualify as 'property' or 'rights to property' within the compass of the federal tax lien legislation." Drye v. United States, 528 U. S. 49, 58 (1999).

A common idiom describes property as a "bundle of sticks" — a collection of individual rights which, in certain combinations, constitute property. See B. Cardozo, Paradoxes of Legal Science 129 (1928) (reprint 2000); see also Dickman v. Commissioner, 465 U. S. 330, 336 (1984). State law determines only which sticks are in a person's bundle. Whether those sticks qualify as "property" for purposes of the federal tax lien statute is a question of federal law.

In looking to state law, we must be careful to consider the substance of the rights state law provides, not merely the labels the State gives these rights or the conclusions it draws from them. Such state law labels are irrelevant to the federal question of which bundles of rights constitute property that may be attached by a federal tax lien. In Drye v. United States, supra, we considered a situation where state law allowed an heir subject to a federal tax lien to disclaim his interest in the estate. The state law also provided that such a disclaimer would "creat[e] the legal fiction" that the heir had predeceased the decedent and would correspondingly be deemed to have had no property interest in the estate. Id., at 53. We unanimously held that this state law fiction did not control the federal question and looked instead to the realities of the heir's interest. We concluded that, despite the State's characterization, the heir possessed a "right to property" in the estate — the right to accept the inheritance or pass it along to another — to which the federal lien could attach. Id., at 59-61.

III

We turn first to the question of what rights respondent's husband had in the entireties property by virtue of state law. In order to understand these rights, the tenancy by the entirety must first be placed in some context.

English common law provided three legal structures for the concurrent ownership of property that have survived into modern times: tenancy in common, joint tenancy, and tenancy by the entirety. 1 G. Thompson, Real Property § 4.06(g) (D. Thomas ed. 1994) (hereinafter Thompson). The tenancy in common is now the most common form of concurrent ownership. 7 R. Powell & P. Rohan, Real Property §51.01[3] (M. Wolf ed. 2001) (hereinafter Powell). The common law characterized tenants in common as each owning a separate fractional share in undivided property. Tenants in common may each unilaterally alienate their shares through sale or gift or place encumbrances upon these shares. They also have the power to pass these shares to their heirs upon death. Tenants in common have many other rights in the property, including the right to use the property, to exclude third parties from it, and to receive a portion of any income produced from it.

Joint tenancies were the predominant form of concurrent ownership at common law, and still persist in some States today. 4 Thompson § 31.05. The common law characterized each joint tenant as possessing the entire estate, rather than a fractional share: "[J]oint-tenants have one and the same interest... held by one and the same undivided possession." 2 W. Blackstone, Commentaries on the Laws of England 180 (1766). Joint tenants possess many of the rights enjoyed by tenants in common: the right to use, to exclude, and to enjoy a share of the property's income. The main difference between a joint tenancy and a tenancy in common is that a joint tenant also has a right of automatic inheritance known as "survivorship." Upon the death of one joint tenant, that tenant's share in the property does not pass through will or the rules of intestate succession; rather, the remaining tenant or tenants automatically inherit it. Id., at 183; 7 Powell §51.01 [3]. Joint tenants' right to alienate their individual shares is also somewhat different. In order for one tenant to alienate his or her individual interest in the tenancy, the estate must first be severed — that is, converted to a tenancy in common with each tenant possessing an equal fractional share. Id., § 51.04[1], Most States allowing joint tenancies facilitate alienation, however, by allowing severance to automatically accompany a conveyance of that interest or any other overt act indicating an intent to sever.

A tenancy by the entirety is a unique sort of concurrent ownership that can only exist between married persons. 4 Thompson § 33.02. Because of the common-law fiction that the husband and wife were one person at law (that person, practically speaking, was the husband, see J. Cribbet et al., Cases and Materials on Property 329 (6th ed. 1990)), Blackstone did not characterize the tenancy by the entirety as a form of concurrent ownership at all. Instead, he thought that entireties property was a form of single ownership by the marital unity. Neither spouse was considered to own any individual interest in the estate; rather, it belonged to the couple.

Like joint tenants, tenants by the entirety enjoy the right of survivorship. Also like a joint tenancy, unilateral alienation of a spouse's interest in entireties property is typically not possible without severance. Unlike joint tenancies, however, tenancies by the entirety cannot easily be severed unilaterally. Typically, severance requires the consent of both spouses or the ending of the marriage in divorce. At common law, all of the other rights associated with the entireties property belonged to the husband: as the head of the household, he could control the use of the property and the exclusion of others from it and enjoy all of the income produced from it. [The husband's control of the property was so extensive that, despite the rules on alienation, the common law eventually provided that he could unilaterally alienate entireties property without severance subject only to the wife's survivorship interest.

With the passage of the Married Women's Property Acts in the late 19th century granting women distinct rights with respect to marital property, most States either abolished the tenancy by the entirety or altered it significantly. Michigan's version of the estate is typical of the modern tenancy by the entirety. Following Blackstone, Michigan characterizes its tenancy by the entirety as creating no individual rights whatsoever: "It is well settled under the law of this State that one tenant by the entirety has no interest separable from that of the other .... Each is vested with an entire title." Long v. Earle, 277 Mich. 505, 517, 269 N. W. 577, 581 (1936). And yet, in Michigan, each tenant by the entirety possesses the right of survivorship. Mich.

Comp. Laws Ann. § 554.872(g) (West Supp. 1997), recodified at § 700.2901(2)(g) (West Supp. Pamphlet 2001). Each spouse — the wife as well as the husband — may also use the property, exclude third parties from it, and receive an equal share of the income produced by it. See §557.71 (West 1988). Neither spouse may unilaterally alienate or encumber the property, Long v. Earle, supra, at 517, 269 N. W., at 581; Rogers v. Rogers, 136 Mich. App. 125, 134, 356 N. W. 2d 288, 292 (1984), although this may be accomplished with mutual consent, Eadus v. Hunter, 249 Mich. 190, 228 N. W. 782 (1930). Divorce ends the tenancy by the entirety, generally giving each spouse an equal interest in the property as a tenant in common, unless the divorce decree specifies otherwise.

In determining whether respondent's husband possessed "property" or "rights to property" within the meaning of 26 U. S. C. § 6321, we look to the individual rights created by these state law rules. According to Michigan law, respondent's husband had, among other rights, the following rights with respect to the entireties property: the right to use the property, the right to exclude third parties from it, the right to a share of income produced from it, the right of survivorship, the right to become a tenant in common with equal shares upon divorce, the right to sell the property with the respondent's consent and to receive half the proceeds from such a sale, the right to place an encumbrance on the property with the respondent's consent, and the right to block respondent from selling or encumbering the property unilaterally.

IV

We turn now to the federal question of whether the rights Michigan law granted to respondent's husband as a tenant by the entirety qualify as "property" or "rights to property" under §6321. The statutory language authorizing the tax lien "is broad and reveals on its face that Congress meant to reach every interest in property that a taxpayer might have." United States v. National Bank of Commerce, 472 U. S., at 719-720. "Stronger language could hardly have been selected to reveal a purpose to assure the collection of taxes." Glass City Bank v. United States, 326 U. S. 265, 267 (1945). We conclude that the husband's rights in the entireties property fall within this broad statutory language.

Michigan law grants a tenant by the entirety some of the most essential property rights: the right to use the property, to receive income produced by it, and to exclude others from it. See Dolan v. City of Tigard, 512 U. S. 374, 384 (1994) ("[T]he right to exclude others" is " 'one of the most essential sticks in the bundle of rights that are commonly characterized as property' " (quoting Kaiser Aetna v. United States, 444 U. S. 164, 176 (1979))); Loretto v. Teleprompter Manhattan CATV Corp., 458 U. S. 419, 435 (1982) (including "use" as one of the "[property rights in a physical thing"). These rights alone may be sufficient to subject the husband's interest in the entireties property to the federal tax lien. They gave him a substantial degree of control over the entireties property, and, as we noted in Drye, "in determining whether a federal taxpayer's state-law rights constitute 'property' or 'rights to property,' [t]he important consideration is the breadth of the control the [taxpayer] could exercise over the property." 528 U. S., at 61 (some internal quotation marks omitted).

The husband's rights in the estate, however, went beyond use, exclusion, and income. He also possessed the right to alienate (or otherwise encumber) the property with the consent of respondent, his wife. Loretto, supra, at 435 (the right to "dispose" of an item is a property right). It is true, as respondent notes, that he lacked the right to unilaterally alienate the property, a right that is often in the bundle of property rights. There is no reason to believe, however, that this one stick — the right of unilateral alienation — is essential to the category of "property."

This Court has already stated that federal tax liens may attach to property that cannot be unilaterally alienated. In United States v. Rodgers, 461 U. S. 677 (1983), we considered the Federal Government's power to foreclose homestead property attached by a federal tax lien. Texas law provided that "'the owner or claimant of the property claimed as homestead [may not], if married, sell or abandon the homestead without the consent of the other spouse.' " Id., at 684-685 (quoting Tex. Const., Art. 16, §50). We nonetheless stated that "[i]n the homestead context . . . , there is no doubt... that not only do both spouses (rather than neither) have an independent interest in the homestead property, but that a federal tax lien can at least attach to each of those interests." 461 U. S., at 703, n. 31; cf. Drye, supra, at 60, n. 7 (noting that "an interest in a spendthrift trust has been held to constitute "'property" for purposes of §6321' even though the beneficiary may not transfer that interest to third parties").

Excluding property from a federal tax lien simply because the taxpayer does not have the power to unilaterally alienate it would, moreover, exempt a rather large amount of what is commonly thought of as property. It would exempt not only the type of property discussed in Rodgers, but also some community property. Community property States often provide that real community property cannot be alienated without the consent of both spouses. See, e. g., Ariz. Rev. Stat. Ann. §25-214(0 (2000); Cal. Fam. Code Ann. §1102 (West 1994); Idaho Code §32-912 (1996); La. Civ. Code Ann., Art. 2347 (West Supp. 2002); Nev. Rev. Stat. Ann. § 123.230(3) (Supp. 2001); N. M. Stat. Ann. §40-3-13 (1999); Wash. Rev. Code §26.16.030(3) (1994). Accordingly, the fact that respondent's husband could not unilaterally alienate the property does not preclude him from possessing "property and rights to property" for the purposes of § 6321.

Respondent's husband also possessed the right of survivorship — the right to automatically inherit the whole of the estate should his wife predecease him. Respondent argues that this interest was merely an expectancy, which we suggested in Drye would not constitute "property" for the purposes of a federal tax lien. 528 U. S., at 60, n. 7 ("[We do not mean to suggest] that an expectancy that has pecuniary value . . . would fall within § 6321 prior to the time it ripens into a present estate"). Drye did not decide this question, however, nor do we need to do so here. As we have discussed above, a number of the sticks in respondent's husband's bundle were presently existing. It is therefore not necessary to decide whether the right to survivorship alone would qualify as "property" or "rights to property" under §6321.

That the rights of respondent's husband in the entireties property constitute "property" or "rights to property" "belonging to" him is further underscored by the fact that, if the conclusion were otherwise, the entireties property would belong to no one for the purposes of § 6321. Respondent had no more interest in the property than her husband; if neither of them had a property interest in the entireties property, who did? This result not only seems absurd, but would also allow spouses to shield their property from federal taxation by classifying it as entireties property, facilitating abuse of the federal tax system. Johnson, After Drye: The Likely Attachment of the Federal Tax Lien to Tenancy-by-the-Entireties Interests, 75 Ind. L. J. 1163, 1171 (2000).

***

Respondent argues that, whether or not we would conclude that respondent's husband had an interest in the entireties property, legislative history indicates that Congress did not intend that a federal tax lien should attach to such an interest. In 1954, the Senate rejected a proposed amendment to the tax lien statute that would have provided that the lien attach to "property or rights to property (including the interest- of such person as tenant by the entirety)." S. Rep. No. 1622, 83d Cong., 2d Sess., 575 (1954). We have elsewhere held, however, that failed legislative proposals are "a particularly dangerous ground on which to rest an interpretation of a prior statute," Pension Benefit Guaranty Corporation v. LTV Corp., 496 U. S. 633, 650 (1990), reasoning that " '[congressional inaction lacks persuasive significance because several equally tenable inferences may be drawn from such inaction, including the inference that the existing legislation already incorporated the offered change.' " Central Bank of Denver, N. A. v. First Interstate Bank of Denver, N. A., 511 U. S. 164, 187 (1994). This case exemplifies the risk of relying on such legislative history. As we noted in United States v. Rodgers, 461 U. S., at 704, n. 31, some legislative history surrounding the 1954 amendment indicates that the House intended the amendment to be nothing more than a "clarification" of existing law, and that the Senate rejected the amendment only because it found it "superfluous." See H. R. Rep. No. 1337, 83d Cong., 2d Sess., A406 (1954) (noting that the amendment would "clarif[y] the term 'property and rights to property' by expressly including therein the interest of the delinquent taxpayer in an estate by the entirety"); S. Rep. No. 1622, at 575 ("It is not clear what change in existing law would be made by the parenthetical phrase. The deletion of the phrase is intended to continue the existing law").

***

We therefore conclude that respondent's husband's interest in the entireties property constituted "property" or "rights to property" for the purposes of the federal tax lien statute. We recognize that Michigan makes a different choice with respect to state law creditors: "[L]and held by husband and wife as tenants by entirety is not subject to levy under execution on judgment rendered against either husband or wife alone." Sanford v. Bertrau, 204 Mich. 244, 247, 169 N. W. 880, 881 (1918). But that by no means dictates our choice. The interpretation of 26 U. S. C. §6321 is a federal question, and in answering that question we are in no way bound by state courts' answers to similar questions involving state law. As we elsewhere have held, "'exempt status under state law does not bind the federal collector.'" Drye v. United States, 528 U. S., at 59. See also Rodgers, supra, at 701 (clarifying that the Supremacy Clause "provides the underpinning for the Federal Government's right to sweep aside state-created exemptions").

V

We express no view as to the proper valuation of respondent's husband's interest in the entireties property, leaving this for the Sixth Circuit to determine on remand. . . .

The judgment of the United States Court of Appeals for the Sixth Circuit is accordingly reversed, and the case is remanded for proceedings consistent with this opinion.

It is so ordered.

7.3.3
Discussion: Notes, Questions, and Problems

7.3.3.1
Discussion Note #7. Feminist perspective of Sawada v. Endo

For a feminist perspective of *Sawada v. Endo*, excerpted above, see Donna Litman, Sawada v. Endo—*Rewritten Opinion in* Feminist Judgments: Rewritten Property Opinions (Eloisa C. Rodriguez-Dod & Elena Marty-Nelson eds., Cambridge University Press 2021). For a discussion of Litman's revised feminist opinion, see

Susan Etta Keller, *Commentary on* Sawada v. Endo—*Rewritten Opinion, in* Feminist Judgments: Rewritten Property Opinions (Eloisa C. Rodriguez-Dod & Elena Marty-Nelson eds., Cambridge University Press 2021).

7.3.3.2

Discussion Problem #8. Alicia's creditor problem

Maria left Blackacre to her two daughters, Alicia and Belinda, as "joint tenants with rights of survivorship and not as tenants in common." Alicia defaulted on a guarantee and a judgment was entered against her. Failing all other collection efforts, Alicia's creditor tries to enforce the judgment against Alicia's half interest in Blackacre. Will Alicia's creditor be successful?

7.4

Severance

It is important to distinguish a ***severance*** of a concurrent ownership from termination of a concurrent ownership. A severance does not terminate the concurrent cotenant relationship. Rather, a severance removes the feature of right of survivorship. For example, assume mom devises a beach house to her four sons as "joint tenants and not as tenants in common." Assume further that one of the sons sells his quarter interest to a friend. The friend did not acquire the interest at the same time or from the same instrument as the sons and thus does not have the unity of time or title. The friend would have a tenancy in common interest, not a joint tenancy interest. Would activities short of selling or giving away a cotenant's interest amount to a severance? For example, would leasing the cotenant's share effectuate a severance? Can a cotenant effectuate a severance and yet retain a concurrent interest in the property?

7.4.1

Porter v. Porter
472 So. 2d 630 (Ala. 1985)

Alabama Supreme Court

ALMON, Justice.

This is an appeal by Mary Jane Porter from a partial summary judgment rendered in favor of Martha Porter. The issue is whether a divorce decree destroyed a joint tenancy with right of survivorship in real estate.   issue

The appellant, Mary Jane Porter, and the late Denis M. Porter were married in 1948. In 1963 they purchased a house and lot in Jefferson County under a deed containing the following habendum clause:

> "[Grantors] do grant, bargain, sell and convey unto the said Denis M. Porter and wife, Mary Jane Porter as joint tenants, with right of survivorship, the following described real estate...."

> "TO HAVE AND TO HOLD unto the said Denis M. Porter and wife, Mary Jane Porter, as joint tenants, with right of survivorship, their heirs and assigns, forever; it being the intention of the parties to this conveyance, that (unless the joint tenancy hereby created is severed or terminated during the joint lives of the grantees herein), in the event one grantee herein survives the other, the entire interest in fee simple shall pass to the surviving grantee, and if one grantee does not survive the other, then the heirs and assigns of the grantee herein shall take as tenants in common."

The appellant and Denis Porter were divorced in 1976. The final judgment of divorce contained the following references to the real property in question:

> "[Fifth] (b) Defendant/Cross-Plaintiff [Mary Jane Porter] shall have the right to exclusive occupancy to the former residence of the parties, property now jointly owned by them until a change in circumstances warrants a modification of this Decree in this respect, and Plaintiff/Cross-Defendant [Denis M. Porter] shall maintain said property in a reasonably good and tenantable condition. Plaintiff/Cross-Defendant [Denis M. Porter] shall maintain adequate insurance on said property; shall pay all charges of utility companies, less charges for long distance telephone calls for persons other than Plaintiff/Cross-Defendant [Denis M. Porter], and shall pay all ad valorem taxes on said property.

211

(c) During the continuance of the obligations of sub-paragraph (b) above:

Plaintiff/Cross-Defendant [Denis M. Porter] shall pay all indebtedness as or before it matures under the present mortgages on the property involved, which payments as under principal will inure in equal proportion to the parties as joint owners."

Sometime after his divorce from appellant, Denis Porter married Martha Porter, appellee, and remained married to her until his death in 1983. There was no modification of the final judgment of divorce in regard to the real property, and neither Denis Porter nor appellant attempted to convey his or her interest in the real property prior to the death of Denis Porter.

appellee arg

Appellee, as executrix of the estate of Denis Porter (later substituted as Martha Porter, individually) filed a complaint for the sale of the property for division. She alleged that Denis Porter's estate was a tenant in common in the property with appellant, claiming that the final judgment of divorce terminated the survivorship provisions of the 1963 deed and made the parties joint owners of the property subject to a sale for division upon petition of either party. Appellant denied any termination of the joint tenancy and moved for summary judgment upon the pleadings and uncontradicted facts presented. Appellee answered by also moving for summary judgment.

The trial court entered a decree of partial summary judgment, finding that "Plaintiff [appellee] and Defendant [appellant] are co-tenants in the property ... and each owns a one-half (1/2) undivided interest therein." ...

The issue in this case is whether the joint tenancy with right of survivorship was destroyed by the 1976 divorce decree. ... *issue*

***

At common law a joint tenancy could be severed by destruction of one of the four unities, i.e., time, title, interest, and possession. *Shrout v. Seale*, 287 Ala. 215, 250 So.2d 592 (1971); II W. Blackstone, *Commentaries on the Laws of England*, ISO-82.

The issue is whether the divorce decree destroyed the unity of possession and converted the joint tenancy with right of survivorship into a tenancy in common by granting exclusive occupancy of the house to appellant. The major distinction between a tenancy in common and a joint tenancy is that the interest held by tenants in common is devisable and descendible, whereas the interest held by joint tenants passes automatically to the last survivor. Thus, if the granting of exclusive possession to appellant destroyed the joint tenancy and converted it into a tenancy in common, appellee would own a half interest in the property through Mr. Porter's will. If the joint tenancy was not destroyed, appellant would own the entire interest by virtue of being the survivor.

Unity of possession requires that the property be held by one and the same undivided possession. 4 G. Thompson, *Commentaries on the Modern Law of Real Property,* § 1776 (1979). Unity of possession means that all joint tenants have a common right to possess and enjoy the property. Possession by one co-tenant is presumed to be possession by all.

appellee arg

Appellee argues that since the divorce decree gave appellant "exclusive occupancy" that means she was given exclusive "possession." This argument concludes that the unity of possession is destroyed, the joint tenancy is destroyed, and a tenancy in common results.

When one or all of the unities of time, title, and interest are destroyed the joint tenancy is severed and a tenancy in common results. This result follows from the rule of law that a tenancy in common requires only one unity, that of possession.

Thus, if we assume that by granting exclusive occupancy to the appellant the unity of possession was destroyed, then the joint tenancy was severed. No other recognized common law joint estate arose and we are left with the conclusion that the divorce court either granted absolute ownership to one of the parties or partitioned the property or some variation of the above. This result is contrary to the divorce decree. The granting of exclusive possession of the house to appellant did not destroy the unity of possession. The divorce decree provides that appellant shall have exclusive occupancy of the house "until a change in the circumstances warrants a modification of this decree in this respect." This retention of jurisdiction, with respect to the jointly owned property, indicates that the court left itself an option to later modify the occupancy or terminate the joint tenancy. This retention of jurisdiction to later modify the decree also indicates that the exclusive occupancy given to the appellant was temporary as opposed to permanent. In *Hamaker v. Hamaker,* 57 Ala.App. 333, 328 So.2d 588 (1976), the Court of Civil Appeals in construing a divorce decree which gave the former wife the occupancy and use of the jointly owned property held that the

"retention of jurisdiction leads us to believe that allowing the wife to use the property was purely a temporary measure and that a future permanent disposition was clearly envisioned."

Id., 57 Ala.App. at 338, 328 So.2d at 592. The mere temporary division of property held by joint tenants, without an intention to partition, will not destroy the unity of possession and amount to a severance of the joint tenancy.

***

A divorce does not necessarily sever a joint tenancy. Although divorcing parties are usually desirous of settling all their property rights, there is no requirement that the divorce modify the previous ownership. A divorce decree which is silent with respect to property held jointly with a right of survivorship does not automatically destroy the existing survivorship provisions. *Summerlin v. Bowden, supra.* The divorce decree is effectively silent as to the status of the property. To hold that the divorce decree severed the joint tenancy in this case would be to convey the property by implication. Real property cannot be conveyed by implication.

The divorce decree did not destroy the joint tenancy with right of survivorship. Consequently, the property vested in the appellant upon the death of her joint tenant, Mr. Porter. The judgment is therefore reversed and the cause remanded.

REVERSED AND REMANDED.

7.4.2

Taylor v. Canterbury
92 P.3d 961 (Colo. 2004)

Colorado Supreme Court

Justice KOURLIS

delivered the Opinion of the Court.

I. INTRODUCTION

issue

The question we address in this case is whether one joint tenant may extinguish a joint tenancy by conveying his interest in real property back to himself as a tenant in common. In the past, courts did not honor such transactions because of two premises: one, that someone could not be both a grantor and a grantee in the same real property transaction; and two, that in order to extinguish a joint tenancy, a joint tenant had to destroy one of the "four unities" of time, title, interest, or possession.

What is not at issue in this opinion is whether a joint tenant may destroy a joint tenancy without the consent of the other joint tenant or tenants. It is indisputable under Colorado law that one joint tenant may unilaterally dissolve the survivorship interest by creating a tenancy in common in lieu of a joint tenancy. However, for a joint tenant to sever the joint tenancy yet remain an owner of the property, courts required the use of a "strawman" transaction whereby the joint tenant executed a deed to a third person, and then a deed back from that third person to the joint tenant-this time as a tenant in common. By transferring legal title to the property held in joint tenancy to a third party, the transferor destroyed the unities of time and title and severed the joint tenancy.

We conclude that this circuitous process is no longer required under Colorado law because the two premises undergirding it are no longer valid. In Colorado and other jurisdictions around the country, joint tenancy law has evolved. The four unities are no longer the compass; rather, the polestar by which joint tenancies are now measured is the intent of the parties. For this reason, we have recognized in recent cases that acts inconsistent with the right of survivorship operate to sever the joint tenancy. Similarly, by operation of statute, the notion that a property owner may not be both the grantor and grantee in the same transaction has evaporated. Currently, the owner of real property may create a joint tenancy by conveying real property back to himself and one or more persons as joint tenants. Hence, the common law notions that once drove the jurisprudence of joint tenancy are gone. In their place are principles that focus on the intent of the property owners.

Therefore, we find no common law or legislative support for preventing a landowner from doing directly what he can do indirectly. We hold that a joint tenant who unilaterally conveys his interest in real property back to himself, with the intent of creating a tenancy in common, effectively severs the joint tenancy as to that joint tenant and the remaining joint tenant or tenants. We reverse the court of appeals and remand the case for further proceedings consistent with this opinion.

II. FACTS AND PROCEDURAL HISTORY

Terrell Taylor (Taylor) was the owner in fee simple of a 666-acre ranch in Fremont County, Colorado. The Petitioner, Noah Taylor, is the personal representative for Taylor, now deceased. On March 4, 1991, Taylor executed a warranty deed that conveyed that property from Taylor as sole owner to Taylor and Lucy I. Canterbury (Canterbury) as joint tenants. The validity of that deed is not in dispute.

In 1997, Taylor executed a second deed: this time a quitclaim deed purporting to transfer the property back to himself and Canterbury as tenants in common. Taylor's manifest intent to sever the joint tenancy between himself and Canterbury, and to create a tenancy in common, could not have been clearer. The second deed stated: "It is my intention by this deed to sever the joint tenancy created by [the 1991 deed], and to create a tenancy in common." The deed was duly recorded on June 16, 1997- the same day it was executed. Taylor died on August 20, 1999.

Canterbury filed an action to quiet title to the property to herself as surviving joint tenant. In that complaint, she also asked the trial court to set aside the 1997 conveyance and award her damages arising out of Taylor's attempted conveyance. Following a bench trial, the trial court found that "as a matter of law, the right of survivorship interest of a joint tenant is an estate in land which vests on the creation of the joint tenancy." Relying on our decision in Lee's Estate v. Graber, 170 Colo. 419, 462 P.2d 492 (1969), the court concluded "that the rights of a joint tenant or joint tenants are vested and fixed at the time of the creation of the joint tenancy" and therefore the 1997 deed failed to effectively sever the joint tenancy between Canterbury and Taylor. On that basis, the court determined that "all interests which Taylor owned ... at the time of his death passed to [Canterbury] pursuant to the 1991 deed."

216

The court of appeals affirmed the trial court's judgment in Canterbury v. Taylor, 74 P.3d 457 (Colo.App.2003), holding that a joint tenant cannot effectively sever a joint tenancy by executing a deed which purports to convey title back to the two individuals as tenants in common. Like the trial court, the court of appeals also relied on our decision in Graber to conclude that once a joint tenancy is created, the rights of each joint tenant are "fixed and vested." Thus, the court concluded that Taylor's unilateral effort to sever the joint tenancy was an improper "form of dominion" over Canterbury's rights to the property. The court also noted that Taylor's conveyance to himself was contrary to the general rule that a grantor and grantee cannot be the same person for purposes of conveying property.

We granted certiorari to address the issue of whether it is "permissible for a joint owner of real estate to sever the joint tenancy by unilaterally conveying his interest in the property back to himself to create a tenancy in common with the other joint tenant." We answer that question in the affirmative. Therefore, we reverse the court of appeals and remand this case for further proceedings consistent with this opinion.

III. ANALYSIS

This case presents an issue of first impression in Colorado: whether the holder of an interest in joint tenancy may unilaterally sever that joint tenancy by conveying property back to himself as a tenant in common. We begin our analysis by discussing the basic characteristics of the two forms of concurrent ownership implicated in this case: tenancies in common and joint tenancies. Next, we analyze the law regarding the termination of joint tenancies in Colorado. Finally, we examine the specific subject of the validity of the transaction at issue in this case and conclude that, in light of the evolution of joint tenancy law in Colorado and other jurisdictions throughout the country, the common law principles that once supported the prohibition against a unilateral self-conveyance no longer have vitality.

A. Tenancy in Common and Joint Tenancy

A tenancy in common is a form of ownership in which each co-tenant owns a separate fractional share of undivided property. United States v. Craft, 535 U.S. 274, 279-80, 122 S.Ct. 1414, 152 L.Ed.2d 437 (2002) (citing to 7 R. Powell & P. Rohan, Real Property § 50.01[1] (M. Wolf ed.2001) (hereinafter Powell)). All co-tenants share a single right to possession of the entire interest. 7 Powell, supra, § 50.01[1]. Each co-tenant also possesses the right to: unilaterally alienate his or her interest through sale, gift or encumbrance; to exclude third parties from the property; and to receive a portion of any income derived from the property. Craft, 535 U.S. at 280, 122 S.Ct. 1414.

joint tenancy

Conversely, joint tenancy is a form of ownership in which each joint tenant possesses the entire estate, rather than a fractional share. Upon the death of one joint tenant, the remaining joint tenant or tenants automatically inherit that tenant's share in the property. Id. ("Upon the death of one joint tenant, that tenant's share in the property does not pass through will or the rules of intestate succession; rather, the remaining tenant or tenants automatically inherit it."). This feature, called the "right of survivorship," is the principal distinction between a joint tenancy and a tenancy in common. Bradley v. Mann, 34 Colo.App. 135, 525 P.2d 492, 493 (1974) ("Upon the death of one of the co-tenants in joint tenancy, the entire undivided interest of the deceased passes, by operation of law, to the surviving co-tenant.").

At common law, joint tenancies were the favored form of concurrent ownership of real property. If property was conveyed to two or more persons, the law presumed that a joint tenancy was intended. 4 David A. Thomas, Thompson on Real Property § 31.06(a) (David A. Thomas ed.1994) (hereinafter Thompson). For purposes of establishing a joint tenancy, the "four unities" of time, title, interest, and possession were essential components. 7 Powell, supra, § 51.01[2] (citing to 2 Blackstone, Commentaries 180. This requirement meant that to create a joint tenancy, "a conveyance had to convey to two or more persons at the same time the same title to the same interest with the same right of possession." 7 Powell, supra, § 51.01[2]. If one of the four unities ceased to exist, a tenancy in common remained. Riddle v. Harmon, 102 Cal.App.3d 524, 162 Cal.Rptr. 530, 531 (1980).

joint tenancy Colorado

Today, in Colorado, joint tenancies are no longer the presumptive form of concurrent ownership of real property. Rather, tenancies in common are favored and the very existence of the joint tenancy is circumscribed by statute. Courts strictly construe instruments purporting to create a joint tenancy and do not recognize joint tenancies created by instruments that lack statutorily prescribed language.

The requirements for establishing a joint tenancy in real property are set forth in section 88-31-101(1), 10 C.R.S. (2008). That provision states:

> No estate in joint tenancy in real property, except when conveyed or devised to executors, trustees, or fiduciaries, shall be created or established unless, in the instrument conveying the property or in the will devising the same, it is declared that the property is conveyed or devised in joint tenancy or as joint tenants. The abbreviation "JTWROS" and the phrase "as joint tenants with right of survivorship" or "in joint tenancy with right of survivorship" shall have the same meaning. Any grantor in any such instrument of conveyance may also be one of the grantees therein.

Thus, to establish a joint tenancy in Colorado, there must only be specific language evidencing the intent to create a joint tenancy. The four unities have been abolished by statute.

B. Termination of Joint Tenancies

We turn to the question of how a joint tenancy may be terminated. In that inquiry, we pause to address the notion that the interests associated with the ownership of real property held in joint tenancy are fixed and vested. That principle comes most recently from our decision in Lee's Estate v. Graber where we addressed the issue of whether "the gift of a joint interest in real estate held jointly with the donor is complete and irrevocable." 462 P.2d at 498. Answering that question affirmatively, we held that "[i]n the case of real property, rights under a joint tenancy are fixed and vested in the joint tenants at the time of the creation of the joint tenancy." Id. at 494. As a result, once a donor creates a joint tenancy, he or she may not convey or otherwise interfere with the property interests vested in the other joint tenant by virtue of the conveyance. . . .

Graber does not hold that the right of survivorship itself is irrevocable or "fixed and vested" and cannot be eliminated without the consent of the other joint tenant or tenants. Indeed, such a holding would fly in the face of years of precedent to the contrary. Even characterizing survivorship as a "right" is somewhat misleading. Rather, survivorship is

219

an expectancy that is not irrevocably fixed upon the creation of the estate; it arises only upon success in the ultimate gamble-survival-and then only if the unity of the estate has not theretofore been destroyed by voluntary conveyance, by partition proceedings, by involuntary alienation under an execution, or by any other action which operates to sever the joint tenancy.

Tenhet v. Boswell, 18 Cal.3d 150, 133 Cal.Rptr. 10, 554 P.2d 330, 334 (1976) (internal citations omitted). Thus, in order for an expectancy of a survivorship interest to become a vested right, one joint tenant must survive the death of another joint tenant during the period of time that the joint tenancy remains intact.

Hence, the right of survivorship is not fixed in such a way as to constrain a joint tenant from changing his mind and abrogating it. Rather, a joint tenant may unilaterally eliminate the survivorship element of the ownership rights, and by doing so, eliminate his own survivorship rights as well.[1] Stated otherwise, a joint tenant has the absolute right to terminate a joint tenancy unilaterally.

In this case, therefore, we are not dealing with whether a joint tenant may sever the tenancy and create a tenancy in common; we are dealing with the question of how that can be accomplished. Historically, whether the severance of a joint tenancy was effective turned on the question of whether the act was sufficient to destroy any of the four unities. Bradley, 525 P.2d at 493. Thus, conveying the property to a third party,[2] transferring legal title into a trust, executing a lien,[3] or foreclosing on a mortgage, were all considered to be effective means of severing a joint tenancy. We also specifically recognized the antiquated convention whereby the joint tenant wishing to terminate a joint tenancy would convey the property to a strawman who would in turn reconvey the property back to the former joint tenant as a tenant in common. The rationale underlying all of these transactions was that because legal title was transferred, the unities of time and title were destroyed, and therefore the joint tenancy, and the survivorship interest associated with it, were destroyed as well.

Along these same lines, mortgages,[4] leases and other encumbrances[5] that did not involve the transfer of legal title were considered insufficient to sever a joint tenancy. Again, the underlying rationale was that because the grantor had not transferred title to the real property, the unities remained intact and the transaction did not sever the joint tenancy.

In stark contrast to traditional common law, "[the modern tendency is to not require that the act of the co-tenant be destructive of one of the essential four unities of time, title, possession or interest before a joint tenancy is terminated." Mann v. Bradley, 188 Colo. 392, 535 P.2d 213, 214 (1975). In Mann, we recognized that a joint tenancy may be terminated by mere agreement between the joint tenants, despite the fact that no property is conveyed or interests alienated. Thus, in determining whether a joint tenancy has been created or severed, we look not to the four unities, but rather to the intent of the parties. Actions that are inconsistent with the right of survivorship may terminate a joint tenancy.

C. Unilateral Self-Conveyance

As we have noted, historically, a joint tenant wishing to sever the joint tenancy used a strawman transaction. That method satisfied the common law proscription that "a conveyance to oneself has no legal consequence and therefore does not destroy any unities." Thompson, supra, § $1.08(b). This "two-to-transfer" artifice stemmed from the English common law feoffment ceremony with livery of seisin. Riddle, 162 Cal.Rptr. at 583. Under the livery of seisin, the grantor of property had to transfer a physical remnant of the land (such as a lump of dirt or a twig) to the grantee. Therefore, the grantor could not be both grantor and grantee simultaneously.

In light of the changes to joint tenancy law in Colorado, the justifications for prohibiting unilateral self-conveyances no longer exist. For example, section 38-81-101 expressly allows the owner of property to become both the grantor and the grantee for purposes of establishing a joint tenancy. This concept directly conflicts with the four unities doctrine and the notion that one could not be a grantor and a grantee. Further, the livery of seisin requirement has been explicitly abolished in Colorado. § 88-80-1083, 10 C.R.S. (2003). In short, none of the underpinnings that led to the artifice of a third-party transfer to sever a joint tenancy have continuing vitality.

Other jurisdictions have similarly concluded that it no longer makes sense to prohibit joint tenants from doing directly what they are already able to do indirectly through a strawman transaction. For instance, in Hendrickson v. Minneapolis Fed. Sav. & Loan Ass'n, 281 Minn. 462, 161 N.W.2d 688 (1968), the Supreme Court of Minnesota rejected the strawman requirement. The court in that case recognized the validity of a "Declaration of Election to Sever Survivorship of Joint Tenancy" by one joint tenant for purposes of severing the joint tenancy.

Similarly, California has rejected the strawman requirement. Riddle 162 Cal.Rptr. at 534. In that case, the court addressed a unilateral self-conveyance like the one at issue here. There, the court relied heavily on the fact that California, like Colorado, allowed for the creation of a joint tenancy by a self-conveyance. In deciding that the grantor need not make use of a strawman to sever the joint tenancy, the court stated that "[in view of the rituals that are available to unilaterally terminate a joint tenancy, there is little virtue in steadfastly adhering to cumbersome feudal law requirements." Id. at 584. Quoting Justice Holmes, the court went on to state that

> [i]t is revolting to have no better reason for a rule of law than that so it was laid down in the time of Henry IV. It is still more revolting if the grounds upon which it was laid down have vanished long since, and the rule simply persists from blind imitation of the past.

Id.

Since Harmon, other states addressing this issue have followed suit. See Minonk State Bank v. Grassman, 95 Ill.2d 392, 69 Ill.Dec. 387, 447 N.E.2d 822, 825 (1983) (holding that conveyance of a joint tenant's property back to herself effectively severed the joint tenancy); In re Estate of Knickerbocker, 912 P.2d 969, 976 (Utah 1996) (holding that a joint tenant may effectively sever a joint tenancy by executing and recording a unilateral self-conveyance).

The exception is Nebraska. In Krause v. Crossley, 202 Neb. 806, 277 N.W.2d 242, 246 (1979), the Supreme Court of Nebraska disallowed the severance of a joint tenancy by a joint tenant who attempted to reconvey property to himself as tenant in common. That court specifically relied upon the notion that in order for title of property to transfer, the grantor and grantee had to be separate individuals.

We conclude, in light of Colorado's statutory and precedential approach to joint tenancy, that a joint tenant may sever a joint tenancy by conveying the property to himself or herself as a tenant in common, without the need for an intermediary strawman. The statute, which permits the grantor and grantee to be one and the same, and which bypasses the four unities, does not preclude such a termination of the joint tenancy. The underlying premises that gave rise to the fiction of the strawman transaction in the first place have disappeared in the law of real property; and the law does not require a futile act. The strawman transaction does not protect the other joint tenant to any greater degree than the direct transfer, and, we repeat, the overriding consideration is that the survivorship interest is not vested.

IV. CONCLUSION

We reverse the court of appeals and thus the trial court's conclusion that the deed from Taylor to Taylor as a tenant in common was not valid for purposes of severing the joint tenancy. Rather, we conclude that Taylor had the right to sever the joint tenancy by means of a conveyance to himself. Taylor retained an undivided one-half interest in the property as a tenant in common at the time of his death in 1999. We return this case to the court of appeals for remand to the trial court for proceedings consistent with this opinion.

Justice COATS,

dissenting.

Today the majority abrogates a limitation on the ability of a joint tenant to defeat his co-tenant's right of survivorship, which has been the law of this jurisdiction since before statehood. Following the lead of California, and a handful of other jurisdictions already doing so, the majority concludes, for the first time, that this venerable principle of property law-that a joint tenant may not unilaterally destroy the tenancy without alienating his own interest-no longer serves a useful purpose and has, in effect, already ceased to exist. Because I disagree with the majority's understanding of the current state of the law; its policy choice in derogation of the right of survivorship; and its decision to act in the face of existing (and I believe conflicting) legislation, I respectfully dissent.

***

We have not previously recognized the ability of a joint tenant to unilaterally terminate a joint tenancy except by divesting himself of his joint interest in it. While nothing has prohibited a former joint tenant from reacquiring, as a tenant in common, the proportionate share he formerly held as a joint tenant, his initial conveyance of that interest to a third party terminates the joint tenancy, once and for all. Although the majority derisively refers to a re-conveying third party as a "straw man," such a series of conveyances, regardless of any prior agreements or expectations of the parties, is in no sense a meaningless ritual or legal fiction.

To the contrary, until today, unless a joint tenant was actually divested of his interest in the property, whatever his hope or expectation concerning re-conveyance, the joint tenancy was not severed; and if the joint tenant retained an enforceable right of return, he had not been divested of his interest. As the majority acknowledges, this jurisdiction has never before found a severance to occur upon a mere encumbrance of property over which the tenant retained the right of repayment. See Webster v. Mauz, 702 P.2d 297 (Colo.App.1985) ("[M]ere encumbering of one's own interest in joint tenancy is insufficient to sever...."); cf. Energy Fuels, 618 P.2d at 1119 (joint tenancy is severed by operation of law upon execution sale, after default on deed of trust). Because conveyance to a third party always involves some risk, I disagree that the requirement to actually alienate one's interest provides no more protection to a joint tenant than re-conveyance to oneself, or that it amounts to nothing more than a fiction. Ironically, it is the conveyance of property to oneself that has all the earmarks of a fictitious transaction.

Nor do I find support for the majority's assertion that joint tenancy law in Colorado has evolved to a point at which "the polestar by which joint tenancies are now measured is the intent of the parties." Maj. op. at 962. The "modern tendency" with regard to the termination of joint tenancies, to which the majority alludes apparently does not refer to unilateral action at all but rather derives from prior decisions finding an effective termination by the agreement of both co-tenants. See Mann v. Bradley, 188 Colo. 392, 535 P.2d 213 (1975)(property settlement associated with divorce proceedings. And while the legislature has sought to avoid the unintended creation

224

of rights of survivorship since before statehood, see 1861 Colo. Sess. Laws 66, it has never suggested the abrogation of existing restrictions on the termination of such rights. See § 38-88-101, 10 C.R.S. (2003).

To the extent that the majority's conclusion today is intended to represent an evolution of the common law, it ventures into a field long acknowledged to have been preempted by the legislature. And to the extent that it intends its announcement today to rest on the construction of the statutes already regulating the area, I do not believe its conclusions are supported by accepted principles of statutory interpretation.

More than a half century ago, the general assembly modified the common law by abrogating the prohibition against creating a joint tenancy by the conveyance of a grantor, in part, to himself. See § 4, C40 C.R.S. (1985). Because the current statute, § 38-31-101, 10 C.R.S. (2008), on its face, merely provides an exception to existing limitations for creating a joint tenancy, the majority finds nothing in that statute that would conflict with extending that same exception to severing a joint tenancy. See maj. op. 968. The maxim at law, however, is to the contrary. By expressly articulating one, and only one, exception to the long-accepted rule of property law, the legislature would normally be understood to have rejected other unarticulated exceptions. See Beeghly v. Mack, 20 P.3d 610, 613 (Colo.2001) ("expressio unius exclusio alterius"). A rule of strict construction is especially true of property statutes in derogation of the common law.

In context, it seems clear enough that the legislature intended to, and did, eliminate a hurdle to the creation of a right of survivorship, as long as the right was created deliberately and with an unchallengeable understanding of the consequences. Eliminating a similar hurdle to the termination of the right of survivorship could easily have been accomplished at the same time by the legislature, had it intended to do so. Doing so without the same evidentiary safeguards, as the majority does today, runs directly counter to the clear legislative purpose. In light of the clear and settled state of the law on this point, it is not surprising that the issue has not before been squarely presented to this court.

The majority looks to other states for support, but even by its count, a mere handful of states have abrogated the requirement that the interest of a joint tenant be conveyed to another in order for severance of the joint tenancy to occur. Tellingly, of the extreme minority – a mere half-dozen or so – jurisdictions abrogating the requirement, either by case law or statute, virtually all include some recording requirement to ensure that notice is at least possible, and to limit abuses. Even if I considered the majority's policy choice to be sound, and even if I considered the court free to make that choice in light of existing legislation, I would nevertheless be reluctant to strike down well-established formalities without replacing them with other protections, as the legislature has done with regard to the creation of joint tenancies.

Because I believe the court's action in striking down a principle of property law accepted for scores, if not hundreds, of years and validated by our own legislature is neither wise nor the proper function of the judiciary, I respectfully dissent.

1. We are aware that the ability of one joint tenant to sever the tenancy risks a circumstance where a joint tenant may terminate the survivorship right of other co-tenants while retaining his or her own. For example,

> [a] joint tenant may execute an undisclosed severance, deposit the severing instrument with a third person, and instruct the third person to produce the instrument if the severing joint tenant dies first so the severed half may pass to his or her heirs or devisees. However, if the other joint tenant dies first, the secret severing instrument may be destroyed so that the surviving joint tenant will take the other half of the property by survivorship, thereby becoming owner of the entire property.

England v. Young, 233 Cal.App.3d 1, 284 Cal.Rptr. 361, 363 (1991); see also Samuel M. Fetters, An Invitation to Commit Fraud: Secret Destruction of Joint Tenant Survivorship Rights, 55 Fordham L.Rev. 173, 179 (1986). However, the possibility of such concealment exists even with the strawman requirement. We do note that after California abolished the strawman requirement in Riddle v. Harmon, 102 Cal.App.3d 524, 162 Cal.Rptr. 530, (1980), the California General Assembly took the opportunity to enact legislation to close this loophole. Specifically, California passed legislation requiring that all instruments purporting to unilaterally sever a joint tenancy be recorded for purposes of providing other joint tenants with constructive notice of the severance. See England, 284 Cal.Rptr. at 363-64; Cal. Civ.Code § 683.2 (West 2004). In the case before the court today, Taylor did record the severance deed, so we do not opine on whether the failure to do so would have made a difference. [Editorial Note: This is footnote 2 of the opinion.]

2. See Carmack v. Place, 188 Colo. 303, 535 P.2d 197, 198 (1975) ("It is well established that an owner in joint tenancy is free to convey his undivided share of property so held, and that upon conveyance by one joint tenant to a third party, the latter becomes a tenant in common with the remaining joint tenant(s)."). [Editorial Note: This is footnote 3 of the opinion.]

3. See First Nat'l Bank of Southglenn v. Energy Fuels Corp., 200 Colo. 540, 618 P.2d 1115, 1118 (1980) (holding that joint tenancy is severed when interest of joint tenant in real property is subject to execution and sale by a judgment creditor). [Editorial Note: This is footnote 5 of the opinion.]

4. Some authority supports the position that in a title theory state, the mere act of mortgaging a piece of property is sufficient to sever a joint tenancy because legal title to the property is actually transferred. 7 R. Powell & P. Rohan, Real Property § 51.04[1][c] (M. Wolf ed.2001). However, in lien theory states such as Colorado, see § 38-35-117, 10 C.R.S. (2003), merely mortgaging property does not transfer legal title and is therefore insufficient to sever a joint tenancy. See Powell, supra, § 51.04{1][cl. [Editorial Note: This is footnote 7 of the opinion.]

5. See Webster v. Mauz, 702 P.2d 297, 298 (Colo.App.1985) (stating that merely encumbering one's own interest in joint tenancy is insufficient to sever a joint tenancy). [Editorial Note: This is footnote 9 of the opinion.]

7.4.3

Reicherter v. McCauley
283 P.3d 219 (Kan. 2012)
Kansas Court of Appeals

Hill, J.:

In this appeal, we must decide if one joint tenant, 10 days before his death, can effectively destroy a joint tenancy interest in a tract of real estate and replace it with a tenancy in common tenant by signing a quitclaim deed to himself and giving it to his lawyer for recording. Guided by the clearly manifested intent of the party making the conveyance here and because jointly owned property is freely transferable, we hold that the transfer of title was effective upon delivery of the deed to the grantor's lawyer for recording. We affirm the district court's ruling.

Two cousins jointly owned 80 acres.

Richard F. Reicherter and his cousin, Douglas M. Reicherter, acquired an 80-acre farm in Marshall County in 1990, as joint tenants with rights of survivorship. Years later, when Richard was residing in a care facility, he signed a quitclaim deed on December 18, 2009, that conveyed his interest in the 80 acres to himself in an apparent attempt to sever the joint tenancy and create a tenancy in common. After signing, Richard gave the deed to his attorney, Rodney Symmonds, for recording. On December 22, 2009, Symmonds mailed Richard's quitclaim deed along with a filing fee to the Marshall County Register of Deeds.

Then, Richard died on December 28, 2009. One day after his death, the Marshall County Register of Deeds recorded Richard's quitclaim deed. Douglas Reicherter was unaware that Richard had executed and filed a quitclaim deed until after Richard's death. There was no express agreement between Richard and Douglas preventing Richard from severing the joint tenancy.

Barbara J. McCauley was appointed executrix of Richard's estate. Naming McCauley as the defendant, Douglas and his wife filed a quiet title action in Marshall County seeking title to the entire 80-acre tract. McCauley counterclaimed claiming a half ownership interest and sought partition of the farm. Douglas opposed this action.

Both sides sought summary judgment. Ruling that Richard clearly intended to sever the joint tenancy and he could convey his interest to himself unimpeded and could thus create a tenancy in common, the district court granted Executrix McCauley s motion and denied Douglas' motion for summary judgment. The district court also held that the joint tenancy was severed when Richard, prior to his death, delivered the quitclaim deed to his attorney for filing. Later, the district court clarified that during the summary judgment hearing Douglas waived any argument that there was an oral agreement in which Douglas gave consideration for the joint tenancy to Richard in exchange for the same benefits and burdens from the land upon Richard's death.

The issue

Douglas Reicherter contends the unilateral attempt at self-conveyance by Richard was ineffective in destroying the joint tenancy ownership they had in the 80 acres. In Douglas' view, since the deed was not recorded until after Richard's death, it did not affect his surviving ownership of the entire tract as he had no prior notice of Richard's intent to sever the joint tenancy. He asks us to reverse the district court and order the court to quiet title to the 80 acres in his favor.

Executrix McCauley contends the joint tenancy to the tract was effectively severed and a tenancy in common was created when Richard signed the quitclaim deed to himself and then gave it to his lawyer for recording. In her view, Richard was not required to give notice to Douglas of his intent and recording the deed after Richard's death did not nullify Richard's intent of severing the joint tenancy. She asks us to affirm the district court.

***

Because the material facts in this case are not in dispute, resolution of this appeal requires a review of the district court's legal conclusions. . . .

Joint ownership of property in Kansas

Generally speaking, there are two ways to jointly own property in Kansas, either as tenants in common or as joint tenants with rights of survivorship. When considering the ownership of real estate, the law presumes a tenancy in common is created unless the deed or other conveyance creating the estate unequivocally conveys a joint tenancy to two or more persons or entities. K.S.A. 58-501. There is no question here that before Richard's death, he and Douglas owned this 80-acre farm as joint tenants.

Before this appeal, it has been argued in other cases that a joint tenant could not unilaterally change ownership of property because of the joint tenancy. But that argument has been rejected by a panel of this court in *Campbell v. Black,* 17 Kan. App. 2d 799, 804, 844 P.2d 759 (1993). In a case where just prior to her death a woman changed the ownership of some joint tenancy accounts, the *Campbell* court held: "[A] joint tenancy may be terminated (1) by mutual agreement of die parties, (2) by course of conduct indicating tenancy in common, or (3) by operation of law upon destruction of one or more of the required unities (time, title, interest, and possession). [Citation omitted.]" 17 Kan. App. 2d at 804. This language was quoted with apparent approval by the Supreme Court in *Nicholas v. Nicholas,* 277 Kan. 171, 186, 83 P.3d 214 (2004), where the court said: "This approach is consistent with the modem trend of looking to the parties' intent as the operative test of whether a joint tenancy has been severed rather than depending upon the traditional doctrine of the four unities."

We have no doubt that Richard intended to sever the joint tenancy. At the summary judgment hearing, Douglas stipulated that the district court would not have to make a determination regarding Richard's intent because Richard demonstrated a clear intent to sever the joint tenancy by signing the quitclaim deed and giving it to his lawyer. Given that Richard's intent is not at issue, the remaining questions are whether self-conveyance is effective in Kansas and whether Richard's delivery of the quitclaim deed to his attorney effectively severed the joint tenancy or whether the failure to record the deed until after Richard's death thwarted Richard's intent.

We address the question of self-conveyance.

No Kansas court has ruled on the issue of whether one joint tenant can unilaterally sever a joint tenancy by executing a quitclaim deed conveying his or her interest in the real estate to himself or herself as a tenant in common. For the three reasons given below, we hold that a joint tenant can self-convey and thus destroy a joint tenancy in this case where there are just two joint tenants.

First, under Kansas law, it is clear that any joint tenant may unilaterally sever his or her joint tenancy interest in real property and create a tenancy in common by conveying his or her interest to a third person. *Hall v. Hamilton,* 233 Kan. 880, 885,

230

667 P.2d 350 (1983). Had Richard conveyed his interests in this real estate to a third person the joint tenancy would have been changed to a tenancy in common with ownership of the tract held in common between that third party and Douglas upon delivery of the deed. We point this out to emphasize that whatever interest a joint owner has in real estate it is freely transferable, that is, it can be sold or given to someone else. There is no need for the party seeking transfer of ownership to first give notice to, or obtain the consent of, the remaining tenant to effectuate the conveyance.

Second, where the intent to create a joint tenancy is clearly manifested, a joint tenancy may be *created* by a transfer to persons as joint tenants from an owner or a joint owner *to himself or herself* and one or more persons as joint tenants. The Supreme Court ruled that a self-conveyance can create a joint tenancy. The all important factor is the clarity with which the grantor's intent is expressed at the time the transaction is initiated. *Winsor v. Powell,* 209 Kan. 292, 299, 497 P.2d 292 (1972). Then, in *In re Estate of Lasater,* 30 Kan. App. 2d 1021, 1023-25, 54 P.3d 511 (2002), this court noted that a decedent's quitclaim deed created a joint tenancy. Logically, we see no reason for a distinction between the method used to create or sever a joint tenancy. Just as a grantor can create a joint tenancy by unilaterally transferring ownership to himself or herself, so should a grantor be able to sever a joint tenancy through self-conveyance.

Third, other jurisdictions have found that unilateral self-conveyance severs a joint tenancy and have dispensed with the old requirements of deeding property to a straw man. We find their reasoning persuasive. See *Riddle v. Harmon,* 102 Cal. App. 3d 524, 162 Cal. Rptr. 530 (1980); *Countrywide Funding Corp. v. Palmer,* 589 So. 2d 994 (Fla. Dist. App. 1991); *Minonk State Bk. v. Grassman,* 103 Ill. App. 3d 1106, 432 N.E.2d 386 (1982); *Hendrickson v. Minneapolis Fed. Sav. & Loan Assn.,* 281 Minn. 462, 161 N.W.2d 688 (1968); *In re Knickerbocker,* 912 P.2d 969 (Utah 1996); see *In Re Estate of Johnson,* 739 N.W.2d 493 (Iowa 2007); *Taylor v. Canterbury,* 92 P.3d 961 (Colo. 2004); *Johnson v. MacIntyre,* 356 Md. 471, 740 A.2d 599 (1999); *Matter of Fuss,* 151 Misc. 2d 689, 573 N.Y.S.2d 586 Sur. Ct. (1991).

This reasoning leads us to rule in favor of Richard's estate. Upon effective delivery during the grantor's life, a quitclaim deed by a joint tenant to himself or herself as a tenant in common effectively severs the joint tenancy and creates a tenancy in common. Obviously, because of the facts of this case, we limit this ruling to a case where there are just two joint tenants.

We consider the effect of the recording statute.

Douglas hangs his hat on one of the recording statutes. He argues that under K.S.A. 58-2223, the execution of the quitclaim deed creating the tenancy in common was not effective until December 29, 2009, the date filing in Marshall County. We are not convinced that the recording statute can be used to thwart Richard's clear intent to sever the joint tenancy.

Douglas' argument ignores well-settled law in Kansas that title to real estate vests at the time of delivery of the deed. To transfer title through a deed, the grantor must cause the deed to be effectively delivered during the grantor's life. Recording is not necessary to effectively deliver a deed. When a deed that is duly executed and acknowledged is found in a third-party's possession, it is presumed that the grantor delivered the deed. Conversely, the law presumes the grantor did not effectively deliver the deed when a deed is signed and acknowledged but the grantor retains control of the deed. Here, Richard signed the deed and gave it to his attorney for filing. We see no other steps that Richard needed to take to effectively deliver the deed.

A brief review of the recording statutes is helpful at this point. K.S.A. 58-2221 provides: "Every instrument in writing that conveys: (a) Real estate; . . . (d) . . . may be recorded in the office of register of deeds of the county in which such real estate is situated." Then, K.S.A. 58-2222 establishes that every instrument recorded shall "impart notice to all persons of the contents thereof; and all subsequent purchasers and mortgagees shall be deemed to purchase with notice." In turn, K.S.A. 58-2223, the statute relied upon by Douglas, states: "No such instrument in writing shall be valid, *except between the parties thereto,* and such as have actual notice thereof, until the same shall be deposited with the register of deed for record." (Emphasis added.)

Obviously, these recording statutes should be construed together as statutes *in pari materia. Luthi v. Evans,* 223 Kan. 622, 629, 576 P.2d 1064 (1978). The *Luthi* court concluded the legislature intended that the purpose of recording instruments of conveyance was to impart constructive notice to subsequent purchasers or mortgagees. 223 Kan. at 629. This is why the exception in K.S.A. 58-2223 is important. Clearly, according to this law, unrecorded deeds are effective for the parties to the deed.

Here, as the only party to the deed, the recording statute did not bar the conveyance of Richard's interest as a joint tenant in the 80 acres to himself as tenant in common upon delivery of the deed to his attorney. Since the deed was effective upon delivery, then the joint tenancy was severed by his actions. Thus, the district court's ruling on this point is correct. Richard had, indeed, severed the joint tenancy several days before his death.

We affirm the ruling of the district court in favor of the estate.

7.4.4

Tenhet v. Boswell
554 P.2d 330 (Cal. 1976)

Supreme Court of California

MOSK, J.

A joint tenant leases his interest in the joint tenancy property to a third person for a term of years, and dies during that term. We conclude that the lease does not sever the joint tenancy, but expires upon the death of the lessor joint tenant.

Raymond Johnson and plaintiff Hazel Tenhet owned a parcel of property as joint tenants. Assertedly without plaintiff's knowledge or consent, Johnson leased the property to defendant Boswell for a period of 10 years at a rental of $150 per year with a provision granting the lessee an "option to purchase."[1] Johnson died some three months after execution of the lease, and plaintiff sought to establish her sole right to possession of the property as the surviving joint tenant. After an unsuccessful demand upon defendant to vacate the premises, plaintiff brought this action to have the lease declared invalid. The trial court sustained demurrers to the complaint, and plaintiff appealed from the ensuing judgment of dismissal.

***

II

An understanding of the nature of a joint interest in this state is fundamental to a determination of the question whether the present lease severed the joint tenancy. Civil Code section 683 provides in part: "A joint interest is one owned by two or more persons in equal shares, by a title created by a single will or transfer, when expressly declared in the will or transfer to be a joint tenancy. . . ." This statute, requiring an express declaration for the creation of joint interests, does not abrogate the common law rule that four unities are essential to an estate in joint tenancy: unity of interest, unity of time, unity of title, and unity of possession.

The requirement of four unities reflects the basic concept that there is but one estate which is taken jointly; if an essential unity is destroyed the joint tenancy is severed and a tenancy in common results. Accordingly, one of two joint tenants may unilaterally terminate the joint tenancy by conveying his interest to a third person. Severance of the joint tenancy, of course, extinguishes the principal feature of that estate—the *jus accrescendi* or right of survivorship.[2] Thus, a joint tenant's right of survivorship is an expectancy that is not irrevocably fixed upon the creation of the estate; it arises only upon success in the ultimate gamble—survival—and then only if the unity of the estate has not theretofore been destroyed by voluntary conveyance, by partition proceedings, by involuntary alienation under an execution, or by any other action which operates to sever the joint tenancy.

Our initial inquiry is whether the partial alienation of Johnson's interest in the property effected a severance of the joint tenancy under these principles. It could be argued that a lease destroys the unities of interest and possession because the leasing joint tenant transfers to the lessee his present possessory interest and retains a mere reversion. Moreover, the possibility that the term of the lease may continue beyond the lifetime of the lessor is inconsistent with a complete right of survivorship.

On the other hand, if the lease entered into here by Johnson and defendant is valid only during Johnson's life, then the conveyance is more a variety of life estate *pur autre vie* than a term of years. Such a result is inconsistent with Johnson's freedom to alienate his interest during his lifetime.

We are mindful that the issue here presented is "an ancient controversy, going back to Coke and Littleton." (2 Am. Law of Prop. (1952) § 6.2, p. 10.) Yet the problem is like a comet in our law: though its existence in theory has been frequently recognized, its observed passages are few. Some authorities support the view that a lease by a joint tenant to a third person effects a complete and final severance of the joint tenancy. Such a view is generally based upon what is thought to be the English common law rule.

Others adopt a position that there is a temporary severance during the term of the lease. If the lessor dies while the lease is in force, under this view the existence of the lease at the moment when the right of survivorship would otherwise take effect operates as a severance,' extinguishing the joint tenancy. If, however, the term of the lease expires before the lessor, it is reasoned that the joint tenancy is undisturbed because the joint tenants resume their original relation. The single conclusion that can be drawn from centuries of academic speculation on the question is that its resolution is unclear.

As we shall explain, it is our opinion that a lease is not so inherently inconsistent with joint tenancy as to create a severance, either temporary or permanent.

Under Civil Code sections 683 and 686 a joint tenancy must be expressly declared in the creating instrument, or a tenancy in common results. This is a statutory departure from the common law preference in favor of joint tenancy.[3] Inasmuch as the estate arises only upon express intent, and in many cases such intent will be the intent of the joint tenants themselves, we decline to find a severance in circumstances which do not clearly and unambiguously establish that either of the joint tenants desired to terminate the estate.

If plaintiff and Johnson did not choose to continue the joint tenancy, they might have converted it into a tenancy in common by written mutual agreement. They might also have jointly conveyed the property to a third person and divided the proceeds. Even if they could not agree to act in concert, either plaintiff or Johnson might have severed the joint tenancy, with or without the consent of the other, by an act which was clearly indicative of an intent to terminate, such as a conveyance of her or his entire interest. Either might also have brought an action to partition the property, which, upon judgment, would have effected a severance. Because a joint tenancy may be created only by express intent, and because there are alternative and unambiguous means of altering the nature of that estate, we hold that the lease here in issue did not operate to sever the joint tenancy.

III

Having concluded that the joint tenancy was not severed by the lease and that sole ownership of the property therefore vested in plaintiff upon her joint tenant's death by operation of her right of survivorship, we turn next to the issue whether she takes the property unencumbered by the lease.

In arguing that plaintiff takes subject to the lease, defendant relies on *Swartzbaugh* v. *Sampson* (1936), 11 Cal.App.2d 451. In that case, one of two joint tenants entered into lease agreements over the objection of his joint tenant wife, who sought to cancel the leases. The court held in favor of the lessor joint tenant, concluding that the leases were valid.

But the suit to cancel the lease in *Swartzbaugh* was brought during the lifetime of both joint tenants, not as in the present case after the death of the lessor. Significantly, the court concluded that "a lease to all of the joint property by one joint tenant is not a nullity but is a valid and supportable contract *in so far as the interest of the lessor in the joint property is concerned.,"* (Italics added; *id.* at p. 458.) During the lifetime of the lessor joint tenant, as the *Swartzbaugh* court perceived, her interest in the joint property was an undivided interest in fee simple that encompassed the right to lease the property.

By the very nature of joint tenancy, however, the interest of the nonsurviving joint tenant extinguishes upon his death. And as the lease is valid only "in so far as the interest of the lessor in the joint property is concerned," it follows that the lease of the joint tenancy property also expires when the lessor dies.

This conclusion is borne out by decisions in this state involving liens on and mortgages of joint tenancy property. In *Zeigler v. Bonnell* (1942), 52 Cal.App.2d 217, the Court of Appeal ruled that a surviving joint tenant takes an estate free from a judgment lien on the interest of a deceased cotenant judgment debtor. The court reasoned that "The right of survivorship is the chief characteristic that distinguishes a joint tenancy from other interests in property. . . . The judgment lien of [the creditor] could attach only to the interest of his debtor .... That interest terminated upon [the debtor's] death." *(Id.* at pp. 219-220.) After his death "the deceased joint tenant had no interest in the property, and his judgment creditor has no greater rights." *(Id.* at p. 220.)

A similar analysis was followed in *People* v. *Nogarr* (1958) 164 Cal.App.2d 591 [330 P.2d 858, 68 A.L.R.2d 992], which held that upon the death of a joint tenant who had executed a mortgage on the tenancy property, the surviving joint tenant took the property free of the mortgage. The court reasoned (at p. 594) that "as the mortgage lien attached only to such interest as [the deceased joint tenant] had in the real property[,] when his interest ceased to exist the lien of the mortgage expired with it."

As these decisions demonstrate, a joint tenant may, during his lifetime, grant certain rights in the joint property without severing the tenancy. But when such a joint tenant dies his interest dies with him, and any encumbrances placed by him on the property become unenforceable against the surviving joint tenant. For the reasons stated a lease falls within this rule.

Any other result would defeat the justifiable expectations of the surviving joint tenant. Thus if A agrees to create a joint tenancy with B, A can reasonably anticipate that when B dies A will take an unencumbered interest in fee simple. During his lifetime, of course, B may sever the tenancy or lease his interest to a third party. But to allow B to lease for a term continuing *after* his death would indirectly defeat the very purposes of the joint tenancy. For example, for personal reasons B might execute a 99-year lease on valuable property for a consideration of one dollar a year. A would then take a fee simple on B's death, but would find his right to use the property—and its market value—substantially impaired. This circumstance would effectively nullify the benefits of the right of survivorship, the basic attribute of the joint tenancy.

On the other hand, we are not insensitive to the potential injury that may be sustained by a person in good faith who leases from one joint tenant. In some circumstances a lessee might be unaware that his lessor is not a fee simple owner but merely a joint tenant, and could find himself unexpectedly evicted when the lessor dies prior to expiration of the lease. This result would be avoided by a prudent lessee who conducts a title search prior to leasing, but we appreciate that such a course would often be economically burdensome to the lessee of a residential dwelling or a modest parcel of property. Nevertheless, it must also be recognized that every lessee may one day face the unhappy revelation that his lessor's estate in the leased property is less than a fee simple. For example, a lessee who innocently rents from the holder of a life estate is subject to risks comparable to those imposed upon a lessee of joint tenancy property.

More significantly, we cannot allow extraneous factors to erode the functioning of joint tenancy. The estate of joint tenancy is firmly embedded in centuries of real property law and in the California statute books. Its crucial element is the right of survivorship, a right that would be more illusory than real if a joint tenant were permitted to lease for a term continuing after , his death. Accordingly, we hold that under the facts alleged in the complaint the lease herein is no longer valid.

***

[T]he judgment is reversed.

1. The lease did not disclose that the lessor possessed only a joint interest in the property. To the contrary, the "option to purchase" granted to the lessee, which might more accurately be described as a right of first refusal, implied that the lessor possessed a fee simple. It provided in part: "Lessee is given a first exclusive right, privilege and option to purchase the house and lot covered by this lease.... If so purchased, Lessor will convey title by grant deed on the usual form subject only to easements or rights of way of record and liens or encumbrances specifically agreed to by and between Lessor and Lessee. Lessor shall furnish Lessee with a policy of title insurance at Lessor's cost...." [Editorial Note: This is footnote 2 of the opinion.]

2. The rule is, nihil de re accrescit ei, qui nihil in re quando jus accrescent habet. (2 Co. Litt. *188.) Literally, no part of the estate accrues to him who has nothing in the estate when the right accrues. In modern parlance, what you have is what you get. [Editorial Note: This is footnote 3 of the opinion.]

3. Because the feudal system was opposed to a division of tenures, estates in joint tenancy were favored at common law. Like the laws of primogeniture, joint tenancy was founded "on the principle of the aggregation of landed estates in the hands of a few, and opposed to their division among many persons." (Siberell v. Siberell (1932) 214 Cal. 767, 771 [7 P.2d 1003], quoting DeWitt v. San Francisco (1852) 2 Cal. 289, 297.) Despite the obsolescence of its original purpose, the estate of joint tenancy remains a popular form of property ownership in California on the ground that it avoids the delay and administrative expenses of probate. [This is footnote 5 of the opinion.]

7.4.5

Discussion: Notes, Questions & Problems

7.4.5.1

Discussion Question #9. Termination of a tenancy by the entireties?

How are tenancies by the entireties severed or terminated?

7.4.5.2

Discussion Question #10. Does slaying sever a joint tenancy?

Review the following excerpt of Fla. Stat. § 732.802 and ask yourselves what result if a joint tenant kills a cotenant.

> **732.802 Killer not entitled to receive property or other benefits by reason of victim's death.—**
>
> (1) A surviving person who unlawfully and intentionally kills or participates in procuring the death of the decedent is not entitled to any benefits under the will or under the Florida Probate Code, and the estate of the decedent passes as if the killer had predeceased the decedent. Property appointed by the will of the decedent to or for the benefit of the killer passes as if the killer had predeceased the decedent.

(2) Any joint tenant who unlawfully and intentionally kills another joint tenant thereby effects a severance of the interest of the decedent so that the share of the decedent passes as the decedent's property and the killer has no rights by survivorship. This provision applies to joint tenancies with right of survivorship and tenancies by the entirety in real and personal property; joint and multiple-party accounts in banks, savings and loan associations, credit unions, and other institutions; and any other form of co-ownership with survivorship incidents.

7.4.5.3

Discussion Question #11. Does mortgage sever a joint tenancy?

Review footnote 7 of *Taylor v. Canterbury*, excerpted above, regarding execution of a mortgage by a cotenant. What is the difference between a lien theory state and a title theory state for mortgages and under which theory might a mortgage create a severance?

7.4.5.4

Discussion Problem #12. Jillian wants a mortgage problem

Assume Jillian, a joint tenant with a one-third interest in a large property, wants to obtain a significant loan from a lender. Jillian offers the lender a mortgage of her interest in the joint tenancy as security for the loan. What should the lender require before making the loan and obtaining the mortgage?

7.5

Separate Property and Community Property

There are two different systems for allocating spousal property rights in the United States – the **separate property** system and the **community property** system. The vast majority of states are separate property states. The separate property system derived from the English common law. The community property states derive their

240

system primarily from the Spanish and French civil systems. The following states are community property states: Arizona, California, Idaho, Louisiana, New Mexico, Nevada, Texas, Washington, and Wisconsin.

In separate property states, also referred to as title states or common law states, marital status alone does not affect ownership of property during the marriage. A spouse whose sole name appears on the title to property is deemed the owner. In addition, despite being married, a spouse retains separate ownership of all that the spouse earns during the marriage. This treatment of ownership applies during an ongoing marriage. In the event of a divorce, the family law system in separate property states generally determines ownership of the property. The family law courts in the separate property states use the concept of equitable distribution to divide the property between the divorcing spouses. If the marriage does not end in divorce but, rather, ends at death, the analysis is different and title during the marriage can be a very important factor. What happens in a separate property state if a spouse attempts to disinherit their surviving spouse, for example, by devising all the property to a friend? Almost all separate property states provide a system by which a surviving spouse who was disinherited could choose to receive a surviving spouse's elective share of the deceased spouse's property.

In community property states, title is not determinative. In those states, notwithstanding how the property is titled, each spouse acquires an ownership interest in one-half of the property the other spouse earns during the marriage. In fact, community property refers to property acquired during the marriage that is not deemed separate property in that community property regime. Generally, in community property states, some property retains separate property status despite the marriage. Property that would be deemed separate property in community property states includes property owned by either spouse prior to the marriage and property acquired by either spouse during the marriage by gift or inheritance. How is property in community property states upon divorce? Generally, the divorcing spouses keep their separate property and community property is divided either equally or by equitably depending on the community property jurisdiction. At death, there is no elective share in community property states because property earned during the marriage is already community property. Thus, at death, a spouse can dispose of separate property and one-half of community property.

7.5.1
Discussion: Notes, Questions, and Problems

7.5.1.1
Discussion Question #13. Separate or community property?

Does your state follow a separate property system or a community property system?

7.5.1.2
Discussion Question #14. Spousal elective share?

Why do community property states not provide for a surviving spouse to elect a spousal elective share at the death of the first spouse?

7.6
Homestead

The term *homestead* is used to refer to several different concepts. For example, the term homestead may be used to refer to the allowance for a reduction of real property taxes for an owner's principal residence. The term homestead is also used for provisions in many states that provide protection of a principal residence from certain creditors of the owner. It is the creditor protection aspect of homestead that we focus on in the property course.

What homestead protection is available against creditors? Some states limit their homestead protections only to certain dollar amounts. Other states limit the protection to the physical size of the property. Other states limit homestead protection by both dollar and size. The states vary widely as to the dollar amount or size of the property that could be protected from creditors.

Compare the dollar limits in the Missouri statute excerpted below with the dollar limits in the California statute excerpted below.

> **Mo. Rev. Stat. § 513.475. Homestead defined — exempt from execution — spouses debarred from selling, when.** — 1. The homestead of every person, consisting of a dwelling house and appurtenances, and the land used in connection therewith, not exceeding the value of fifteen thousand dollars, which is or shall be used by such person as a homestead, shall, together with the rents, issues and products thereof, be exempt from attachment and execution. The exemption allowed under this section shall not be allowed for more than one owner of any homestead if one owner claims the entire amount allowed under this subsection; but, if more than one owner of any homestead claims an exemption under this section, the exemption allowed to each of such owners shall not exceed, in the aggregate, the total exemption allowed under this subsection as to any one homestead.
>
> 2. Either spouse separately shall be debarred from and incapable of selling, mortgaging or alienating the homestead in any manner whatever, and every such sale, mortgage or alienation is hereby declared null and void; provided, however, that nothing herein contained shall be so construed as to prevent the husband and wife from jointly conveying, mortgaging, alienating or in any other manner disposing of such homestead, or any part thereof.

Cal. Civ. Proc. § 704.730. Amount of homestead exemption

(a) The amount of the homestead exemption is the greater of the following:

> (1) The countywide median sale price for a single-family home in the calendar year prior to the calendar year in which the judgment debtor claims the exemption, not to exceed six hundred thousand dollars ($600,000).
>
> (2) Three hundred thousand dollars ($300,000).

(b) The amounts specified in this section shall adjust annually for inflation, beginning on January 1, 2022, based on the change in the annual California Consumer Price Index for All Urban Consumers for the prior fiscal year, published by the Department of Industrial Relations.

Some states do not limit their homestead real property protection to a dollar amount. For example, Florida, Kansas, and Texas limit homestead protection for real property by physical size, rather than by dollar amount. Compare the homestead provisions in Florida an Iowa excerpted below.

Fla. Const. art. X, § 4. Homestead; exemptions.—

(a) There shall be exempt from forced sale under process of any court, and no judgment, decree or execution shall be a lien thereon, except for the payment of taxes and assessments thereon, obligations contracted for the purchase, improvement or repair thereof, or obligations contracted for house, field or other labor performed on the realty, the following property owned by a natural person:

> (1) a homestead, if located outside a municipality, to the extent of one hundred sixty acres of contiguous land and improvements thereon, which shall not be reduced without the owner's consent by reason of subsequent inclusion in a municipality; or if located within a municipality, to the extent of one-half acre of contiguous land, upon which the exemption shall be limited to the residence of the owner or the owner's family; . . .

(b) These exemptions shall inure to the surviving spouse or heirs of the owner.

(c) The homestead shall not be subject to devise if the owner is survived by spouse or minor child, except the homestead may be devised to the owner's spouse if there be no minor child. The owner of homestead real estate, joined by the spouse if married, may alienate the homestead by mortgage, sale or gift and, if married, may by deed transfer the title to an estate by the entirety with the spouse. If the owner or spouse is incompetent, the method of alienation or encumbrance shall be as provided by law.

Kan. Stat. Ann. § 60-2301. Homestead; extent of exemption. … a homestead to the extent of 160 acres of farming land, or of one acre within the limits of an incorporated town or city, or a manufactured home or mobile home, occupied as a residence by the owner or by the family of the owner, or by both the owner and family thereof, together with all the improvements on the same, shall be exempted from forced sale under any process of law, and shall not be alienated without the joint consent of husband and wife, when that relation exists; but no property shall be exempt from sale for taxes, or for the payment of obligations contracted for the purchase of such premises, or for the erection of improvements thereon. The provisions of this section shall not apply to any process of law obtained by virtue of a lien given by the consent of both husband and wife, when that relation exists.

7.6.1
Discussion: Notes, Questions, and Problems

7.6.1.1
Discussion Question #15. Homestead protection?

New Jersey and Pennsylvania do not provide for homestead protection against creditors. Would lenders in those states be more likely to lend monies to borrowers than lenders in states that provide unlimited dollar amount homestead protection?

7.6.1.2
Discussion Question #16. Florida homestead and creditors?

Review the Florida homestead provision, excerpted above. Which types of creditors could force the sale of the real property despite homestead?

8

Chapter 8 · Estates in Land and Future Interests

The laws governing future interests and estates in land are best understood by discussing—albeit cursorily—the history of the feudal system of property in England. Although the history of common law property began before the year 1066, for our purposes in studying the development of the common law property system, we can start with the Battle of Hastings in 1066 and the Norman conquest of England.

In 1066, William the Duke of Normandy, subsequently referred to as William the Conqueror, conquered England and applied the rigid feudal system of land ownership when allocating land to his followers and others. Under the feudal system, land was the source of almost all wealth. In order to maintain control of the grantees of the vast land interests and to ensure a stream of income from the grantees, when William parceled out land to his loyal followers, he did not grant them title to the land outright. Had he done that, they might not have been as inclined to continue to support him in the future. Instead, the land grantees were viewed as tenants who held "of" the king in reward for their past efforts and in exchange for certain requirements, including oaths of loyalty, payment of services, and responsibility for incidents. For our purposes, we focus on some of the requirements for obtaining the land – each tenant agreed to make certain payments (referred to as *services)* and was responsible for certain *incidents*. There were different types of services required but the primary service usually took the form of knights for battle. This type of service was appropriately called knight service. In addition to service, the land holders were also required to pay incidents. There were basically five incidents: relief, aids, escheat, wardship, and marriage. Relief was a form of inheritance tax requiring the tenant's heir to pay for the privilege of taking his predecessor's place. The incident of aids required the tenant to make contributions in certain emergencies such as payments of ransom if the feudal lord or king were kidnapped. The incident of escheat provided for forfeiture of the land if the tenant

246

was convicted of a felony or if the tenant died without heirs. The incident of wardship gave the feudal lord the right to rents and profits from the land during the minority of the deceased tenant's heir. The incident of marriage allowed the lord to arrange marriages, which had financial benefits.

Generally, the most profitable of the incidents to the lord were relief, wardship, marriage, and escheat. A mechanism that helped ensure that a tenant's incident responsibility was clear was the concept of **seisin**. Basically, in feudal times, transfers of title to land required a ceremony consisting of a physical act on the land referred to as the ceremony of livery of seisin or feoffment with livery of seisin. The ceremony usually consisted of the transferor and transferee walking onto the land and the owner picking up a twig or clump of dirt and transferring it into the hands of the new owner. In feudal times, the ceremony was critical, in part, because there was no modern system of land records, the bargain and sale deed was not yet recognized by the law courts, and most people could not read. It was necessary to transfer land with sufficient ceremony so the event would be marked in the minds of the community and give notice to interested persons, especially the feudal lord. Land could only be transferred voluntarily by this ceremony because it was essential that someone be "seized" of a parcel of land at all times as the person who was seized was responsible for the incidents. If seisin was suspended, or if it was unclear who held seisin, then the feudal lord could lose the benefit of those incidents attached to title. Thus, it was important that there not be a gap in seisin. You were introduced to the concept of seisin when you read *Taylor v. Canterbury,* excerpted above in Chapter 7. Recall that in *Taylor,* the court noted that, under the system of seisin, title could not transfer where the grantor was also the grantee because one person could not conduct the feoffment ceremony of transferring a clump of land or some sticks just to himself.

8.1

Estates in Land

Seisin applied to freehold estates, not to non-freehold estates. The freehold estates are the fee simple, the fee tail, and the life estate. The non-freehold estates are the four leasehold interests: the tenancy for a fixed term (also referred to as the estate for years), the periodic tenancy, the tenancy at will, and the tenancy at sufferance. You will study the characteristics of non-freehold interests when we discuss landlord and tenant. Our discussion here will focus primarily with the freehold estates. Freehold estates are either fee simple or non-fee simple estates. As you read the text and cases, you should refer to the diagram of estates in land included below.

Determining which type of estate the grantee obtained depends on how much the grantor intended to convey. Recall from our examination of gifts in Chapter 5 that there is no precise way to know how much the grantor intended to convey – instead we rely on circumstantial evidence – the most important of which is the language used (the words of grant in the instrument). In making this examination, words used by grantors are classified into different categories. We distinguish between two categories of words: words of purchase and words of limitation.

Words of purchase describe the grantee – the purchaser – the one to whom the conveyance is being made. By contrast, **words of limitation** describe the limits placed on the estate, if any, on the time dimension. For example, Owen, the owner of land referred to as Blackacre, executes a deed that provides the following language: "to Albert for life." In that instance, the words of purchase are "to Albert" and, thus, we know that Albert is the grantee. The words "for life" are words of limitation denoting a time dimension of the estate. In this case, Albert's estate terminates at his death and Albert has a life estate, not a fee simple. What if the words used had been "to Albert and his heirs?" How are those words interpreted? See *Woelk v. Luckhardt*, excerpted below. Note also that, at common law, the words "and his heirs" were necessary to convey a fee simple absolute. In fact, the court in *Hardage v. Stroope*, 58 Ark. 303, 24 S.W. 490, 493 (1893), vividly explained as follows:

> No equivalent words would answer the purpose. If the conveyance was not made to a man and his heirs, the grantee only took a life estate, notwithstanding the estate was limited by such phrases as "to A. forever," or "to A. and his successors," and the like. An express direction that the

grantee should have the fee simple in the land would not have supplied the place of the word "heirs."

The modern interpretation is that if no words of limitation are attached to the interest the grantor conveyed a fee simple.

8.1.1

Woelk v. Luckhardt
277 N.W. 836 (Neb. 1938)

Nebraska Supreme Court

Munday, District Judge.

This is an appeal by Walter J. Luckhardt, administrator with will annexed of the estate of John Luckhardt, deceased, and others, from an order of the district court for Lancaster county in a proceeding in equity, wherein the district court as an appellate court reversed and set aside an order of the county court directing said administrator to make a partial distribution of the personal property of said estate.

John Luckhardt died testate in Lancaster county, Nebraska, in March, 1935. His last will and testament was made in 1920. The sole legatee and executrix of said will, Amalia Luckhardt, wife of John Luckhardt, died in 1934. Before her marriage to Luckhardt she had previously been married and had two sons by the former marriage, who are the appellees herein. By her marriage to John Luckhardt she had four children. The will was offered for probate by petition in the usual form by Walter J. Luckhardt. The petition, among other things, set out the death of the aforesaid executrix and legatee and named the six children as interested parties. The county court admitted the will to probate and appointed Walter J. Luckhardt administrator with will annexed. No appeal was taken from this order. So far the proceedings were amicable. In April, 1935, said administrator filed an inventory showing the amount of the assets of the estate as $111,505.76. Later said administrator filed a petition in the county court praying for an order permitting him to make a partial distribution of the personal assets of the estate to the four children of John and Amalia Luckhardt. The appellees, William and Samuel Woelk, then filed a petition in the county court asking that said distribution be made to all the six children of said Amalia Luckhardt as substitutionary legatees under said will. The question was squarely raised in the county court, whether all six children of Amalia Luckhardt were entitled to participate in the distribution of the estate, or only the four children of Amalia Luckhardt, who were the issue of her marriage with John Luckhardt. The county court ordered the distribution to the four children of John Luckhardt. The appellees herein appealed to the district court, where the cause was tried on the same pleadings as in the county court. The district court reversed the order of the county court and held that each of the six children of Amalia Luckhardt was entitled to share equally in the distribution. The four children of John and Amalia Luckhardt with said administrator have appealed to this court.

***

This brings us to the construction of the disputed clause in the will: "I give, devise and bequeath, unto my beloved wife Amalia Luckhardt all the property, real and personal, and effects of every name and nature which I now have, may die possessed of, or may be entitled to, her heirs and assigns forever." There was no residuary clause.

It is axiomatic to say that the intention of the testator controls in the construction of a will if it is consistent with the rules of law. But the plain and certain rules of law should not be set aside except in favor of an equally plain and certain disposition of the testator. Do the words "her heirs and assigns forever" in the will describe the nature of the estate given to the beneficiary, or do they describe the persons who are to take? Or, putting it differently, are they words of limitation or purchase? Under the common law the words were used to indicate that the entire property was given absolutely, and, if real estate, that it was given in fee simple. By statute in this state such words are no longer necessary to convey the fee title. Formerly these words were an intensified form of expression of an absolute gift. Although not now necessary to convey title, they are still quite often used to give greater certainty that a devise was intended to be absolute.

The court in *Jackson v. Alsop*, 67 Conn. 249, 34 Atl. 1106, uses this language: "Where the word 'assigns' is added to the word 'heirs,' it is almost impossible to read the whole phrase otherwise than as words of limitation, and not as intended to create an estate in any other person. 2 Redfield on Wills, 82; *Grafftey v. Humpage,* 1 Beavan, 46; *Holloway v. Clarkson,* 2 Hare, 521, 523."

In *Loveren v. Donaldson,* 69 N. H. 639, 45 Atl. 715, a similar phrase was under consideration and the following language used: "But the use of the words 'her heirs and assigns forever,' immediately following the name of the devisee or legatee, are not alone sufficient to express this intention and to prevent a lapse. These words have a well-settled construction, by which they are held to be merely words of limitation used to describe the nature of the estate given to the beneficiary, and not to express an intention that a lapse should be avoided by the substitution of the heirs, in place of a predeceased devisee or legatee. Where words and terms like these have a well-settled and well-understood meaning, they will not be given a different one, unless it appears that the testator employed them in a different sense and intended to express a different meaning. Cressey *v. Wallace,* 66 N. H. 566." See *Matter of Clark,* 175 N. Y. 139, 67 N. E. 212.

Therefore, we conclude the inference to be drawn from the phrase "her heirs and assigns forever" as used in the instant case is not sufficient to show other intent than the original meaning, of the words at common law, that the words are of limitation and are not to be used in a substitutionary sense.

***

There is no doubt that the testator and his stepsons, the appellees, were on the best of terms and that the appellees manifested a filial attitude towards him. However, those facts are not relevant under the circumstances above indicated. In the instant case we think the sentiment expressed in *Cleaver v. Cleaver,* 39 Wis. 96 (1875), is quite pertinent: " 'It is an unfortunate case, but the law is clear. The legacy lapsed by the death of the legatee in the life of the testator.' . . . 'and we are sorry for it.'. . . "

We, therefore, conclude that the trial court was in error in its construction of the will and that only the four children of the testator and Amalia Luckhardt should share in the distribution. The judgment of the district court is reversed and the case remanded, with directions to enter judgment for the appellants in accordance with this opinion.

Reversed.

8.1.2
Diagram of Estates in Land

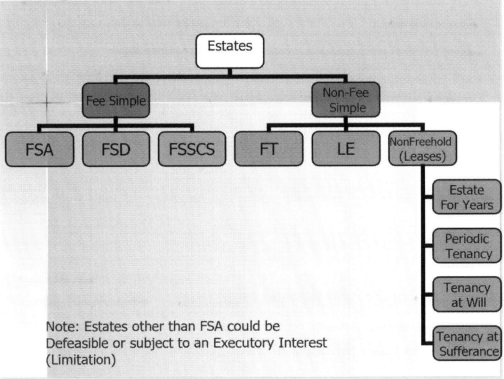

Note: Estates other than FSA could be Defeasible or subject to an Executory Interest (Limitation)

8.1.3
Fee Simple Estates

A *fee simple* estate is an estate with the possibility of indefinite duration. A fee simple may be *absolute* or *defeasible*. If it is absolute, there is no future interest connected to that property. A *future interest* – unlike a *present interest*, which is possessory immediately when the interest is created – becomes possessory, if at all, at some point in the future. If instead of conveying a fee simple absolute, the grantor conveys a defeasible fee, the fee simple may terminate or may be cut short sometime in the future. There are, in turn, two basic types of defeasible fees: the *fee simple determinable* and the *fee simple subject to condition subsequent.*

When a grantor conveys a fee simple absolute, the grantor has conveyed the entire estate and has not retained any interest in the estate. By contrast, when a grantor conveys a defeasible fee, the grantor has not conveyed the entire estate. When a grantor conveys a *fee simple determinable*, the grantor retains a *possibility of reverter*. When a grantor conveys a *fee simple subject to condition subsequent*, the grantor retains a *right of re-entry*, also referred to as a right of entry or a power of termination.

8.1.3.1

Mahrenholz v. County Board of School Trustees
417 N.E.2d 138 (Ill. App. Ct. 1981)

Illinois Appellate Court

Mr. JUSTICE JONES

delivered the opinion of the court:

This case involves an action to quiet title to real property located in Lawrence County, Illinois. Its resolution depends on the judicial construction of language in a conveyance of that property. The case is before us on the pleadings, plaintiffs' third amended complaint having been dismissed by a final order. The pertinent facts are taken from the pleadings.

On March 18, 1941, W. E. and Jennie Hutton executed a warranty deed in which they conveyed certain land, to be known here as the Hutton School grounds, to the trustees of School District No. 1, the predecessors of the defendants in this action. The deed provided that "this land to be used for school purpose only; otherwise to revert to Grantors herein." W. E. Hutton died intestate on July 18,1951, and Jennie Hutton died intestate on February 18,1969. The Huttons left as their only legal heir their son Harry E. Hutton.

The property conveyed by the Huttons became the site of the Hutton School. Community Unit School District No. 20 succeeded to the grantee of the deed and held classes in the building constructed upon the land until May 30, 1973. After that date, children were transported to classes held at other facilities operated by the District. The District has used the property since then for storage purposes only.

Earl and Madeline Jacqmain executed a warranty deed on October 9, 1959, conveying to the plaintiffs over 390 acres of land in Lawrence County and which included the 40-acre tract from which the Hutton School grounds were taken. When and from whom the Jacqmains acquired the land is not shown and is of no consequence in this appeal. The deed from the Jacqmains to the plaintiffs excepted the Hutton School grounds, but purported to convey the disputed future interest. . .

.

On May 7, 1977, Harry E. Hutton, son and sole heir of W. E. and Jennie Hutton, conveyed to the plaintiffs all of his interest in the Hutton School land. This document was filed in the recorder's office of Lawrence County on September 7, 1977. . . .

The plaintiffs filed a complaint in the circuit court of Lawrence County on April 9, 1974, in which they sought to quiet title to the school property in themselves, by virtue of the interests acquired from the Jacqmains. This complaint was amended but later dismissed on defendants' motion.

A second amended complaint was filed on September 7, 1977. This alleged that the plaintiffs owned the property through the conveyance from Harry Hutton. The defendants moved to dismiss this complaint because (1) the plaintiffs did not meet the equitable requirements which would entitle them to have title quieted in them, and (2) Harry Hutton had no interest in the school property, as he never acted to re-enter it. The second amended complaint was dismissed on August 17, 1978, by an order which did not specify the reasons for the decision.

The plaintiffs filed a third amended complaint on September 13, 1978. This complaint recited the interests acquired from the Jacqmains and from Harry Hutton. On March 21, 1979, the trial court entered an order dismissing this complaint. In the order the court found that the

> "[W]arranty deed dated March 18, 1941, from W.E. Hutton and Jennie Hutton to the Trustees of School District No. 1, conveying land here concerned, created a fee simple subject to a condition subsequent followed

by the right of entry for condition broken, rather than a determinable fee followed by a possibility of reverter."

Plaintiffs have perfected an appeal to this court.

issue

The basic issue presented by this appeal is whether the trial court correctly concluded that the plaintiffs could not have acquired any interest in the school property from the Jacqmains or from Harry Hutton. Resolution of this issue must turn upon the legal interpretation of the language contained in the March 18, 1941, deed from W. E. and Jennie Hutton to the Trustees of School District No. 1:

> "this land to be used for school purpose only; otherwise to revert to Grantors herein."

In addition to the legal effect of this language we must consider the alienability of the interest created and the effect of subsequent deeds.

The parties appear to be in agreement that the 1941 deed from the Huttons conveyed a defeasible fee simple estate to the grantee, and gave rise to a future interest in the grantors, and that it did not convey a fee simple absolute, subject to a covenant. The fact that provision was made for forfeiture of the estate conveyed should the land cease to be used for school purposes suggests that this view is correct.

The future interest remaining in this grantor or his estate can only be a possibility of reverter or a right of re-entry for condition broken. As neither interest may be transferred by will nor by *inter vivos* conveyance (Ill. Rev. Stat. 1979, ch. 30, par. 37b), and as the land was being used for school purposes in 1959 when the Jacqmains transferred their interest in the school property to the plaintiffs, the trial court correctly ruled that the plaintiffs could not have acquired any interest in that property from the Jacqmains by the deed of October 9, 1959.

alt arg

Consequently this court must determine whether the plaintiffs could have acquired an interest in the Hutton School grounds from Harry Hutton. The resolution of this issue depends on the construction of the language of the 1941 deed of the Huttons to the school district. As urged by the defendants, and as the trial court found, that deed conveyed a fee simple subject to a condition subsequent, followed by a right of re-entry for condition broken. As argued by the plaintiffs, on the other hand, the deed conveyed a fee simple determinable followed by a possibility of reverter. In either case, the grantor and his heirs retain an interest in the property which may become possessory if the condition is broken. We emphasize here that although section 1 of "An Act relating to Rights of Entry or Re-entry for breach of condition subsequent and possibilities of reverter" effective July 21, 1947 (Ill. v. Stat. 1979, ch. 30, par. 37b) provides that rights of re-entry for condition broken and possibilities of reverter are neither alienable nor devisable, they are inheritable. The type of interest held governs the mode of reinvestment with title if reinvestment is to occur. If the grantor had a possibility of reverter, he or his heirs become the owner of the property by operation of law as soon as the condition is broken. If he has a right of re-entry for condition broken, he or his heirs become the owner of the property only after they act to retake the property.

It is alleged, and we must accept, that classes were last held in the Hutton School in 1973. Harry Hutton, sole heir of the grantors, did not act to legally retake the premises but instead conveyed his interest in that land to the plaintiffs in 1977. If Harry Hutton had only a naked right of re-entry for condition broken, then he could not be the owner of that property until he had legally re-entered the land. Since he took no steps for a legal re-entry, he had only a right of re-entry in 1977, and that right cannot be conveyed *inter vivos*. On the other hand, if Harry Hutton had a possibility of reverter in the property, then he owned the school property as soon as it ceased to be used for school purposes. Therefore, assuming (1) that cessation of classes constitutes "abandonment of school purposes" on the land, [and] (2) that the conveyance from Harry Hutton to the plaintiffs was legally correct, . . . the plaintiffs could have acquired an interest in the Hutton School grounds if Harry Hutton had inherited a possibility of reverter from his parents.

The difference between a fee simple determinable (or determinable fee) and a fee simple subject to a condition subsequent, is solely a matter of judicial interpretation of the words of a grant. As Blackstone explained, there is a fundamental theoretical difference between a conditional estate, such as a fee simple subject to a condition subsequent, and a limited estate, such as a fee simple determinable.

"A distinction is however made between a *condition in deed* and a *limitation,* which Littleton denominates also a *condition in law.* For when an estate is so expressly confined and limited by the words of it's [sic] creation, that it cannot endure for any longer time than till the contingency happens upon which the estate is to fail, this is denominated a *limitation-,* as when land is granted to a man, *so long as* he is parson of Dale, or *while* he continues unmarried, or *until* out of the rents and profits he shall have made 500 £. and the like. In such case the estate determines as soon as the contingency happens, (when he ceases to be parson, marries a wife, or has received the 500£.) and the next subsequent estate, which depends upon such determination, becomes immediately vested, without any act to be done by him who is next in expectancy. But when an estate is, strictly speaking, upon *condition in deed* (as if granted expressly *upon condition* to be void upon the payment of 40£. by the grantor, or *so that* the grantee continues unmarried, or *provided* he goes to York, etc.) the law permits it to endure beyond the time when such contingency happens, unless the grantor or his heir or assigns take advantage of the breach of the condition, and make either an entry or a claim in order to avoid the estate." (Emphasis in original.) 2 W. Blackstone, Commentaries *155.

A fee simple determinable may be thought of as a limited grant, while a fee simple subject to a condition subsequent is an absolute grant to which a condition is appended. In other words, a grantor should give a fee simple determinable if he intends to give property for so long as it is needed for the purposes for which it is given and no longer, but he should employ a fee simple subject to a condition subsequent if he intends to compel compliance with a condition by penalty of a forfeiture.

Following Blackstone's examples, the Huttons would have created a fee simple determinable if they had allowed the school district to retain the property *so long as* or *while* it was used for school purposes, or *until* it ceased to be so used. Similarly, a fee simple subject to a condition subsequent would have arisen had the Huttons given the land *upon condition that* or *provided that* it be used for school purposes. In the

1941 deed, though the Huttons gave the land "to be used for school purpose only, otherwise to revert to Grantors herein," no words of temporal limitation, or terms of express condition, were used in the grant.

The plaintiffs argue that the word "only" should be construed as a limitation rather than a condition. The defendants respond that where ambiguous language is used in a deed, the courts of Illinois have expressed a constructional preference for a fee simple subject to a condition subsequent. Both sides refer us to cases involving deeds which contain language analogous to the 1941 grant in this case.

We believe that a close analysis of the wording of the original grant shows that the grantors intended to create a fee simple determinable followed by a possibility of reverter. Here, the use of the word "only" immediately following the grant "for school purpose" demonstrates that the Huttons wanted to give the land to the school district only as long as it was needed and no longer. The language "this land to be used for school purpose only" is an example of a grant which contains a limitation within the granting clause. It suggests a limited grant, rather than a full grant subject to a condition, and thus, both theoretically and linguistically, gives rise to a fee simple determinable.

The second relevant clause furnishes plaintiffs' position with additional support. It cannot be argued that the phrase "otherwise to revert to grantors herein" is inconsistent with a fee simple subject to a condition subsequent. Nor does the word "revert" automatically create a possibility of reverter. But, in combination with the preceding phrase, the provisions by which possession is returned to the grantors seem to trigger a mandatory return rather than a permissive return because it is not stated that the grantor "may" re-enter the land.

The terms used in the 1941 deed, although imprecise, were designed to allow the property to be used for a single purpose, namely, for "school purpose." The Huttons intended to have the land back if it were ever used otherwise. Upon a grant of exclusive use followed by an express provision for reverter when that use ceases, courts and commentators have agreed that a fee simple determinable, rather than a fee simple subject to a condition subsequent, is created. Our own research has uncovered cases from other jurisdictions and sources in which language very similar to that in the Hutton deed has been held to create a fee simple determinable:

"[A conveyance] 'for the use, intent and purpose of a site for a School House * * * [and] whenever the said School District removes the School House from said tract of land or whenever said School House ceases to be used as the Public School House * * * then the said Trust shall cease and determine and the said land shall revert to [the grantor and his heirs.]' " *(Consolidated School District v. Walter* (1954), 243 Minn. 159, 160, 66 N.W.2d 881, 882.)

" '[I]t being absolutely understood that when said land ceases to be used for school purposes it is to revert to the above grantor, his heirs.' " *(United States v. 1119.15 Acres of Land* (E.D. Ill. 1942), 44 F. Supp. 449.)

" 'That I, S.S. Gray (Widower), for and in consideration of the sum of Donation to Wheeler School District to be used by said Wheeler Special School District for school and church purposes and to revert to me should school and church be discontinued or moved.' " *(Williams v. Kirby School District No. 32* (1944), 207 Ark. 458, 461, 181 S.W.2d 488, 490.)

"It is understood and agreed that if the above described land is abandoned by the said second parties and not used for school purposes then the above described land reverts to the party of the first part." *(School District No. 6 v. Russell* (1964), 156 Colo. 75, 76, 396 P.2d 929, 930.)

"[T]o B and C [trustees of a school district] and their heirs and successors for school purposes and to revert to the grantor when it ceases to be so used." Restatement of Property §44, comment 1, illustration V (1936).

Thus, authority from this State and others indicates that the grant in the Hutton deed did in fact create a fee simple determinable. We are not persuaded by the cases cited by the defendants for the terms of conveyance in those cases distinguish them from the facts presented here.

***

The estate created in *Latham v. Illinois Central R.R. Co.* (1912), 253 Ill. 93, 97 N.E. 254, was held to be a fee simple subject to a condition subsequent. Land was conveyed to a railroad in return for the railroad's agreement to erect and maintain a passenger depot and a freight depot on the premises. The deed was made to the grantee, " 'their successors and assigns forever, for the uses and purposes hereinafter mentioned, and for none other.' " (253 Ill. 93, 96.) Those purposes were limited to " 'railroad purposes only.' " (253 Ill. 93, 96.) The deed provided "that in case of non-user of said premises so conveyed for the uses and purposes aforesaid, that then and in that case the title to said premises shall revert back to [the grantors], their heirs, executors, administrators and assigns.' " (253 Ill. 93, 96-97.) The property was granted to the railroad to have and hold forever, " 'subject, nevertheless, to all the conditions, covenants, agreements and limitations in this deed expressed.' " (253 Ill. 93, 97.) The estate in *Latham* may be distinguished from that created here in that the former was a grant "forever" which was subjected to certain use restrictions while the Hutton deed gave the property to the school district only as long as it could use it.

***

holding

We hold, therefore, that the 1941 deed from W. E. and Jennie Hutton to the Trustees of School District No. 1 created a fee simple determinable in the trustees followed by a possibility of reverter in the Huttons and their heirs. Accordingly, the trial court erred in dismissing plaintiffs' third amended complaint which followed its holding that the plaintiffs could not have acquired any interest in the Hutton School property from Harry Hutton. We must therefore reverse and remand this cause to the trial court for further proceedings.

decision

We refrain from deciding the following issues: (1) whether the 1977 conveyance from Harry Hutton was legally sufficient to pass his interest in the school property to the plaintiffs, (2) whether Harry Hutton effectively disclaimed his interest in the property in favor of the defendants by virtue of his 1977 disclaimer, and (3) whether the defendants have ceased to use the Hutton School grounds for "school purposes."

Reversed and remanded.

8.1.3.2

Canova Land & Inv. Co. v. Lynn
856 S.E.2d 581 (Va. 2021)

Supreme Court of Virginia

OPINION BY JUSTICE WILLIAM C. MIMS

In this case, the Court decides whether a deed restriction for the use of a particular church was an unreasonable restraint on alienation.   ᵢₛₛᵤₑ

I. BACKGROUND AND MATERIAL PROCEEDINGS BELOW

In 1875, Edna and Levi Lynn executed a deed granting one acre of land to the Woodbine Baptist Church ("Woodbine") "in exchange for five dollars." The deed states in relevant part:

> the said Trustees will hold said property for the use and benefit of the Baptist Church (commonly called the "New School") and that they will allow the proper authorities of said Church to use it for the worship of God in accordance with the customs and regulations of said Church and the laws of Virginia: The being those confirmed by the Circuit Court of Prince William at the May Term thereof for the said church known as the "Woodbine" Baptist Church, said property to revert to the grantors or their heirs if it ceases to be used for the purposes expressed in the deed.

Woodbine, which since its inception had been an unincorporated association, continued to use the land until 2006, when its trustees gifted it to the Woodbine Family Worship Center and Christian School ("Woodbine Worship Center"), a Virginia corporation. The land continued to be used for worship by the corporation.

In 2007, Woodbine Worship Center received a loan of $1,373,000 from Virginia Commerce Bank. The loan was secured by a deed of trust, in which Woodbine Worship Center granted all of its "present and future right, title and interest" in a five-acre parcel of land, including the one acre conveyed by the 1875 deed. The bank's title search of the property extended only to the year 1900, so it did not disclose the 1875 deed.

Woodbine Worship Center defaulted on the loan in 2011. Canova Land and Investment Company ("Canova"), a wholly owned subsidiary of United Bank, acquired title to the property at a foreclosure sale in September 2012. Canova has not taken possession of, attempted to sell, or used the property due to concerns about implicating the reverter clause in the deed. Woodbine Worship Center continues to use the land for worship.

Canova brought suit to quiet title to the property in the Circuit Court of Prince William County, claiming that the reverter clause in the 1875 deed should be voided as an unreasonable restraint on alienation. It asserted that because the deed by its terms allows use only by the "Woodbine Baptist Church," the restraint is irrationally limited in scope and should be voided as contrary to public policy. It also argued that upholding the deed restriction would hinder its efforts to develop the larger five-acre parcel, thus preventing it from being put to its most efficient use.

Appellees Carolyn Lynn and Cheryl Crawford, descendants of Edna and Levi Lynn, argued that the restraint in the 1875 deed only affects Canova's use, rather than its ability to alienate, and is therefore valid. They also argued that it "is the creator of its own alleged misfortune" because it failed to search the title prior to 1900. As to the reasonableness of the restriction, they note that Virginia precedent clearly recognizes a charitable exception to the rule against restraints on alienation, citing this Court's opinion in *County School Board of Scott County v. Dowell*, 190 Va. 676, 680, 58 S.E.2d 38 (1950). Appellees Unknown Heirs of Levi and Edna Lynn also countered Canova's claim that the restraint is unreasonably limited in scope. They argued that the restriction allows for use by the broader Baptist denomination and "not merely the Woodbine Congregation," and is therefore sufficiently general.

The parties went to trial in July 2019. The circuit court dismissed Canova's complaint with prejudice, but suspended the dismissal after Canova filed a post-trial motion. After reconsidering, the circuit court ultimately dismissed the complaint with prejudice in January 2020, finding that the reverter clause was a reasonable land use restriction imposed on a charitable gift. The court explained in its letter opinion that the deed granted a fee simple determinable subject to a possibility of reverter and not a fee simple absolute. Therefore, in acquiring the restricted property from

Woodbine Worship Center, Canova "ha[d] acquired no more than its predecessor in title had." Relying upon *Dowell*, the circuit court also reasoned that a landowner has the right to grant a defeasible fee when the land is transferred for charitable purposes. On appeal, Canova claims that the 1875 deed imposes an unreasonable restraint on its ability to alienate the property. It assigns error to the lower court's finding that the restraint was reasonable in scope. We granted the petition for appeal.

[handwritten margin note: plaintiff arg.]

II. ANALYSIS

The interpretation of a deed is a mixed question of law and fact that this Court reviews de novo. It is axiomatic that "a lawful owner, as a general rule, has the power to convey his real property to whomever he wishes under whatever conditions they agree to." *Hamm v. Hazelwood*, 292 Va. 153, 157, 787 S.E.2d 144 (2016). In interpreting the Lynns' 1875 deed, we must give full effect to their intent unless such intent is inconsistent with the law.

One limitation on a grantor's absolute right to transfer property is the rule against restraints on alienation. "A condition totally prohibiting the alienation of a vested fee simple estate or requiring a forfeiture upon alienation is void." *Edwards v. Bradley*, 227 Va. 224, 228, 315 S.E.2d 196 (1984). However, reasonable restraints are generally valid. *See Hamm*, 292 Va. at 159, 787 S.E.2d 144 (noting that lesser forms of restraint are not "per se repugnant," and will be upheld if "under all the circumstances of the case, the restraint is found to be reasonable") (quoting Restatement (Second) of Property: Donative Transfers § 4.2 (1983)). Additionally, we use a "liberal interpretation to uphold" deeds involving land granted for charitable purposes. *Shenandoah Valley Nat'l Bank v. Taylor*, 192 Va. 135, 148, 63 S.E.2d 786 (1951).

The 1875 deed granted Woodbine a fee simple determinable subject to the possibility of reverter, not a fee simple absolute. The deed language is comparable to the deed in *Dowell*, in which we found that a deed granting land to trustees of a local school district "so long as it is used for a public school" conveyed a valid defeasible fee. 190 Va. at 687, 689, 58 S.E.2d 38. We held that the limitation on the grant proved it "was not intended to be and was not in fact an absolute fee simple, but an estate whose duration should exist and continue until the happening of a specified event." *Id.* at 689, 58 S.E.2d 38.

As in *Dowell*, the Lynns never intended to grant a fee simple absolute to the Woodbine congregation. They used conditional language that is typical of a defeasible fee by specifying that the property will revert to the grantors "if it ceases to be used for the purposes expressed in the deed." As the circuit court correctly stated, "There is ample authority in Virginia that restrictions triggering reverters of fee simple determinable estates are generally valid." When a grantor clearly intends to create a limited estate, we are less inclined to find the condition imposed on the grant to be unreasonable.

Canova agrees that the deed creates a fee simple determinable, but it maintains that the restriction is nevertheless "all-encompassing" and constitutes an unreasonable restraint on alienation. It points to the Restatement (Second) of Property to buttress its claim that a forfeiture restraint on alienation must be "reasonable under all the circumstances of the case." Restatement (Second) of Property: Donative Transfers § 4.2 (1983). However, § 3.4 of the same Restatement distinguishes restraints on use, explaining that "a restraint on the use that may be made of transferred property by the transferee is not a restraint on alienation, as that term is used in this Restatement." While there is "no precise rule" for determining whether a restraint controls the use of property or its alienation, we look to the form of the restraint, the reasons for imposing the restraint, and the practical effect of the restraint when making our decision. *See id.*

Regarding form, the language of the deed granting land to Woodbine "to *use* it for the worship of God" clearly suggests that this is a restraint on use. (Emphasis added.) Additionally, the Lynns clearly stated their reason for imposing the restraint: "for the worship of God." That too suggests that the restraint focuses on the use of the property. Nonetheless, Canova claims that the "all-encompassing" nature of the reverter clause makes it a restraint on alienation in practical effect, if not in form.

Canova claims that this case is comparable to *Dunlop v. Dunlop*, in which we held that a reverter clause requiring a son to forfeit three-fourths of his father's business if he attempted to sell any part of it was unreasonable because it was unlimited in time and scope. 144 Va. 297, 309, 132 S.E. 351 (1926). We disagree. The testator in that case granted a fee simple absolute, suggesting that he wanted his son to have "absolute control and complete ownership of [his business]." *Id.* at 305, 132 S.E. 351. By contrast, the Lynns' deed conveyed a defeasible fee to Woodbine.

***

In arguing that the 1875 deed restraint is unreasonable, Canova has adopted an overly restrictive interpretation that would create significant unintended consequences for church landowners. Under Canova's interpretation, the deed permits use only by Woodbine as the congregation existed in 1875. We disagree. At oral argument, Canova conceded that, under its interpretation, the deed may have been violated when Woodbine incorporated in 2006 to become the Woodbine Worship Center, a transition adopted by countless congregations in Virginia once incorporation was permitted. Indeed, following Canova's interpretation to its logical conclusion, if Woodbine changed its denominational affiliation – such as joining or leaving the Southern Baptist Convention, for example – the subsequent use by the newly-affiliated entity could constitute a violation of the restraint in the deed. To adopt such a narrow and rigid interpretation would ignore the practical realities of individual congregations and denominations over decades and even centuries. The more reasonable interpretation of the deed is that the land must be used "for the worship of God" by a congregation that generally follows the tenets of Baptist churches.

***

We have recognized that "public policy is at the heart" of challenges involving restraints on alienation. *Lipps v. First American*, 223 Va. 131, 137, 286 S.E.2d 215 (1982). In *Lipps*, we noted that determining whether a restraint is reasonable requires "considering whether [the restraint] is such only as to afford a fair protection to the interest of the party in favor of whom it is given, and not so large as to interfere with the interest of the public." *Id.* at 136, 286 S.E.2d 215.

. . . Canova claims that upholding the restraint would significantly limit its ability to develop the land for arguably more efficient purposes, and would, to quote Minor, "put the lands of the living in the cold grip of the hands of the dead." 1 Frederick D.G. Ribble, Minor on Real Property § 553, at 720 (2d ed. 1928). We sympathize with these concerns, but we cannot agree that Canova's legitimate interest in robustly developing the larger parcel of land it has acquired outweighs the equally legitimate interest in protecting and promoting charitable giving. To hold otherwise, as appellees have noted, would put into jeopardy innumerable charitable gifts with restraints like those included in the Lynns' deed. In light of the significant chilling effect that such a holding could have on charitable giving, we cannot agree that Canova's interest in developing all of its acquired land should take priority.

Because the Lynns' deed granted Woodbine a fee simple subject to the possibility of reverter, the reverter by its terms is a restraint on use, and the reverter is not unreasonable in light of the charitable context in which it was given, we affirm the circuit court's decision to uphold the 1875 deed as valid.

III. CONCLUSION

For these reasons, we affirm the Circuit Court of Prince William County's dismissal of Canova's complaint.

Affirmed.

8.1.3.3

El Dorado Land Co. v. City of McKinney
395 S.W.3d 798 (Tex. 2013)

Supreme Court of Texas

Justice DEVINE

delivered the opinion of the Court.

The issue in this inverse condemnation lawsuit is whether a reversionary interest, consisting of the grantor's right to purchase real property on the occurrence of a future event, is a sufficient property interest to support an inverse condemnation claim. The trial court concluded it was not and dismissed the case. The court of appeals affirmed the trial court's judgment, holding that the grantor's retained right was not a compensable property interest under the Takings Clause of the Texas Constitution. 349 S.W.3d 215, 216, 218 (Tex.App.Dallas 2011) (citing TEX. CONST, art I, § 17). Because we conclude that the reversionary interest here is a compensable property interest, we reverse and remand to the trial court.

I

In 1999, El Dorado Land Company sold several acres of land to the City of McKinney for use as a park. El Dorado's special warranty deed provided that the conveyance was "subject to the requirement and restriction that the property shall be used only as a Community Park." If the City decided not to use the property for that purpose, the deed further granted El Dorado the right to purchase the property. The deed labeled this right an option and set the option's price at the amount the City paid or the property's current market value, whichever was less. El Dorado also had the right to inspect the property and to close on the purchase within ninety days after inspection.

Ten years after acquiring the property, the City built a public library on part of the land. The City did not offer to sell the property to El Dorado or otherwise give notice before building the library. After learning about the library, El Dorado notified the City by letter that it intended to exercise its option to purchase. El Dorado's letter further asked the City within ten days to acknowledge its obligations under the deed and to suggest an acceptable closing date.

After the City failed to acknowledge El Dorado's rights under the deed, El Dorado sued for inverse condemnation. The City responded with a plea to the jurisdiction. In its plea, the City argued that El Dorado's claim did not involve a compensable taking of property but a mere breach of contract for which the City's governmental immunity had not been waived. The trial court agreed, sustaining the City's plea and dismissing El Dorado's lawsuit. The court of appeals similarly agreed and affirmed the trial court's judgment.

II

The dispute here continues over the nature of El Dorado's interest in this land. El Dorado argues that its right to purchase this property is a real property interest, in the nature of a reversionary interest, and more particularly described as a right of reentry. The City, on the other hand, contends that El Dorado's option is not a real property interest but a mere contract right. As such, the City argues that the option is unenforceable against it absent an express waiver of the City's governmental immunity. Because the Legislature has not chosen to waive governmental immunity

267

for this particular type of contract claim, the City concludes that the court of appeals correctly affirmed the dismissal of El Dorado's claim.

The court of appeals similarly reasoned that the deed restriction and option were merely contract rights that were not compensable against a governmental entity under the Texas Constitution. *See* 349 S.W.3d at 218 (observing that inverse condemnation claims have "traditionally involved interests in real property and not the alleged taking of property interests created under contract"). The court accordingly "reject[ed] El Dorado's argument that, pursuant to the deed provision, it held a reversionary interest or the 'possibility of reverter' in the property." *Id.* While we agree that the deed did not create a possibility of reverter, we disagree that El Dorado did not retain another type of reversionary interest in the property.

El Dorado refers to its reversionary interest as a right of reentry. A right of reentry is a "future interest created in the transferor that [may] become possessory upon the termination of a fee simple subject to a condition subsequent." Restatement (Third) of Property: Wills and Other Donative Transfers § 25.2 cmt. b (hereafter Restatement (Third) of Property); *see also Davis v. Vidal,* 105 Tex. 444, 151 S.W. 290, 292-93 (1912) (describing a right of reentry as "a contingent reversionary interest in the premises resulting from the conveyance of an estate upon a condition subsequent where there has been an infraction of such condition").

Under the deed, El Dorado's possessory interest was contingent on the property's use. If the City violated the deed restriction, El Dorado retained the power to terminate the City's estate.[1] The deed referred to this power or right as an option, but it effectively functioned as a power of termination, or as El Dorado labels it, a right of reentry. El Dorado's deed conveyed a defeasible estate ("a fee simple subject to a condition subsequent") to the City with El Dorado retaining a conditional future interest — the power to terminate the City's defeasible estate on the occurrence of a condition subsequent. We have previously equated this right to an estate or interest in land. *Davis,* 151 S.W. at 293; *see also* Restatement of Property § 153(l)(a) & cmt. a (noting that the term future interest includes an interest in land which "may become a present interest" and is "sufficiently broad to include ... powers of termination").

Contrary to the court of appeals, we conclude that El Dorado retained a reversionary interest in the property. We likewise disagree with the court of appeals' analysis of El Dorado's claim as a contract right dependent on a statutory waiver of the City's governmental immunity. A statutory waiver of immunity is unnecessary for a takings claim because the Texas Constitution waives "governmental immunity for the taking, damaging or destruction of property for public use." *Steele v. City of Houston*, 603 S.W.2d 786, 791 (Tex.1980).

El Dorado's claim is that the City took or destroyed its reversionary interest in the property by refusing either to convey the property or to condemn El Dorado's interest. The issue then is whether El Dorado's reversionary interest can support a takings claim under the Texas Constitution. Tex. Const. art. I § 17. El Dorado submits that it can under our decision in *Leeco Gas & Oil Co. v. Nueces County*, 736 S.W.2d 629 (Tex.1987).

III

Leeco, like this case, involved a restricted conveyance of land to a governmental entity that later sought to avoid the deed restriction. The land in that case was donated to Nueces County for use as a park, and the deed included a restrictive covenant requiring that use. *Leeco*, 736 S.W.2d at 630. The grantor retained a reversionary interest, described as a possibility of reverter, in the event the land was not used as a park.

Nueces County subsequently decided to use the land for another purpose and sought to condemn the grantor's reversionary interest. Although the land was worth millions of dollars, the trial court awarded only nominal damages for the grantor's reversionary interest, and the court of appeals affirmed that award. We reversed and remanded, concluding that the grantor's reversionary interest was worth more than nominal damages.

Relying on the Restatement of Property, we observed that a possibility of reverter was a protected property interest, the value of which depended upon the imminence of possession. We explained that a nominal valuation would be appropriate for the government taking such property only "when the event upon which the possessory estate in fee simple defeasible is to end is not probable within a reasonably short period of time." *Id.* at 631. Conversely, we explained that nominal damages would be inappropriate if the defeasible event was reasonably certain to occur in the near future or had already occurred. Under those circumstances, we said the compensable value of the reversionary interest should be measured by the amount "the value of the unrestricted fee exceeds the value of the restricted fee." *Id.* at 631-32. *Leeco* thus recognizes that a future interest in real property is compensable under the Takings Clause, Tex. Const, art. I, § 17, and that the owner of such an interest is entitled to a condemnation award.

The court of appeals' opinion does not directly address *Leeco,* but arguably attempts to distinguish the decision by observing that the deed in this case did not include a possibility of reverter. 349 S.W.3d at *218.* While we agree it did *not,* as previously explained, we do not accept the court's further conclusion that El Dorado's deed did not create a reversionary interest. *See id.* (rejecting El Dorado's argument that "it held a reversionary interest or the 'possibility of reverter' in the property"). As El Dorado argues, the deed restriction and option created in El Dorado a right of reentry, which is a reversionary interest, albeit of a different type than the possibility of reverter reserved in *Leeco.*

The City argues that *Leeco* is distinguishable on this ground because a possibility of reverter is materially different from the right or option reserved by El Dorado. At oral argument, the City elaborated on the distinction, explaining that *Leeco's* reversionary interest was different because it was self-executing, whereas the right retained by El Dorado was not. While we agree that Leeco's possibility of reverter and El Dorado's right of reentry are different types of reversionary interests, it is not apparent why their technical differences make one a compensable property interest and the other a worthless right. In both, the termination of the possessory estate rests on the occurrence of a condition subsequent imposed upon the conveyance. That a right of reentry requires its holder to make an election does not make it any less a property right, particularly where as here the holder has made the required election.

Historically, the law divided future interests into five types: (1) remainders, (2) executory interests, (3) reversions, (4) possibilities of reverter, and (5) rights of entry.

Restatement (Third) of Property § 25.2 cmt. a. Remainders and executory interests are future interests created in persons other than the grantor. Reversions, possibilities of reverter, and rights of entry are interests that remain with the grantor. *Id.; see also* Restatement (Third) of Property § 25.2 cmt. b (noting their classification "as reversionary future interests, because they were retained by the transferor"). Collectively, the types of future interests that remain with the grantor are reversionary interests and may be viewed "as claims to property that the grantor never gave away." Powell on Real Property § 20.02[1].

***

. . . Under Texas law, the possibility of reverter and the right of reentry are both freely assignable like other property interests. . . . Simply put, both the possibility of reverter and the right of reentry are future interests in real property. *See* Lewis M. Simes & Allan F. Smith, the Law of Future Interests § 1 (2d ed.1956) (defining a future interest as "an interest in land or other things in which the privilege of possession or of enjoyment is future and not present"). And *Leeco* recognizes that a future interest in real property is compensable under the Takings Clause. 736 S.W.2d at 631-32 (citing Restatement of Property § 53). We accordingly reject the City's argument that *Leeco* is distinguishable merely because it involved a different type of reversionary interest.

***

Finally, the City argues that *Leeco* is procedurally distinguishable because the county initiated the condemnation proceedings, whereas in this case El Dorado commenced an inverse condemnation case. . . .

When private property is taken for a public purpose, our constitution requires that the government compensate the owner. TEX. CONST. art I, § 17. A condemnation proceeding is the formal process by which that compensation is determined. But when the government takes private property without paying for it, the owner must bring suit for inverse condemnation. The action is termed "inverse" because it is initiated by the private property owner instead of the government, but its purpose and procedure are generally no different.

In summary, we conclude that the reversionary interest retained by El Dorado in its deed to the City is a property interest capable of being taken by condemnation. We express no opinion, however, on whether a taking has occurred in this case. We reverse and remand to the trial court for it to determine whether the City violated its deed restrictions by building a public library on a part of the land dedicated for use as a community park and, if so, to what extent the City has taken El Dorado's interest in the restricted property.

1. This power, referred to in the deed as the option to purchase, is also known at common law by other names, such as a right of entry for condition broken, a right of reentry for breach of condition subsequent, or a power of termination. See 3 Richard R. Powell, Powell on Real Property § 20.01[1] (2000) ("The term 'power of termination' is used by the Restatement and by some courts, but most courts and most lawyers employ the term 'right of entry for condition broken.'"); see also 34 Tex. Jur.3d Estates § 8 at 546 (2010) (noting that "a future interest" may be "characterized as a right of reentry for breach of condition subsequent or, in other words, an estate subject to a power of termination"). [Editorial Note: This is footnote 3 of the opinion.]

8.1.4
Life Estates

A grantor could convey less than a fee estate. For example, a grantor could convey a *life estate* or a leasehold interest. The life estate is a very descriptive name. As expected, a life estate terminates on the death of the life tenant. A variation of a life estate is referred to as a life estate *pur autre vie*. In that case, the grantee's estate is based on the life of another and terminates at death of the measuring life.

8.1.4.1

Knopf v. Gray
545 S.W.3d 542 (Tex. 2018)

Supreme Court of Texas

PER CURIAM

This case involves the construction of a will bequest of a tract of land. The primary issue presented is whether the testator intended to devise a fee-simple interest or a life-estate interest to her son. Both the trial court and the court of appeals held that the will unambiguously devised a fee-simple interest, entitling the son to summary judgment. We disagree and reverse the court of appeals' judgment.

Vada Wallace Allen's will disposed of her entire estate, including the land at issue in this case-approximately 316 acres of land in Robertson County. The provision through which she devised that land states:

> NOW BOBBY I leave the rest to you, everything, certificates of deposit, land, cattle and machinery, Understand the land is not to be sold but passed on down to your children, ANNETTE KNOPF, ALLISON KILWAY, AND STANLEY GRAY. TAKE CARE OF IT AND TRY TO BE HAPPY.

The provision thus begins with a residuary bequest to her son, William Robert "Bobby" Gray. That residuary bequest is immediately followed by instructional language referencing the "land" included in the residuary and Bobby's children. Two of those children, Annette Knopf and Stanley Gray (collectively, Knopf), are the petitioners here.

Bobby and his wife, Karen, conveyed the land at issue in fee simple to Polasek Farms, LLC, via multiple warranty deeds. Knopf sued Bobby, Karen, and Polasek Farms (who collectively are the respondents here), seeking a declaratory judgment that Allen devised only a life estate to Bobby, thus precluding him from delivering a greater interest to Polasek Farms.

Polasek Farms and Knopf filed cross-motions for summary judgment. The trial court granted Polasek Farms' motion in two separate rulings and rendered final judgment for the respondents, finding that the contested provision contained an invalid disabling restraint, the will vested Bobby with a fee-simple interest in the property, and Knopf received no remainder interest. A divided court of appeals affirmed, agreeing with the trial court's findings and concluding that the will's language regarding passing the land on down to the children was merely an instruction to Bobby rather than a gift to the children. 541 S.W.3d 200, ----, 2017 WL 131863 (Tex.

App. Waco 2017) (mem. op.). The dissenting justice would have held that the provision's meaning was ambiguous and thus improper for resolution on summary judgment. *Id.* at ---- (Gray, C.J., dissenting).

We review summary judgments de novo. . . .

The cardinal rule of will construction is to ascertain the testator's intent and to enforce that intent to the extent allowed by law. We look to the instrument's language, considering its provisions as a whole and attempting to harmonize them so as to give effect to the will's overall intent. We interpret the words in a will as a layperson would use them absent evidence that the testator received legal assistance in drafting the will or was otherwise familiar with technical meanings.

Here, the parties dispute whether Allen intended to devise to Bobby a fee-simple interest in the land at issue or only a life estate. "An estate in land that is conveyed or devised is a fee simple unless the estate is limited by express words," TEX. PROP. CODE § 5.001(a), but the law does not require any specific words or formalities to create a life estate. Therefore, the words used in the will must only evidence intent to create what lawyers know as a life estate. A life estate is generally defined as an "estate held only for the duration of a specified person's life." *Life Estate* , BLACK'S LAW DICTIONARY (10th ed. 2014). Thus, a will creates a life estate "where the language of the instrument manifests an intention on the part of the grantor or testator to pass to a grantee or devisee a right to possess, use, or enjoy property during the period of the grantee's life." *Fin. Freedom Senior Funding Corp. v. Horrocks* , 294 S.W.3d 749, 755 (Tex. App. Houston [14th Dist.] 2009, no pet.).

As noted, the contested provision in Allen's will states:

> NOW BOBBY I leave the rest to you, everything, certificates of deposit, land, cattle and machinery, Understand the land is not to be sold but passed on down to your children, ANNETTE KNOPF, ALLISON KILWAY, AND STANLEY GRAY. TAKE CARE OF IT AND TRY TO BE HAPPY.

Knopf argues that the instructional language in the second clause, read in conjunction with other language throughout the will, demonstrates Allen's intent to grant Bobby a life estate with the remainder interest going to her grandchildren. The respondents counter that the instructional language confirms Allen's intent to devise the land to Bobby in fee simple. In the alternative, they argue that the instructional language either constitutes an invalid disabling restraint, is nontestamentary, or is technically insufficient to create a life estate.

Beginning with the contested provision itself, the parties focus largely on the meaning of the specific phrase "passed on down." However, this line of semantic argument misses the analytical forest for the trees. The provision's meaning depends on its overall intent, so narrow concentration on the possible meanings of three words is a diversion. We need only read the provision as a whole to see a layperson's clearly expressed intent to create what the law calls a life estate. Reading all three clauses together, Allen grants the land to Bobby subject to the limitations that he not sell it, that he take care of it, *and* that it be passed down to his children. This represents the essence of a life estate; a life tenant's interest in the property is limited by the general requirement that he preserve the remainder interest unless otherwise authorized in the will. *See, e.g.*, *Richardson v. McCloskey*, 276 S.W. 680, 685 (Tex. 1925) (stating that life tenants take the property's benefits with corresponding burdens of repair and upkeep); *Moody v. Pitts*, 708 S.W.2d 930, 936 (Tex. App.-Corpus Christi 1986, no writ) (recognizing the duty of life tenants not to destroy remainder interests except as authorized by the will); *Maxwell v. Harrell*, 183 S.W.2d 577, 580 (Tex. Civ. App.-Austin 1944, writ ref'd w.o.m.) (noting that a life tenant cannot alienate property to "defeat the estate of the remaindermen"). Allen's words in the contested provision unambiguously refer to elements of a life estate and designate her grandchildren, the petitioners, as the remaindermen. The language thus clearly demonstrates that the phrase "passed on down," as used here, encompasses a transfer upon Bobby's death.

Reading the provision in the context of the entire document only cements this conclusion. Allen devised her entire estate to various family members, including approximately one dozen specific bequests to her grandchildren. She also selectively repeated the sentiment that certain property not be sold but be "passed on" or "given" or "handed down" to the devisees' children. Thus, the will as a whole indicates an intent to keep her property in her family and to bequeath certain property to multiple generations. Reading the contested provision to grant Bobby a life estate and to grant Knopf the remainder interest is fully consistent with the overall intent of the document.

The respondents attempt to rebut Knopf's interpretation by characterizing the words "the land is not to be sold" as an invalid disabling restraint on sale, as the trial court and court of appeals held. A disabling restraint is an attempt by the grantor, through the terms of a transfer, "to invalidate a [grantee's] later transfer of that [granted] interest, in whole or in part." RESTATEMENT (SECOND) OF PROPERTY § 3.1 (Am. Law Inst. 1983). The respondents would thus have us pluck a fragment out of context, construe it in isolation, strike it, and then return to the remaining text. This proposed approach inverts the analytical process and defies our rules of will construction. The nature of a granted interest (e.g., fee simple versus life estate) must be resolved *before* a court may determine whether a restraint on that interest is valid because the restraint's validity depends on the type of interest granted. To the point, inherent in a life estate is a restraint on alienation of the remainder interest. Accordingly, the phrase "the land is not to be sold" is an integral part of Allen's expression of intent to create a life estate. The respondents' suggested methodology would also violate our contextual approach to will construction and our rule against rewriting wills to arrive at a presumed intent. *Shriner's Hosp. for Crippled Children v. Stahl*, 610 S.W.2d 147, 151 (Tex. 1980) (noting that intent is derived from the words actually used and that courts cannot redraft wills to reflect presumed intent).

The respondents' remaining arguments also ultimately beg the question of the contested provision's intended meaning. For example, they contend that the instructional language following the residuary bequest is precatory, or nontestamentary, language with no legal effect. But whether language is precatory or testamentary is itself a question of intent. Our determination that the provision clearly expresses Allen's intent to grant a life estate establishes that the instructional language *is* testamentary. Moreover, the fact that Allen selectively used these phrases evidences that she intended they have some effect.

Finally, the respondents also claim that any ambiguity in the contested provision favors them because a testator must clearly reduce a bequest from a fee simple to a life estate. However, in light of our holding that the provision unambiguously conveyed a life estate, we need not address this argument.

* * * *

Accordingly, . . . we grant Knopf's petition for review, reverse the court of appeals' judgment, and render judgment that the will granted Bobby Gray a life estate and the petitioners the remainder interest in the property at issue. The case is remanded to the trial court for further proceedings consistent with this opinion.

8.1.5
Fee Tails

As noted above, the freehold estates include the fee simple, the *fee tail*, and the life estate. Our discussion of non-fee simple estates primarily focuses on life estates and leaseholds because jurisdictions in the United States have either abolished or significantly modified the fee tail. Nonetheless, a brief mention of fee tail is warranted because the States vary in how they interpret or treat attempted fee tail language. The fee tail originated as a means to keep real property within a bloodline from generation to generation. The typical language for conveyance of a fee tail is "O to A and the heirs of his body."

8.1.5.1
Doe on Demise of See v. Craigen
35 Va. 449 (1836)
Supreme Court of Appeals of Virginia

Testator devises to his daughter [Phoebe Couchman] the upper half of his plantation, but should she die without heirs of her own body, then the said half of the plantation to be divided between the son in law and the son of the testator: Held, [Phoebe Couchman] took by the will an estate tail in the land devised to her, which the statute for abolishing entails converted into a fee simple, and barred the contingent remainder limited on the estate tail.

George See, late of Hardy county, by his last will and testament, dated September 3, 1803, and recorded June 11, 1811, made the following devise (among others): "I give and bequeath to my daughter Phoebe Couchman the upper half of my plantation, to be equally divided between her and John Craigen as to quality and quantity; but should my said daughter die without heirs of her own body, it is then my will and desire that said half of my plantation should be divided between my son in law John Craigen and my son Adam See."

Phoebe Couchman entered upon the land devised to her by the will of the testator, and held it until her death. She died in the year 1832, without any child or descendant living at the time of her death, having first duly made and published her last will and testament, by which she devised the land given her by the will of George See deceased, to Adeline Louisa Craigen, in fee simple, if she had right to devise the same. Adeline Louisa Craigen entered into the land so devised to her, and held possession by virtue of that devise.

In May 1833, John Doe, lessee of Adam See (to whom a moiety of the land was devised by the will of George See, in case Phoebe Couchman should die without heirs of her body) brought an action of ejectment in the circuit superior court of law and chancery for Hardy county, against Adeline Louisa Craigen, for an undivided moiety of the land which had been devised as aforesaid to Phoebe Couchman. . . .

The circuit court decided that the law, upon the case agreed, was for the defendant, and rendered judgment accordingly. To which judgment a *supersedeas* was allowed.

CARR, J.

In spite of the ingenious argument of the counsel for the plaintiff in error, I am of opinion, that according to the spirit and meaning of the law, and the clear and uniform course of our decisions, the estate given to Phoebe Couchman was a fee tail, changed by our act into a fee simple, and the devise over void.

CABELL, J.

I think the case a very plain one, and that the judgment ought to be affirmed.

***

TUCKER, P.

This is a question upon a clause of the will of George See, dated in 1803, in the following words: "I give and bequeath to my daughter Phoebe Couchman the upper half of my plantation, to be equally divided between her and John Craigen; but should my said daughter die without heirs of her own body," then over. There are other provisions of the will, which are strongly relied on as demonstrative of the testator's intention; but they are entirely unimportant in the view of the case which I shall take.

This court has, by its various decisions, at length placed beyond further dispute a point which has been most earnestly debated on various occasions. It has been contended, that when a question arises whether an estate tail is created by the language of the testator, which is converted into a fee by the statute, the act of 1785, dispensing with words of inheritance in the creation of an estate in fee simple, may be resorted to, to enlarge the estate of the first taker into a fee, and thereby avoid the consequences which ensue if the words of limitation to him are construed to give only a life estate. Thus in the case at bar, the limitation is to Phoebe Couchman, without superadded words of inheritance ; and then it is provided that if she dies without heirs of her body, the estate shall go over. Here the words "if she dies without heirs of her body" do not amount to a devise to the heirs of her body, after the determination of her estate for life, and the consequence would be that if she takes but an estate for life, her issue can never take anything. The law of England would therefore construe this clearly an estate tail. But if, under our law, you consider Phoebe as taking a fee by the operation of the act of 1785, then there is a good devise to her of the fee, with a limitation over upon her dying without heirs of the body, by way of executory devise; and thus the whole line of her descendants wilt take according to the manifest general intent, without the necessity of creating an estate tail.

This use of the statute has been attempted in many cases, but has been repeatedly overruled. I have struggled for it myself in more than one case, but have found myself in the woful minority of one. I must therefore surrender; . . .

***

For these reasons I am of opinion to affirm the judgment.

BROCKENBROUGH, J.

I concur in affirming the judgment.

8.1.6
Discussion: Notes, Questions, and Problems

8.1.6.1
Discussion Note #1. Alienability of possibility of reverter and right of re-entry

In *Mahrenholz v. County Board of School Trustees*, excerpted above, an Illinois prohibited lifetime alienation or devises of both a possibility of reverter and a right of re-entry. By contrast, into *El Dorado Land Co. v. City of McKinney*, excerpted above, the court noted that in under Texas law, "the possibility of reverter and the right of reentry are both freely assignable like other property interests." Most states align with the view in Texas that both the possibility of reverter and the right of re-entry are alienable.

8.1.6.2
Discussion Question #2. Restraint on alienation?

Review the discussion on restraints on alienation in *Canova Land & Inv. Co. v. Lynn*, excerpted above, and *Knopf v. Gray*, excerpted above, and the following language in two different conveyances of Blackacre. The first conveyance provides as follows: "O to A so long as Blackacre is used as a farm, otherwise to revert to grantor." The second conveyance provides as follows: "O to A and his heirs but the land is not to be sold." Which of these two, if any, might run afoul of the restriction on alienation rule and why?

8.1.6.3
Discussion Question #3. Fee tail statute?

As noted in *Doe on Demise of See v. Craigen*, excerpted above, if a grant uses fee tail language, Virginia law provides that the estate converts into a fee simple absolute.

Compare the statutory response to fee tail language under Virginia law to the statutory response in Florida found in Fla. Stat. § 689.14, which provides as follows:

> **689.14** **Entailed estates.**—No property, real or personal, shall be entailed in this state. Any instrument purporting to create an estate tail, express or implied, shall be deemed to create an estate for life in the first taker with remainder per stirpes to the lineal descendants of the first taker in being at the time of her or his death. If the remainder fails for want of such remainderman, then it shall vest in any other remaindermen designated in such instrument, or, if there is no such designation, then it shall revert to the original donor or to her or his heirs.

If you were the recipient of a conveyance that uses fee tail language, would you prefer to be governed by a statute patterned after the Virginia statute or the Florida statute, and why?

8.1.6.4

Discussion Problem #4. Blackacre conveyance to County Hospital problem

Assume Owen conveys Blackacre **"to County Hospital forever so long as the land is used for hospital purposes; if the land ceases to be used for hospital purposes, the conveyance shall be null and void."** What are the words of purchase? Does the purchaser have a present interest or a future interest? What are the words of limitation? What estate does the purchaser have? Did the grantor retain an interest in Blackacre? If so, what is the grantor's retained interest?

8.1.6.5

Discussion Problem #5. Conveyance to Alina problem

Assume that last year Oliver conveyed Blackacre to Alina as follows: **"to Alina for life."** Assume that the conveyance did not contain any other language of conveyance. What are the words of purchase? Does the purchaser have a present interest or a future interest? What are the words of limitation? What estate does the purchaser

present possessory interest

have? Did the grantor retain an interest in Blackacre? If so, what is the grantor's retained interest? Assume further that Xavier is very interested in leasing Blackacre for his new retail business. Xavier would like to enter into a 15-year lease for Blackacre. What would you recommend Xavier do in this situation?

[handwritten margin note: protect Xavier lease alina dies owner must be on lease, if dead get heirs]

8.1.6.6

Discussion Problem #6. Conveyance to caretaker problem

Assume that Annabelle has been taking care of Olivia's mother for many years. Last year, Olivia conveyed Blackacre as follows: **"to Annabelle for the life of my mother."** What are the words of purchase? Does the purchaser have a present interest or a future interest? What are the words of limitation? What estate does the purchaser have? Did the grantor retain an interest in Blackacre? If so, what is the grantor's retained interest?

[handwritten margin note: O has reversion mother has nothing]

8.2

Future Interests

Up until now, we have been discussing future interests retained by a grantor, such as a possibility of reverter, right of re-entry, and reversion. We noted that a grantor with a fee simple absolute could convey a life estate in Blackacre to A and retain the reversion. Or a grantor could convey a fee simple determinable to A and retain a possibility of reverter. We have also discussed that a grantor could convey a fee simple subject to condition subsequent to A and retain a right of re-entry.

Instead of retaining the future interest, however, the grantor could, at the time of the grant of the present possessory interest to A, grant the future interest to another grantee. For example, a grantor with a fee simple absolute could convey a life estate in Blackacre to A and the future interest to B. How do we classify that future interest in B? The future interest to B is a ***remainder*** if it meets the definition of a remainder. In order for a future interest to be deemed a remainder, it must be a future interest in someone other than the grantor that will become a present possessory estate, if ever, immediately upon the natural expiration of prior non-fee simple estates created simultaneously with it. If the future interest in the grantee does not meet the definition of remainder, then it is classified as an ***executory interest***. In fact, the definition of an executory interest is a future interest in a grantee that does not meet the definition of a remainder. As you will see, once you decide whether a future interest in a grantee is a remainder or an executory interest, you then will need to determine which type of remainder or which type of executory interest the grantee was granted.

As you read the text and cases, you should refer to the diagram of future interests included below.

8.2.1
Diagram of Future Interests

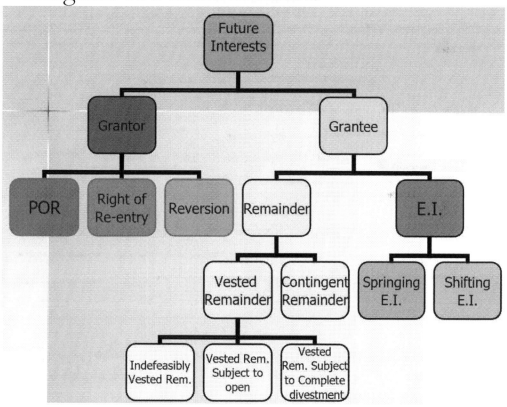

8.2.2

Remainders

Recall that in order for a future interest to be deemed a remainder the interest must meet the definition of remainder, which is a *future interest in someone other than the grantor that will become a present possessory estate*, if ever, immediately upon the natural expiration of prior non-fee simple estates created simultaneously with it. There are two types of remainders – the ***vested remainder*** and the ***contingent remainder***. In order for a remainder to be deemed a ***vested remainder***, at the time the interest is created, there must be (1) at least one identifiable person who would be ready to take should the interest become possessory immediately and (2) no condition precedent attached to the grant. A ***contingent remainder*** is a remainder that does not meet the definition of vested remainder.

There are three different types of vested remainders – the ***indefeasibly vested remainder***, the ***vested remainder subject to open***, and the ***vested remainder subject to complete divestment***. The indefeasibly vested remainder cannot be destroyed or diluted. The vested remainder subject to open is a remainder in a class. The vested remainder subject to complete divestment has a condition subsequent. There is only one type of contingent remainder. The contingent reminder can be recognized because it arises when there is a condition precedent or when there is not an identified grantee at the time of the grant. A grantee is not identifiable when the grantees are all unborn or unascertained at the time of the grant.

8.2.2.1

Jackson v. Don Johnson Forestry, Inc.
830 S.E.2d 659 (N.C. Ct. App. 2019)

Court of Appeals of North Carolina

DILLON, Judge.

This is an appeal and cross-appeal by a number of parties from a summary judgment order entered in this case involving alleged damages caused by the unauthorized cutting of timber from a certain tract of land.

I. Background

In 1982, Z. J. Burden died, bequeathing a large tract of land (the "Property") to his lineal descendants. Specifically, pursuant to Mr. Burden's will, Mr. Burden's five children, or the survivor(s) of them, received a life estate in the Property; and the fee simple remainder interest was held by those grandchildren of Mr. Burden who were alive at the death of the last of Mr. Burden's five children. That is, the Property would not pass in fee simple absolute to Mr. Burden's grandchildren until *all* of his children had died, and would only pass to those grandchildren who survived all of Mr. Burden's five children.

Mr. Burden's will also granted to his children, or the survivor(s) of them, during the life tenancy, the right to sell any timber growing on the Property that was at least twelve (12) inches in diameter for any reason they saw fit, without having to share the proceeds from the sale with the remaindermen-grandchildren.

In early 2014, Florida Bazemore was the sole surviving child of Mr. Burden and, therefore, was the sole owner of the life estate in the Property. After entering a nursing home, Mrs. Bazemore signed a General Power of Attorney, naming her husband, William Bazemore, and two others as her attorneys-in-fact.

Shortly thereafter, Mr. Bazemore entered into a broker's agreement with Defendant Don Johnson Forestry, Inc. (the "Broker"), to procure a buyer for the timber growing on the Property. The Property had not been timbered since the mid-1980's. The Broker procured an offer from Defendant East Carolina Timber, LLC, (the "Timber Buyer") to purchase the timber growing on the Property.

In March 2014, Mr. Bazemore signed an agreement to sell the timber growing on the Property to the Timber Buyer.

During the summer of 2014, the Timber Buyer cut a number of trees from the Property, paying $130,000; $122,000 of this money was paid to the Bazemores, and the remainder was paid to the Broker for its brokerage commission.

In May 2015, Mr. Bazemore died. Two months later, in July 2015, Mrs. Bazemore died. Upon her death, the Property passed to Mr. Burden's then-living grandchildren *per stirpes* in fee simple absolute.

In October 2015, several of Mr. Burden's grandchildren (the "Grandchildren") commenced this action against the Broker and the Timber Buyer for cutting timber from the Property during Mrs. Bazemore's life tenancy. The Grandchildren sought double the value of the timber cut, pursuant to N.C. Gen. Stat. § 1-539.1.

The Broker and Timber Buyer each answered denying liability. And the Timber Buyer asserted a third-party complaint against the estates of Mr. and Mrs. Bazemore's estates for indemnity.

In November 2017, after a hearing on summary judgment motions, the trial court entered a summary judgment order, which did three things: (1) it granted the Broker's motion for summary judgment, thereby dismissing the Grandchildren's claims against it; (2) it granted the Grandchildren's motion for summary judgment on their claims against the Timber Buyer, awarding $259,596 in double damages; and (3) it granted the Timber Buyer's motion for summary judgment against Mr. and Mrs. Bazemore's estates for indemnity. Each part of the summary judgment order was timely appealed. For the reasons stated below, we affirm in part, reverse in part, and remand for further proceedings, as detailed in Section III (Conclusion) below.

II. Analysis

A. Mrs. Bazemore's Rights in the Trees During Her Life Tenancy

Rights in a particular piece of property have been described as a "bundle of sticks" or "bundle of rights," where various people/entities could own different rights in that property. These rights include the right to timber the property.

Mr. Burden, as the fee simple absolute titleholder, owned substantially all of the "sticks" or "rights" in the Property. When Mr. Burden died, he left some of the "sticks" to Mrs. Bazemore, as a life tenant, and other "sticks" to the Grandchildren, as remaindermen. Important to the present case are the sticks owned by Mrs. Bazemore and by the Grandchildren relating to the timber on the Property.

Mr. Burden bequeathed to Mrs. Bazemore a life estate, which carries with it some rights in the trees. Specifically, our Supreme Court has held that, absent some other express grant, a life tenant's right to cut timber from her land is limited. That is, a life tenant is allowed to "clear tillable land to be cultivated for the necessary support of

[her] family," and she may "also cut and use timber appropriate for necessary fuel" or to build structures on the property. *Dorsey v. Moore* , 100 N.C. 41, 44, 6 S.E. 270, 271 (1888). Further, a life tenant is permitted to harvest and sell sufficient timber needed to maintain the property. However, a life tenant commits waste if she cuts timber "merely for sale,--to sell the timber trees, and allow them to be cut down and manufactured into lumber for market[:]"

It would take from the land that which is not incident to the life-estate, and the just enjoyment of it, consistently with the estate and rights of the remainder-man or reversioner. The law intends that the life-tenant shall enjoy his estate in such reasonable way as that the land shall pass to the reversioner, as nearly as practicable unimpaired as to its natural capacities, and the improvements upon it.

Moore , 100 N.C. at 44, 6 S.E. at 271 (citations omitted).

Mr. Burden, however, bequeathed to Mrs. Bazemore more "sticks" in the timber than that normally held by a life tenant, as was his right as the fee simple owner. *See Fletcher v. Bray* , 201 N.C. 763, 767-68, 161 S.E. 383, 385-86 (1931). Specifically, in addition to bequeathing to Mrs. Bazemore the "sticks" in the timber normally reserved for a life tenant, Mr. Burden bequeathed to Mrs. Bazemore the *unfettered* right to cut and sell any tree with a diameter of twelve (12) inches or more (hereinafter the "Large Trees") during her life tenancy. This arrangement was similar to that in *Fletcher v. Bray* , where the fee simple owner bequeathed a life estate in certain property to his wife *and* the right to dispose of the trees thereon *for any reason* during her life tenancy, with the remainder to his nephews and nieces in fee simple. Our Supreme Court held that this arrangement was lawful:

The court holds the opinion that the standing timber was severed by the testator from the fee and the absolute dominion thereof given the wife, and such severance was designed for her benefit rather than for the benefit of [the remaindermen]. Therefore, [wife], upon the sale of the timber, was entitled to hold the proceeds in her own right as her own property [and had the right to bequeath the proceeds as she saw fit].

Id. at 768, 161 S.E. at 386.

Therefore, Mrs. Bazemore had the unfettered right *during her life tenancy* to profit from any Large Tree, pursuant to Mr. Burden's will. However, her right to the smaller trees during her life tenancy was limited to that of a life tenant.

B. The Grandchildren's Right to Seek Relief as Remaindermen

Where there is an unauthorized cutting of trees during a life tenancy, the remaindermen may seek relief. But the type of relief that a remainderman can seek depends on whether his interest is vested or contingent.

Our Supreme Court has held that a *vested* remainderman or reversioner has many remedies. Specifically, he "has his election either to bring trover for the value of the tree after it is cut, or an action [for trespass] on the case in the nature of waste, in which, besides the value of the tree considered as timber, he may recover damages for any injury to the inheritance which is consequent upon the destruction of the tree." *Burnett v. Thompson*, 51 N.C. 210, 213 (1858). Indeed, the right to bring an action for waste has been codified in Chapter 1, Article 42 of our General Statutes.

However, owners of a *contingent* future interest "cannot recover damages for waste already committed, [but] they are entitled to have their [contingent] interests protected from [future] threatened waste or destruction by injunctive relief." *Gordon v. Lowther* , 75 N.C. 193, 193 (1876) ; *see also Peterson v. Ferrell* , 127 N.C. 169, 170, 37 S.E. 189, 190 (1900) (holding that both vested and contingent remaindermen have the right to seek an injunction to protect against future waste); *Edens v. Foulks* , 2 N.C. App. 325, 331, 163 S.E.2d 51, 54 (1968) (stating that "[i]t is well settled in this State, as in other states, that a contingent remainderman is entitled to an injunction to prevent a person in possession from committing future waste").

In the present case, the Timber Buyer argues that the Grandchildren have no standing to sue *for damages* because they were mere contingent remaindermen when the trees were cut. Indeed, their interest was contingent on their surviving Mrs. Bazemore. We conclude, though, that it is irrelevant whether the Grandchildren's remaindermen interest in the Property may have been contingent under Mr. Burden's will: They did not bring suit until after Mrs. Bazemore's death, after their interest became a *vested* fee simple interest. Though neither party cites a case on point on this issue, we conclude that once a contingent remainderman's interest vests, he may bring suit for damages, even for acts committed during the life tenancy. Indeed, in discussing the limited right of a contingent remainderman to seek only injunctive relief, our Supreme Court stated that a contingent remainderman "could not maintain [an] action [for damages] *during the life of the first taker*." *Latham v. Roanoke R. & Lumber Co.*, 139 N.C. 9, 51 S.E. 780, 780 (1905) (emphasis added). Our Supreme Court reasoned that, during the life tenancy, it is impossible to know what, if any, damage any particular contingent remainderman will suffer or which remainderman will vest and actually will suffer the damage. But once the life tenancy terminates, this concern disappears.

Further, our General Assembly has provided that *any* remainderman whose interest has become a vested present interest may sue for damages for timber cut during the preceding life tenancy. N.C. Gen. Stat. § 1-537 (2017) ("Every heir may bring action for waste committed on lands ... of his own inheritance, as well in the time of his ancestor as in his own.")

Therefore, we conclude that the Grandchildren do have standing to seek relief for damage caused by any unauthorized cutting of timber on the Property which occurred during Mrs. Bazemore's life tenancy.

C. The Large Trees

grandchildren arg.

The Grandchildren argue that they are entitled to damages for the trees which were cut, contending that the contract between Mr. Bazemore (purportedly signed on behalf of Mrs. Bazemore) and the Timber Buyer was not validly executed.

We conclude that the Grandchildren have no claim regarding the Large Trees.

Even if the contract was not valid, any claim pertaining to the cutting of Large Trees, which occurred during the life tenancy of Mrs. Bazemore, belonged to Mrs. Bazemore alone, and now to her estate. That is, the Large Trees belonged to Mrs. Bazemore during the life tenancy pursuant to the express grant in Mr. Burden's will, and they were severed from the property during the life tenancy. Unlike typical remaindermen, because of Mr. Burden's express grant to Mrs. Bazemore (and the other life tenants), the Grandchildren had no rights in the Large Trees during the life tenancy; and, therefore, they had no rights in the Large Trees which were severed from the Property during the life tenancy. Therefore, assuming that the Large Trees were cut without Mrs. Bazemore's authorization, it is Mrs. Bazemore who suffered. The Grandchildren can make no claim for waste of their inheritance since Mr. Burden had "severed" the Large Trees from the fee that they were entitled to inherit. And they have no claim for trover, as the Large Trees, once cut, belonged to Mrs. Bazemore.

D. The Small Trees

We conclude that the Grandchildren are entitled to any damage caused by the cutting of trees less than twelve (12) inches in diameter (hereinafter the "Small Trees") by the Timber Buyer. Mrs. Bazemore's interest in the Small Trees was only that of a life tenant, as Mr. Burden did not expressly grant her any additional rights in the Small Trees in his will. And there was no evidence offered at summary judgment suggesting that the Small Trees were cut for any reason other than for profit, which, as explained above, is not permissible for a life tenant to authorize.

The Timber Buyer argues that it is entitled to summary judgment, in any event, because the Grandchildren failed to put on any evidence showing that any of the trees cut by the Timber Buyer were, in fact, Small Trees. However, we conclude that there was *enough* evidence presented to survive summary judgment on this point. Specifically, the contract with the Timber Buyer provided that the Property would be "clear cut," suggesting that *all* of the marketable trees on the Property would be cut, not just the Large Trees. Further, there is evidence which identifies the types of trees actually cut by the Timber Buyer, including trees used for "pulp" and "chip-in-saw." Such are typically made from smaller trees, less than twelve (12) inches in diameter.

It certainly would have been better if the Grandchildren had offered an affidavit of a witness who expressly stated that at least one Small Tree was cut. However, we conclude that the record was sufficient to create an issue of fact that at least one Small Tree was cut, and therefore sufficient to reach the jury on the question of damages.

***

F. Liability of Timber Buyer

Our Supreme Court has held that a third party may be liable for wrongfully cutting timber to a remainderman whose interest has vested, specifically, for trover (the value of the trees) or for "an action on the case in the nature of waste" (the damage to the land). *Burnett*, 51 N.C. at 213.

Our Supreme Court has held that even if the third party contracts with the life tenant to cut timber, the third party is still liable to the remaindermen if any cutting is unauthorized. *Dorsey*, 100 N.C. at 45, 6 S.E. at 272. It is no excuse that the third party acted under a contract with the life tenant, where the life tenant, otherwise, had no right to have the timber cut:

> The judgment, it seems, is founded upon the supposition that the contract between the life-tenant in possession and the [third party], purporting to give them the right to cut and remove the timber, had the legal effect to exempt [the third party] from liability to the [remaindermen] on such account. *This was a misapprehension of the law applicable.*

Id. at 45-6, 6 S.E. at 272.

Therefore, we conclude that the Timber Buyer is liable to the Grandchildren for any damage caused by the cutting of the Small Trees.

But we further conclude that the Timber Buyer is not liable for double damages pursuant to N.C. Gen. Stat. § 1-539.1. Specifically, our Court has held that a third party is not liable for double damages under this statute if the third party was not trespassing on the land itself when the cutting occurred. *Matthews v. Brown*, 62 N.C. App. 559, 561, 303 S.E.2d 223, 225 (1983). In *Matthews*, a timber company had the contractual right to enter upon a tract of land and cut some trees, but the evidence demonstrated that the company cut more trees than it was authorized to cut. We held that the award of damages for the unauthorized cutting of trees was appropriate, but that the doubling of the award was not since the company was lawfully on the land. *Id.* at 561, 303 S.E.2d at 225 (holding that N.C. Gen. Stat. § 1-539.1 does not apply unless the defendant was a "trespasser to the land"). In the present case, the Timber Buyer was authorized by Mr. Bazemore, who was acting within his apparent authority as Mrs. Bazemore's agent, to enter the Property and was therefore not a trespasser.

***

III. Conclusion

The Grandchildren were entitled to summary judgment on the issue of *liability* against the Timber Buyer for damages caused by any Small Trees cut from the Property. Therefore, that portion of the summary judgment order is affirmed.

There is, however, a genuine issue of material fact as to the *damages* suffered by the Grandchildren for the Small Trees which were cut. Therefore, we reverse that portion of the summary judgment order granting the Grandchildren judgment as to the amount of damages, and we remand this issue for trial.

As the issue of damages has yet to be decided, we vacate that portion of the summary judgment order awarding costs to the Grandchildren from the Timber Buyer. The trial court may consider this issue at the conclusion of the trial.

The Timber Buyer is not liable to the Grandchildren for any Large Trees as a matter of law. Therefore, we reverse that portion of the summary judgment order granting the Grandchildren judgment on liability and for damages as to the Large Trees, and we remand with instructions to enter summary judgment for the Timber Buyer on this issue.

The Timber Buyer is not liable to the Grandchildren pursuant to N.C. Gen. Stat. § 1-539.1 for double damages, as a matter of law, for any damages which may be found for the cutting of the Small Trees. Therefore, we reverse that portion of the summary judgment order granting summary judgment for the Grandchildren on this issue, and we remand with instructions to enter summary judgment for the Timber Buyer on this issue.

***

AFFIRMED IN PART, REVERSED IN PART, REMANDED IN PART.

8.2.3

Executory Interests

As discussed above, a future interest in a grantee that is not a remainder is referred to as an ***executory interest***. There are two types of executory interests – the ***springing executory interest*** and the ***shifting executory interest***. The springing executory interest is an executory interest that must, in order to become possessory, divest the grantor following a certain period of time during which no other grantee is entitled to possession. The shifting executory interest is an executory interest that must, in order to become possessory, divest or cut short some interest in another grantee.

8.2.3.1

Martin v. Seeley
142 N.Y.S.3d 252 (N.Y. App. Div. 2021)

Supreme Court, Appellate Division, Fourth Department, New York

MEMORANDUM AND ORDER

It is hereby ORDERED that the judgment so appealed from is unanimously affirmed without costs.

Memorandum: Plaintiffs commenced this action seeking, inter alia, a declaration adjudicating their right of first refusal with respect to a 1.9-acre parcel of land located on Hanover Road in Silver Creek (the premises). Defendants appeal from a judgment denying their cross motion for summary judgment dismissing the complaint and declaring the right of first refusal to be null and void. We affirm.

In July 2009, plaintiffs contracted to purchase from defendant Willard L. Seeley and defendant Doris J. Seeley (Seeley defendants) a home with approximately 3.5 acres of land on Hanover Road. Included in the purchase contract, an addendum to that contract, and the warranty deed conveying the property from the Seeley defendants to plaintiffs was a right of first refusal on the premises, which the Seeley defendants had retained, and which is adjacent to the property purchased by plaintiffs. As set forth in the deed, plaintiffs' right of first refusal would be triggered upon the Seeley defendants' receipt of a bona fide offer to purchase the premises, which would then require the Seeley defendants to give written notice of the offer to plaintiffs within five days of receiving the offer. Plaintiffs would then have 10 days from receipt of the notice to notify the Seeley defendants of their intent to purchase the premises on at least the same terms and conditions as the bona fide offer. In fall 2017, the Seeley defendants received and accepted an offer from defendant Todd T. Schilling to purchase approximately 10 acres of land, including the premises. In November 2017, defendants' attorney sent written notice of Schilling's offer to plaintiffs at the mailing address listed for them on the 2009 purchase contract and deed, but not to the Hanover Road residence that plaintiffs purchased from the Seeley defendants pursuant to that contract and deed, and the United States Postal Service returned the notice as "not deliverable as addressed." The Seeley defendants sold the premises to Schilling in December 2017.

Defendants contend that the right of first refusal in the deed is void as against the rule against perpetuities as codified in EPTL 9-1.1 (b) because the right of first refusal is not personal to plaintiffs and may be exercised by their heirs and distributees more than 21 years after plaintiffs' deaths. We reject that contention. EPTL 9-1.1 (b) provides that "[n]o estate in property shall be valid unless it must vest, if at all, not later than twenty-one years after one or more lives in being at the creation of the estate and any period of gestation involved." "EPTL 9-1.3 (b) and the common-law rule of construction which it codifies embody the unexceptionable propositions that parties who make grants of real property interests presumably intend their grants to be effective and that reviewing courts should, if at all possible, avoid constructions which frustrate their intended purposes" (*Morrison v. Piper*, 77 N.Y.2d 165, 173-174, 565 N.Y.S.2d 444, 566 N.E.2d 643 [1990]).

Here, the deed indicates that the right of first refusal is for the benefit of plaintiffs only, and that it may only be exercised by plaintiffs personally. The provision provides, in relevant part, "[t]his [r]ight of [f]irst [r]efusal shall run with the land and inure to and be for the benefit of the [plaintiffs] but not their successors and assigns tenants subtenants licensees mortgagees and possession [sic] and invitees." We reject defendants' contention that plaintiffs' interest could vest in their heirs and distributees more than 21 years after plaintiffs' deaths inasmuch as it would not be possible for the right to vest in plaintiffs' heirs and distributees without also necessarily vesting in their successors and assigns. We note that "[t]here is nothing in the language of the deed—if read as a whole in an effort to discover the purpose sought to be achieved (see Matter of Carmer, 71 N.Y.2d 781, 785, 530 N.Y.S.2d 88, 525 N.E.2d 734 [1988]; Matter of Thall, 18 N.Y.2d 186, 192, 273 N.Y.S.2d 33, 219 N.E.2d 397 [1966])—suggesting that the parties had the intention of creating the invalid remote interests which defendants' construction imputes to them" (Morrison, 77 N.Y.2d at 174, 565 N.Y.S.2d 444, 566 N.E.2d 643). Where, as here, no "contrary intention appears" (EPTL 9-1.3 [a]), we must presume that the parties "intended the [interest] to be valid" (EPTL 9-1.3 [b].

 alt arg.

Defendants also contend that the right of first refusal is void for lack of consideration because the contract included plaintiffs' purchase of a house for $155,000 and contained no right of first refusal. We reject that contention. A right of first refusal is subject to the statute of frauds, which provides that "[a] contract ... for the sale[ ] of any real property, or an interest therein, is void unless the contract or some note or memorandum thereof, expressing the consideration, is in writing, subscribed by the party to be charged" (General Obligations Law § 5-703 [2]). Contrary to defendants' contention, the purchase contract provided that plaintiffs would receive a single family dwelling, several acres of land, and "the right of first refusal on the open land behind the grapes" for a purchase price of $155,000. The addendum to the purchase contract also provided that "the [c]ontract includes a [r]ight of [f]irst [r]efusal to the Purchasers of vacant land behind the grape vineyards, which are to be retained by the Sellers," and the deed conveying the dwelling, the land, and the right of first refusal expressed consideration "of One and More Dollars ($1.00 & More) lawful money of the United States paid by the Grantees."

We further conclude that defendants are not entitled to summary judgment dismissing the complaint on the ground that plaintiffs failed to exercise their right of first refusal in a timely manner. Contrary to defendants' contention, questions of fact exist whether the Seeley defendants complied with the deed's requirement that they provide written notice to plaintiffs of any bona fide offers to purchase the premises within five days of receipt of the bona fide offer. Although defendants' attorney attempted to send written notice to plaintiffs on November 14, 2017, he sent the notice to a mailing address that was "current" for plaintiffs as of August 31, 2009, rather than to the Hanover Road residence that plaintiffs purchased from the Seeley defendants in August 2009. Consequently, the notice was returned by the post office as "not deliverable as addressed" and "unable to forward." Prior to Schilling's purchase of the premises in December 2017, Willard L. Seeley and Schilling were informed by the attorney who represented both Schilling and the Seeley defendants in the transaction that the notice sent to plaintiffs had been returned as undeliverable, and both Willard L. Seeley and Schilling testified that they knew plaintiffs were living on Hanover Road. Nonetheless, no effort was made to provide notice to plaintiffs at their current known address. Thus, plaintiffs were unaware of Schilling's offer to purchase the premises and they had no opportunity to exercise their right of first refusal. Inasmuch as a plain reading of the purchase contract, the addendum to that contract and the deed, or a simple address search by defendants' attorney, would have verified that plaintiffs had been living at the Hanover Road address since they took possession of that property from the Seeleys in 2009, we conclude that a question of fact exists whether the Seeley defendants complied with the notice requirement in the right of first refusal.

Finally, even assuming, arguendo, that it was reasonable for defendants' attorney, in November 2017, to send notice to plaintiffs' former mailing address after plaintiffs purchased a residence from the Seeley defendants in 2009, we conclude that a question of fact exists whether the written notice sent on November 14, 2017 was timely. The deed required the Seeley defendants to provide written notice to plaintiffs within five days of receiving an offer, and according to the deposition testimony of defendant Schilling, he made a purchase offer to the Seeley defendants in October and entered into an agreement with them to purchase the premises and other property during the week of October 10-17, 2017, which was approximately one month before defendants' attorney sent notice to plaintiffs' former mailing address.

8.2.4

Discussion: Notes, Questions, and Problems

8.2.4.1

Discussion Note #7. Express survivorship language

In *Jackson v. Don Johnson Forestry, Inc.*, excerpted above, Z.J. Burden's will provided a life estate to his five children and the remainder to "those grandchildren of Mr. Burden who were alive at the death of the last of Mr. Burden's five children." The court found the devise to the grandchildren created a contingent remainder rather than a vested remainder. Note the express requirement of survivorship for the grandchildren.

8.2.4.2

Discussion Note #8. Law of waste

In *Jackson v. Don Johnson Forestry, Inc.*, excerpted above, the court addresses the doctrine of waste between a life tenant and a remainderman. The law of waste is also relevant as between landlords and tenants.

8.2.4.3

Discussion Problem #9. Conveyance to Alicia and Bob problem

Assume that Oscar conveyed Blackacre as follows: **"to Alicia for life, then to Bob and his heirs."** Note that when classifying the interests and estates for this conveyance you would need to analyze the conveyance for both Alicia and Bob. What are the words of purchase? Does the first purchaser listed in the instrument have a present interest or a future interest? If it is a present interest, continue to that purchaser's estate. If it is a future interest, you would classify the first purchaser's future interest before describing the estate. What estate is the first purchaser's interest is in? Once you have classified the interests and estates of the first purchaser, do the same for the second purchaser listed in the instrument. Does the second purchaser listed in the instrument have a present interest or a future interest? If it is a future interest, is it a remainder (apply the definition) or is it an executory interest? If it is a remainder, is it vested (apply the definition) or is it contingent? If it is vested, is the vested remainder an indefeasibly vested remainder, a vested remainder subject to open, or a vested remainder subject to complete divestment? What estate is the second purchaser's interest is in? Did the grantor retain an interest in Blackacre? If so, what is the grantor's retained interest?

8.3

Steps for Analyzing Interests and Estates

As you have seen, many terms and definitions developed over the course of history to classify interests and estates in property. To determine the interests and estates created by a grantor in an instrument, we recommend employing the following steps.

For **step one**, identify the words of purchase to determine the grantees in the instrument.

For **step two**, classify the interest of the first purchaser/grantee listed in the instrument and determine whether that first purchaser has a present interest or a future interest. Recall that an interest is deemed a present interest when it is possessory immediately when the interest is created. The purchaser's interest is a future interest when possession is delayed until sometime in the future. If the interest is a present interest, you would move on to step three. If, however, the interest is deemed a future interest, you would then classify which type of future interest the purchaser obtained.

For **step three**, after determining the interest of the purchaser, you must review the instrument to find the words of limitation attached to that purchaser's interest to determine the purchaser's estate.

For **step four**, if there is more than one purchaser listed in the instrument, repeat both step two and step three for each additional purchaser in the order in which each purchaser appears in the instrument.

For **step five**, review the instrument to determine whether the grantor has retained an interest in the property and describe what interest the grantor retained, if any.

For **step six**, determine the common law rules applicable in the jurisdiction and apply those rules. These common law rules are discussed below. As you will see, the most famous – or infamous – is the Rule Against Perpetuities. As you work through this step six, be sure to apply any other applicable common law rules first and save the Rule Against Perpetuities for last.

8.4
Common Law Rules

Recall that, after classifying the interests and estates of the various purchasers in an instrument, the recommended steps described above require you to determine whether any of the common law rules continue to apply in your jurisdiction and analyze what effect, if any, such rules have on the interests and estates created. The sections below discuss the common law rules of the Doctrine of Worthier Title, the Rule in Shelley's Case, the Merger Doctrine, and the Rule Against Perpetuities. You should also review the note on the Doctrine of Destructibility of Contingent Remainders.

8.4.1
Doctrine of Worthier Title

Under the **_Doctrine of Worthier Title_**, if a grantor conveyed a present interest to a grantee and in the same instrument conveyed a future interest to the grantor's own heirs, the future interest was deemed a reversion in the grantor rather than a remainder in the grantor's heirs. As discussed by the court in *Hatch v. Riggs National Bank*, excerpted below, the Doctrine of Worthier Title can be traced back to the feudal system and was designed largely to ensure that certain incidents, which were payable when property descended upon death rather than when it was obtained by purchase, were paid—"whereby descent is deemed 'worthier' than purchase." Where it continues to apply, the Doctrine of Worthier Title is limited to conveyances, not to devises. Moreover, it is deemed a rule of construction designed to construe the grantor's intent, not a rule of law. However, the rebuttable presumption that applies is in favor of its application. Thus, as explained by the court in *Hatch*, to overcome the rebuttable presumption that a reversion was intended, in instances where the grantor in fact truly intended a remainder, the intent of creating a remainder must be clearly expressed in the instrument.

8.4.1.1

Hatch v. Riggs National Bank
361 F.2d 559 (D.C. Cir. 1966)

United States Court of Appeals for the District of Columbia Circuit

LEVENTHAL, Circuit Judge.

Appellant seeks in this action to obtain modification of a trust she created in 1923. The income terms of the trust instrument are of a spendthrift character, directing the trustees to pay to the settlor for life all the income from the trust estate "for her own use and benefit, without the power to her to anticipate, alienate or charge the same * * Upon the death of the settlor-life tenant, the trustees are to pay over the corpus as the settlor may appoint by will; if she fails to exercise this testamentary power of appointment, the corpus is to go to "such of her next of kin * * * as by the law in force in the District of Columbia at the death of the * * * [settlor] shall be provided for in the distribution of an intestate's personal property therein." No power to appoint the corpus by deed, nor any power to revoke, alter, amend or modify the trust, was expressly retained by appellant, and the instrument states that she conveys the property to the trustees "irrevocably."

Appellant does not claim that the declaration of trust itself authorizes her to revoke or modify the trust. In effect she invokes the doctrine of worthier title, which teaches that a grant of trust corpus to the heirs of the settlor creates a reversion in the settlor rather than a remainder in his heirs. She claims that since she is the sole beneficiary of the trust under this doctrine, and is also the settlor, she may revoke or modify under accepted principles of trust law.

The District Court, while sympathizing with appellant's desire to obtain an additional stipend of $5000 a year, out of corpus, "to accommodate recently incurred expenses, and to live more nearly in accordance with her refined but yet modest tastes," felt that denial of the requested relief was required by this court's decision in Liberty National Bank v. Hicks, 84 U.S.App.D.C. 198, 173 F.2d 631, 9 A.L.R.2d 1355 (1948). Summary judgment was granted for appellees. We affirm.

* * *

worthier doctrine

The doctrine of worthier title had its origins in the feudal system which to a large extent molded the English common law which we inherited. In its common law form, the doctrine provided that a conveyance of land by a grantor with a limitation over to his own heirs resulted in a reversion in the grantor rather than creating a remainder interest in the heirs. It was a rule of law distinct from, though motivated largely by the same policies as, the Rule in Shelley's Case. Apparently the feudal overlord was entitled to certain valuable incidents when property held by one of his feoffees passed by "descent" to an heir rather than by "purchase" to a transferee. The doctrine of worthier title — whereby descent is deemed "worthier" than purchase — remained ensconced in English law, notwithstanding the passing of the feudal system, until abrogated by statute in 1833.

Cardozo landmark opinion

The doctrine has survived in many American jurisdictions, with respect to inter vivos conveyances of both land and personalty, as a common law "rule of construction" rather than a "rule of law." In Doctor v. Hughes, 225 N.Y. 305, 122 N.E. 221 (1919), Judge Cardozo's landmark opinion reviewed the common-law history of the doctrine and concluded that its modern relevance was as a rule of construction, a rebuttable presumption that the grantor's likely intent, in referring to his own heirs, was to reserve a reversion in his estate rather than create a remainder interest in the heirs. Evidence might be introduced to show that the grantor really meant what he said when he spoke of creating a remainder in his heirs. "Even at common law," wrote Cardozo, "a distinction was taken between grants to the heirs as such, and grants where the reference to heirs was a mere *descriptio personarum*." But to overcome the presumption that a reversion rather than a remainder was intended, "the intention to work the transformation must be clearly expressed." 122 N.E. at 222.

In the decades that followed, the worthier title doctrine as a rule of construction with respect to inter vivos transfers won widespread acceptance. The "modern" rationale for the rule is well stated in an opinion of the Supreme Court of California:

> It is said that where a person creates a life estate in himself with a gift over to his heirs he ordinarily intends the same thing as if he had given the property to his estate; that he does not intend to make a gift to any particular person but indicates only that upon his death the residue of the trust property shall be distributed according to the general laws governing succession; and that he does not intend to create in any persons an interest which would prevent him from exercising control over the beneficial interest. * * * Moreover, this rule of construction is in accord with the general policy in favor of the free alienability of property, since its operation tends to make property more readily transferable.

[handwritten margin note: modern rationale]

While the weight of authority, as just indicated, supports the retention of the doctrine of worthier title (unlike its common-law brother, the Rule in Shelley's Case) as a rule of construction, there has been substantial and increasing opposition to the doctrine.

The views of the critics of the doctrine, which we find persuasive against its adoption, and borne out by the experience of the New York courts in the series of cases which have followed Doctor v. Hughes, *supra,* may be summarized as follows. The common-law reasons for the doctrine are as obsolete as those behind the Rule in Shelley's Case. Retention of the doctrine as a rule of construction is pernicious in several respects.

First, it is questionable whether it accords with the intent of the average settlor. It is perhaps tempting to say that the settlor intended to create no beneficial interest in his heirs when he said "to myself for life, remainder to my heirs" when the question is revocation of the trust, or whether creditors of the settlor's heirs should be able to reach their interest. But the same result is far from appealing if the settlor-life beneficiary dies without revoking the trust and leaves a will which makes no provision for his heirs-at-law (whom he supposed to be taken care of by the trust). In short, while the dominant intent of most such trusts may well be to benefit the life tenant during his life, a subsidiary but nevertheless significant purpose of many such trusts may be to satisfy a natural desire to benefit one's heirs or next of kin. In the normal case an adult has a pretty good idea who his heirs will be at death, and probably means exactly what he says when he states in the trust instrument, "remainder to my heirs."

It is said that the cases in which such is the grantor's intent can be discerned by an examination into his intent; the presumption that a gift over to one's heirs creates a reversion can thereby be rebutted in appropriate cases. But the only repository of the settlor's intent, in most cases, will be the trust instrument itself. Nor would it be fruitful or conducive to orderly and prompt resolution of litigation to engage in searches for other sources of intent. In the typical case of this genre — a stark, unqualified "to myself for life, remainder to my heirs" — the instrument will send forth no signals of contrary intent to overcome the presumption that only a reversion was intended. Yet this is precisely the class of cases in which settlors are likely to have intended to create beneficial interests in their heirs.

***

We see no reason to plunge the District of Columbia into the ranks of those jurisdictions bogged in the morass of exploring, under the modern doctrine of worthier title, "the almost ephemeral qualities which go to prove the necessary intent." The alleged benefit of effectuating intent must be balanced against the resulting volume of litigation and the diversity and difficulty of decision. We are not persuaded that the policy of upholding the intention of creators of trusts is best effectuated by such a rule of construction, with its accompanying uncertainty.

The rule we adopt, which treats the settlor's heirs like any other remainder-men, although possibly defeating the intention of some settlors, is overall, we think, an intent-effectuating rule. It contributes to certainty of written expression and conceptual integrity in the law of trusts. It allows heirs to take as remaindermen when so named, and promises less litigation, greater predictability, and easier drafting. These considerations are no small element of justice.

We hold, then, that the doctrine of worthier title is no part of the law of trusts in the District of Columbia, either as a rule of law or as a rule of construction. Any act or words of the settlor of a trust which would validly create a remainder interest in a named third party may create a valid remainder interest in the settlor's heirs. It follows that the District Court was correct in granting summary judgment for appellees in this case, since appellant's action is based on the theory that she was the sole beneficiary and hence could revoke the "irrevocable" trust she had created.

***

Affirmed.

8.4.2
Rule in Shelley's Case

The court in *Hatch* reminds us that the ***Rule in Shelley's Case***, much like the Doctrine of Worthier Title, derived from the feudal system as another way of closing attempts to avoid paying the incidents – closing a tax loophole. The Rule in Shelley's Case provides that when a single instrument created a freehold estate in a grantee and also created a contingent remainder in that grantee's heirs, and the estates were both legal or both equitable, the contingent remainder in the grantee's heirs would convert to a remainder in the freehold grantee. A freehold includes a life estate and a fee tail. A fee tail is unusual and, thus, we can rephrase the Rule in Shelley's Case as follows: The Rule in Shelley's Case applies when a single instrument creates a life estate in a grantee and also creates a contingent remainder in that grantee's heirs, and the estates are both legal or both equitable, the contingent remainder in the grantee's heirs convert to a remainder in the life estate grantee. Note that if the Rule in Shelley's Case applies, such that the life estate holder will also be deemed have the remainder, you would need to apply the merger doctrine to see if the lesser estate is merged into the larger. The merger doctrine is discussed below.

8.4.2.1

Rogers v. Kaylor
299 S.W.2d 204 (Ark. 1957)

Arkansas Supreme Court

Ed. E. McFaddin, Associate Justice.

The question presented is whether the deed, here, comes within the Rule in Shelley's Case.

In 1908, John and Callie Tenniswood conveyed the three lots here involved to their daughter, Johnie Tenniswood. The granting clause of the deed recited: ". . . do hereby give, bargain, sell and convey unto the said Johnie Tenniswood during her natural life, and unto heirs and assigns forever . . ." The *habendum* clause recited: "To have and to hold the same unto the said Johnie Tenniswood during her natural life, and unto her heirs and assigns forever . . ." The grantee, Johnie Tenniswood, became Mrs. Johnie Rogers, and in due time executed warranty deeds which purported to convey to the grantees — through whom the appellees claim — the entire fee to the three lots conveyed to her by her father and mother, as aforesaid.

Upon the death intestate of Mrs. Johnie Tenniswood Rogers, the appellants, as her children and heirs at law, brought this suit against appellees to recover the three lots. The appellants claimed that under the said deed to their mother, Mrs. Johnie Tenniswood Rogers, she took only a life estate and that the appellants, as her heirs, took the remainder in fee. The appellees claimed that, under the Rule in Shelley's Case, Mrs. Johnie Tenniswood Rogers owned the fee in the lots which she had duly conveyed. The Trial Court ruled in favor of the appellees; and this appeal resulted.

The ruling of the Trial Court was correct. This case presents the perfect application of the classic "Rule in Shelley's Case," which rule, most succinctly stated, is, that when the first taker takes an estate of freehold and in the same instrument there is a remainder to his heirs by way of limitation, then the first taker takes the fee estate. Here, the conveyance was to Johnie Tenniswood, ". . . during her natural life and unto heirs and assigns forever"; and, under the rule in Shelley's Case, Johnie Tenniswood took the fee title.

. . . We have many cases discussing the Rule in Shelley's Case, and the textbooks and annotations on the Rule in Shelley's Case are legion. Our own case of *Hardage* v. *Stroope* conclusively settles the question here presented. Mrs. Johnie Tenniswood Rogers took the fee under the deed to her, and the appellants cannot prevail.

Affirmed.

In re the Estate of Hendrickson
736 A.2d 540 (N.J. Super. Ct. Ch. Div. 1999)

New Jersey Superior Court, Chancery Division

FISHER, P.J.Ch.

It seems unimaginable that a court, near the end of this millennium, would be asked to consider the application of the long-abolished "Rule in Shelley's Case." Yet, this anachronistic doctrine — like Banquo's Ghost — has raised its hoary head and must be addressed not as an academic puzzle but as the key to a very real and substantial property dispute.

Wycoff Hendrickson ("Wycoff") died in 1928. His will, executed eight years earlier, states in part:

> I give and devise to my son Earle W. Hendrickson, my farm (known as Mulberry Hill Farm) situated near Imlaystown, in the County of Monmouth and State of New Jersey *during the term of his natural life,* he to have the right to occupy, possess and enjoy the same and receive the rents, issues and profits, he to pay the taxes and keep said farm up during his life time and *after the decease of my said son I give and devise the said farm to such person or persons as shall be his sole heir or heirs in land in fee simple.*

Verified Complaint, 112 (emphasis added). Earle Hendrickson ("Earle") died on May 31, 1997 setting in motion — after the passage of nearly 70 years — a dispute as to whether Wycoff, by this language, conveyed to Earle a fee simple (if the Rule in Shelley's Case applies) or merely a life estate (if it does not). If the former, defendants Elizabeth A. Olson and Nancy L. Nicholson ("Earle's devisees") are entitled to the property; if the latter, then the property passes to those who were Earle's heirs at the time of his death, namely, defendants Elizabeth S. Corson, Kathryn Deacon, Marie Field Sharbaugh, Carol Lynn Gasslein, Bonnie Joyce Weaver and Robert Weaver ("Earle's heirs").

Consideration of the Rule in Shelley's Case seems odd because its place in the common law was abrogated in this State in 1934. But our Legislature then declared only that the "rule of the common law, known as the Rule in Shelley's Case, shall not be applicable to any interest in property *created by any instrument to take effect hereafter."* *N.J.S.A.* 46:3-14. Because Wycoff's will was probated in 1928, it remains unaffected by *N.J.S.A.* 46:3-14. . . .

***

rule

The Rule in Shelley's Case provides that "where an instrument gave a man a freehold and, by the same instrument, the remainder was given to his 'heirs,' the first taker had a fee simple if the remainder was to his heirs generally, and a fee tail if the remainder was to the heirs of his body." 4 Bowe-Parker, *Page on Wills* (1961), § 37.15 at p. 617. Here, the practical effect of the application or avoidance of the Rule in Shelley's Case can be summarized as follows: . . . did Wycoff's Will transfer to Earle

question

a fee simple, which he could freely devise by way of his own Will, or did Wycoff merely devise a life estate which terminated upon Earle's death and would thereafter pass to certain persons, described as being Earle's heirs, by way of Wycoff's Will? Because Earle's devisees and his heirs are not the same persons, the application or avoidance of the Rule in Shelley's Case controls the disposition of the property.

The Rule in Shelley's Case is not only an anachronism — what one commentator referred to as " 'exhibit A' in the museum of legal antiques," I *American Law of Property* (1952), § 4.40 at p. 479 — but a doctrine which runs contrary to all modern thought on the interpretation of wills.[1]It unabashedly causes a transfer of an interest in property greater than what may have been the actual or probable intent of the testator. . . .

As mentioned, in 1920, when Wycoff's Will was executed, and in 1928, when it was probated, the Rule in Shelley's Case was part of our common law. Considering its emergence from the mist of feudal England, it seems strange that the Rule in Shelley's Case would ever be followed in this country. But with our adoption of English common law, along came the Rule in Shelley's Case — a rule possessing no salutary purpose, surviving through the march of centuries only because of tradition and legislative inertia. Having no mission but to ensnare the unwary, it is hardly imaginable that a seasoned attorney in 1920 would have chosen words to intentionally invite application of the Rule in Shelley's Case.

life estate

A conveyance of a life estate with the remainder to the life tenant's heirs undoubtedly presupposes an intent to keep the property in the family after the death of the life tenant. It does not presuppose an intent to convey a fee simple; that could have been accomplished in this case, for example, by Wycoff simply saying "I give to Earle my farm" without the convoluted language quoted earlier. There can be no question, and the parties do not dispute, that Wycoff intended to give Earle only a life estate in the farm. But the Rule in Shelley's Case was designed to avoid the testator's intention to create both a life estate and a remainder interest in the life tenant's heirs by transforming the life tenant's interest into a fee simple. The challenge faced by the scrivener of a Will, during the reign of the Rule in Shelley's Case, was to capture the testator's desire to ensure the retention of the property in the family without tripping over the Rule in Shelley's Case. Scanning the landscape of New Jersey's common law at that time, Wycoff's attorney would have been confronted with a number of decisions of the State's highest court on the subject.

rule's purpose

In 1896, the Court of Errors and Appeals found the Rule in Shelley's Case to attach to a devise to A for life, and "afterwards to descend unencumbered to his lawful heirs." As had been the understanding for centuries before, the Court described the rule as "one of law and not of construction," and disregarded the intention of the testator as being "of no account whatsoever." *Lippincott, supra,* 59 *N.J.L.* at 243-244, 28 *A. 587.* . . . However, the last decision of the Court of Errors and Appeals on the subject — prior to the creation of Wycoff's Will— was *Peer v. Hennion, supra,* 77 *N.J.L.* 693, 76 *A.* 1084, where the Court found a particular choice of words to have successfully avoided application of the Rule in Shelley's Case.

An undiscerning eye might view as enigmatic the decisional law of this State at the time Wycoff's Will was drafted, executed and probated. But there is, contrary to the argument of Earle's devisees, a difference between the language which *Lippincott* and the others found to have caused the invocation of the Rule in Shelley's Case and the language which *Peer* found to have avoided it. For example, like the words examined in *Lippincott* mentioned above, the court in *Neill* considered a devise to A "and to go to his heirs at his death," 96 *N.J.Eq.* at 479, *126 A.* 608, and in *Forman,* the conveyance was to A "for and during his natural life, and at his death to his heirs forever," 104 *N.J.Eq.* at 404, 145 *A.* 867. The language of the conveyances considered in *Martling, Armour* and *Woodbridge* is similar. A conveyance to "A for life and at his death to his heirs," so those courts said, compelled the application of the Rule in Shelley's Case notwithstanding the conveyor's contrary intent. But in *Peer,* the Court of Errors and Appeals found the doctrine did not attach to a slightly different provision, namely: to A "for and during her natural life, and after her decease I do give and devise to such person or persons as shall be her heir or heirs of land." 77 *N.J.L.* at 694-695, 76 *A.* 1084. In short, the difference between the decisions of the Court of Errors and Appeals in *Lippincott* and *Marbling,* on the one hand, and *Peer,* on the other, can be summarized very simply. The conveyances in the former cases gave the remainder, after the life estate, to the life tenant's "heirs"; in *Peer,* the remainder was given to "such person or persons as shall be [the life tenant's] heir or heirs." That permitted the Court in *Peer* to conclude the testator was merely describing the persons to whom the remainder was conveyed and not persons to whom the property would descend. . . . *Peer* had done it. *Peer* — or, rather, the attorney who drafted that Will — found the words which would talismanically ward off the Rule in Shelley's Case. Similarly, the Will drafted by Wycoff's attorney, and which Wycoff executed, gave the farm to Earle "during the term of his natural life," and after Earle's life, gave the farm *"to such person or persons* as shall be his sole heir or heirs in land in fee simple" (emphasis added). Wycoff invoked Peer's words and avoided the Rule in Shelley's Case.

The argument of Earle's devisees that the Rule in Shelley's Case applies and that they are entitled to the property in question is rejected. Judgment will accordingly be entered.

1. The purpose behind this 600 year old doctrine is elusive. While commentators have suggested a number of reasons for its creation, the rule is generally understood to have arisen in medieval England as a means to "prevent the use of a device which would otherwise deprive the overlord of the fruits of his seignoiy [seigniory]." American Law of Property, supra, § 4.40 at p. 478; Page on Wills, supra, § 37.15 at

p. 619. In other words, it might have been analogous to any number of provisions which a modern day scrivener might insert into a document to avoid a taxable event. [Editorial Note: This is footnote 6 of the opinion.]

8.4.3

Merger Doctrine

The court in **Swanson v. Swanson**, excerpted below, noted that the merger doctrine is an established property law principle that applies "whenever a greater estate and a less coincide and meet in one and the same person, without any intermediate estate, ..." In those instances, the lesser estate is "immediately annihilated, or, in the law phrase, it is said to be merged, that is, sunk or drowned in the greater."

8.4.3.1

Swanson v. Swanson
856 N.W.2d 705 (Minn. Ct. App. 2014)

Court of Appeals of Minnesota

CLEARY, Chief Judge.

Respondent brought an action to partition property under Minn.Stat. § 558.01. Appellant opposed the partition and brought a motion for summary judgment. The district court denied the motion for summary judgment and held that respondent could bring a partition action under section 558.01. The district court found that partition by sale was appropriate after a partition hearing. Because we conclude that respondent's remainder and life estate merge to create a fee simple, and because the owner of a fee simple interest is not a tenant in common with the owner of a remainder interest under section 558.01, we reverse.

FACTS

Respondent Marian Swanson and her late husband conveyed a future interest in two properties to their children, Kristin Schumacher and appellant Terrence Swanson, by quit claim deeds executed on January 26, 1996. One property was a homestead located in Babbitt, Minnesota, and the other was a cabin located on White Iron Lake in Lake County, Minnesota. The deeds created a life estate in the two properties for respondent and reserved undivided one-half remainder interests for respondent's daughter and appellant. Respondent's husband died on October 20, 2007. Respondent's daughter and her then husband conveyed their one-half remainder interests back to respondent through quit claim deeds recorded on November 9, 2012.

After respondent received the remainder interests, she brought an action for partition. Appellant moved for summary judgment. The major issue at the summary judgment hearing was whether respondent could bring an action for partition under Minnesota law depending on how the district court classified her property interests. Respondent argued that she had a life estate subject to appellant's undivided one-half remainder in the properties, and a fee simple estate in the other half created by merging her life estate and undivided one-half remainder interests. Respondent argued that the owner of a fee simple interest could bring an action to partition against an undivided one-half remainder under section 558.01. Appellant argued that respondent could not bring an action for partition under Minnesota law. The district court denied appellant's motion for summary judgment in all respects and said that respondent was a "life tenant to the subject properties and an owner of one-half of the remainder in the two properties." The district court reasoned that the remainder and life estate together were an "undivided one-half fee simple (which encompasses both a present and future interest)."

The district court held a partition hearing. At the hearing, respondent argued for partition by sale because one of the properties was a homestead that could not be partitioned in kind without great expense, and the other property was a cabin that could not be divided because of lake-front and septic regulations. The district court found that partition by sale was appropriate. Appellant timely filed an appeal under Minn.Stat. § 558.215 (2012).

ISSUES

I. Did appellant waive the right to challenge the district court's characterization of respondent's property interests?

II. Should Minnesota apply the merger doctrine when a person's life estate and remainder interests are united?

III. Does respondent have the requisite property interest under section 558.01 to bring an action for partition?

ANALYSIS

I.

In its summary judgment order, the district court held that respondent had the necessary property interests to bring an action for partition. Respondent unpersuasively argues that appellant waived the property interest issue at the partition hearing. . . .

Here, the order for partition provides the basis for appeal pursuant to Minn.Stat. § 558.215. . . . Because the district court found in its summary-judgment order that respondent had standing to bring an action for partition under section 558.01, this court can review the order.

II.

Respondent has a life estate and an undivided one-half remainder interest in the properties. Appellant has an undivided one-half remainder interest in the properties subject to respondent's life estate and argues that respondent does not have the requisite property interests to bring an action for partition. In the summary judgment order, the district court held that "[respondent] is the owner of a life estate and a one-half undivided remainder interest which give[s] her the requisite ownership interest to bring an action in partition." Later in the same order, the district court stated that respondent had an "undivided one-half fee simple (which encompasses both a present and future interest)." When appellant challenged the characterization of respondent's property interests at the partition hearing, the district court referenced the summary judgment order. Given the language in the summary judgment order, it is unclear whether the district court applied merger, permitted the partition action to go forward as between two owners of remainder interests, or both.

When the material facts of a case are not in dispute, this court applies a de novo standard of review to determine whether the trial court erred in its application of the law on a motion for summary judgment. . . . Because no published Minnesota appellate court decision has addressed whether the merger doctrine applies when someone holds both a life estate and remainder in the same property at the same time, we address the issue for the first time.

The supreme court has applied the merger doctrine in other situations instructive here. It has applied merger where the same person owns the dominant and servient estates with an easement. *Pergament v. Loring Props., Ltd.,* 599 N.W.2d 146, 149 (Minn.1999) ("[A]n easement that benefits the dominant estate and burdens the servient estate is extinguished when fee title to each estate is united in one owner."). The supreme court has also used merger when the same person acquires title to a property and a mortgage on that property. *Davis v. Pierce,* 10 Minn. 376, 378 (1865). In deciding whether the mortgage and title merge, courts look to the intent of the parties to determine whether the mortgage is extinguished. *Id.; Losleben v. Losleben,* 199 Minn. 227, 230, 271 N.W. 463, 464 (1937). For example, in certain cases the owner of the property who also holds a first mortgage might want to keep the mortgage interest separate so it can be satisfied if the property is sold. *Losleben,* 199 Minn. at 231, 271 N.W. at 465.

The application of the merger doctrine in this case would be similar to the application of merger involving easements. In the case of easements, there is no reason to maintain a distinction between the servient estate, dominant estate, and the easement, because the same person owns all three. Similarly, there is no reason to maintain the separation of a remainder and life estate when the same owner holds them together. Maintaining the separation would lead to a confusing mix of legal duties that one person would owe to herself. For example, the life tenant would owe a duty to herself to pay interest and taxes and keep the premises in reasonable repair.

Because the use of merger in this circumstance is an issue of first impression, this court may also look for guidance from foreign jurisdictions that have addressed the issue. Many foreign courts hold that if someone holds both a life estate and a remainder in the same property at the same time, the property rights merge into a fee simple.[1] Additionally, an established property law principle is that "whenever a greater estate and a less coincide and meet in one and the same person, without any intermediate estate, the less is immediately annihilated, or, in the law phrase, it is said to be merged, that is, sunk or drowned in the greater." 1 Herbert T. Tiffany et al., *The Law of Real Property* § 70 (3d ed.1976) (citing 2 William Blackstone, *Commentaries* § 177). Applying this principle to the facts of the case, the life estate, the lesser estate, merges into the remainder, the greater estate.

Given the use of the merger doctrine in other contexts in Minnesota and the persuasive authority of foreign courts, we hold that the doctrine applies in Minnesota when a life estate and remainder interest are united in one owner. More specifically, the life estate (the lesser estate) is merged in the remainder (the greater estate) and is thereby extinguished.

III.

After applying merger, respondent has a one-half fee simple interest in the properties. Appellant has a remainder in the other half of the properties subject to respondent's life estate. We must next address, as a matter of first impression, whether the owner of a fee simple interest can bring an action for partition against the owner of a remainder interest under section 558.01. In its summary judgment order, the district court held that respondent could bring an action for partition. We reverse the district court because the owner of a fee simple interest is not a tenant in common with the owner of a remainder interest under section 558.01.

***

Section 558.01 describes who can bring an action for partition:

> When two or more persons are interested, as joint tenants or as tenants in common, in real property in which one or more of them have an estate of inheritance or for life or for years, an action may be brought by one or more of such persons against the others for a partition thereof according to the respective rights and interests of the parties interested therein....

Minn.Stat. § 558.01. The statute, then, has two requirements regarding who can bring an action for partition: the person must be interested in real property as a tenant in common or joint tenant, and one or more of them must have "an estate of inheritance or for life or for years." *Id.*

314

Respondent argued that she was a tenant in common with appellant, while appellant argued they were not tenants in common under section 558.01. Tenants in common must share the same right to possession in the property. 2 Herbert T. Tiffany et al., *The Law of Real Property* § 426 (3d ed. 1976) ("Tenancy in common is characterized by unity of possession.... The unity of possession means unity of right of possession and not possession in fact."). Since tenants in common must have the same right to possession, section 558.01 requires tenants in common in real property to share a present possessory interest or a future interest. Thus, the tenants in common could have fee simple interests, or the tenants in common could have remainder interests. *See Heintz v. Wilhelm,* 151 Minn. 195, 197, 186 N.W. 305, 305 (1922) (permitting an owner of a remainder interest to bring an action for partition against another owner of a remainder subject to the life estate). However, the statute does not permit the owner of a fee simple interest to bring a partition action against the owner of a remainder interest, or vice versa.

Respondent's daughter conveyed her undivided one-half remainder to respondent. Respondent also had a life estate in the properties. The two interests merged to give respondent a fee simple interest in one-half of the properties and a life estate in the other half. Appellant has an undivided one-half remainder interest subject to respondent's life estate. The fee simple is an estate in possession, Minn.Stat. § 500.07 (2012), whereas the remainder is a future estate. Minn.Stat. § 500.11 (2012). Because respondent has a present possessory interest and appellant has a future interest, they do not share the same right to possession and are not tenants in common under the plain meaning of section 558.01. Respondent therefore does not have a right to bring an action for partition.

Respondent cites several foreign cases for the proposition that the owner of a fee simple interest can bring an action for partition against the owner of a remainder interest. However, the statutes in the cases cited by respondent are distinguishable from section 558.01. In *Bosley v. Burk,* the Maryland court allowed the owner of a one-third fee simple to bring an action for partition against the owner of the other two-thirds remainder interest. 154 Md. 27, 139 A. 543, 543–44 (1927). But the partition statute in Maryland is broader than Minnesota's, it includes any "joint tenant, tenant in common, or any parcener or *any concurrent owner,* whether claiming by descent or purchase." *Id.* at 544 (emphasis added). . . .

Respondent also argues that a fee simple encompasses both a present and future estate, and that she can bring an action for partition under the future estate of the fee simple. Respondent does not cite any legal authority for this proposition, and it is contrary to property law principles. *See* Restatement (Third) of Prop.: Wills & Donative Transfers § 24.2 (2011) (stating that a fee simple is "never followed by a future interest"). While it is true that a fee simple is descendible or devisable, that does not mean that it also encompasses a future interest. For example, in this case respondent has a fee simple in half the properties without a future interest, such as a reversion or remainder. No one else necessarily has a future interest in the fee simple as respondent could choose to convey it in any number of ways before her death.

***

DECISION

Under the doctrine of merger, a life estate is extinguished when title to the life estate and title to a remainder interest in the property are united in one owner. The owner of a fee simple is not a tenant in common with the owner of a remainder interest under section 558.01, and respondent does not have the right to bring an action for partition. The district court's order is reversed.

Reversed.

1. See Larmon v. Larmon, 173 Ky. 477, 191 S.W. 110, 112 (1917) ("Thus, if there be a tenant for years, and the reversion in fee simple descends to or is purchased by him, the term of years is merged in the inheritance, and shall never exist any more."); Gray v. Shinn, 293 Ill. 573, 127 N.E. 755, 758–59 (1920) (applying merger "when an estate for life and the next vested estate in remainder or reversion meet in the same person"); Allen v. Anderson, 44 Ind. 395, 399 (1873) (merging life estate in greater estate acquired by deed); Wagner v. Maskey, 353 N.W.2d 891, 893 (Iowa Ct.App.1984) (stating that merger only occurs "when the life tenancy and the remainder interest are owned by the same person"); Bosley v. Burk, 154 Md. 27, 139 A. 543, 544 (1927) ("Upon the purchase of the life estate in the whole and the

remainder as to one undivided third by the appellant, all of the requisites necessary to constitute a merger were present."); Brown v. Long Bell Co., 138 Miss. 548, 103 So. 353, 355 (1925) (merging life estate with remainder when life tenant conveyed her interest to remainderman); Treiber v. Citizens State Bank, 598 N.W.2d 96, 97 (N.D.1999) (merging a life estate with remainder interest in two-thirds of the property to create fee simple in two-thirds). [Editorial Note: This is footnote 2 of the opinion.]

8.4.4

Rule Against Perpetuities

The circumstances that led to the development of the common law *Rule Against Perpetuities* existed in the 1600s, including the rise of the indestructible executory interest. Executory interests became recognized by the law courts in 1636 after the passage of the famous Statute of Uses, which executed the use. Unlike contingent remainders, which could have been destroyed by the Destructibility of Contingent Remainder rule, there was nothing comparable to limit executory interests.

The Rule Against Perpetuities, which served to place limits on executory interests and other non-vested future interests, can be traced to the *Duke of Norfolk's Case*, 3 Ch. Cas. 1, 22 Eng. Rep. 931 (Ch. 1682). In addition to curbing dead hand control, other purposes for the Rule Against Perpetuities were to ensure that real property and other resources are freely in commerce and readily alienable and to limit private express trusts.

The Rule Against Perpetuities developed over time. Understanding the Rule Against Perpetuities requires first recognizing which interests are vulnerable to it. The types of interests that are vulnerable to the Rule Against Perpetuities are executory interests, contingent remainders, and vested remainders subject to open (or other future interests if in a class, such as a vested remainder subject to complete divestment in a class). Notice that present interests are not vulnerable to the Rule Against Perpetuities. Moreover, future interests in a grantor are also not vulnerable. Therefore, possibilities of reverter, rights of re-entry, and reversions are not vulnerable to the Rule Against Perpetuities. Neither are indefeasibly vested remainders.

An interest that is vulnerable to the Rule Against Perpetuities – executory interest, contingent remainder, or class gift – would need to be tested to see if it violates the Rule Against Perpetuities. Note that, when testing a vulnerable interest against the Rule Against Perpetuities, the concern is with an interest vesting beyond the perpetuities period or, when dealing with a class gift, with someone joining the class beyond the perpetuities period. If the concern could occur beyond the perpetuities period, the vulnerable interest violates the Rule Against Perpetuities and is void.

The **perpetuities period** is lives in being at the time the interest is created plus 21 years. One way to test whether the vulnerable interest violates the Rule Against Perpetuities is to ask whether the concern could occur more than 21 years after a life in being. Relevant **lives in being** are: (1) the grantor, if living at the time the interest is created; (2) purchasers listed in the instrument; (3) others related to persons named in the instrument, sometimes referred to as a member of an intervening generation; and (4) someone mentioned in the instrument under a perpetuities savings clause. When testing these levels of lives in being, if any person proves the concern impossible, the interest does not violate the Rule Against Perpetuities and you stop testing. Such life in being who can prove the concern impossible is deemed a **validating life**. If, however, you have tested all the relevant levels and the concern could occur beyond the perpetuities period – no validating life was found – the vulnerable interest violates the Rule Against Perpetuities and must be stricken from the instrument.

There are three interesting twists regarding class gifts and the Rule Against Perpetuities. First, although vested remainders subject to open are vested at their inception, for purposes of the Rule Against Perpetuities they are nevertheless deemed vulnerable. Second, an open class cannot serve as a validating life. Third, if even only one potential person could join the class beyond the perpetuities period, the entire class gift is void under the "all or nothing rule" for class gifts.

8.4.4.1

Malone v. Guynes
250 S.W.3d 260 (Ark. Ct. App. 2007)

Arkansas Court of Appeals

Jhon Mauzy Pittman, Chief Judge.

The appellant owns a house in a residential subdivision subject to several restrictive covenants, including a prohibition against construction of multifamily dwellings. Appellant attempted to build a duplex in the subdivision in violation of the covenant limiting use to single-family residences. Appellees, who are owners of other lots in the subdivision, sued to enjoin construction. Both sides moved for summary judgment; the trial court granted summary judgment to appellees. On appeal, appellant contends that the trial court erred in granting appellees' motion for summary judgment, arguing that the restrictive covenant is void as violative of the rule against perpetuities and, in the alternative, that the covenant limiting construction to single-family dwellings was unenforceable because other restrictive covenants had been violated in the past.

Appellant's first argument is without merit. The Arkansas Constitution forbids "perpetuities" but does not describe them. Ark. Const, art. 2, § 19. The doctrine of perpetuities is a creation of the common law that arose out of conflict between courts striving to maintain the alienability of property and feudal lords attempting to amass and control wealth over generations. It has its origins in *The Duke of Norfolk's Case*, 3 Ch. Cas. 1, 22 Eng. Rep. 931 (Ch. 1682), a case involving a donative transfer of land to family members that attempted to control the ownership of the property by future generations through a series of contingent interests. There, Lord Chancellor Nottingham held that any future interest is good if based on a contingency that must occur within lives in being, expressly leaving undecided the question of "the utmost Limitation of a Fee upon a Fee." *Id.* at 37, 22 Eng. Rep. 953. That question remained undecided for 150 years before being settled in *Cadell v. Palmer*, 1 Cl. & F. 372 (H.L. 1833), as a gross term of twenty-one years after a life or lives in being. *See generally* John Chipman Gray, *The Rule Against Perpetuities* (3d ed. 1915). This formulation was soon thereafter adopted in Arkansas. Stated in modern terms, the rule against

319

perpetuities prohibits the creation of future interests or estates which by possibility may not become vested within the life or lives in being at the time of the testator's death or the effective date of the instrument creating the future interest, and twenty-one years thereafter. If there is any possibility that the interest will vest beyond the limits of the rule, the transaction is void.

Here, the rule against perpetuities does not apply because appellant's interest in the property vested immediately. The Arkansas Supreme Court upheld a residential community assessment covenant of indefinite duration in *Kell v. Bella Vista Village,* 258 Ark. 757, 528 S.W.2d 651 (1975), holding that nothing in the covenant kept that appellant's interest from immediately vesting. The restrictive covenants do not prevent the interest from vesting, but are merely contractual proscriptions against certain uses.

> Restrictions against a particular use of property do not restrict the alienation of such property, since the owner of the fee can convey it at his or her pleasure, nor do they tend to perpetuity, since the person who is entitled to the rights or privileges created or secured by the restriction can at any time release them. A restrictive covenant limiting the use of lots in a subdivision to residential purposes, and prohibiting their use for commercial purposes, does not restrain alienation or violate the rule against perpetuities even if it is of indefinite duration. Similarly, the rule limiting the duration of restraints on alienation is not applicable to a restrictive covenant in a deed that no buildings should ever be erected on a certain part of the land conveyed; consequently the restriction, even though created to endure forever, is valid and enforceable.

20 Am. Jur. 2d *Covenants* § 165 (2006).

Appellant next argues that none of the covenants . . . can be enforced because some have been violated, e.g., those involving setback requirements and prohibition of mobile homes, with the result that the subdivision lacks a general plan of development. This argument also lacks merit. The primary test of the existence of a general plan for development or improvement of a tract of land divided into a number of lots is whether substantially common restrictions apply to all lots of like character or similarly situated. Here, appellant has shown only a relatively few violations of other restrictions in the covenants. The fact that other violations have occurred does not always constitute acquiescence or waiver of the restrictions, and the breach of the covenant by the developer not only must be substantial but also must be a breach of the same restriction. Appellant has shown no prior breach of the restriction against multifamily dwellings, and we therefore find no error.

Affirmed.

8.4.4.2

Atlantic Richfield Co. v. Whiting Oil & Gas Corp.
320 P.3d 1179 (Colo. 2014)

Colorado Supreme Court

JUSTICE MARQUEZ

delivered the Opinion of the Court

We granted certiorari review to address a doctrine that has been described as "long cherished by law school professors and dreaded by most law students: the infamous rule against perpetuities." Byke Constr. Co. v. Miller, 140 Ariz. 57, 680 P.2d 193, 194 (Ct.App.1984). Specifically, we have been asked to determine whether section 15-11-1106(2), C.R.S. (2013), which provides for reformation of nonvested property interests to avoid the harsh consequences of the common law rule against perpetuities, requires a court to reform a revocable option negotiated as part of a commercial contract entered into before May 31, 1991 (the effective date of the Statutory Rule Against Perpetuities Act).

The common law rule against perpetuities was developed to curb excessive "dead-hand control" of property retained in families through intergenerational transfers. Restatement (Third) of Prop.: Servitudes § 8.3 cmt. b (2000). Like rules against restraints on alienation, the rule against perpetuities stems from a general policy that frowns upon the withdrawal of property from commerce. The rule against perpetuities furthered this policy by voiding property interests that may vest too remotely. Under the common law rule, a non-vested property interest is void unless it is certain to vest, if at all, within twenty-one years after the death of a life in being at the time the interest was created.

At issue here is section 15-11-1106(2), which appears in the Statutory Rule Against Perpetuities Act ("Act"). See §§ 15-11-1101 to -1216, C.R.S. (2013). In Colorado, the Act – which was modeled on the Uniform Statutory Rule Against Perpetuities ("US-RAP") – supersedes the common law rule for nonvested property interests created after May 31, 1991. § 15-11-1107(2), C.R.S. (2013). The common law rule still applies to nonvested property interests created prior to that date. Under the Act, all donative transfers created after May 31, 1991 (with the exception of trusts and powers of appointment) are valid so long as the property interest created vests or terminates within ninety years of its creation. § 15-11-1102.5, C.R.S. (2013). The statutory rule thus adopts a "wait and see" approach under which no interest is invalid unless and until it actually fails to vest within the statutory period.

§ 15-11 Section 15-11-1106(2) of the Act is a reformation provision that requires courts, upon request, to reform nonvested interests created prior to May 31, 1991 to bring them into compliance with the common law rule. The parties before us dispute whether section 15-11-1106(2) applies broadly to permit reformation of all nonvested property interests that predate the Act, or whether it applies more narrowly to reform only the types of nonvested interests that remain subject to the statutory rule against perpetuities, thus precluding reformation of the commercial option at issue here. Regardless of the breadth of interests potentially subject to reformation, section 15-11-1106(2) applies only to reform interests that are determined in a judicial proceeding to "violate this state's rule against perpetuities as that rule existed before May 31, 1991." *applies to*

PP
trial In this case, the trial court concluded that the revocable option at issue here, granted as part of a negotiated commercial agreement, violated the common law rule against perpetuities. Pursuant to section 15-11-1106(2), the court inserted a savings clause to prevent the option from being voided by the common law rule and ruled that the option holder was entitled to specific performance of the reformed option. The court of appeals affirmed the trial court judgment, concluding that the trial court properly

applied section 15-11-1106(2) to reform the option. In so doing, the court of appeals expressly declined to reach the question of whether the revocable option was subject to the common law rule.

We granted review to examine whether section 15-11-1106(2) authorized the trial court to reform the option at issue here. In so doing, we consider, as a threshold matter, whether the option violated the common law rule, and conclude that it did not. The commercial option negotiated by the parties posed no practical restraint on alienation because it was fully revocable at any time before its exercise. Therefore, the option did not violate the common law rule against perpetuities as that rule was construed in our case law prior to passage of the Act. Because the option here did not violate the common law rule against perpetuities, it was valid as originally negotiated by the parties and no reformation was necessary. Accordingly, we affirm the judgment of the court of appeals on different grounds and do not reach the Petitioner's arguments that section 15-11, 1106(2) does not provide for the reformation of nondonative, commercial instruments, or that the lower courts' application of that section to the option here was unconstitutionally retrospective.

I.

Beginning in 1968, Petitioner Atlantic Richfield Company ("ARCO") and Respondent Equity Oil Company (now known as Whiting Oil & Gas) ("Equity") entered into a series of agreements to develop oil shale on a number of properties, including a property in western Colorado known as the Boies Block. An option contained within one of these agreements is the source of the current controversy.

A.

In 1968, ARCO and Equity entered into an agreement ("1968 Agreement") in which ARCO committed two million dollars to fund Equity's research into methods of recovering oil shale from several properties. In return, Equity conveyed a partial interest in the properties to ARCO, thereby allowing ARCO to share in any future profits from oil shale production. Specifically, and as relevant here, Equity conveyed half of its undivided fifty-percent interest in the Boies Block to ARCO. The 1968 Agreement further provided that if oil shale was not in commercial production by

1988, Equity would convey an additional interest in the Boies Block to ARCO ("Additional Conveyance").

additional Conveyance

By 1982, Equity's research had not led to commercial production of oil shale. In 1983, following a year of negotiations, ARCO and Equity agreed to an amendment postponing the Additional Conveyance. That 1983 amendment is at issue here. As an incentive to complete its research, ARCO granted Equity a non-exclusive option ("1983 option") to buy back the interest in the Boies Block that ARCO had previously acquired from Equity as part of the 1968 Agreement. Pursuant to the 1983 amendment, Equity's right to exercise the option would not expire until 11:59 p.m. on February 1, 2008. Importantly, the parties agreed that "ARCO shall retain the sole and exclusive right to cancel this Option at any time during its term," with the exception that Equity was granted a right of first refusal if ARCO received an offer from another party to buy its interest in the Boies Block. The parties' agreement set an initial price at which the 1983 option could be exercised, but provided for annual market-based adjustments tethered to the annual percentage change in ARCO's published benchmark price for West Texas sour crude oil.

Equity's research never led to commercial production of oil shale from the properties. In the early 2000s, Equity sought to acquire ARCO's interest in the Boies Block after discovering that the property contained valuable reserves of natural gas. In 2003, ARCO rejected an initial offer by Equity to purchase the Boies Block for $10,000, but took no action to revoke the 1983 option. Then, in 2006, Equity attempted to exercise the 1983 option. The 1983 option had not considered natural gas production in its exercise price valuation, instead tying the exercise price to ARCO's West Texas sour crude benchmark. When Equity attempted to exercise the option in 2006, the purchase price for the property – as determined by the option's valuation formula – was significantly below the property's 2006 market value. ARCO refused to convey the interest in the Boies Block to Equity.

B.

Equity sued ARCO for specific performance of the 1983 option. ARCO moved for judgment on the pleadings, arguing that, as a matter of law, the 1983 option was void ab initio because the twenty-five year option period violated the common law rule against perpetuities. In response, Equity argued that the common law rule against perpetuities does not apply to cancelable or revocable interests. Equity argued that because the 1983 option could be cancelled at ARCO's sole and exclusive discretion, the option imposed no practical restraint on ARCO's property interests and did not violate the policies of the common law rule. Alternatively, Equity argued that even if the 1983 option violated the common law rule, the court was required to reform the option by inserting a savings clause pursuant to section 15-11-1106(2).

The trial court denied ARCO's motion for judgment on the pleadings. The court agreed with ARCO that the twenty-five year option, as written, violated the common law rule against perpetuities because it could be exercised more than twenty-one years after the parties entered into the 1983 amendment. However, the court denied judgment on the pleadings because the option could be reformed under section 15-11-1106(2).

Following a bench trial on the remaining issues in the case, the court reformed the option pursuant to section 15-11-1106(2) by inserting a savings clause terminating the option "unless it is exercised no later than twenty-one years after the death of [former Equity president] Paul M. Dougan." The trial court concluded that Equity was entitled to specific performance of the reformed option, and imposed a constructive trust on ARCO's interest in the Boies Block until ARCO delivered the deed required by the court's judgment.

In a 2-1 decision, the court of appeals affirmed the trial court's judgment, rejecting ARCO's argument that the reformation provision does not apply to commercial, nondonative transfers. The majority also rejected ARCO's argument that the trial court's reformation of the 1983 option constituted an unconstitutional retrospective application of section 15-11-1106(2).

The majority reasoned that, by its own terms, section 15-11-1106(2) applies to "nonvested property interests" and does not exclude interests arising from nondonative transfers. The majority noted that some versions of the USRAP adopted in other states expressly exclude interests arising from nondonative transfers from the operation of the entire act, including the reformation provision, and not just from the vesting requirements of the new statutory rule Accordingly, those states' reformation provisions generally would not apply to commercial transactions. In contrast, Colorado's version of the USRAP contains a narrower exclusion of such interests, exempting them only from the vesting requirements of the statutory rule against perpetuities. Thus, the majority reasoned, the general assembly did not intend to exclude such interests from application of the reformation provision in section 15-11-1106(2).

The majority further reasoned that applying the reformation provision broadly to all interests invalidated under the common law rule comports with the legislature's "major policy goal" to "make interests valid whenever possible." . . . Because it concluded that the trial court properly applied the reformation provision, the court of appeals expressly declined to address Equity's argument that it should affirm the trial court on the grounds that the 1983 option did not violate the common law rule against perpetuities because ARCO could cancel the option at any time.

***

ARCO petitioned this court to review the court of appeals' decision, and we granted certiorari review. We affirm, albeit on different grounds.

II

Because section 15-11-1106(2) applies to reform only nonvested interests that violate the common law rule against perpetuities, we first determine, as a thresh old matter, whether the 1983 option violated the common law rule.

We first review the origins and development of the common law rule and the commentary criticizing its application to commercial instruments. In so doing, we acknowledge that the vesting period of the common law rule, based on lives in being plus twenty-one years, makes little sense in the world of commercial transactions. Indeed, for this reason, nonvested interests arising out of commercial transactions are now excluded from the vesting requirements of the statutory rule. Many courts, including our own, have struggled with the application of the common law rule to commercial transactions. Over time, we have avoided applying the rule against perpetuities to certain types of interests in commercial settings where we have concluded that the purposes of the common law rule would not be advanced. Upon reexamination of our more recent cases involving non-donative, commercial transactions, we conclude that we effectively have been applying a general rule against unreasonable restraints on alienation, rather than the rule against perpetuities in its classic formulation. The current Restatement (Third) of Property acknowledges this modern trend in the treatment of options and preemptive rights such as rights of first refusal Restatement (Third) of Prop.: Servitudes § 3.3 (2000).

. . . Because it was fully revocable, the option did not violate the common law rule against perpetuities, either as construed in our case law prior to passage of the Act, or even as strictly formulated. Accordingly, we hold that the 1983 option was valid as originally negotiated by the parties and no reformation was necessary. We therefore affirm the judgment of the court of appeals on different grounds and do not reach ARCO's arguments that section 15-11-1106(2) does not apply to reform nondonative, commercial instruments, or that the lower courts' application of that section to the option here was unconstitutionally retrospective.

***

B.

The common law rule against perpetuities arose in England in response to landowners' attempts to control their land in perpetuity. The English courts, having deemed it generally good policy to keep property marketable by limiting restraints on its alienation, developed the rule against perpetuities to "curb excessive dead-hand control of property retained in families through intergenerational transfers." Restatement (Third) of Prop.: Servitudes § 3.8 cmt. b (2000). The rule served to "avoid fettering real property with future interests dependent upon contingencies unduly remote which isolate the property and exclude it from commerce and development for long periods of time, thus working an indirect restraint upon alienation." First Nat'l Bank & Trust Co. v. Sidwell Corp., 234 Kan. 867, 678 P.2d 118, 127 (1984). Like rules against unreasonable restraints on alienation, the rule against perpetuities stems from a general policy against withdrawal of property from commerce, and accordingly aims to keep property freely transferable.

The rules against unreasonable restraints on alienation generally aim to keep assets available for commerce by applying different types of limits depending on the nature of the property, the purpose of the restraint, and its potential for harm. . . .

By contrast, the rule against perpetuities evolved more specifically as a limitation on family gift transactions; that is, the rule developed to address indirect restraints on alienation placed on real property by landowners seeking to preserve their land for their lineal descendants. The rule accomplished this by voiding contingent future interests that may vest too remotely in time. Under Professor Gray's classic distillation of the common law rule, which has been generally adopted in Colorado, "[n]o interest is good unless it must vest, if at all, not later than twenty-one years after some life in being at the creation of the interest." John Chipman Gray, The Rule Against Perpetuities 191 (Roland Gray ed., 4th ed. 1942). Importantly, because the rule developed to address concerns regarding excessively long family settlements, the perpetuities period-twenty one years after some life in being at the creation of the interest-was tailored to fit the needs of family gift transactions. W. Barton Leach, Perpetuities in Perspective: Ending the Rule's Reign of Terror, 65 Harv. L.Rev. 721, 737 (1952). This court first recognized and applied the common law rule against perpetuities in 1896. See Chilcott v. Hart, 23 Colo. 40, 54, 45 P. 391, 396 (1896).

In the late 19th century, courts began to view the rule against perpetuities as a generalized statement purporting to apply to all contingent interests in property, and therefore began to apply the rule to commercial land transactions, including, among other things, options and rights of first refusal. Restatement (Third) of Prop.: Servitudes § 8.3 cmt. b (2000). The line of case law applying the rule to options generally can be traced back to the 1882 English case of London & S.W. Ry. Co. v. Gomm, 20 Ch. 562 (1882). See, e.g., Rocky Mountain Fuel Co. v. Heflin, 148 Colo. 415, 421, 366 P.2d 577, 580 (1961) (citing London & S.W. Ry. Co. for the proposition that options to purchase real estate are subject to the rule against perpetuities). Courts reasoned that because an option to purchase land is specifically enforceable, the option holder has an equitable interest in the land that is contingent upon the exercise of the option. Reasoning that contingent interests in land are void unless they must vest within the period of perpetuities, courts concluded that an option to purchase that can be exercised beyond the period of perpetuities is void under the rule.

The application of the common law rule to nondonative, commercial transactions has been sharply criticized. For well over half a century, commentators have argued that the rule against perpetuities should not be applied to commercial transactions. These commentators have contended that, even assuming it is desirable to impose some sort of restriction on the equitable interests created by specifically enforceable contracts, the perpetuities period of the common law rule does not offer an appropriate limitation: "lives in being" and "21 years" have "no significance in the world of commercial affairs." Leach, Perpetuities in a Nutshell, supra at 661; see also Lewis M. Simes & Alan F. Smith, The Law of Future Interests 159 (Alan F. Smith ed., 2d ed. 1956) ("[The] rule against perpetuities was designed primarily to restrict family settlements and not commercial transactions, and ... an option to purchase land is nearly always a part of a commercial transaction. As an original proposition, it might have been better for the courts to hold that all option contracts are outside the rule against perpetuities."); T. Bergin et al., Preface to Estates in Land & Future Interest 207-08 (2d ed. 1984) ("[The rule against perpetuities is obviously not suited to the commercial transaction.").

***

In recent years, some courts have adopted the Restatement's view that both commercial options and rights of first refusal fall beyond the ambit of the common law rule against perpetuities. See, e.g., Bauermeister v. Waste Mgmt. Co., 280 Neb. 1, 783 N.W.2d 594, 600 (2010) (holding that the rule against perpetuities is inapplicable to a contractual option); Old Port Cove Holdings, Inc. v. Old Port Cove Condo. Assoc. One, Inc., 986 So.2d 1279, 1287-88 (Fla.2008) (adopting the "modern" view that options and rights of first refusal should be "analyzed under the rule against unreasonable restraints ... [and] are not subject to the common law rule against perpetuities") (citing Jesse Dukeminier, A Modern Guide to Perpetuities, 74 Cal. L.Rev. 1867, 1908 (19868) ("The modern trend, however, has been to free preemptive options from the Rule and to subject them instead to the rule against unreasonable restraints on alienation.")); Shaver, 81 CalRptr.2d at 598 (observing that "the purpose of the rule against perpetuities was found to be inapt to commercial arrangements").

Courts adopting the Restatement approach observe that neither the historical purpose of the rule against perpetuities, nor public policy, is served by applying the rule to commercial transactions. . . .

***

C.

We recognize that our court has struggled with the application of the common law rule against perpetuities in the commercial arena, which has led to a convoluted and imprecise body of case law. This court has stated, without analysis, that the application of the common law rule to "ordinary options" is "firmly established," Atchison, 170 Colo. at 306, 463 P.2d at 302, and that the "rule applies to both options and preemptive rights," Perry v. Brundage, 200 Colo. 229, 234, 614 P.2d 362, 366 (1980). Close review of our cases addressing options and preemptive rights, however, reveals that in our struggle to apply the rule against perpetuities to commercial instruments, we have blurred the distinction between the common law rule against perpetuities and the rule against unreasonable restraints on alienation. . . . Yet in so doing, we have effectively shifted the inquiry to the reasonableness of the restraint and away from a strict application of the rule focused on the remoteness of vesting.

***

D.

We turn now to the 1983 option before us. Because the 1983 option was fully revocable by ARCO at any time, . . . we conclude that the 1983 option does not violate the common law rule against perpetuities, either as construed in our case law prior to passage of the Act, or even as strictly formulated.

As discussed above, ARCO and Equity, both sophisticated commercial entities, agreed to the option as part of the 1983 amendment following a year of arms-length negotiations. Equity and ARCO were joint owners of the Boies Block at the time the 1983 amendment was negotiated. Pursuant to the 1983 amendment, the option allowed Equity to buy back the interest in the Boies Block that ARCO had previously acquired from Equity as part of the 1968 Agreement. The parties agreed that Equity could exercise the option "at any time until 11:59 p.m. on February 1, 2008, unless the Option is cancelled pursuant to the provisions hereinafter set forth." Under the terms of the agreement, ARCO retained "the sole and exclusive right to cancel this Option at any time during its term."

Looking to whether the purposes of the common law rule are served, . . . we conclude that the 1983 option did not discourage valuable improvements to the land. Equity and ARCO were joint owners of the Boies Block, and therefore the option did not discourage Equity from improving the land. At the same time, the option did not discourage ARCO from investing in the land because it faced no risk of loss, given that it could cancel the 1983 option at any time.

***

More fundamentally, the 1983 option posed no practical restraint on ARCO's ability to improve or sell the property because ARCO reserved the express right to cancel the option at any time and for any reason. Unlike an ordinary option, which creates an absolute right to purchase property at the demand of the option holder, the 1983 option here was fully revocable by ARCO. Consequently, it did not prevent the improvement or conveyance of the property or otherwise violate the policies of the common law rule. In other words, because it could extinguish the option at any time at its sole discretion, ARCO retained full power to develop or dispose of the property.

Professor Gray, who articulated the classic formulation of the common law rule against perpetuities, long ago acknowledged that "[if] the owner of the present interest in property is at liberty to destroy a future interest, that interest is not within the scope of the Rule Against Perpetuities." Gray, supra, at 510; see also id. at 512 ("an interest, which is presently destructible, is not subject to the Rule against Perpetuities"). This principle was articulated by the Maryland Court of Appeals in Fitzpatrick v. Mercantile-Safe Deposit & Trust Co.:

> So long as one person has an unrestricted present power to alienate absolutely and in fee simple for his own benefit no future interest can be

void under the rule against perpetuities. For the policy of the rule to prevent the restriction of practical alienability is not violated.

220 Md. 534, 155 A2d 702, 709-10 (1959) (quoting Lewis M. Simes & Frank A. Smith, The Law of Future Interests 232-88 (John A. Borron, Jr. ed., 3d ed. (2004))). In short, where a conveyor retains the absolute power to destroy a future interest through the power of revocation, the rule against perpetuities is not implicated. Restatement (First) of Property § 378 cmt. a. (1944).

For these reasons, the 1983 option did not violate the common law rule against perpetuities. . . . Because the 1983 option was never subject to the rule against perpetuities, there was no need to reform it with a savings clause.

. . . Accordingly, we affirm the judgment of the court of appeals on different grounds.

8.4.5
Discussion: Notes, Questions, and Problems

8.4.5.1
Discussion Note #10. Destructibility of Contingent Remainders

Under the common law, the Doctrine of Destructibility of Contingent Remainders provided that, unless a contingent remainder shall vest at or before the termination of all estates prior to it in possession, it shall be destroyed. In almost all jurisdictions, the Doctrine of Destructibility of Contingent Remainders no longer applies, or has been modified to convert a contingent remainder that has not vested at the time of possession into a springing executory interest. See, for example, Nev. Rev. Stat. Ann. § 111.102, excerpted below.

> **111.102. Abolishment of doctrine of destructibility of contingent remainders**
>
> A contingent remainder is not destroyed by the termination of the preceding estate before the satisfaction of the condition upon which the remainder is

contingent. If the condition is subsequently satisfied, the remainder takes effect in the same manner as a springing or shifting executory interest. The purpose of this section is to abolish the doctrine of the destructibility of contingent remainders.

8.4.5.2

Discussion Note #11. Merger in other contexts

As noted in *Swanson v. Swanson*, excerpted above, the merger doctrine also arises in contexts other than estates in land and future interests. For example, merger can also occur with easements, servitudes, and mortgages.

8.4.5.3

Discussion Note #12. Perpetuities period

The period for the Rule Against Perpetuities is lives in being plus 21 years. What if the transaction involves corporate entities and the instrument does not refer to human lives? The courts have handled such scenarios by limiting the perpetuities period to 21 years from the creation of the interest. See, e.g., *C & D Investment Co. v. Gulf Transport Co.*, 526 So.2d 526 (Miss.1988); *Symphony Space, Inc. v. Pergola Properties, Inc.*, 669 N.E.2d 799 (1996).

8.4.5.4

Discussion Question #13. Right of first refusal and Rule Against Perpetuities?

In *Martin v. Seeley*, excerpted above, the plaintiff had a right of first refusal, which is a type of executory interest. Executory interests are vulnerable to the common law Rule Against Perpetuities. Why did the right of first refusal in *Martin v. Seeley* not violate the common law Rule Against Perpetuities?

8.4.5.5

Discussion Problem #14. Alexis' graduation problem

Grandmother was very proud upon hearing that Alexis was admitted to law school. When Alexis started her first year of law school, Grandmother executed and delivered to her a deed conveying Blackacre as follows: **"to Alexis upon her graduation from law school."** Assume that in this jurisdiction the Rule Against Perpetuities is applied in its common law form. Before analyzing the applicability of the Rule Against Perpetuities to this conveyance, classify the interests and estates created. What are the words of purchase? Does the purchaser have a present interest or a future interest? If it is a present interest, continue to that purchaser's estate. If it is a future interest, is it a remainder (apply the definition) or is it an executory interest? If it is a remainder, is it vested (apply the definition) or is it contingent? If instead of a remainder you determine that it is an executory interest, is it springing (apply the definition) or is it shifting (apply the definition)? What estate is the purchaser's interest in? Did the grantor retain an interest in Blackacre? If so, what is the grantor's retained interest? Are any of the interests vulnerable to the Rule Against Perpetuities? Note that only contingent remainders, executory interests, and future interests in a class are vulnerable to the Rule Against Perpetuities. If after classifying the interests and estates created you determine that Alexis has one of the vulnerable interests, then you must test her interest to see if it violates the Rule Against Perpetuities. Note that a vulnerable interest does not violate the Rule Against Perpetuities if, at the moment the interest is created, it is impossible for the condition to be met or for someone to join the class beyond the perpetuities period. Could the condition of Alexis' graduating law school occur more than 21 years after a life in being's death? Is there a validating life for the conveyance to Alexis?

8.4.5.6

Discussion Problem #15. Multiple common law rules problem

Assume that Olympia conveyed Blackacre as follows: **"to my son Albert for life, then to Albert's children for life, then to Albert's grandchildren and their heirs."** Assume that at the time of the conveyance Albert had one child, Junior, but that Albert had no grandchildren yet. Assume further that in this jurisdiction the Rule in Shelley's Case, the Doctrine of Worthier Title, the Rule of Merger, and the Rule Against Perpetuities all apply in their common law forms. Classify the interests and estates created by this conveyance and analyze whether any of them would be affected by the common law rules.

9
Chapter 9 · Easements and Licenses

In chapter 8, we discussed estates in land. In this chapter, we cover **easements**, which are not estates in land but are **interests in land**. This chapter also discusses **licenses**, which are neither estates in land nor interests in land but are nevertheless important to introduce in property law.

You may be familiar with certain common easements, such as those that allow for ingress and egress. Other common easements are utility easements. Before addressing how easements are created, transferred, interpreted as to scope, and terminated, it helps to classify easements pursuant to the following categorizations: (1) appurtenant or in gross; (2) affirmative or negative; (3) specific or general; and (4) exclusive or nonexclusive.

An easement is **appurtenant** if it benefits a parcel of land. That is, an easement is appurtenant if, in addition to benefitting the easement holder, the existence of the easement increases the use, value, or utility of land. An easement is **in gross** if the easement does not benefit land.

When an easement is appurtenant, the estate that benefits from the easement is referred as the **dominant estate** or the dominant tenement. The estate that is burdened by the easement is referred to as the **servient estate** or servient tenement. An easement in gross only has a servient estate.

An easement is **affirmative** if it provides the easement holder with the right to use or act on the servient estate. A type of affirmative easement, referred to as a **profit à prendre** or a profit, allows the holder of the easement to also appropriate something of value from the land. A **negative easement** provides the easement holder the right to prevent the owner of the servient estate from doing something on the servient estate.

An easement is characterized as a **specific easement** when the easement is geographically limited. Thus, a specific easement holder only has the right to use a particular part of the servient estate. A **general easement** does not provide specification as to where the easement holder's right may be exercised on the servient estate.

An easement is deemed *exclusive* if the easement prohibits similar easements from existing concurrently. And easement is *nonexclusive* where there could be similar easements at the same time.

As mentioned above, a license does not grant an interest in land. A *license* is permission from the *licensor* to the *licensee* to use or perform an act on the licensor's property. Licenses are generally intended as temporary and limited as to purpose. Although the general rule is that a license can be revoked freely by the licensor, there are certain circumstances that may prohibit such free revocation.

9.1
Creation of Easement

There are three main ways by which an easement may be created: (1) *expressly* by agreement of the parties, (2) by *implication*, and (3) by *prescription*.

9.1.1
Express by Grant or Reservation

The best way for an easement to be created is by the express agreement of the parties. As noted above, an easement is an interest in land. Thus, the requirements for a land transfer must be met. Notably, an easement must comply with the Statute of Frauds. An express easement can be created by *grant* or *reservation*. An easement is created by grant when the owner of the servient estate grants an easement to the easement holder. An easement is created by reservation when the owner of the dominant estate coveys land but retains an easement on the conveyed land. The reserved easement is stated in the deed conveying the land.

9.1.1.1

Corbett v. Ruben
290 S.E.2d 847 (Va. 1982)

Supreme Court of Virginia

POFF, J.,

delivered the opinion of the Court.

Bernard R. Corbett and Marie Bullock, d/b/a C & E partnership (collectively, Corbett), filed a bill of complaint against Ralph H. Ruben and Dorothy K. Ruben (collectively, Ruben) seeking to remove a cloud on Corbett's title. The chancellor entered a decree in favor of Ruben on cross motions to strike the pleadings, and we summarize the facts as stated in the pleadings and the stipulations of the parties.

In 1962, Al Baker Maintenance Company, a partnership (the Maintenance Company), owned two parcels of land located at 212-14 South Payne Street (parcel #1) and 219-21 South Payne Street (parcel #2). By a document styled "Declaration and Easement" recorded that year (the 1962 document) the Maintenance Company attempted to impress a perpetual automobile parking easement upon the whole of parcel #1 as an appurtenance to parcel #2 on which the Maintenance Company planned to construct an apartment building.

In 1964, after the building had been completed, the Maintenance Company conveyed parcel #2 to Lewis & Thos. Saltz, Inc., and parcel #1 to Albert E. Baker, Thomas Saltz's partner in the Maintenance Company. Later that year, Baker and his wife signed, acknowledged, sealed, and recorded a document styled "Corrected Declaration of Easement" (the 1964 document). Describing parcel #1 by metes and bounds, the 1964 document recited that the 1962 document had misdefined the scope and term of the easement and that the Bakers "wish to correct . . . and redefine this easement". The 1964 document then stated that the Bakers

> hereby create and establish an easement for the off-street parking of seven (7) passenger automobiles on [parcel #1] for the use and benefit of the owner and occupants of the apartments located on [parcel #2], said easement [described by metes and bounds], the duration of this easement to be co-extensive with the life of the building constructed [on parcel #2] and shall terminate when that structure no longer stands.

This document further provided that the Bakers "covenant and agree that the said easement shall be a covenant running with the title to" parcel #1.

Corbett, successor in title to parcel #1, maintained that a landowner cannot make one portion of his estate subservient to another portion and that the 1962 document was void. Ruben, successor in title to parcel #2, agreed, the case proceeded on that theory, and we treat the agreement as the law of the case. The chancellor ruled that the 1964 document, despite its references to the void document, "is by its terms a grant of an express easement appurtenant to [parcel #2] and. that [parcel #1] is servient thereto".

corbett arg. 1

Appealing from that ruling, Corbett argues that the 1964 document was void because "one may not modify, change, redefine or otherwise correct that which is null and void." Corbett misconceives the ruling. The question is not whether one document can breathe life into another which was void *ab initio.* The chancellor did not rule that the 1964 document validated the 1962 document; he held that the 1964 document was "by its [own] terms a grant of an express easement", and we address our inquiry to that holding.

Corbett arg. 2

Yet, the 1964 document is inoperative, Corbett asserts, because it "does not make an express grant of an easement". Corbett seems to assume an imperative the law does not impose. Neither statutory nor common law requires a grantor to employ words of art so long as "the intention to 'grant' is so manifest on the face of the instrument that no other construction could be put upon it". *Albert* v. *Holt,* 137 Va. 5, 10, 119 S.E. 120, 122 (1923). *See generally,* 3 R. Powell, The Law of Real Property ¶ 407, at 34-33, 34-34 (1981); Conard, "Words Which Will Create an Easement", 6 Mo. L. Rev. 245, 264-66 (1941). We believe the words "hereby create and establish" employed by the Bakers signify such an intent.

***

corbett arg 3

Assuming the 1964 document created an easement, Corbett maintains that it is not an easement appurtenant, as the chancellor ruled, but an easement in gross, *i.e.,* an easement with a servient estate but no dominant estate, an easement personal to the grantee. *See Stokes Inc.* v. *Matney,* 194 Va. 339, 344, 73 S.E.2d 269, 271 (1952). And, Corbett says, an easement in gross is not transferable.

In *Coal Corporation* v. *Lester,* 203 Va. 93, 97-99, 122 S.E.2d 901, 904-05 (1961), we reaffirmed the principles that an easement is not presumed to be one in gross; that the intent of the parties is the crucial determinant; that one of the tests of appurtenancy is whether the easement is a useful adjunct to the property; and that an easement appurtenant is one capable of being transferred and inherited while an easement in gross is not.[1]

The easement reviewed in *Coal Corporation* was granted "forever", *id.* at 97, 122 S.E.2d at 904, and Corbett argued at bar that an easement is not appurtenant unless its tenure is permanent. We did not consider such an argument in that case, and nothing in our analysis supports the inference Corbett draws. Even when the grant is made without term, courts may presume that an appurtenant easement was intended to terminate when the purpose for which it was created can no longer be served. When "the easement is intended to endure so long only as the purpose of its creation can be regarded as still existent, the possible duration of the easement corresponds to that of an estate in fee determinable rather than to that of an estate in fee simple." 3 H. Tiffany, The Law of Real Property § 760, at 210 (3d ed. 1939) (footnote omitted).

If courts can presume an easement appurtenant was intended to be determinable, there is no reason why a landowner cannot expressly make it so. Rejecting Corbett's argument, we adopt such a rule.

Pursuing his theory that permanency is essential, Corbett submits that an easement is not appurtenant unless the grantor specifically provides that its life extend to the grantee and his "heirs, successors and assigns". While such words are "language which strongly tends to preclude the idea of [an easement] in gross", *French* v. *Williams*, 82 Va. 462, 468, 4 S.E. 591, 594 (1886), they were not considered essential to a grant of an easement appurtenant at common law. Absent a statutory change in the common law rule, we apply it here.

Bringing to bear the principles reviewed in *Coal Corporation*, we hold that the 1964 document created an easement, that the easement is appurtenant to parcel #2, and that parcel #1 is servient thereto.

Even so, Corbett insists that neither the burden nor the benefit passed by conveyance to successors in title in this case. We disagree.

Under the explicit language of the 1964 document, the burden was affixed to parcel #1 as a "covenant running with the title". That document was signed, acknowledged, sealed, and recorded by the grantors. Thus, the title Corbett acquired was burdened by the easement, an encumbrance he accepted with constructive, if not actual, notice.

Clearly, the benefit of the easement passed with the title to parcel #2. It is wholly immaterial whether the easement was described in the deeds in Ruben's chain of title. " '[T]he easement . . . continues to adhere to the dominant estate to which it is appurtenant and passes with it to the grantee thereof, though not specifically mentioned. . . .' Minor on Real Property (2nd Ed.), page 124." *Stokes Inc.* v. *Matney,* 194 Va. at 344, 73 S.E.2d at 272. "Every deed conveying land shall ... be construed to include all . . . appurtenances of every kind . . . ." Code § 55-50.

***

Finding no error below, we will affirm the chancellor's decree.

Affirmed.

1. After our decision in Coal Corporation, the General Assembly amended Code § 55-6 (which provides what property interests may be "disposed of by deed or will") to include "easements in gross". Acts 1962, c. 169. [Editorial Note: This is footnote 2 of the opinion.]

9.1.2

Easement by Implication

Under the common law, there are two primary ways in which an easement is created by implication of law – ***strict necessity*** and ***quasi-easement***. In some situations, an easement is implied by grant or reservation even though the easement is not expressed in the instrument. Basically, when the surrounding facts are such that the parties must have intended that the easement be included in an instrument, an easement may be implied. Note, an easement may only be created by implication by strict necessity or quasi-easement if there is an instrument that satisfies the statute of frauds into which the terms of the easement can be implied. The easement created by implication would be construed as if the words creating the easement were included in the instrument.

An implied easement by strict necessity occurs where the parties must have intended to create an easement. An easement of strict necessity does not exist prior to the transfer of the land but, rather, arises because of the conveyance of the land. Three elements are necessary to create an implied easement by ***strict necessity***: (1) land in common ownership; (2) severed into two or more parcels; and (3) the severance creates the strict need for the easement.

Another easement by implication arises by quasi-easement. In these circumstances, an owner who owns two parcels of land burdens one parcel for the benefit of the other parcel. Physically, the appearance is just like an easement, except that the burdened and benefited land are owned by the same person. Thus, the law does not recognize the use as an easement. When either the burdened parcel or the benefited parcel is transferred and the other parcel is retained, the law views this as if the grantor and the grantee must have intended the apparent quasi-easement to continue despite the transfer of ownership of one parcel. If the elements for a quasi-easement are met, the quasi-easement is transformed into an actual easement. Generally, the elements for a ***quasi-easement*** to transform into an actual easement are the following: (1) a single owner burdened one parcel for the benefit of another parcel; (2) the benefit is reasonably necessary for the benefited parcel; (3) the single owner transferred one parcel and retained the other; and, (4) at the time of the severance, the burden was apparent. The term quasi-easement is sometimes referred to as an easement created by implication by prior use.

Although strict necessity and quasi-easement are the main ways that an easement can be impliedly created under the common law, in some instances, a license could be deemed to be an easement by implication by ***estoppel***. Licenses are discussed below.

9.1.2.1

Bartkowski v. Ramondo
219 A.3d 1083 (Pa. 2019)

Supreme Court of Pennsylvania

JUSTICE WECHT

We granted allowance of appeal to consider whether a landowner must prove impossibility of alternative access arising from zoning and regulatory prohibitions or conditions of the land in order to establish an easement by necessity.

The facts pertinent to this appeal are not in dispute. Kenneth Ramondo and Theresa-Cecelia Ramondo ("the Ramondos") purchased a property in Chester County (the "Ramondo property") on July 16, 1991. The Ramondo property is of a type known as a "flag lot," because it is consists of both a main portion (the "flag") and a narrow strip (the "pole") that connects the main portion to a public street. The pole portion of the Ramondo property is approximately twenty-five feet wide and opens onto Garrett Mill Road. The Ramondo pole extends six hundred feet from Garrett Mill Road to the main portion of the Ramondo property—the flag portion—which is approximately 5.62 acres. Thaddeus J. Bartkowski, III, and Crystal Anne Crawford ("the Bartkowskis") bought the neighboring property ("the Bartkowski property"), also a flag lot, on December 11, 2012. The pole of the Bartkowski property, also measuring twenty-five feet wide, abuts and runs parallel with the Ramondos' pole. The flag portion of the Bartkowski property is approximately 5.25 acres.

The portion of land at issue in this appeal involves the adjoining Ramondo and Bartkowski poles, upon which the Ramondos constructed a driveway (the "Ramondo driveway") that provides them access to Garrett Mill Road. The Ramondo driveway begins on the Bartkowski pole, and extends up that pole for approximately three hundred feet. At that point, the Ramondo driveway crosses onto the Ramondo pole and continues on that pole to the main portion of the Ramondo property. The Bartkowskis use neither their pole nor the Ramondo pole to access their own flag portion, as they instead make use of an earlier-granted easement which passes over an adjacent property.

At one time, the Ramondo property and the Bartkowski property were both owned by a common grantor, Adrian and Margaret Teaf ("the Teafs"). In 1967, the Teafs recorded a subdivision map which laid out, among other properties, the Ramondo and Bartkowski parcels. Both parcels were vacant, wooded lots, and neither pole contained a driveway providing access to the flag portions of these parcels. On April 19, 1968, the Teafs conveyed the Bartkowski property to Herbert and Margaret

Mansmann ("the Mansmanns"). The Mansmanns did not construct a driveway on their pole. Rather, the Mansmanns, and all subsequent owners of the Bartkowski property, shared a driveway with the owners of the parcel south of the flag portion of the Bartkowski property, the Coulstons. The Coulston driveway is located on the side of the Coulston property farthest from the Bartkowski pole. As noted, an easement for this driveway use was recorded prior to the Bartkowskis' arrival.

The Mansmanns built a single-family home on the Bartkowski property in 1969 and still lived there when the Ramondos purchased the neighboring Ramondo property in 1991. In order to build a home on the vacant property, the Ramondos first needed to construct a driveway. Before doing so, Kenneth Ramondo invited his neighbors, including the Coulstons and the Mansmanns, to "walk the property line to see if anybody had a problem with where the driveway was going." . . . None of the neighbors objected to the Ramondos' proposed placement of the driveway. Nonetheless, although the lower portion of the Ramondo driveway would traverse the Mansmanns' property, no easement securing such access was executed or recorded.

The Ramondos completed construction of their driveway in 1992 and their home in 1993. The Ramondos placed the driveway in its current location due to numerous legal and physical impediments that precluded the placement of the driveway entirely on their pole. First, a stream runs through the lower portion of the Ramondo pole and into Ridley Creek, which flows across from and parallel to Garrett Mill Road. Second, the area in which the stream crosses the Ramondo pole is a flood plain. Third, a utility pole sits just off Garrett Mill Road in the middle of the Ramondo pole and services a utility line that runs under the Ramondo driveway. Fourth, portions of the Ramondo pole are very steeply sloped.

In 1995, the Ramondos paved the driveway, which had previously been gravel-surfaced. The Ramondos resurfaced the driveway in 2000 and installed a guardrail along the edge of the steep slope. In 1993, and again in 2004, the Ramondos executed mortgages on their property in favor of Barclays and USAA, respectively. Neither of the legal descriptions of the Ramondo property attached to the mortgage documents included the portion of the Ramondo driveway that is situated on the Bartkowski pole.

In 2003, the Mansmanns conveyed the Bartkowski property to F. Ramondo, Inc., the Ramondo family's business. During the years that F. Ramondo, Inc. owned the property, Kenneth Ramondo was an officer of the company. On May 2, 2007, F. Ramondo, Inc. conveyed the property to James and Marianne Bianco ("the Biancos"). The Biancos conveyed the property to the Bartkowskis on December 11, 2012. When the Bartkowskis purchased their property, they were aware that the Ramondos used the Ramondo driveway to access their home. The Bartkowskis also knew that the Biancos had used the shared Coulston driveway to access the home on the Bartkowski property.

In 2013, the Bartkowskis approached the Ramondos about the Ramondo driveway's encroachment upon the Bartkowskis' pole. On June 30, 2015, the Bartkowskis, through their attorney, sent the Ramondos a cease and desist letter demanding that the Ramondos stop using the portion of the Ramondo driveway that is on the Bartkowskis' pole.

On July 16, 2015, the Bartkowskis filed an action in ejectment and trespass, alleging that the Ramondos improperly constructed their driveway on the Bartkowski property. On July 31, 2015, the Ramondos filed a counterclaim alleging that they acquired title to the disputed area by adverse possession or through the doctrine of consentable lines. Alternatively, the Ramondos claimed a property interest in the driveway by way of an easement by prescription, necessity, or implication.

The Bartkowskis and Ramondos decided to forego a trial, agreeing instead to submit a stipulated fact record and joint exhibits, as well as memoranda of law, to the court. The Bartkowskis submitted a site survey which identified in detail the Bartkowski and Ramondo properties and their respective poles, as well as the location of the Ramondo driveway. Both parties submitted expert reports.

The Ramondos' expert, Daniel Malloy, P.E., a civil engineer, concluded that the current location of the Ramondo driveway is the "only method to reach their home." . . . Malloy noted that, in some places along the Ramondo pole, the slope is a 50% grade, which leaves "a portion of the Ramondo's [pole] sit[ting] more than ten feet

345

below the elevation of the existing driveway." In order to install a driveway on the Ramondos' pole, Malloy opined, it would be necessary to either "construct the driveway at the lower grade of their property or elevate their driveway to remain close to the elevation of the driveway they currently use." Neither of these options are viable solutions, Malloy explained, because of environmental and zoning regulations.

A thirty-foot wide stream runs through the lower portion of the Ramondos' pole before flowing under Garrett Mill Road, creating a flood plain in the entire area. Malloy opined that constructing the driveway at the lower grade would require installation of a retaining wall on the Ramondo pole in order to comply with Willistown Township zoning ordinances regarding wetlands and prohibitive slopes. Construction of a retaining wall would in turn require the placement of fill into the floodplain, which is prohibited both by township ordinances and by the Federal Emergency Management Agency (FEMA). These same ordinances and regulations, Malloy opined, would likewise prohibit the Ramondos from elevating their pole to the elevation of the Bartkowski pole. The only option, therefore, would be to relocate the stream.

Malloy posited that, in order to relocate the stream onto the neighboring property, the Ramondos would need the approval not only of their neighbor, but also of the township and the Pennsylvania Department of Environmental Protection ("DEP"). This approval would be difficult to obtain, Malloy explained, because neither the township nor the state allows streams to be relocated unless a "significant reason" exists to do so. Malloy posited that the construction of a driveway, especially where one exists in close proximity, "does not fall into a category the State or Township would consider a significant reason" to relocate a waterway. Building a bridge over the stream, Malloy contended, would implicate many of the same ordinances and environmental concerns. In total, Malloy summarized the extensive number of permits that the Ramondos would be required to obtain from both the township and the DEP:

> They include an Erosion and Sedimentation permit, Highway Occupancy
> Permit to connect to Garrett Mill [Road], a PADEP permit GP7 (minor

road crossing) and possibly a GP 15 (residential construction in wetlands). The Township will require zoning relief since the construction of a driveway in steep slopes, flood plains, and/or riparian buffer is prohibited by Willistown Township's Environmental Ordinance (Section 73) and by the Zoning Code (Section 119).

Finally, even assuming that all the environmental and zoning issues could be overcome, which Malloy characterized as "highly unlikely," constructing a driveway within the Ramondo pole also would require the relocation of the utility pole. Malloy estimated this cost alone at approximately $10,000. For all of these reasons, Malloy concluded that "the amount of regulatory relief and permitting needed to install a new driveway on the Ramondos' property from the State and the Township will be extremely extensive making the construction of a parallel driveway all but impossible.". Additionally, Malloy posited that "[t]he amount of engineering required to satisfy the permitting agencies will be a significant percentage of the cost to construct the new driveway (which in itself will be prohibitive)." Malloy further advised that "it will be many, many months, if not years before the approvals may be obtain[ed], if at all," and opined that "[i]t is very likely that all the required permits would never be approved."

The Bartkowskis' expert, Denny L. Howell, P.E., a civil engineer, issued a rebuttal report challenging Malloy's conclusions. Howell acknowledged that the terrain of the Ramondos' pole is "steep," and agreed with Malloy that construction thereon "would require relief from Willistown [o]rdinances as it pertains to steep slope disturbance, riparian buffer disturbance as well as flood plain disturbance." . . . Despite these obstacles, Howell concluded that "this relief is not unreasonable." Howell posited that, "[s]etting aside the necessary [o]rdinance relief ... construction of the driveway is feasible," and estimated that the construction cost would be approximately $75,000. On the likelihood that the Ramondos could obtain the necessary environmental and zoning relief, Howell concluded that "it is well within reason to expect that these variances could be obtained."

. . .The trial court concluded that the Ramondo property was "not landlocked," and that, although the Ramondos presented evidence that gaining approval from the

Township to relocate the driveway "may be difficult," the Ramondos did not "demonstrate impossibility and thus necessity."

***

In an unpublished memorandum, a divided panel of the Superior Court affirmed in part and vacated in part. On the Ramondos' easement by necessity claim, the Superior Court agreed with the trial court's reasoning to the effect that the Ramondos failed to establish necessity. . . .

***

We granted allowance of appeal in order to consider whether, when seeking to establish an easement by necessity, a landowner must prove impossibility of alternative access arising from zoning and regulatory prohibitions or other conditions.

The Ramondos argue that the only element at issue in this appeal is whether access upon the Ramondo driveway is necessary. The Ramondos characterize their need for access as one of strict necessity, distinguishing their circumstances from those cases in which this Court or the Superior Court have concluded that a landowner's claim for a particular desired access is one of mere convenience. The Ramondos maintain that the "regulatory prohibitions" and the "practical and financial impossibility of relocating the stream and driveway," result in their property being landlocked.

***

. . . Accordingly, the Ramondos ask that we reverse the order of the Superior Court and hold that they have established grounds for an easement by necessity over the Bartkowski property.

***

This appeal calls upon us to clarify the requirement of "strict necessity" as it relates to the establishment of an easement by necessity. This is a question of law over which our standard of review is *de novo* and our scope of review is plenary.

As noted above, the three fundamental requirements for an easement by necessity are:

> 1) the titles to the alleged dominant and servient properties must have been held by one person; 2) this unity of title must have been severed by a conveyance of one of the tracts; and 3) the easement must be necessary in order for the owner of the dominant tenement to use his land, with the necessity existing both at the time of the severance of title and at the time of the exercise of the easement.

Youst, 94 A.3d at 1075. We have long recognized that a "right of way from necessity over the land of another ... is always of strict necessity." *Ogden v. Grove*, 38 Pa. 487, 491 (1861) (internal citations and quotation marks omitted). Thus, a right of way never exists "when a man can get to his own property through his own land," and "[c]onvenience is no foundation for the claim." *Id.*

Here, the first two elements have been met. The titles to the Ramondo and Bartkowski properties were once held by a common grantor (the Teafs), and unity of title was severed in 1967 when the Teafs subdivided the land. Thus, the only factual dispute before the trial court concerned whether the Ramondo driveway's encroachment upon the Bartkowski pole was "necessary in order for the [Ramondos] to use [their] land, with the necessity existing both at the time of the severance of title and at the time of the exercise of the easement." *Youst*, 94 A.3d at 1075.

The question presented hinges not upon whether the Ramondos in fact satisfied this element but, rather, upon the validity of the lower courts' conclusions that the Ramondos did not establish necessity because they failed to prove that constructing a new driveway on their pole "could not be done." By equating strict necessity with impossibility, the lower courts increased the Ramondos' burden beyond what this Court previously has required. Our research has not uncovered, nor did either party present, any case from this Court or our intermediate appellate courts holding that a party seeking access across a neighboring property must prove absolute impossibility of alternative access in order to establish strict necessity.

As is evident from our easement by necessity jurisprudence, the concept of strict necessity always is contrasted with the notion of convenience. *See Ogden*, 38 Pa. at 491; *Graff*, 673 A.2d at 1032 ("An easement implied on the grounds of necessity is always of *strict necessity*; it never exists as a mere matter of convenience."). Our precedents provide little insight on the meaning of "necessity" beyond these opposing principles. Without question, these two concepts—strict necessity and mere convenience—sit at opposite ends of a continuum that encompasses a significant amount of gray area. One scholar has opined that, although the necessity element is the "fulcrum on which way of necessity cases balance," this "seemingly black-and-white concept ... is really gray." 11 JEFFREY R. SANG, AM. JUR. PROOF OF FACTS 3D 601, § 6 (2019). There is no formulaic or canonical standard that constitutes "strict necessity," leaving each case to turn on its facts.

To require a party to prove utter impossibility of alternative access is to stretch "strict necessity" beyond its intended meaning. This effectively would limit a landowner's entitlement to an easement by necessity to circumstances in which the property is completely surrounded and landlocked by other properties, such that there is literally no means of ingress and egress. This Court has never so held. On this subject, a decision of the Idaho Court of Appeals is particularly instructive. In *MacCaskill v. Ebbert*, 112 Idaho 1115, 739 P.2d 414 (Idaho Ct. App. 1987), the court was asked to determine whether an easement by necessity may arise where the property is landlocked, not for want of legal access, but because the topographical characteristics of the land make legal access impassable. The court refused to limit the circumstances under which an easement by necessity may arise to landlocked properties, reasoning that, "there are cases where a tract of land, though not totally landlocked in a legal sense, cannot yield a beneficial use because the sole legal access is inadequate for the purposes to which the property naturally might be put." *Id.* at 418. The court continued:

> Obviously, one seeking an easement need not show that a legally available route is absolutely impossible to use. There are few natural obstacles that could not be surmounted by modern engineering if unlimited resources were committed to the task. On the other hand, neither is it sufficient merely to show that the legally available route would be inconvenient or expensive. Rather, an easement by necessity should be granted only if the difficulty or expense of using the legally available route is so great that it renders the parcel unfit for its reasonably anticipated use.

Id. at 419 (citation and emphasis omitted). We agree with the *MacCaskill* court that literal impossibility of alternative access is an unworkable standard. As the Idaho court acknowledged, with enough money and modern resources, creation of an alternative means of access can never be considered truly and utterly impossible.

This analysis also comports with other jurisdictions' formulations of "strict necessity." *See, e.g., Ashby v. Maechling,* 356 Mont. 68, 229 P.3d 1210, 1215 (2010) ("The element of strict necessity requires that there is no practical access to a public road from the landlocked parcel."); *Beery v. Shinkle,* 193 S.W.3d 435, 441 (Mo. Ct. App. 2006) ("Strict necessity has been interpreted to mean the absence of a reasonably practical way to and from plaintiff's land that the plaintiff has a legally enforceable right to use."); *Thompson v. Whinnery,* 895 P.2d 537, 541 (Colo. 1995) (*en banc*) (internal quotation marks omitted) ("[I]n evaluating whether an easement is necessary for access over difficult terrain[,] we must determine whether there is a practical inability to have access any other way than by a way of necessity."); *Hitchman v. Hudson,* 40 Or.App. 59, 594 P.2d 851, 858 (1979) ("An easement of necessity will not be implied where the claimant has other practicable ways of ingress or egress or could obtain the necessary way by a reasonable expenditure"). These descriptions of "strict necessity" demonstrate that the standard is not "hopelessly inelastic for sensible application to varying sets of facts." *Mitchell v. Castellaw,* 151 Tex. 56, 246 S.W.2d 163, 168 (1952). Common to these descriptions, and absent from the reasoning of the courts below in the instant case, is a focus upon the practicability of constructing alternative access. Where it is manifestly impracticable, even though theoretically possible, to create ingress and egress across one's own property, the landowner may establish that a right of way over a neighboring property is "strictly necessary" in the legal sense.

The expense of constructing alternative access may be one of many relevant factors in determining whether access across a neighboring property is "strictly necessary." The Maryland Court of Appeals considered as much, while maintaining a "strict necessity" standard:

> If the cost of constructing a road over one's land as a means of access to the
> public highway would require unreasonable expense out of proportion to

the value of the land, then there exists such necessity for a way over the grantor's land as to justify recognition of a way by implication. But the court will not recognize a way of necessity if another road to the public highway can be made without unreasonable expense, even though the other road may be much less convenient. Mere inconvenience will not be sufficient to justify the finding of a way of necessity.

Condry v. Laurie, 184 Md. 317, 41 A.2d 66, 68 (1945); *see also Bluffs Owners Ass'n, Inc. v. Adams*, 897 So.2d 375, 378 (Ala. Civ. App. 2004) ("[T]he issue is not whether the right-of-way sought is, of all possible routes, the nearest and most convenient means to access ... the property; instead, the landowner seeking the easement must show that any other alternate-access route would require unreasonable expense disproportionate to the value of the property."); 3 TIFFANY REAL PROPERTY § 794 (3d ed. 2018) ("[I]f the cost of the construction of a road over one's own land, as a means of access to any particular portion thereof, would involve very great expense, out of proportion to the value of the land itself, there is such a necessity for a way over another's land as to justify the recognition of a way of necessity."). These cases demonstrate that, although the cost or difficulty of constructing alternative access may not always, or even often, be sufficient by itself to warrant burdening another's property, there may be a tipping point at which it becomes manifestly unreasonable to require a party to expend a disproportionate amount of money in order to access a parcel.

***

Based on the foregoing analysis, we hold that the courts below erred in holding that a landowner must establish impossibility of alternative access before a court will grant an easement by necessity. To be sure, the strict necessity standard remains a daunting hurdle to overcome for a landowner seeking an easement by necessity. Given the sanctity of property rights, this is as it should be. Nevertheless, neither our case law, nor the persuasive reasoning from other states imposing a "strict necessity" standard, supports a requirement that a landowner prove utter impossibility of alternative access. Such a burden risks becoming insurmountable, and, as such, as unworkable as it is unjust.

Determining whether a landowner has established necessity is a fact-intensive question, which defies a one-size-fits-all, bright-line standard. The central inquiry is whether, absent the recognition of an easement, the proposed dominant estate will be left without a means of ingress and egress, rendering the property inaccessible and, thus, unusable. *See, e.g., Bodman v. Bodman*, 456 Pa. 412, 321 A.2d 910, 912 (1974) ("An easement by necessity may be created when after severance from adjoining property, a piece of land is without access to a public highway."). A court must evaluate the asserted necessity by assessing whether this untenable outcome will result in practice, not merely by asking whether some remote alternative is hypothetically possible in the abstract. Each case will require individualized consideration of multiple factors, including, but not limited to: the existence of zoning restrictions and the likelihood that the party can obtain the necessary variances or exceptions; the existence of state or federal regulations that prohibit certain uses of the land in question; the topography of the land and the practicability of constructing alternative access; the environmental consequences of construction; the costs involved; and, of course, whether and to what extent these impediments existed at the time of severance. This list of factors is non-exclusive, as future cases may well present additional circumstances relevant to the establishment of necessity. As in this case, expert opinions often will be necessary in order to establish that any legal or physical barriers cannot or are exceedingly unlikely to be overcome. Although some degree of speculation is inherent in the assessment of such future outcomes, this is a question of the credibility of the evidence and the weight to be afforded thereto, which are matters that we entrust to the discretion of the fact-finder.

We do not intend to dilute or diminish the rigors of the "strict necessity" standard. Nor do we intend to imply that the presence of one or more, or even all, of the above-listed circumstances automatically establishes strict necessity. These considerations are intended only to guide courts in navigating the "gray area" between sheer impossibility and mere convenience. As the quantity and quality of hurdles obstructing a party's ability to create an alternative means of access mount, so too does a court's prerogative to find that strict necessity has been established.

The Superior Court affirmed the trial court's order denying the Ramondos an easement by necessity based upon the theory that establishing necessity requires proving impossibility of alternative access. This was error. Accordingly, we reverse the order of the Superior Court, and we remand the matter for further proceedings consistent with this Opinion.

***

9.1.2.2

Schmidt v. Eger
289 N.W.2d 851 (Mich. Ct. App. 1980)

Michigan Court of Appeals

Per Curiam.

Plaintiff appeals as of right the judgment of the trial court in favor of defendants denying the relief requested in plaintiffs complaint.

Plaintiff leased two lots of an industrial complex to a corporation controlled by the defendants on November 12, 1968. Plaintiff subsequently became the owner of a small area of property at the southern end of the two lots, and this property also became a part of the defendants' leasehold. In 1969, this new area was developed, a lawn established, and a ditch put in. This ditch carries water off other land owned by plaintiff and is the subject of the instant case. Testimony differed as to when it was first developed; plaintiff testified that the work done in 1969 was a modification of a ditch that had existed prior to the acquisition of the property to the south of the original two lots, although he had previously given answers to written interrogatories stating that the ditch was first put in simultaneously with the other improvements. Defendant Frank Eger testified that the ditch did not exist prior to the establishment of the leasehold, but that it was constructed after he commenced occupation.

A history of litigation between the parties commenced in 1972 when defendants' corporation brought suit seeking specific performance of an option to purchase the property that was contained in the lease. A consent judgment was entered and defendants took title to the property. On October 9, 1973, defendants announced to plaintiff their intention to grade and level that portion of the property that contained the ditch, a manhole, access structures, and buried drain tile. Plaintiff filed suit seeking an injunction against the defendants prohibiting them from interfering with the drainage ditch. Accelerated judgment was granted to defendants, but this Court reversed and remanded for trial. . . . Judgment was for defendants and plaintiff has appealed as of right. . . .

I.

Plaintiff claims the drainage ditch represents an easement by implied reservation. To establish an implied easement, three things must be shown: (1) that during the unity of title an apparently permanent and obvious servitude was imposed on one part of an estate in favor of another, (2) continuity, and (3) that the easement is reasonably necessary for the fair enjoyment of the property it benefits. *Harrison v Heald*, 360 Mich 203; 103 NW2d 348 (1960), *Rannels v Marx*, 357 Mich 453; 98 NW2d 583 (1959). The party asserting the easement has the burden of proving the claim by a preponderance of the evidence. The trial court found that the continuity element was established, given the nature of drains, and we agree. Our discussion is limited to the remaining two elements.

A. Necessity

On the necessity element, the trial court held that plaintiff needed to establish that the easement was *strictly* necessary before it would be implied. We hold that this was error, and that plaintiff needed only to establish that the easement was *reasonably* necessary. We do note, however, that some confusion in this regard is justified, as Michigan law has been less than clear on the point and as easements by implication may arise under different circumstances.

An implied easement may arise in essentially two ways. First, it can be implied from necessity. In this situation, an estate has been severed, leaving the dominant estate without a means of access. Before an easement will be implied in this situation, the party who would assert the easement must establish that it is strictly necessary for the enjoyment of the property. Mere convenience, or even reasonable necessity, will not be sufficient if there are alternative routes, even if these alternatives prove more difficult or more expensive. All implied easements are based on the presumed intent of the parties, but this sort is additionally supported by the public policy favoring the productive and beneficial enjoyment of property. Easements implied from necessity have been recognized in Michigan as requiring a showing of strict necessity. This sort of implied easement is not dependent on the existence of any established route or quasi-easement prior to the severance of the estate by the common grantor; it is first established after the severance.

The easement with which we are involved in the instant case is of a different type, what Dean Cribbet refers to as easements implied from quasi-easements. It requires that at the severance of an estate an obvious and apparently permanent servitude already exists over one part of the estate and in favor of the other. It also requires a showing of necessity, but whether that necessity needs to be "strict", or only "reasonable", traditionally has depended on whether the easement claimed was an implied *grant,* or an implied *reservation.*

It appears to be the position of a majority of jurisdictions that an implied grant of an easement requires only a showing of reasonable necessity, while an implied reservation of an easement in the grantor requires a showing of strict necessity. The difference seems based on the idea that a grantor will not be allowed to derogate from the grant by alleging to retain interests which the deed purports to convey. . . .

Several Michigan cases have adopted this position, and held that when an implied reservation is involved, as in the instant case, a showing of strict necessity is required. *Brown v Fuller,* 165 Mich 162; 130 NW 621 (1911), *von Meding v Strahl,* 319 Mich 598, 605-606; 30 NW2d 363 (1948), *Wilson v Anglin,* 72 Mich App 212; 249 NW2d 360 (1976). An apparent minority of jurisdictions hold that there is no difference between a grant and a reservation for the purposes of implying an easement from an existing servitude or quasi-easement, and that only reasonable necessity is required for both. Despite the holdings in the cases cited above, this seems to be the most recent position adopted by our Supreme Court. In *Harrison v Heald, supra,* the Supreme Court was faced with the question whether the rules governing easements by implied grant also controlled implied reservation of easements. The Court quoted language from *Rannels v Marx, supra,* which *Rannels* had in turn quoted from *Rischall v Bauchmann,* 132 Conn 637; 46 A2d 898; 165 ALR 559 (1946), and noted that the language used, including that referring to an element of reasonable necessity, applied equally to grants and reservations. The *Harrison* Court was criticized for relying on dicta rather than its own prior holdings in reaching this result, and alternatively for failing to adopt the new course after squarely addressing the issue. While it is true that the Supreme Court in *Harrison* did not specifically direct itself to the precise issue of what quantum of necessity was to be required in cases of implied reservations, as opposed to implied grants, it is clear that it intended the same rules to apply to each. We thus view *Harrison* as controlling, and as requiring only a showing of reasonable necessity, regardless of whether a grant or reservation is sought to be implied. To the extent that post-*Harrison* decisions of this Court may be read to require a showing of strict necessity when an implied reservation is involved, it is our opinion that they were wrongly decided.

Applying a test of reasonable necessity to the facts of the instant case, we hold plaintiff sufficiently established this element. The trial court found that the several alternative drainage plans open to the plaintiff would require considerable work. One of the expert witnesses who testified placed the cost of a new drainage system at between $30,000 and $35,000. Under the facts and circumstances of this case, the effort and expense were great enough for implication of the easement to be reasonably necessary.

B. *Apparentness*

In order to establish his easement, plaintiff also needs to show that it was apparent at the date of severance. The testimony conflicted as to whether the drain existed prior to November 12, 1968, the date of the lease, but the trial court found that it did not, that it instead came into existence in 1969. The lease contained an option to purchase the property, and on June 22, 1973, the defendants purchased the property they had been leasing. Since the trial court held that the necessity element had not been established, it felt that it was unnecessary to decide the question of when severance took place, but remarked that if called upon to do so, the appropriate date of severance would have been the date of the lease. Since we reach a different result on the necessity element, we must decide the date of severance. If, as the trial court suggested, that date is the date of the lease, then plaintiff has failed to establish the element of apparentness since the drain was found to have first come into existence after the date of the lease. If, on the other hand, the plaintiff is right in asserting that severance did not take place until 1973 when defendants took title to the land, then the easement was apparent and plaintiff will have shown all the elements necessary to the establishment of an implied easement.

We have found no Michigan cases directly on point, but our analysis of the purpose of the severance requirement leads us to conclude that the appropriate date of severance is the date of the lease.

Simply put, a severance is required because it is legally impossible to have an "easement" in your own land. If a person owns two adjacent tracts of land and imposes a servitude on one tract for the benefit of the other, there exists only a quasi-easement that may ripen into a full easement when one of the tracts is conveyed. A lease is a conveyance of property for a term, and while the grantor retains a reversionary interest in the land, the right to use and possess the land has passed to the lessee. It is for this reason that while an easement cannot exist over one part of a person's land in favor of another part when both parts remain in that person's possession, an easement may exist when one part is conveyed to a lessee. See *Powers v Harlow*, 53 Mich 507; 19 NW 257 (1884), 5 Restatement Property, § 475, p 2976 (Illustration 1). The Restatement's drafters, when addressing the issue of severance, wisely chose to speak in terms of the severance of a single *possessory interest*. 5 Restatement Property, § 474, pp 2972-2975. The lessor, having conveyed his possessory interest in a tract of land for a period of time, must establish his right to use an easement in the land conveyed in the manner generally provided for establishing easements. In the instant case the defendants took a possessory interest in the land in 1968. In 1973 they joined with this possessory interest all the other property interests in the land that the deed conveyed. Given the nature and purpose of the severance requirement, we hold that the date of severance cannot be placed in the middle of a continuous possessory interest, but must instead be placed at the point where the possessory interest first arose, which in this case is November 12, 1968, the date of the lease. Because the trial court found that the drain did not come into existence until 1969, we hold that it was not "apparent" as of the date of severance. Plaintiff thus failed to satisfy one of the necessary elements, and the trial court did not err in holding that he failed to establish an implied easement.

***

III.

Plaintiff's final argument that he has an easement because the lease and deed each contained general language conveying the property subject to easements reserved to the grantor is without merit. The deed listed several specifically defined easements that were reserved to the plaintiff, but made no mention of the drain which is the subject of this appeal. There was no express easement in the drain as such, and, as noted above, plaintiff has failed to establish an implied easement.

Affirmed.

9.1.2.3

Safran Family Trust v. Hughes Prop. Mgmt.
105 N.E.3d 652 (Ohio Ct. App. 2018)

Court of Appeals of Ohio, Sixth District, Ottawa County

JENSEN, J.

Appellant, Hughes Property Management, appeals the judgment of the Ottawa County Court of Common Pleas, following a bench trial, which granted easements over appellant's land in favor of appellee, Safran Family Trust. For the reasons that follow, we affirm.

I. Facts and Procedural Background

For ease of discussion, we note at the outset that Ken Hughes owns Hughes Property Management, and we will refer to them individually or in the collective as appellant. Likewise, we note that John and Janet Safran are the trustees and beneficiaries of the Safran Family Trust, and we will refer to them as appellees.

On September 28, 2015, appellees initiated the present matter by filing a seven-count complaint in which they sought implied easements by necessity, estoppel, and implication for both ingress and egress and for access to water and sewer.

The matter proceeded to a bench trial at which the following facts were adduced. The property in question was part of the Avalon on the Bay Subdivision, and was initially owned by the Gough Trust. Appellees have maintained a trailer on Lot 1 on the southeastern corner of the Gough Trust property since 1986. Lot 1 is landlocked, with Lot 2 bordering it on the west, and Lot 3 bordering both Lots 1 and 2 on the north. To the east is additional property not owned by the Gough Trust, and not relevant to this appeal. To the south is the Sandusky Bay.

In 2006, appellees purchased Lot 1 from the Gough Trust. After purchasing the land from the Goughs, and in reliance on promises made regarding the conveyance of easements, appellees purchased and constructed a new double-wide mobile home on the lot, costing over $140,000. In particular, the Goughs agreed to convey an easement across Lot 2 for ingress and egress. The recorded easement, however, designated a 15-foot strip of land along the southern border of Lot 2, which is submerged in the Sandusky Bay. Nevertheless, appellees continued to use a gravel U-shaped drive across Lot 2 from Bayview Drive as they had always done. In addition, appellees and the Goughs agreed that appellees would arrange for separate billing for water and sewer with the Ottawa County Sanitary Engineer's office. At the time, appellees received water from a community pump station through a pipe that was partially below ground and partially above ground. Later, that source was shut off, and appellees received water from another neighbor. When the county demanded that appellees discontinue receiving water from a neighbor, appellees installed a water tank. As for sewer service, the sewer line for appellees' mobile home runs east to west, and is partially on the southern portion of Lot 3 and the northern portion of Lot 2.

Towards the end of 2012, the Gough Trust sought to sell the rest of its property in Avalon on the Bay, including Lots 2 and 3. On October 19, 2012, the Gough Trust entered into an agreement with Howard Hanna Real Estate Services to be its agent for the sale. On the "Exclusive Right to Sell Agreement," the Goughs disclosed that the property was encumbered by an easement for the owner of Lot 1 to get to his property, and by an easement for the owner of Lot 1 to tie into the county's water lines. Notably, a written easement for water and sewer lines was executed on October 24, 2012, granting appellees access across Lot 2. However, that easement was never recorded.

In January 2013, appellant entered into negotiations with the Gough Trust to purchase the property. On January 3, 2013, appellant received and initialed the "Vacant Land Seller's Description of the Property," which indicated that there were "encroachments, easements, shared driveways, party walls, or similar conditions that may affect title to the property," and which referred appellant to the "Disclosures on Seller's Agreement." Tomi Johnson, the Gough Trust's real estate agent, testified that she believes the seller's disclosures regarding the easements were transmitted to appellant, and the purchase agreement offered by appellant also indicated that appellant had received the "Residential Property Disclosure Form." Furthermore, the purchase agreement signed by appellant on January 3, 2013, included an Addendum A, stating that appellant's offer was contingent upon "Accepted written agreement with Mr. and Mrs. John Safran regarding the easements for water and sewer lines and driveway location." Appellant's real estate agent, Mary Kay Michel, who is also appellant's sister, testified that the contingency written in Addendum A was in her handwriting. Subsequently, the contingency was crossed out, and appellant initialed the crossed-out contingency on January 15, 2013. The parties dispute who crossed out the contingencies and when he or she did it.

Appellant testified that a title search was conducted before closing, and revealed only that the property was encumbered by the easement for ingress and egress, which appellant determined was located underwater. Appellant further testified that he had no knowledge of the easement regarding sewer and water access, and that he did not receive the seller's disclosure of that easement. In addition, he testified that when he received the draft of the purchase agreement to sign on January 3, 2013, the contingencies in Addendum A were already crossed off. Ultimately, the sale was completed.

Following the sale, appellant and appellees had at least one conversation about where appellees could locate their water line. John Safran testified that appellant told him they would figure it out when appellant began constructing his home. Appellant testified that he was unsure what to do because he did not think that an easement existed. Relevant to the location of the water and sewer lines, Steve Lange of the Ottawa County Sanitary Engineer's Office testified that the county's sewer lines terminate near Bayview Drive at a manhole approximately on the boundary between Lots 2 and 3, and the county's water line terminates at a fire hydrant approximately 20 feet to the north of the manhole, located on Lot 3. He testified that the county could not extend the sewer lines to the south because of the potential for infiltration from Lake Erie. However, he stated that a 15-foot easement running east to west across the northern boundary of Lot 3 would be adequate for providing water and sewer access to appellee's mobile home on Lot 1.

trial court

After the trial, the court entered its judgment granting the easements. The court found that appellant had knowledge of the easement issues at the time of the purchase. Thus, the trial court granted appellees an easement by necessity and/or estoppel for access at the present location of the graveled U-shaped drive. In addition, the trial court granted appellees a sewer easement by implication and estoppel where the sewer line is currently located. Finally, the trial court granted an easement by implication and estoppel for a water line.

II. Assignments of Error

Appellant has timely appealed the trial court's judgment. . . .

III. Analysis

. . . Appellant contends that the trial court abused its discretion when it granted easements for access and for water and sewer. . . .

"[A]n easement may be created by specific grant, prescription, or implication which may arise from the particular set of facts and circumstances." *Campbell v. Great Miami Aerie No. 2309, Fraternal Order of Eagles*, 15 Ohio St.3d 79, 80, 472 N.E.2d 711 (1984). Here, the trial court granted an access easement by necessity and/or estoppel, and granted an easement for water and sewer by implication and/or estoppel.

"An implied easement is based upon the theory that whenever one conveys property, he or she includes in the conveyance whatever is necessary for its beneficial use and enjoyment and retains whatever is necessary for the use and enjoyment of the land retained." *Arkes v. Gregg* , 10th Dist. Franklin No. 05AP-202, 2005-Ohio-6369, 2005 WL 3220209, ¶ 11. Implied easements are not favored in the law, "being in derogation of the rule that written instruments shall speak for themselves." *Ciski v. Wentworth* , 122 Ohio St. 487, 172 N.E. 276 (1930), paragraph one of the syllabus. Nonetheless, an easement by implication may arise where the following elements appear:

> (1) A severance of the unity of ownership in an estate; (2) that before the separation takes place, the use which gives rise to the easement shall have been so long continued and obvious or manifest as to show that it was meant to be permanent; (3) that the easement shall be reasonably necessary to the beneficial enjoyment of the land granted or retained; (4) that the servitude shall be continuous as distinguished from a temporary or occasional use only. *Id.*

"An implied easement may be implied either by prior use or by necessity." *Yowonske v. MDB Constr. Co.*, 7th Dist. Belmont No. 09 BE 10, 2010-Ohio-4185, 2010 WL 3482692, ¶ 20 (12th Dist.). However, if the plaintiff is attempting to establish an implied easement by necessity, the plaintiff must show that the easement is strictly necessary under the third prong, rather than reasonably necessary.

In contrast to implied easements, an easement by estoppel arises when "an owner of property misleads or causes another in any way to change the other's position to his or her prejudice." *Kienzle v. Myers* , 167 Ohio App.3d 78, 2006-Ohio-2765, 853 N.E.2d 1203, ¶ 20 (6th Dist.). "Where an owner of land, without objection, permits another to expend money in reliance upon a supposed easement, when in justice and equity the former ought to have disclaimed his conflicting rights, he is estopped to deny the easement." *Id.*

In its first assignment of error, appellant challenges several findings of the trial court. First appellant contests the trial court's finding that neither party knew that the recorded access easement designated land that was submerged. Appellant contends that appellees were aware of the recorded easement's deficiency, yet took no action to correct the issue. However, appellant does not argue how appellees' knowledge of the submerged easement undermines the conclusion that access across the graveled U-turn on Lot 2 is necessary to enter Lot 1. Thus, we find that this argument is not meritorious in demonstrating that the trial court's grant of an implied easement by necessity for ingress and egress is against the manifest weight of the evidence.

Next, appellant argues that the trial court found that appellees had expended $250,000 in reliance on the Goughs' promises regarding the easements, when the testimony indicated that appellees spent only $140,000. We find this discrepancy to be meaningless, because even an expenditure of $140,000 would be sufficient to demonstrate that appellees acted in reliance on the promises from the Goughs. Thus, this argument is meritless.

Finally, appellant challenges the trial court's finding that it had prior knowledge of the easements when it purchased Lots 2 through 9 in 2013. This argument relates to appellant's position, taken throughout its first and second assignments of error, that to the extent appellees have a claim for implied easements or easements by estoppel, those easements have arisen based on the actions of the Gough Trust, not appellant. On this reasoning, appellant concludes that because appellees failed to protect their interest by acquiring and recording the easements, it is appellees who should suffer the consequences from their lack of diligence, not appellant. Indeed, the Ohio Supreme Court has recognized that the equitable right of an implied easement "is not enforceable against a bona fide purchaser for value who has no actual or constructive notice of such easement." *Renner v. Johnson* , 2 Ohio St.2d 195, 207 N.E.2d 751 (1965), paragraph three of the syllabus; *see also* R.C. 5301.25(A) ("Until so recorded or filed for record, [written easements] are fraudulent insofar as they relate to a subsequent bona fide purchaser having, at the time of purchase, no knowledge of the existence of that former deed, land contract, or instrument.").

Here, however, the evidence demonstrates that appellant had prior knowledge of the easements. The "Vacant Land Seller's Description of the Property" disclosed that there were easements or other encumbrances on the property that appellant was buying, and referred appellant to the Seller's Disclosures, which referenced the access and water easements. The seller's real estate agent testified that she believes the disclosures were transmitted, and the purchase agreement offer signed by appellant indicated that it had received the disclosures. Moreover, appellant's own offer was made contingent upon "Accepted written agreement with Mr. and Mrs. John Safran regarding the easements for water and sewer lines and driveway location." This contingency was handwritten by appellant's real estate agent. Regardless of when the contingency was crossed out, we hold that its presence, combined with the other evidence relating to the disclosure of the easements, supports the trial court's finding that appellant had prior knowledge of the easements at the time it purchased the property. Therefore, appellant is not a bona fide purchaser, and the implied easements are enforceable.

Accordingly, appellant's first and second assignments of error are not well-taken.

Finally, in his third assignment of error, appellant argues that the trial court's grant of an easement to appellees violated its constitutional right to the inviolate enjoyment of its property. Appellant concludes that the trial court's judgment renders Lot 2 useless for the purpose of constructing a lakeside home, and therefore the judgment constitutes an uncompensated taking.

***

Here, however, the property was not "taken for public use." Rather, the trial court settled a land dispute between two private entities. . . .

Accordingly, appellant's third assignment of error is not well-taken.

IV. Conclusion

For the foregoing reasons, the judgment of the Ottawa County Court of Common Pleas is affirmed. . . .

Judgment affirmed.

9.1.2.4

Discussion: Notes, Questions, and Problems

9.1.2.4.1

Discussion Question #1. Easement created by statute?

Some states allow for the creation of an easement by statute. For an example of a jurisdiction that allows for a statutory easement, see Fla. Stat. § 704.01, excerpted below. Review carefully subsections (1) and (2). Is subsection (1) similar to the common law easement implied by strict necessity. How does subsection (2) differ from the analysis under common law for easements by implication? Note that Florida has also enacted Fla. Stat. § 704.04, excerpted below. What is the effect of that statute? If you were a state legislator, what changes would you propose, if any, for these statutes?

704.01 Common-law and statutory easements defined and determined.—

(1) IMPLIED GRANT OF WAY OF NECESSITY.—The common-law rule of an implied grant of a way of necessity is hereby recognized, specifically adopted, and clarified. Such an implied grant exists where a person has heretofore granted or hereafter grants lands to which there is no accessible right-of-way except over her or his land, or has heretofore retained or hereafter retains land which is inaccessible except over the land which the person conveys. In such instances a right-of-way is presumed to have been granted or reserved. Such an implied grant or easement in lands or estates exists where there is no other reasonable and practicable way of egress, or ingress and same is reasonably necessary for the beneficial use or enjoyment of the part granted or reserved. An implied grant arises only where a unity of title exists from a common source other than the original grant from the state or United States; provided, however, that where there is a common source of title subsequent to the original grant from the state

366

or United States, the right of the dominant tenement shall not be terminated if title of either the dominant or servient tenement has been or should be transferred for nonpayment of taxes either by foreclosure, reversion, or otherwise.

(2) STATUTORY WAY OF NECESSITY EXCLUSIVE OF COMMON-LAW RIGHT.—Based on public policy, convenience, and necessity, a statutory way of necessity exclusive of any common-law right exists when any land, including land formed by accretion, reliction, or other naturally occurring processes, or portion thereof, which is being used or is desired to be used for a dwelling or dwellings or for agricultural or for timber raising or cutting or stockraising purposes is shut off or hemmed in by lands, fencing, or other improvements by other persons so that no practicable route of egress or ingress is available therefrom to the nearest practicable public or private road in which the landlocked owner has vested easement rights. The owner or tenant thereof, or anyone in their behalf, lawfully may use and maintain an easement for persons, vehicles, stock, franchised cable television service, and any utility service, including, but not limited to, water, wastewater, reclaimed water, natural gas, electricity, and telephone service, over, under, through, and upon the lands which lie between the said shut-off or hemmed-in lands and such public or private road by means of the nearest practical route, considering the use to which said lands are being put; and the use thereof, as aforesaid, shall not constitute a trespass; nor shall the party thus using the same be liable in damages for the use thereof, provided that such easement shall be used only in an orderly and proper manner.

704.04 Judicial remedy and compensation to servient owner.—When the owner or owners of such lands across which a statutory way of necessity under § 704.01(2) is claimed, exclusive of the common-law right, objects or refuses to permit the use of such way under the conditions set forth herein or until she or he receives compensation therefor, either party or the board of county commissioners of such county may file suit in the circuit court of the county wherein the land is located in order to determine if the claim for said easement exists, and the amount of compensation to which said party is entitled for use of such easement. When said easement is awarded to the owner of the dominant tenement, it shall be in compliance with § 704.01(2) and shall exist so long as such easement is reasonably necessary. The court, in its discretion, shall determine all questions, including the type, duration, extent, and location of the easement, the amount of compensation, and the attorney's fees and costs to be awarded to either party for unreasonable refusal to comply with the provisions of § 704.01(2), provided that if either of said parties so requests in her or his original pleadings, the amount of compensation may be determined by a jury trial. The easement shall date from the time the award is paid.

9.1.2.4.2

Discussion Question #2. Quasi-easement in Corbett v. Ruben?

Review *Corbett v. Ruben*, excerpted above. Would the elements for a quasi-easement have been met in that case?

9.1.3

Easement by Prescription

We have discussed easements created expressly and easements created by implication. We noted that an easement may also be created by **prescription** based on long use and certain actions by the claimant. You will likely be familiar with many of the elements required for a prescriptive easement because they overlap with the concepts you studied in Chapter 6 on adverse possession. Unlike with adverse possession, however, in cases involving a prescriptive easement, the successful claimant does not obtain title to the estate or possessory rights. Rather, a successful claimant for a prescriptive easement obtains an easement, which is an interest in land, not an estate in land. For example, for a successful claim of prescriptive easement, the claimant would need to show that the use was open and notorious and continuous, and met such additional elements for the time period required by the jurisdiction.

There are two theories used to recognize the prescriptive easement – the *lost grant* theory and the **adverse use** theory. The court in *State ex rel. Haman v. Fox*, excerpted below, explained that the lost grant theory provides a presumption that, due to long possession, "there must have originally been a grant, from the owner to the claimant, which had become lost during the course of time." The lost grant theory has fallen out of favor and most states follow the adverse use theory. While at first blush the differences between the theories may appear slight, the distinction could produce a different outcome. An element required under the lost grant theory is different than an element required under the adverse use theory. Under the lost grant theory, the claimant must show that the owner of the servient estate acquiesced to the use. Acquiescence is viewed as submission to the use – not a grant of permission. By contrast acquiescence plays no role in the adverse use theory.

9.1.3.1

State ex rel. Haman v. Fox
594 P.2d 1093 (Idaho 1979)

Idaho Supreme Court

McFADDEN, Justice.

This is an action brought by the Prosecuting Attorney of Kootenai County on behalf of the people of the state of Idaho to establish public rights in and to privately owned water front property on Lake Coeur d'Alene. The district court determined that the public had no right or interest in the property and gave judgment to the property owners. We affirm.

THE FACTS

Defendants-respondents C. R. W. Fox and Eileen Fox, husband and wife, and Burgess K. McDonald, personal representative of the estate of Carmelita K. McDonald, deceased, own adjoining residential properties in the City of Coeur d'Alene. The properties consist of two residential lots in the Lake Shore Addition Plat together with two water front parcels abutting the waters of Lake Coeur d'Alene. The water front property is separated from the platted lots by Lake Shore Drive, a dedicated public street. Respondents' homes and yards are in the platted lots to the north of Lake Shore Drive. The water front lots to the south of Lake Shore Drive are for the most part sandy beach. The beach lots are adjoined on both sides by other privately owned lots, which together comprise what is commonly known as Sander's Beach. The beach has no public access other than from the lake itself. But the public does have access to the lake via a deeded right-of-way to the west of respondents' property and via a ten-foot wide pathway to the east of respondents' property.

Respondents' beach property extends south from Lake Shore Drive to the ordinary mean high water mark of Lake Coeur d'Alene. Their adjoining lots have a combined lake frontage of 250 feet and a depth of from 60 to 75 feet. The property is subject to the seasonal fluctuations of high water in the spring and low water in the late summer and fall. The property is also subject to the washings and erosive forces of the lake.

For many years, at least since the 1920's, respondents and their predecessors have maintained seawalls to protect a portion of their property immediately south of Lake Shore. Drive from the erosive forces of the lake. In 1971 respondents obtained the necessary building permits from the City of Coeur d'Alene and constructed a new concrete seawall. The new wall is a three-sided structure extending approximately 20 feet closer to the lake than the earlier walls and running the entire 250 feet across respondents' property. The wall does not interfere with swimming or boating on the lake, nor does it extend to the ordinary high water mark of the lake. The wall has, however, eliminated the public use of the enclosed area for sunbathing, picnicking and other related activities. It is this 20 feet by 250 feet enclosed area which is in dispute here.

This action was brought to force respondents to remove the seawall and to permanently enjoin them from further interfering with the alleged right of the public to use the enclosed areas. The complaint alleged that for over thirty years the general public had enjoyed complete freedom to use the beach for recreational purposes. It was alleged that by virtue of such public use respondents had impliedly dedicated the property to the general public or in the alternative that the public had acquired an easement thereon by prescription or by custom. It was also alleged that the wall interfered with the public trust in which the waters of the lake are held. After a trial to the court sitting without a jury, the people of the state of Idaho were adjudged to have no right or interest whatever to the property. The requested injunctive relief was denied, and judgment was entered in favor of respondents. This appeal followed.

STANDING

No governmental agency is in any way affiliated with this litigation and no rights of the State in its capacity as sovereign are concerned here. Nor does the City of Coeur d'Alene or Kootenai County claim any interest to this property. The action is brought by the Prosecuting Attorney for Kootenai County, but is brought solely on behalf of the people at large, i. e., the general public of the state.

***

We are of the opinion that the legislative grant of authority to the prosecuting attorney to prosecute actions in which "the people are interested" amounts to a statutory grant of standing in the instant case. The statute empowers the prosecuting attorney to call upon the courts of this state for vindication of public rights which for all practical purposes would otherwise go unprotected. The rights contended for here are of this nature. This court therefore holds that this action is properly brought under I.C. § 31-2604(1) by the prosecuting attorney.

THE MERITS

A. Easement by Prescription.

Appellant claims a right on behalf of the general public of this state to use private property for recreational purposes. In order to establish such a right by prescription, a party must submit "reasonably clear and convincing proof of open, notorious, continuous, uninterrupted use, under a claim of right, with the knowledge of the owner of the servient tenement, for the prescriptive period." *West v. Smith*, 95 Idaho 550, 557, 511 P.2d 1326, 1333 (1973) (footnotes omitted). The prescriptive right cannot arise, however, if the use of the land is with the permission of the owner.

After hearing the testimony of some seventeen witnesses on the use of respondents' property, the trial court found "that the use herein by the public was open, notorious, continuous, and uninterrupted and with the knowledge of the defendants [respondents] for more than the prescriptive period." The court further found, however, that the public use was in fact "a permissive use" and that "the evidence herein does not establish an adverse or hostile use by the plaintiff [appellant] against the interest of the defendants [respondents] nor any act on the part of any member of the public that would give' notice to the defendants [respondents] that the public was claiming an interest adverse to them." The court therefore concluded that no public rights had been established by prescription.

These findings, if supported by substantial and competent evidence in the record, will not be disturbed on appeal. We have carefully reviewed the record and conclude that there is substantial and competent evidence to support these findings. Even so, the court's finding that the use was by permission of respondents can only be sustained from that point in time in which respondents held title to the property. Respondents Fox acquired their property in 1948. Carmelita McDonald, now deceased, acquired hers in 1924. Appellant contends that the prescriptive rights to use the beach were acquired prior to 1948 and 1924, and that respondents took their fee interests subject to the already established public rights. We find it unnecessary to answer this contention. For the reasons stated below, this court is of the opinion that the "general public" or "the people of the state of Idaho" as distinguished from specific individuals cannot, absent specific statutory authorization, acquire prescriptive rights to private property.

As a starting point, it is important that the underlying legal rationale of a prescriptive right be discussed. Many courts have relied upon the fiction of the "lost-grant," i. e. it was presumed, from long possession under claim of right and with acquiescence of the owner, that there must have originally been a grant, from the owner to the claimant, which had become lost during the course of time. Under the lost grant rationale, courts have held that the general public, considered apart from legally organized or political entities, could not acquire prescriptive rights because they could not receive a grant. *Rosemann v. Adams,* 398 S.W.2d 855 (Mo.1966); *Morgan v. McLoughlin,* 5 N.Y.2d 1041, 185 N.Y.S.2d 801, 158 N.E.2d 498 (1959); *Ivons-Nispel, Inc. v. Lowe,* 347 Mass. 760, 200 N.E.2d 282 (1964); *Bioletti v. Sindoni,* 135 N.J.Eq. 609, 39 A.2d 634 (1944). In *Ivons-Nispel, Inc. v. Lowe, supra,* in a case almost identical to the case at bar, the Supreme Judicial Court of Massachusetts stated that "We are of opinion that 'persons of the local community' and the 'general public' are too broad a group to acquire by prescription an easement to use private beaches for bathing and for recreational purposes, (citations omitted.)" 200 N.E.2d at 283.

Although Idaho long ago abandoned the fiction of the lost grant, we reach the same result as the Massachusetts court in holding that the general public cannot acquire prescriptive rights in private property. In *Last Chance Ditch Co. v. Sawyer,* an action brought by the property owner to enjoin 89 persons from permitting waste water to flow into the canal, 35 Idaho 61, 66-67, 204 P. 654, 655 (1922), the court stated

> We are of the opinion, however, that the recognized fiction of a lost grant should not be given such controlling efficacy. While it is true that the statute of limitations does not in terms apply to the acquisition of title to an easement by prescription, it is generally held that by analogy such statutes are applicable. The use of an easement constitutes a direct invasion of the dominion of the proprietor of the land, and the statute forbids maintenance of an action to prevent such use as has been enjoyed openly, continuously, adversely, and with the acquiescence of the owner for a period of five years or more. The statute announces the policy of the law. It does not appear to be founded upon the fiction of a lost grant, but upon the proposition that it is the policy of the state to discourage litigation of matters which, through the lapse of time, should be considered as settled. We think the acquiescence of the owner of land in case of continuous and adverse user of an easement is presumed, and can be disproved only by showing acts upon his part which interrupt the continuity of the use, or by appropriate action in court to prevent its continuance.

The statute of limitations discussed in *Last Chance Ditch Co., supra,* upon which prescriptive rights in Idaho are based, is I.C. § 5-203. This statute in effect gives an owner five years to take the necessary and appropriate legal action to have an unauthorized use of his property stopped. If the owner of the property fails to eject the trespasser or enjoin the unauthorized use, after five years his right to do so will be barred. But as against whom would the owner be barred? Only those who had actually made open, notorious, continuous, uninterrupted use, under a claim of right, with the knowledge of the owner, for the five year period. Those persons who had not made such use could be enjoined from further interfering with the owner's superior rights.

In *West v. Smith, supra,* where an individual claimant asserted a prescriptive right to moor his houseboat in front of another person's privately owned lake front lot and to maintain a catwalk onto the owner's property, this court held that any prescriptive right there acquired was purely personal to the individual claimant. The prescriptive right belonged exclusively to the actual user, and not to guests or assignees. The private owner could therefore exclude all others from making any unapproved use of his property.

As in *West v. Smith, supra,* the rights contended for here are in the nature of an easement in gross. Being a personal right, the rule is that one individual's prescriptive use cannot inure to the benefit of anyone else. Personal prescriptive rights are confined to the actual adverse user and are limited to the use exercised during the prescriptive period. The fact that hundreds of individuals have made use of respondents' property for the. prescriptive period does not bar respondents from enjoining all future trespass to the property. Nor does the use of respondents' property by certain neighbors or friends or even total strangers accrue or inure to the benefit of others. We therefore hold that, the "people of the State of Idaho" as distinguished from specific individuals cannot acquire prescriptive rights in and to private property absent some express statutory authority. The one situation where the legislature has allowed such public prescriptive rights is in public highways. When a right-of-way has been used by the general public for a period of five years and has been maintained at public expense, the right-of-way becomes a public highway. *See* I.C. § 40-103 and *Meservey v. Gulliford,* 14 Idaho 133, 93 P. 780 (1908). No similar statute applies to the facts of this case. The district court's denial of the prescriptive easement is affirmed.

B. Dedication.

appellant arg.: Appellant contends that respondents have made an implied dedication of their property to the public. The district court put the burden on appellant to prove that respondents had by their acts or omissions intended to dedicate the land to public use. The court found that this burden had not been sustained. We concur.

The fundamental principles in this state regarding implied dedications are found in *Village of Hailey v. Riley,* 14 Idaho 481, 495, 95 P. 686, 691 (1908), quoted with approval in *Simmons v. Perkins,* 63 Idaho 136, 143, 118 P.2d 740, 744 (1941):

> It is no trivial thing to take another's land without compensation, and for this reason the courts will not lightly declare a dedication to public use. It is elementary law that an intention to dedicate upon the part of the owner must be plainly manifest.
>
> And while long continued user, without objection, and with the knowledge and consent of the owner is some evidence of a right in the public, still there must be joined to that user an intention upon the part of the owner to dedicate, or no dedication will be consummated; for the long-continued user by the public without objection by the owner is entirely consistent with a license to the public to use the land, and therefore evidence of long-continued user alone will not support a finding of fact that a dedication was created. Neither will a finding of fact of mere long-continued user support a conclusion of law that a public highway was created. As previously stated, in order to constitute a dedication of a highway by evidence *in pais,* there must be convincing evidence that the owner intended to appropriate the land to the public use.

Appellant urges this court to adopt the reasoning of the California per curiam decisions, *Gion* v. *City of Santa Clara* and *Dietz v. King,* 2 Cal.3d 29, 84 Cal.Rptr. 162, 465 P.2d 50 (1970), for the proposition that five years uninterrupted public use of private property creates a conclusive presumption of the owner's intent to dedicate. We decline the opportunity. Instead we adhere to the rule that a party claiming a right by dedication bears the burden of proof on every material issue. The intent of the owner to dedicate his land to public use must be clearly and unequivocally shown and must never be presumed.

***

The district court found as a fact that "none of the present defendants [respondents] nor any of their predecessors ever intended to make any dedication of the disputed area to public use . ... The plaintiff [appellant] did not carry his burden of proof in this regard." Our review of the record discloses substantial and competent evidence to support this finding. Respondents exercised dominion over the property by at various times personally ousting unwelcome users; at other times they enlisted the aid of the city police to do so. Trash cans mistakenly put on the property by the city were ordered removed by respondents. The deed executed in 1923 by John Taylor and Edith Taylor, respondents predecessors in title, conveying to the City of Coeur d'Alene a public right-of-way to the lake over property located to the west of respondents' property expressly limited the public rights to the narrow right of way and expressly prohibited interference with the rights of the private owners. This instrument, together with respondents' own affirmative acts of dominion and unequivocal testimony at trial negative any intent to dedicate the property to the public.

C. Custom.

Another theory advanced by appellant is that the public has by customary usage acquired recreation rights to respondents' property. This theory is based upon the English common law of custom, defined as: "a usage or practice of the people, which, by common adoption and acquiescence, and by long and unvarying habit, has become compulsory, and has acquired the force of a law with respect to the place or subject-matter to which it relates." Black's Law Dictionary 461 (rev. 4th ed. 1968). By the law of custom, the general public could, after many years of unrestricted common usage, acquire rights over private property. *Post v. Pearsall*, 22 Wend. 425 (N.Y.Ct.Err.1839); 2 W. Blackstone, Commentaries 263; 2 G. Thompson, supra, § 335.

The acquisition of a right through custom in England required that the use "must have continued from time immemorial, without interruption, and as a right; it must be certain as to the place, and as to the persons; and it must be certain and reasonable as to the subject matter or rights created." 3 H. Tiffany, Law of Real Property, § 935 at 623 (3d ed. 1939). Virtually all commentators are agreed that, until recently, the law of custom was a dead letter in the United States. Aside from two New Hampshire cases decided in the 1850's no state had applied the doctrine. As recently as 1935 New York refused to accept customary usage as a means of claiming an easement in a private beach for bathing and boating. The doctrine was exhumed, however, by the Supreme Court of Oregon in *State ex rel. Thornton v. Hay*, 254 Or. 584, 462 P.2d 671 (1969), where it was held that the public had acquired customary rights to a privately owned dry sand stretch of beach on the Oregon sea coast. Because of the tract-by-tract limitations inherent in the prescription theory, the Oregon court chose to apply custom to claimed public use of oceanfront lands.

Whether the doctrine exists in this state is a matter of first impression. I.C. § 73-116 provides that "[t]he common law of England, so far as it is not repugnant to, or inconsistent with, the constitution or laws of the United States, in all cases not provided for in these compiled laws, is the rule of decision in all courts of this state." There being no statute which expressly or impliedly rejects the doctrine of custom, this court is of opinion that the doctrine does obtain in Idaho.

The district court applied the law of custom to the facts of this case and concluded that the requisite elements had not been established. The first element, use from time immemorial, means that the use has existed for so long that "the memory of man runneth not to the contrary." *State ex rel. Thornton v. Hay, supra,* 462 P.2d at 677. In the instant case, the district court found that usage commenced as early as 1912. We agree with the district court that this does not constitute "from time immemorial." The second requirement, that the use must be uninterrupted, is not met because of the fact that respondents had personally and with police assistance removed members of the public from their land. Without further burdening this opinion, suffice it to say that of the seven essential elements of a customary right, the trial court found adversely to appellant on six of them. We find ample evidence in the record to support the findings, and we therefore affirm the district court's denial of any customary rights in this case.

D. Public Trust.

Appellant's final argument is that respondents' lake front property is imbued with a public trust under the principles of the public trust doctrine. That doctrine's leading authority, Professor Sax of the University of Michigan School of Law, articulates the following as the "central substantive thought in public trust litigation":

> [w]hen a state holds a resource which is available for the free use of the general public, a court will look with considerable skepticism upon *any* governmental conduct which is calculated *either* to relocate that resource to more restricted uses *or* to subject public uses to the self-interest of private parties.

J. Sax, *The Public Trust Doctrine in Natural Resource Law: Effective Judicial Intervention,* 68 Mich.L.Rev. 473, 490 (1970) (emphasis in text).

It is undisputed that the land in contention here is private property, traceable to a patent from the United States Government in 1892. It is also undisputed that the seawall constructed by respondents lies above the ordinary mean high water mark of the lake and that it in no way interferes with navigability or the public's use of the lake's waters. Since no natural resource owned by the state is involved here the public trust doctrine is inapposite. The district court judgment is affirmed in all respects. Costs to respondents.

9.1.3.2
White v. Ruth R. Millington Living Trust
785 S.W.2d 782 (Mo. Ct. App. 1990)
Missouri Court of Appeals

MAUS, Judge.

The plaintiffs by Count I seek a declaration they have acquired an easement for ingress and egress by prescription. By Count II, in the alternative, they seek the establishment of a private road of necessity under § 228.340. The defendant tendered to the plaintiffs an easement in the south eighteen feet of her property for the construction of a road. The judgment of the trial court declared the plaintiffs shall be entitled to the tendered easement and denied relief upon the petition. The plaintiffs appeal.

The following is a summary of the facts. The . . . plaintiffs' 318 acres joins the defendant's 320 acres on the east. Neither tract is fenced. Except for a machine shed and cabin constructed by plaintiffs, neither tract is improved. The tracts are located in a wooded, sparsely settled area of Wayne County.

The earliest history and description of the tracts and roads involved were given by witnesses Peck West and Dee West, his wife. They lived in the area for approximately thirty years. The later history and description of the area and road were also related by the parties and other witnesses.

At all relevant times, an improved county road has extended generally north and south along the west side of the defendant's tract. An unimproved dirt road (road A) meanders through the woods, west to east, from the county road across the defendant's tract to the plaintiffs' tract. Road A varies in width and is bordered by trees, many of substantial size. The plaintiffs claim an easement by prescription in road A across the defendant's tract. *plaintiffs claim*

At one time, road A extended east through and beyond the plaintiffs' tract, approximately two and one-half miles to the McGee store, which is located on County Highway TT. When road A, beyond the plaintiffs' property, was abandoned is not clear. Witness Martin White was over that portion of the road in a four-wheel drive vehicle around 1972. Subsequently, a ditch was cut across that road just east of the plaintiffs' tract. Peck West testified that in recent years that portion of the road had become so "plugged up" that he couldn't ride a horse on the road beyond the plaintiffs' property.

***

Road B, also an unimproved dirt road, runs northeast from a point on the county road, well south of the defendant's tract. Road B extends northeast to the southwest corner of the plaintiffs' tract. . . .

The plaintiffs bought their tract by a contract for deed on October 16, 1972. They subsequently received a warranty deed. The plaintiffs, and members of their family, used the tract for recreational purposes. Plaintiff Willis White was 70 years old at the time of trial, December 20, 1988. The plaintiffs have five sons. The plaintiffs and/or members of their family came to the tract to spend most weekends since the plaintiffs bought the tract. Initially, the plaintiffs placed a travel trailer on the tract. The five brothers built a machine shed on plaintiffs' tract using road A to haul materials. They later converted a portion of the machine shed into living quarters, or a cabin. The plaintiffs thought road A was a public road. They primarily used road A in going to and coming from their property. From time to time they graded and filled holes on that road. In the earlier years, when it was wet, they used road B, to avoid causing ruts in road A. At the time of trial, road B had become impassible by vehicle.

timber deed

The plaintiffs bought their tract subject to a "timber deed" in favor of John E. Haggett. The timber deed sold all timber ten inches in diameter and above to Haggett and granted him eighteen months in which to remove that timber. He used road A in removing the timber. In an unexplained manner, the defendant learned of his use and directed that he stop using road A unless he paid her $50 per month for the privilege. To avoid delay, Haggett made the payments for several months. When he quit cutting timber, Haggett repaired the road at defendant's request. He said he "hauled gavel [sic] back in there and I had my bulldozer down there, you know, to level and so forth."

The defendant lived in Advance, Missouri. She bought her tract in 1968. She knew of the existence of road A at that time. She considered it a logging road, a type of road commonly found in the area. She did collect $50 per month from Haggett for his use of the road through March 1974. It was difficult for her to estimate how often she saw the tract. She surmised that she had been there once a year since she bought it. Some of her family and friends used the tract for hunting. On more than one occasion in the 1970's she caused barbed wire to be placed across road A at its junction with the county road to bar unauthorized use of the road. The wire was removed. At one time she caused a cable to be placed across road A for that purpose. It, too, was removed. She did not know the plaintiffs were using road A. No one, including her family members, reported to her that the plaintiffs were using road A.

Defendant acknowledged that exhibits D through S (photographs) showed road A in substantially the condition it had been in through the time she owned her tract. Those photographs unmistakably show a well-defined dirt road through the woods.

On July 12, 1983, plaintiff Willis White called the defendant and asked permission to cut some trees along road A. Defendant testified this was the first she knew plaintiffs were using the road. Negotiations between the plaintiffs and the defendant to establish the plaintiffs' right to use the road were futile. On March 19, 1987, the defendant wrote to Willis White. That letter included the following two paragraphs.

"Under no circumstances will your continued use of the logging road which crosses our property be tolerated unless you acknowledge in writing, within ten days of the date of this letter, that your use of the road has been and will be with our express permission only.

As previously indicated, I would be willing to enter into an agreement with you providing for your occasional permissive use of the road for a period of time. However, should you fail to acknowledge in writing that your use has been and will continue to be permissive, an appropriate legal action will be instituted in Wayne County, Missouri, to obtain a court order prohibiting your further use."

The plaintiffs did not terminate their use of road A. They filed this action on August 10, 1987.

The plaintiffs' basic contention is that the overwhelming weight of the evidence established they had acquired an easement for ingress and egress over the route described as road A by prescription and that the trial court misapplied the law in finding they had not acquired such an easement. The fundamental requirements for the acquisition of an easement by prescription are well established.

"The elements that establish an easement by prescription have been outlined and considered in detail in countless decisions. The requirements have been summarized: 'An easement by prescription may be established by use which is shown to have been continuous, uninterrupted, visible and adverse for a period of ten years.' *Guerin v. Yocum,* [506 S.W.2d 46, 47 (Mo.App.1974)]." *Orvis v. Garms,* 638 S.W.2d 773, 776 (Mo.App.1982).

Of course, those fundamental elements have been refined and amplified where necessary by reason of the issues raised in individual cases. Such amplifications relevant to this case include the following.

adverse

> "To be adverse, it is only necessary for the use to proceed without recognition of the owner's authority to permit or prohibit the use; it is not necessary that the user intend to violate the owner's rights." *Johnston v. Bates,* 778 S.W.2d 357, 362 (Mo.App.1989).

A use may be continuous within the meaning of the above requirement, even though it is not daily.

continuous

> "'Continuous enjoyment' simply means that the claimant must exercise the use as frequently as convenience or necessity requires consistent with the character of the property and the nature of the easement asserted." Bruce & Ely, The Law of Easements and Licenses in Land, Para. 5.05[1], p. 5-24 (1988).

***

It is not required that the adverse use be exclusive.

> "[T]he fact that the right-of-way traveled by plaintiffs was in fact used by other people did not preclude establishment of an easement by prescription in plaintiffs." *Beldner v. General Electric Company,* 451 S.W.2d 65, 75 (Mo.1970). "The claim of right need not be a claim to possess title as in adverse possession, but it may be a nonexclusive right to use the property." *Fenster v. Hyken,* supra at 870.

The trial court made detailed Findings of Fact and Conclusions of Law. Those Findings substantially included the facts set forth in the above statement of the evidence. The Conclusions of Law included the following.

> *"The crucial element lacking* in plaintiffs' claim in Count I for an easement by prescription is that of notice. The uncontroverted evidence presented before the court is that defendant, or even residents within the area of Road A, have either *never received any actual notice* of plaintiffs' use of logging Road A or, received no such notice until July of 1983. Plaintiffs therefore did not

present proof that they have engaged in the requisite type of use of the roadway, with notice, for a period of ten (10) years and that, at the time of trial, such use, although possibly satisfying all other elements of easement by prescription, only satisfied all of the essential elements, including that of notice, for a little over five (5) years. *For these reasons,* relief requested by plaintiff [sic] in Count I, seeking establishment of an easement by prescription, must be denied." (Emphasis added.)

notice

This is a clear determination by the trial court the plaintiffs established all the elements required for the acquisition of an easement by prescription in the route described as road A, but denied relief because plaintiffs did not prove the defendant had actual notice of their adverse use. The defendant seeks to sustain the judgment upon that basis. The issue presented in her brief is stated in the following terms. "Constructive notice of use is not sufficient." In support of that position, she argues: "Appellants would now have the Court hold that constructive notice of a use or possession will suffice to divest a property owner of its interest. The only constructive notice of ownership interest or claims of ownership interest accorded by the law is that in the recording of enforceable instruments and deeds in a recorder's office which are by statute sanctioned with the authority and ability to provide constructive notice by the mere act of recording." In denying relief, the trial court erroneously declared and applied the law.

It is generally recognized that to establish an easement by prescription, it is not necessary the owner of the servient estate have actual knowledge of an adverse use.

***

"If the user is open, adverse, notorious, peaceable, and uninterrupted, the owner of the servient land is charged with knowledge of such user and his acquiescence in it is implied." Thompson on Real Property, Easements § 341, p. 204 (1980 Repl.) (footnote omitted.)

"The landowner need not have actual knowledge of adverse usage. Rather, the claimant must prove that the use was sufficiently open and notorious to apprise a diligent owner of its existence. In other words, the usage must be of such a nature as to charge the landowner with constructive notice." Bruce

& Ely, The Law of Easements and Licenses in Land, Para. 5.04, pp. 5-19 — 5-20 (1988).

That principle has been established as the law of this state by the Supreme Court at an early date. In *Boyce v. Missouri Pac. R. Co.,* 168 Mo. 583, 68 S.W. 920 (1902), the Supreme Court was considering whether or not a railroad company had acquired an easement by prescription. In holding that it had, the Supreme Court established the law of this state in the following language.

> "Theoretically the use and easement are with the knowledge and acquiescence of the owner as much as is the adverse possession of a defendant in ejectment. For the law presumes that every man knows the condition and status of his land, and if any one ousts him, or trespasses upon his land, or enters into possession and sets up an adverse claim thereto, and the owner does not ask legal aid to dispossess him within the time limited for bringing such actions, the law assumes that the owner has acquiesced in the adverse claim.... In point of fact, the owner, like these owners, may have had no actual knowledge, and therefore did not expressly acquiesce; but the law implies knowledge, and therefore consent. This is as true of claims to easements as it is to claims to the land itself." *Id.* 68 S.W. at 922-923.

***

The doctrine has been consistently followed.

***

> "The notice, however, 'can be constructive or implied' from circumstantial evidence." *Johnston v. Bates,* supra at 362.

In the trial court, and in this court, the defendant has emphasized portions of the evidence to establish she had no actual notice of the plaintiffs' use of road A. Such evidence, of course, included her testimony that she had no actual knowledge. It also included testimony that no member of her family or their guests saw or reported use by the plaintiffs. She also in part relied upon the fact that Peck West, who lived in the immediate vicinity for thirty years, never saw the plaintiffs using road A.

This evidence does support the conclusion defendant had no actual notice of the plaintiffs' use. However, as above noted, lack of such actual notice does not defeat the plaintiffs' claim.

Even the defendant's evidence supports the conclusion that the plaintiffs' use was sufficient to provide constructive notice of that use. The members of defendant's family were there only a few days each year. Yet they acknowledged the existence of the road. The defendant was there perhaps only one day each year. The photographs in evidence taken May 21, 1988 establish that road A was well defined. The defendant acknowledged that road A had been in substantially the same condition since 1968. Witness Dee West described road A as better than the average logging road. The defendant acknowledged there had been adverse use of that road by placing wire across road A several times in the 1970's. She knew the wire was later removed. When asked why she placed barbed wire across road A the first time, she replied, "We could see where cars were pulling in, or vehicles were pulling in."

The undisputed evidence established that the plaintiffs and members of their family used road A virtually each weekend since 1972. The plaintiffs' use was readily apparent from the improvements that were placed upon the plaintiffs' property during the period of time in question. The net effect of the evidence in respect to the issue of constructive notice, was established by two witnesses called by the defendant. Witness Mike Clark had lived in the area and had been familiar with road A for twenty-five years. He said, "[i]t's a beaten path" and even though he had not seen anyone using the road, "I knew someone was using it."

When asked if he had seen Willis White use the road, witness Peck West testified as follows:

> "A. Well, actually see him, I couldn't say that I have.
>
> Q. Okay.
>
> A. But I do know that he uses the road."

The weight of the evidence established the plaintiffs' use of road A was sufficient to afford the defendant constructive notice of that use. *Johnston v. Bates,* supra. In denying the plaintiffs' relief, because they did not prove the defendant had actual notice of that use, the trial court misapplied the law and the judgment must be reversed.

The judgment of the trial court is reversed. The cause is remanded for the entry of a judgment granting the plaintiffs relief upon Count I of the petition and declaring they have established by prescription an easement appurtenant to the tract owned by them for ingress and egress to that tract over road A as located by the survey in evidence. . . . The cause is remanded for further proceedings consistent with this opinion.

9.2

Scope and Transferability of Easement

With an express easement, the parties have an opportunity to clearly state the terms of the easement, including its scope and transferability. Sometimes, however, even with express easements, the parties fail to include these various terms. In those cases, and certainly in cases of easements created by implication or prescription, the courts may be called upon to determine the missing terms.

9.2.1

SRB Inv. Co., Ltd v. Spencer
463 P.3d 654 (Utah 2020)

Supreme Court of Utah

Chief Justice Durrant, opinion of the Court:

Introduction

SRB Investment Company sought access to its property through a prescriptive easement crossing land owned by the Spencer family. The district court determined that SRB had established this easement. But the court prohibited SRB from using the easement for any reason other than to access the SRB property for the purposes of ranching or farming. Because the court improperly focused on the purposes for which SRB's land would be used, rather than on the purpose for which the relevant portion of the Spencer property would be used, we reverse its determination and remand for a new determination regarding the scope of the easement. On remand, the court should take a flexible approach to determining the scope of the prescriptive easement—an approach that permits changes in the use of the parties' respective property rights so long as those changes do not *materially* increase the burden imposed on either party.

Background

For well over twenty years, Norman Carroll used a road crossing real property owned by the Spencer family to access his own property. But in 2005, Mr. Carroll sold his property to SRB Investment Company. Although Mr. Carroll had principally used his property only for ranching and farming, SRB purchased the property with the intent to use it as a cabin vacation spot for its members.

Some time after SRB purchased the property, the Spencers objected to SRB's continued use of the portion of the road crossing the Spencer property. In response, SRB filed this action in order to regain access to the property.

After a one-day bench trial, the district court determined that SRB had acquired a prescriptive easement across the Spencer property. And, citing Utah case law, it held that the scope of the easement needed to be limited to its historical usage. In determining the easement's historical usage, the court found that "almost all of the relevant evidence" came from Mr. Carroll's deposition testimony.

Based on Mr. Carroll's testimony, the court held the following: (1) the easement was limited to "vehicular travel in daily uses for farming and ranching purposes, and uses at random times for random reasons" and (2) "[m]ultiple house buildings on the SRB Parcel are outside the scope of the prescriptive easement's historic[al] usage, but a camp or other [temporary] building or vehicle that is ancillary to farming and ranching used on the SRB Property would not be outside the scope." SRB appealed this determination. . . .

* * *

Analysis

SRB argues the district court erred in defining the scope of the easement based on how SRB used its own property during the prescriptive period. Instead, SRB argues that the court should have defined the scope of the easement based on how SRB used the Spencer's property during that period. We agree and remand this case to the district court for a new determination, consistent with the legal principles outlined in this opinion, regarding the easement's scope.

We have long held that "the extent of a prescriptive easement is measured and limited by its historic[al] use during the prescriptive period." The district court cited this rule in limiting the scope of the easement across the Spencer property. But, in so doing, the court limited the use of the easement to "vehicular travel in daily uses for farming and ranching purposes, and uses at random times for random reasons." It also appeared to limit SRB's use of SRB's own property by stating that "[m]ultiple house buildings on the SRB Parcel are outside the scope of the prescriptive easement's historic[al] usage, but a camp or other [temporary] building or vehicle that is ancillary to farming and ranching uses on the SRB Property would not be outside the scope." By limiting the scope of the easement in this way, the district court erred.

The district court erred because it erroneously equated the "purpose" for which SRB's property—the dominant estate—was used with the "extent" of the easement's historical use over the Spencer property—the servient estate. This is inconsistent with basic principles underlying the prescriptive easement doctrine.

When the principles underlying the prescriptive easement doctrine are considered, together with our case law, an important distinction between a prescriptive easement's "type" (or "purpose") and a prescriptive easement's "scope" emerges. Under this distinction, a prescriptive easement's type should be categorized broadly based on the general purpose for which the easement over the servient estate has historically been used. And a prescriptive easement's scope should be defined with particularity based on the nature, or extent, of that historical use. We discuss this distinction in greater detail before applying it to the facts of this case.

I. There is an Important Distinction Between a Prescriptive Easement's Type and Its Scope

"It is elementary that the use of an easement must be as reasonable and as little burdensome to the servient estate as the *nature* of the easement and its *purpose* will permit." Although our case law has never explicitly distinguished between a prescriptive easement's type—as defined by its historical *purpose*—and its scope—as defined by the *nature* of its historical use—such a distinction is implicit in our previous prescriptive easement cases and is consistent with well-established prescriptive easement principles.

Our case law clearly establishes that there are different types of prescriptive easements.[1] The most common type of prescriptive easement is an access easement, or, in other words, an easement for ingress or egress across the servient estate.[2] But we have also recognized other types of easements, such as easements for the purposes of recreation, logging, and irrigation. And we have explained that an easement "for one purpose gained by user cannot be turned into a[n] [easement] for another purpose if the latter adds materially to the burden of the servient estate." For this reason, the "first step in determining whether the holder of an easement is entitled to make a particular use challenged by the owner of the servient estate is to determine whether the use falls within the *purposes* for which the [prescriptive easement] was created."

But the purpose for which a prescriptive easement was created is not the only limiting factor in defining the easement. We have also explained that the extent of a prescriptive easement is measured and limited by the nature of the use made during the prescriptive period. Utah courts often refer to this second form of limitation as the "scope" of the easement.[3]

Thus our case law establishes that a prescriptive easement should be defined generally by type—based on the purpose for which it was acquired—as well as specifically by scope—based on the nature and extent of the easement's historical use. But even though an easement's type and scope both work to define the extent of the rights enjoyed through a prescriptive easement, the limitations imposed by the type and scope should be analyzed separately.

II. The Type of a Prescriptive Easement Should be Defined Broadly Based on the Purpose for Which the Servient Estate was Used

Because a prescriptive easement acquired "for one purpose ... cannot be turned into a[n] [easement] for another purpose if the latter adds materially to the burden of the servient estate," the "outcome in any particular case" may hinge on "the level of generality with which the purpose is defined." So, for example, the purpose of the easement in this case could be broadly defined as an easement to access the dominant estate. Or, as the district court's order illustrates, it could be narrowly defined as an easement to access the dominant estate for farming and ranching activities. But our case law suggests that the type, or purpose, of a prescriptive easement should be defined broadly.

For example, in describing the purpose of an access easement, we typically characterize the purpose as being to access another property without further identifying the purpose for which that property was being accessed. Likewise, we have defined easements used for "recreational purposes" without specifically identifying the types of recreation. And we have discussed an easement for "the purpose of discharging" water "across the premises of the plaintiffs" without discussing the purpose for which the water would be used. So our case law suggests that when describing the easement's purpose we need only do so in broad terms.

Accordingly, courts should construe the general purpose of a prescriptive easement broadly. And once this general purpose is determined, any use of the servient estate that is for another purpose is impermissible unless the burden imposed on the servient estate by the change is immaterial.

In applying this rule to this case, the factual findings of the district court suggest that the purpose of the prescriptive easement at issue is to provide access to SRB's property. The court held that "the essentially unrefuted testimony of Norman H. Carroll clearly and convincingly establish[ed] that a prescriptive easement was created" to access "the SRB Parcel." Accordingly, the general purpose of the easement should be defined broadly as being for access to SRB's property, and any use of the servient estate, other than for access to the SRB property, should be deemed permissible only if it does not materially add to the burden imposed by the access easement.

III. The Extent, or Scope of Permissible Use, of a Prescriptive Easement Should be Limited by the Nature of its Historical Use

In contrast to the broad characterization of a prescriptive easement's purpose, our case law suggests that we must define the specific nature, or scope, of the easement's historical use with particularity. This is so because "the extent of a prescriptive [right]

is measured and limited by its historic[al] use during the prescriptive period."[4] And that right "cannot be enlarged to place a greater burden or servitude" on the servient estate.[5] In other words, the extent of a prescriptive easement is measured by the burden historically imposed on the servient estate during the prescriptive period. Because the ultimate aim in determining the extent (or scope) of a prescriptive easement is to limit the burden on the servient estate to what had been imposed historically, courts should consider only those factors that are helpful in determining the nature of the historical burden imposed on the servient estate.

A. The scope of a prescriptive easement must be limited by the burdens imposed by its historical use

There are a number of factors that courts consistently consider in determining the scope of a prescriptive easement. As discussed above, the purpose of considering these factors is to determine the burden that has historically been placed on the servient estate. With this purpose in mind, courts almost always consider the physical dimensions of the historical use of the servient estate. They also consider the frequency and intensity of the use, as well as the effect of the use on the aesthetic and economic value of the property.

For example, in *Crane v. Crane*, we considered the appropriate scope of a prescriptive easement for access. The prescriptive easement in question had been used historically to transport approximately 150 cattle each spring, and 400 cattle each fall, across the property. Based on this historical use, the district court held that the easement could be used "one day in the spring of each year and up to ten days in the fall of each year." And the court limited the use to "up to 350 head of cattle during the 10 days in the fall." In reviewing this decision, we held that the district court "appropriately limit[ed] the easement in gross to the nature and extent of the use by which it was acquired." But we noted that even though the district court limited the number of cattle in the fall, it failed to do so in the spring. Accordingly, we modified the district court's order to include this additional limitation. In this way, we ensured that the burden—stated in terms of the frequency and intensity of the use—imposed on the servient estate by the judicially recognized prescriptive easement did not exceed the burden that had historically been imposed.[6]

Even though courts will almost always consider the physical dimensions of the land used, as well as the frequency and intensity of that use, the "ultimate criterion" in determining the scope of a prescriptive easement is that of avoiding increased burdens on the servient estate. So courts should consider any and all factors that may contribute to that burden.

For instance, in determining the scope of access easements, courts often consider the mode of transportation that has historically been used for access. But, importantly, this factor is considered only where the mode of transportation affects the burden placed on the servient estate. For example, in *Gillmor v. Carter*, the district court reserved for trial the question of whether the defendant "had obtained a prescriptive right to personally travel over [an easement] by jeep, passenger car or panel truck," but it enjoined him from using a road "for the purpose of hauling salt or other minerals from the Great Salt Lake." The defendant appealed this determination. On appeal, we explained that although the defendant had testified that he had used the road for over twenty years, his use of the road "did not include use of trucks for hauling heavy tonnage." Because "hauling salt in heavy tonnages" would have imposed an additional "burden" on the servient estate than what was imposed by his use of smaller vehicles, we affirmed the district court's decision. Thus our decision in *Gillmor* confirms that courts should consider any factors that may contribute to the overall burden imposed on the servient estate by the easement.[7]

B. *The subjective purpose in using an easement is relevant only to the extent it sheds light on the nature of the historical burden imposed on the servient estate*

Although, in determining the scope of a prescriptive easement, courts may consider a wide variety of factors, the subjective purpose for which a prescriptive easement is used should be considered only to the extent it is helpful in determining the nature of the burden historically placed on the servient estate. This is so because the purpose for which an easement holder uses the servient estate does not, in and of itself, burden the servient estate.

For example, in *Jesurum v. WBTSCC Limited Partnership*, the New Hampshire Supreme Court determined the scope of an easement providing access to a public beach across a private golf course. The owner of the golf course argued that the easement "should be limited in scope to digging for worms and searching for shellfish because the first recorded use of [the easement across the golf course] was limited to those purposes." But the court explained that this "argument confuse[d] the public use made of [the golf course] with the public use made of [the beach]." Because the subjective purpose the prescriptive users may have had in using the easement was "irrelevant" to the burden imposed by the easement, the court correctly held that that purpose was "not germane to the determination of the scope of the easement." So the decision in *Jesurum* illustrates that in many cases, the purpose for which a prescriptive easement is used will not materially contribute to the burden imposed by that use.

But there may be instances where the purpose for which an easement is used provides the best evidence of the burden imposed on the servient estate. For example, in *Bolton v. Murphy* we considered the "nature or character of the use" of an access easement in a rural farming community. In that case, a large number of plaintiffs claimed a prescriptive easement across the land of a neighbor to access a public highway. The group of plaintiffs had used the easement for roughly fifty years to access their respective farms and homes. Because the easement had been used so widely and for so long, the court was forced to articulate the scope of the easement in broad terms. It held that the easement could be used "for the purposes that roads are ordinarily used for by farmers in the vicinity." In other words, in the absence of evidence of more specific limiting factors, the court in *Bolton* properly considered the purposes for which roads in the area were typically used as the best evidence of the burden imposed on the servient estate.

Accordingly, in determining what the historical burden has been on a servient estate, courts may consider the subjective purpose for which an easement is used, but only to the extent it provides relevant evidence of the scope of that burden.

C. The use of the dominant estate is likewise relevant only to the extent it sheds light on the nature of the historical burden imposed on the servient estate

Similarly, an easement holder's use of the dominant estate may be considered in determining the scope of an easement, but only to the extent it provides information regarding the nature of the burden on the servient estate. Our decision in *Robins v. Roberts* illustrates this point.

393

In *Robins*, the owner of the dominant estate replaced an earthen dam on his own property with a larger cement dam. Although the owner of the dominant estate had previously acquired a prescriptive easement to flood a portion of the servient estate by using his dam, the owner of the servient estate attempted to restrain the owner of the dominant estate "from maintaining" the new cement dam. Because the new cement dam was "five or six inches higher than the old one," the owner of the servient estate argued that its construction had enlarged the flooding easement on the servient estate. But we disagreed. Although we acknowledged that the new dam was "five or six inches higher than the earthen dam it replaced," we explained that "it matters not that the dam itself is larger or occupies more ground" because the dam was not on the servient estate. The only thing that was relevant, we explained, was whether the water flooding the servient estate exceeded the extent of the flooding "that was done by use of the old dam." Because the evidence indicated that "[s]ubstantially the same amount of land [was] irrigated as was irrigated theretofore," we refused to order the owner of the dominant estate to remove his new dam. So our decision in *Robins* illustrates that the nature of the usage of the dominant estate is irrelevant except to the extent it provides information that would be helpful in determining the burden placed on the servient estate.

The reasoning in *Robins* is consistent with the approach followed in other jurisdictions. For example, in *Gaither v. Gaither*, a California court of appeals held that a prescriptive easement that had formerly been used to access the dominant estate, which had historically been used "for farming purposes," could also be used to access recently constructed rental units on the property. In so holding, the court explained that the change did not increase the burden on the servient estate because the change did not affect "the physical objects [(vehicles)] passing over the driveway." In other words, the court found that the purpose for which the dominant estate was being used was irrelevant to a determination of the burden that had historically been imposed on the servient estate. As the decision in *Gaither* illustrates, our case law is consistent with the approach generally followed in other jurisdictions.

Accordingly, the purposes for which the dominant estate is used is relevant to a determination of the permitted uses of a prescriptive easement only to the extent it provides information regarding the nature of the burden imposed on the servient estate. In other words, where a change in the purpose for which a dominant estate is used does not increase the burden imposed on the servient estate, that change is irrelevant in determining the scope of a prescriptive easement.[8]

D. *Utah follows the majority rule that the nature of a use can be altered reasonably*

Although the ultimate criterion in determining the scope of a prescriptive easement is to limit the burden imposed on the servient estate to what has been imposed historically, Utah allows reasonable changes to be made by both the easement holder and the owner of the servient estate so long as it does not materially increase the burden imposed on either party.

We have held that a "right of way for one purpose gained by user cannot be turned into a right of way for another purpose if the latter adds materially to the burden of the servient estate." We have also held that "an alteration in the easement requires the consent of the other party *unless* it can be considered to be of such an immaterial character as would not interfere with the reasonable enjoyment of the easement." And we have held that the "right of the easement owner and the right of the land-owner are not absolute, irrelative, and uncontrolled, but are so limited, each by the other, that there may be a due and reasonable enjoyment of both." As these holdings indicate, in considering changes to the use of an easement or the servient estate, we apply a flexible rule that seeks to accommodate reasonable changes in use.

This rule was applied in our 1976 decision in *North Union Canal Co. v. Newell.* In that case a canal company sought to enjoin the owners of the servient estate from maintaining a fence around their property because it placed a burden on the canal company's easement right to enter the property for the purpose of performing maintenance on its canal. In considering this argument, we observed that whenever "there is ownership of property subject to an easement there is a dichotomy of interests, both of which must be respected and kept in balance." We then noted that the fence constructed on the servient estate "would interfere with the [canal company's] use and enjoyment of its easement." "From this," we explained, "the logical conclusion would seem to be that the fence should be removed." But we declined to order the fence's removal.

In declining to order "such a stringent measure," we explained that "the object to be desired [in easement cases] is to find some accommodation of those conflicting interests, to the maximum advantage and to the minimum disadvantage[ ] of both parties." So with this object in mind, we declined to order the removal of the fence, but we ordered the owners of the servient estate to maintain gates "at reasonable intervals in the fence along the canal bank to allow the [canal company] access thereto as its needs may arise." Accordingly, our decision in *North Union Canal Co.* confirms that, in considering changes to the use of an easement or the servient estate, we apply a flexible rule that seeks to accommodate reasonable changes in use. And our case law suggests that a reasonable change in use is any change that does not materially increase the burden on the servient estate or materially restrict the use of the easement.

This flexible approach is consistent with the approach followed in a majority of jurisdictions.[9] For example, the Alaska Supreme Court has held that "the use made of a prescriptive easement may evolve beyond the original prescriptive uses, [but] new uses cannot substantially increase the burden on the servient estate."[10] And a Connecticut appellate court has explained that one "who has an easement by prescription has the right to do such acts that are reasonable and necessary to effectuate that party's enjoyment of the easement unless it unreasonably increases the burden on the servient tenement."[11]

According to the Maine Supreme Judicial Court, this flexible approach is essential to preserve the usefulness of a prescriptive right over time.[12] And we endorsed a similar rationale in our *Big Cottonwood Tanner Ditch Co.* case. In that case we cited the rule that "the extent of an easement acquired by prescription is measured and limited by the use made during the prescriptive period." But we cautioned against applying this rule "with absolute strictness" because doing so would render the prescriptive right "of no utility whatsoever." Accordingly, our decision in *Big Cottonwood Tanner Ditch Co.* suggests that prescriptive rights, where established, should be construed to preserve their usefulness over time.

In sum, when asked to determine the scope of a prescriptive easement, or whether a particular use is permitted under that easement, courts should consider any and all factors that are helpful in determining the extent of the historical burden on the servient estate. Factors that courts should consider in almost every case are the physical dimensions of the prescriptive use, the frequency and intensity of the use, and the effect of the use on the aesthetic and economic value of the property. Additionally, courts may also consider the subjective purpose for using the easement, as well as the nature of the use of the dominant estate, but only to the extent those factors are helpful in determining the nature of the burden on the servient estate. Finally, in determining the scope of a prescriptive right, courts should take a flexible approach that permits changes of use so long as those changes do not materially burden the servient estate or materially interfere with the prescriptive right.

IV. We Reverse the Judgment of the District Court and Remand for a New Determination Regarding the Scope of the Prescriptive Easement in this Case

With the correct approach to prescriptive easements in mind, we now consider the district court's determination in this case. In determining the easement's historical usage, the court found that "almost all of the relevant evidence" came from Mr. Carroll's deposition testimony. Based on this testimony, the court found that Mr. Carroll's uses had "almost all been farming or ranching related uses, along with trips to and from the SRB Parcel at random times and for random reasons." And after defining the purpose of the easement in this way, the court held the following: (1) the easement was limited to "vehicular travel in daily uses for farming and ranching purposes, and uses at random times for random reasons" and (2) "[m]ultiple house buildings on the SRB Parcel are outside the scope of the prescriptive easement's historic[al] usage, but a camp or other [temporary] building or vehicle that is ancillary to farming and ranching uses on the SRB Property would not be outside the scope." The court erred in making both of these determinations.

A. The district court incorrectly limited the use of the access easement to only those people who would use it with the subjective purpose to farm or ranch on the SRB property

First, the court erred by limiting the use of the access easement to only those people who would use it with the subjective purpose to farm or ranch on the SRB property. As we discussed above, the subjective purpose for which an easement is used is relevant only to the extent it provides evidence regarding the nature of the burden imposed on the servient estate. Thus the court erred in focusing on that fact to the exclusion of all other factors regarding the historical burden on the servient estate.

To be clear, we are not suggesting that, on remand, the court cannot consider the prescriptive users' subjective purpose in using the easement. The fact that the easement was historically used for ranching and farming could be helpful in establishing certain aspects of the burden imposed. For example, evidence related to farming or ranching activities on the SRB property could suggest that, historically, the physical dimensions of the easement were wide enough to allow large trucks, loaded with tractors or crops, to pass through. And, in the absence of better evidence, the fact that the SRB property was used for ranching or farming could also suggest that the nature of the use of the easement was seasonal and that the frequency of the use was less than that of a road leading to a residential or commercial area.[13]

But the fact that the easement was used to access the SRB property by people having the subjective purpose to ranch or farm does not, in and of itself, burden the Spencer property. And for this reason, the district court erred in limiting SRB's future use of the easement to those who use it intending to farm or ranch.

B. The district court incorrectly limited SRB's use of the dominant estate

Second, the district court erred in limiting SRB's use of SRB's own property. Although the limited scope of a prescriptive easement could, in practical effect, limit the uses to which SRB's property could be used, those limitations are not legally imposed by nature of SRB's prescriptive rights in the Spencer property. As we held in our decision in *Robins v. Roberts*, "it matters not" to the Spencers what SRB does on SRB's property because the Spencers have no legal right burdening that property. And even though certain uses of the SRB property could lead to incidental increases on the burden imposed by the easement on the Spencer property, there is no indication that such an increase has occurred or would occur were SRB to build a few family cabins on the SRB property.

The unrefuted deposition testimony of Norman Carroll informs us that the easement was used "sometimes daily in the spring and the harvest time." At another point, he testified that he traveled to his property "all the time"; that he used the easement "without any restrictions"; and that there was never a time that he was not permitted to use the property. And at the end of his testimony, he again testified that he used the road "unrestricted for all th[ose] years," that he "never had to ask for permission," and that he "used it for the operation of [the SRB] property."

In addition to testimony regarding the frequency of the easement's use, there is ample testimony regarding the intensity of that use. Mr. Carroll testified that he regularly drove "big trucks in" across the property. He also testified that he used the road to transport "all the farm equipment," "harvesting equipment," and "the camps." And that it was used to haul water to the livestock and to haul off crops, as well as to transport horses in horse trailers.

So the record contains ample evidence regarding the nature of the burden imposed on the Spencer property by the historical use of the easement. Because this evidence speaks more directly to the burden imposed on the Spencer property than does evidence regarding the historical use of SRB's property, the evidentiary value regarding the use of SRB's property appears to be minimal. And, even more importantly, the Spencers have failed to point to any evidence to suggest that a conversion of the SRB property from a farming and ranching property to a cabin property, with a few cabins, would increase the burden on the servient estate. So the district court erred in imposing restrictions on how SRB may use SRB's property.

In sum, the district court erred by incorrectly limiting the use of the easement to only those people who would use it for the purposes of ranching and farming and by limiting SRB's use of its own property.

Because the district court erred in describing the scope of the prescriptive easement in this case, we remand for a new determination. On remand, the district court should be careful to consider only those factors that provide information regarding the burden that has been imposed historically by the easement on the Spencer property. Because the physical dimensions of the easement do not appear to be disputed, this determination should focus on the frequency and intensity of the use, the effect of the use on the aesthetic and economic value of the property, as well as any other factor relevant in determining the burden the use of the easement has historically imposed on the servient estate. Additionally, in making this determination, the district court should employ a flexible approach that aims "to find some accommodation of [the parties'] conflicting interests, to the maximum advantage and to the minimum disadvantage[ ] of both parties," so that the prescriptive right retains its "utility" for SRB without materially adding to the burden imposed on the Spencers.

Conclusion

When asked to determine the scope of a prescriptive easement, or whether a particular use is permitted under that easement, the ultimate aim of courts should be to preserve the utility of the prescriptive right without materially adding to the burden imposed on the servient estate. For this reason, the focus in a court's analysis should be on the burden historically imposed on the servient estate by the easement's use. In conducting this analysis, courts should almost always consider the physical dimensions of the prescriptive use, the frequency and intensity of the use, and the effect of the use on the aesthetic and economic value of the property. Additionally, courts may consider the subjective purpose for using the easement, as well as the nature of the use of the dominant estate, but only to the extent those factors are helpful in determining the nature of the burden on the servient estate. Finally, in determining the scope of a prescriptive right, courts should take a flexible approach that permits changes of use so long as those changes do not materially burden the servient estate or materially interfere with the prescriptive right. Because the district court's determination of the scope of the prescriptive easement in this case was inconsistent with these principles, we remand for a new determination.

1. See, e.g., Richards v. Pines Ranch, Inc., 559 P.2d 948, 949 (Utah 1977) (distinguishing between an easement established for access and an easement for recreational purposes). [Editorial Note: This is footnote 7 of the opinion.]

2. See, e.g., Orton v. Carter, 970 P.2d 1254 (Utah 1998) (concluding that each party owned an easement over a common lane for access purposes); Crane v. Crane, 683 P.2d 1062 (Utah 1984) (affirming the award of an easement to a grazing association to drive cattle over a limited area of a property twice a year); Richards, 559 P.2d at 948 (awarding the plaintiffs a prescriptive easement to cross over "a rough road across defendant's land"); Richins v. Struhs, 17 Utah 2d 356, 412 P.2d 314 (Utah 1966) (concluding that claimants had established a prescriptive easement to use a

common driveway and bridge approaching the adjoining properties for access purposes); Zollinger v. Frank, 110 Utah 514, 175 P.2d 714, 715 (Utah 1946) (affirming the claimant's right to use a strip of his neighbor's land for "the purpose of traveling" to his land from a public road); Judd v. Bowen, 2017 UT App 56, ¶ 43, 397 P.3d 686 (explaining that "most prescriptive easements consist of one version or another of a right merely to pass over another's land, such as a right-of-way, for purposes related to access or ingress and egress"). [This is footnote 8 of the opinion.]

3. See, e.g., Judd, 2017 UT App 56, ¶ 43, 397 P.3d 686 ("[A] review of cases in which our courts have awarded or affirmed awards of prescriptive easements suggests that the balance has been struck by limiting the scope of a prescriptive easement to the sort of transitory uses which place relatively minimal burdens on the landowner's own use of the property."). [Editorial Note: This is footnote 15 of the opinion.]

4. Valcarce v. Fitzgerald, 961 P.2d 305, 312 (Utah 1998); see also Nyman v. Anchor Dev., L.L.C., 2003 UT 27, ¶ 18, 73 P.3d 357 ("Here, the term 'use' implies an inherent distinction in the property rights conferred by an easement, on the one hand, and outright ownership, on the other. 'A prescriptive easement does not result in ownership, but allows only use of property belonging to another for a limited purpose.' " (citation omitted)). [Editorial Note: This is footnote 21 of the opinion.]

5. Valcarce, 961 P.2d at 312 (internal quotation marks omitted); see also Nielson v. Sandberg, 105 Utah 93, 141 P.2d 696, 701 (1943) ("The use during the prescriptive period is the only indication of the nature and extent of the right acquired. The servient estate can only be subjected to the easement to the extent to which the easement was acquired, and the easement owner cannot change this use so as to put any greater burden upon the servient estate." (citation omitted)). [Editorial Note: This is footnote 22 of the opinion.]

6. The focus on the burdens imposed by a prescriptive use is consistent with equitable principles. This is because, by permitting a prescriptive use to continue uninterrupted for twenty years, the landowner has demonstrated that the burden imposed by the prescriptive use is not too onerous to be born. But the same cannot be said about any change in use that materially increases the burden imposed on the servient estate. See Harvey v. Haights Bench Irr. Co., 7 Utah 2d 58, 318 P.2d 343,

349 (1957) ("Since the right has its inception in the use during that time, its extent and limitations, its burdens and benefits are determined by the nature of that use and the understandings of the parties thereto. Thus any use which would have probably been interrupted by the owner of the servient estate had the owner of the dominant estate attempted such use prior to the expiration of the prescriptive period[ ] is a use which places a greater burden on the servient estate and therefore is beyond the prescriptive right acquired by the dominant estate." (emphasis omitted) (citation omitted)). [Editorial Note: This is footnote 32 of the opinion.]

7. See also Williams v. Slate, 415 S.W.2d 616, 618 (Ky. 1966) ("The easement acquired by prescription was for normal rural transportation purposes. Converting the passway to a haul-road for heavy coal trucks was an entirely new and heavily burdensome use unrelated to that which had theretofore existed."). [Editorial Note: This is footnote 37 in the opinion.]

8. See Restatement (Third) of Prop.: Servitudes § 4.10 cmt. f (Am. Law Inst. 2000) ("If the change in use of the dominant estate, or enterprise benefited by the easement, brings no change in the physical use of the easement, the dominant owner may continue to use the easement."). [Editorial Note: This is footnote 55 in the opinion.]

9. See Restatement (First) of Property § 477 cmt. b (Am. Law Inst. 1944) ("Yet, no use can ever be exactly duplicated. If any practically useful easement is ever to arise by prescription, the use permitted under it must vary in some degree from the use by which it was created. Hence, the use under which a prescriptive interest arises determines the general outlines rather than the minute details of the interest."); Restatement (Third) of Prop.: Servitudes § 4.10 (Am. Law Inst. 2000) ("The manner, frequency, and intensity of the use may change over time to take advantage of developments in technology and to accommodate normal development of the dominant estate or enterprise benefited by the servitude."). [Editorial Note: This is footnote 66 in the opinion.]

10. Price v. Eastham, 75 P.3d 1051, 1058 (Alaska 2003). [Editorial Note: This is footnote 67 in the opinion.]

11. Hoffman Fuel Co. of Danbury v. Elliott, 68 Conn.App. 272, 789 A.2d 1149, 1158 (2002) (citation omitted). [Editorial Note: This is footnote 68 in the opinion.]

12. Gutcheon v. Becton, 585 A.2d 818, 822 (Me. 1991) ("In order to remain useful to the dominant estate it serves, a prescriptive right of way must encompass some flexibility of use, and adapt to natural and foreseeable developments in the use of the surrounding land. When presented with an alleged overburdening of a prescriptive easement, the factfinder must balance the prior use of the right of way established during the prescriptive period against any later changes in the method of use that unreasonably or unforeseeably interfere with the enjoyment of the servient estate by its current owner."). [Editorial Note: This is footnote 69 in the opinion.]

13. We note that, consistent with Utah's flexible approach to easements—which seeks to resolve disputes to the maximum advantage and to the minimum disadvantage of both parties—a party's use of an easement that has historically been used only seasonally should be limited to that seasonal use only where more frequent use would materially increase the burden on the servient estate. [Editorial Note: This is footnote 73 in the opinion.]

9.2.2

Miller v. Lutheran Conference & Camp Ass'n, 200 A. 646 (Pa. 1938)

Supreme Court of Pennsylvania

Opinion by

Mr. Justice Stern,

This litigation is concerned with interesting and somewhat novel legal questions regarding rights of boating, bathing and fishing in an artificial lake.

Frank C. Miller, his brother Rufus W. Miller, and others, who owned lands on Tunkhannock Creek in Tobyhanna Township, Monroe County, organized a corporation known as the Pocono Spring Water Ice Company, to which, in September, 1895, they made a lease for a term of ninety-nine years of so much of their lands as would be covered by the backing up of the water as a result of the construction of a 14-foot dam which they proposed to erect across the creek. The company was to have "the exclusive use of the water and its privileges." It was chartered for the purpose of "erecting a dam . . ., for pleasure, boating, skating, fishing and the cutting, storing and selling of ice." The dam was built, forming "Lake Naomi," somewhat more than a mile long and about one-third of a mile wide.

By deed dated March 20, 1899, the Pocono Spring Water Ice Company granted to "Frank C. Miller, his heirs and assigns forever, the exclusive right to fish and boat in all the waters of the said corporation at Naomi Pines, Pa." On February 17,1900, Frank C. Miller (his wife Katherine D. Miller not joining) granted to Rufus W. Miller, his heirs and assigns forever, "all the one-fourth interest in and to the fishing, boating, and bathing rights and privileges at, in, upon and about Lake Naomi . . . which said rights and privileges were granted and conveyed to me by the Pocono Spring Water Ice Company by their indenture of the 20th day of March, A. D. 1899." On the same day Frank C. Miller and Rufus W. Miller executed an agreement of business partnership, the purpose of which was the erection and operation of boat and bath houses on Naomi Lake and the purchase and maintenance of boats for use on the lake, the houses and boats to be rented for hire and the net proceeds to be divided between the parties in proportion to their respective interests in the bathing, boating and fishing privileges, namely, three-fourths to Frank C. Miller and one-fourth to Rufus W. Miller, the capital to be contributed and the losses to be borne in the same proportion. In pursuance of this agreement the brothers erected and maintained boat and bath houses at different points on the lake, purchased and rented out boats, and conducted the business generally, from the spring of 1900 until the death of Rufus W. Miller on October 11, 1925, exercising their control and use of the privileges in an exclusive, uninterrupted and open manner and without challenge on the part of anyone.

Discord began with the death of Rufus W. Miller, which terminated the partnership. Thereafter Frank C. Miller, and the executors and heirs of Rufus W. Miller, went their respective ways, each granting licenses without reference to the other. Under date of July 13, 1929, the executors of the Rufus W. Miller estate granted a license for the year 1929 to defendant, Lutheran Conference and Camp Association, which was the owner of a tract of ground abutting on the lake for a distance of about 100 feet, purporting to grant to defendant, its members, guests and campers, permission to boat, bathe and fish in the lake, a certain percentage of the receipts therefrom to be paid to the estate. Thereupon Frank C. Miller and his wife, Katherine D. Miller, filed the present bill in equity, complaining that defendant was placing diving floats on the lake and "encouraging and instigating visitors and boarders" to bathe in the lake, and was threatening to hire out boats and canoes and in general to license its guests and others to boat, bathe and fish in the lake. The bill prayed for an injunction to prevent defendant from trespassing on the lands covered by the waters of the lake, from erecting or maintaining any structures or other encroachments thereon, and from granting any bathing licenses. The court issued the injunction.

It is the contention of plaintiffs that, while the privileges of boating and fishing were granted in the deed from the Pocono Spring Water Ice Company to Frank C. Miller, no *bathing* rights were conveyed by that instrument. . . . They further contend that even if such bathing rights ever did vest in Frank C. Miller, all of the boating, bathing and fishing privileges were easements in gross which were inalienable and indivisible, and when Frank C. Miller undertook to convey a one-fourth interest in them to Rufus W. Miller he not only failed to transfer a legal title to the rights but, in attempting to do so, extinguished the rights altogether as against Katherine D. Miller, who was the successor in title of the Pocono Spring Water Ice Company. It is defendant's contention, on the other hand, that the deed of 1899 from the Pocono Spring Water Ice Company to Frank C. Miller should be construed as transferring the bathing as well as the boating and fishing privileges, but that if Frank C. Miller did not obtain them by grant he and Rufus W. Miller acquired them by prescription, and that all of these rights were alienable and divisible even if they be considered as easements in gross, although they might more properly, perhaps, be regarded as licenses which became irrevocable because of the money spent upon their development by Frank C. Miller and Rufus W. Miller.

***

It is impossible to construe the deed of 1899 from the Pocono Spring Water Ice Company to Frank C. Miller as conveying to the latter any privileges of bathing. It is clear and unambiguous. It gives to Frank C. Miller the exclusive right to *fish and boat*. Expressio unius est exclusio alterius. No *bathing* rights are mentioned. This omission may have been the result of oversight or it may have been deliberate, but in either event the legal consequence is the same. It is to be noted that the mortgagee to whom the company mortgaged all its property in 1898 executed in 1902 a release of the fishing and boating rights to the company and to Frank C. Miller, thus validating the latter's title to these rights under the company's deed of 1899, but in this release also the bathing rights are omitted.

But, while Frank C. Miller acquired by grant merely boating and fishing privileges, the facts are amply sufficient to establish title to the bathing rights by prescription. True, these rights, not having been granted in connection with, or to be attached to, the ownership of any land, were not easements appurtenant but in gross. There is, however, no inexorable principle of law which forbids an adverse enjoyment of an easement in gross from ripening into a title thereto by prescription. . . . Certainly the casual use of a lake during a few months each year for boating and fishing could not develop into a title to such privileges by prescription. But here the exercise of the bathing right was not carried on sporadically by Frank C. Miller and his assignee Rufus W. Miller for their personal enjoyment but systematically for commercial purposes in the pursuit of which they conducted an extensive and profitable business enterprise. The circumstances thus presented must be viewed from a realistic standpoint. Naomi Lake is situated in the Pocono Mountains district, has become a summer resort for campers and boarders, and, except for the ice it furnishes, its bathing and boating facilities are the factors which give it its prime importance and value. They were exploited from the time the lake was created, and are recited as among the purposes for which the Pocono Spring Water Ice Company was chartered. From the early part of 1900 down to at least the filing of the present bill in 1929, Frank C. Miller and Rufus W. Miller openly carried on their business of constructing and operating bath houses and licensing individuals and camp associations to use the lake for bathing. This was known to the stockholders of the Pocono Spring Water Ice Company and necessarily also to Katherine D. Miller, the wife of Frank C. Miller no objection of any kind was made, and Frank C. Miller and Rufus W. Miller were encouraged to expend large sums of money in pursuance of the right of which they considered and asserted themselves to be the owners. Under such circumstances it would be highly unjust to hold that a title by prescription to the bathing rights did not vest in Frank C. Miller and Rufus W. Miller which is just as valid, as far as Katherine D. Miller is concerned, as that to the boating and fishing rights which Frank C. Miller obtained by express grant.

We are thus brought to a consideration of the next question, which is whether the boating, bathing and fishing privileges were assignable by Frank C. Miller to Rufus W. Miller. What is the nature of such rights? In England it has been said that easements in gross do not exist at all, although rights of that kind have been there recognized. In this country such privileges have sometimes been spoken of as licenses, or as contractual in their nature, rather than as easements in gross. These are differences of terminology rather than of substance. We may assume, therefore, that these privileges are easements in gross, and we see no reason to consider them otherwise. It has uniformly been held that a profit in gross—for example, a right of mining or fishing—may be made assignable. In regard to easements in gross generally, there has been much controversy in the courts and by textbook writers and law students as to whether they have the attribute of assignability. There are dicta in Pennsylvania that they are non-assignable. But there is forcible expression and even definite authority to the contrary. *Tide Water Pipe Co. v. Bell*, 280 Pa. 104, 112, 113. . . . There does not seem to be any reason why the law should prohibit the assignment of an easement in gross if the parties to its creation evidence their intention to make it assignable. Here, as in *Tide Water Pipe Company v. Bell*, supra, the rights of fishing and boating were conveyed to the grantee—in this case Frank C. Miller— "his heirs and assigns," thus showing that the grantor, the Pocono Spring Water Ice Company, intended to attach the attribute of assignability to the privileges granted. Moreover, as a practical matter, there is an obvious difference in this respect between easements for personal enjoyment and those designed for commercial exploitation; while there may be little justification for permitting assignments in the former case, there is every reason for upholding them in the latter.

The question of assignability of the easements in gross in the present case is not as important as that of their divisibility. It is argued by plaintiffs that even if held to be assignable such easements are not divisible, because this might involve an excessive user or "surcharge of the easement" subjecting the servient tenement to a greater burden than originally contemplated. The law does not take that extreme position. It does require, however, that, if there be a division, the easements must be used or exercised as an entirety. This rule had its earliest expression in *Mountjoy's Case,* which is reported in Co. Litt. 164b, 165a. It was there said, in regard to the grant of a right to dig for ore, that the grantee, Lord Mountjoy, "might assign his whole interest to one, two, or more; but then, if there be two or more, they could make no division of it, but work together with one stock." In *Caldwell v. Fulton,* 31 Pa. 475, 477, 478, and in *Funk v. Haldeman,* 53 Pa. 229, that case was followed, and it was held that the right of a grantee to mine coal or to prospect for oil might be assigned, but if to more than one they must hold, enjoy and convey the right as an entirety, and not divide it in severalty. There are cases in other jurisdictions which also approve the doctrine of *Mountjoy's Case,* and hold that a mining right in gross is essentially integral and not susceptible of apportionment; an assignment of it is valid, but it cannot be aliened in such a way that it may be utilized by grantor and grantee, or by several grantees, separately; there must be a joint user, nor can one of the tenants alone convey a share in the common right.

These authorities furnish an illuminating guide to the solution of the problem of divisibility of profits or easements in gross. They indicate that much depends upon the nature of the right and the terms of its creation, that "surcharge of the easement" is prevented if assignees exercise the right as "one stock," and that a proper method of enjoyment of the easement by two or more owners of it may usually be worked out in any given instance without insuperable difficulty.

In the present case it seems reasonably clear that in the conveyance of February 17, 1900, it was not the intention of Frank C. Miller to grant, and of Rufus W. Miller to receive, a separate right to subdivide and sub-license the boating, fishing and bathing privileges on and in Lake Naomi, but only that they should together use such rights for commercial purposes, Rufus W. Miller to be entitled to one-fourth and Frank C.

Miller to three-fourths of the proceeds resulting from their combined exploitation of the privileges. They were to hold the rights, in the quaint phraseology of *Mountjoy's Case,* as "one stock." Nor do the technical rules that would be applicable to a tenancy in common of a corporeal hereditament apply to the control of these easements in gross. Defendant contends that, as a tenant in common of the privileges, Rufus W. Miller individually was entitled to their use, benefit and possession and to exercise rights of ownership in regard thereto, including the right to license third persons to use them, subject only to the limitation that he must not thereby interfere with the similar rights of his co-tenant. But the very nature of these easements prevents their being so exercised, inasmuch as it is necessary, because of the legal limitations upon their divisibility, that they should be utilized in common, and not by two owners severally, and, as stated, this was evidently the intention of the brothers.

Summarizing our conclusions, we are of opinion (1) that Frank C. Miller acquired title to the boating and fishing privileges by grant and he and Rufus W. Miller to the bathing rights by prescription; (2) that he made a valid assignment of a one-fourth interest in them to Rufus W. Miller; but (3) that they cannot be commercially used and licenses thereunder granted without the common consent and joinder of the present owners, who with regard to them must act as "one stock." It follows that the executors of the estate of Rufus W. Miller did not have the right, in and by themselves, to grant a license to defendant.

The decree is affirmed. . . .

9.3

Termination of Easement

In *Lindsey v. Clark,* excerpted below, the owners of the servient estate attempted to terminate the easement by arguing **abandonment** and **estoppel**. In addition to those two ways, easements could also terminate as follows. An easement could terminate if the servient estate is conveyed to a **bona fide purchaser without notice** of the easement. An express easement could terminate pursuant to **language of termination** in the easement instrument. An easement implied by strict necessity could terminate **when the necessity ends**. An easement could terminate **by prescription**. An easement also could terminate by a governmental **taking** of the servient or dominant estate. An easement could terminate by *release* to the owner of the servient estate. An easement could terminate by *merger* of the servient and dominant estates. An easement could terminate by *misuse*.

9.3.1

Lindsey v. Clark
69 S.E.2d 342 (Va. 1952)

Supreme Court of Appeals of Virginia

Buchanan, J.,

delivered the opinion of the court.

This suit was instituted by the Lindseys to enjoin the Clarks from using a driveway along the north side of the Lindsey lots and to have themselves adjudged the fee simple owners of the two lots claimed by them. The trial court held that the Clarks owned a right of way on the south side of the Lindsey lots and, in effect, put the Lindseys on terms to make it available to them or else allow the Clarks to continue using the one on the north side.

There is no controversy about the controlling facts.

In 1937 the Clarks were the owners of four adjoining lots, Nos. 31, 32, 33 and 34, each fronting 25 feet on the east side of Magnolia avenue in West Waynesboro, and running back 150 feet to a 20-foot alley. The Clark residence was on Nos. 31 and 32.

By deed dated July 24, 1937, the Clarks conveyed to C. W. Six and Mabel G. Six, his wife, the latter being a daughter of the Clarks, the front two-thirds of Lots 33 and 34, being a frontage of 50 feet and extending back 100 feet. On the rear one-third of these two lots Clark erected a dwelling and. garage for rental purposes. After this conveyance the Sixes built a house on their property, approximately 15 feet from the Clark line on the north and about 8 feet from their own line on the south. The Clark deed to the Sixes contained this reservation:

"There is reserved, however, a right-of-way ten (10) feet in width, along the South side of the two lots herein conveyed, for the benefit of the property in the rear."

By deed of January 16, 1939, the Sixes conveyed their property to William H. McGhee and wife, with the same reservation; and by deed of March 16,1944, the McGhees conveyed the property to the Lindseys, without any reservation.

These three deeds were all made with general warranty and both the deed to the Sixes and the deed to the McGhees were duly recorded prior to the date of the deed to the Lindseys.

Notwithstanding that the 10-foot right of way was reserved by Clark along the south .side of the property conveyed to the Sixes, now owned by the Lindseys, Clark proceeded to use it along the north side of the Six property, and has so used it ever since, without objection by the Sixes, or by the McGhees, or by the Lindseys until a few months before this suit was brought. There is no explanation of this change of location. Six, a witness for the Lindseys, testified that Clark stood in the driveway on the north and said, "I am reserving this driveway to get to my back property." The time of that statement is not shown, but the words suggest it was at or before the time of the conveyance to the Sixes. When the McGhees bought the property in 1939, Six pointed out to them the driveway on the north, but the reservation in the deed he made to the McGhees was, as stated, on the south.

In 1946 the Lindseys had their attorney write to Clark, referring to the right of way in the deed to the McGhees, their grantors, and complaining, not of its location, but of its being used for parking purposes. Again, on November 7, 1949, they had their attorney write Clark, calling attention to the fact that the reservation was along the south side of .their property- and complaining about the use of a water line on their property which had not been reserved. The Lindseys, the letter stated, wanted to erect a line fence and suggested a discussion of the matter before this was done.

The Lindseys contend that the Clarks now have no right of way across their property because none was reserved along the north side and the one reserved on the south side has been abandoned and thereby extinguished. The trial court held it had not been abandoned and that holding was clearly right.

Abandonment is a question of intention. A person entitled to a right of way or other easement in land may abandon and extinguish such right by acts *in pais;* and a cessation of use coupled with acts or circumstances clearly showing an intention to abandon the right will be as effective as an express release of the right.

But mere non-user of an easement created by deed, for a period however long, will not amount to abandonment. In addition to the non-user there must be acts or circumstances clearly manifesting an intention to abandon; or an adverse user by the owner of the servient estate, acquiesced in by the owner of the dominant estate, for a period sufficient to create a prescriptive right. Nor is a right of way extinguished by the habitual use by its owner of another equally convenient way unless there is an intentional abandonment of the former way.

The burden of proof to show the abandonment of an easement is upon the party claiming such abandonment, and it must be established by clear and unequivocal evidence.

Clark specifically reserved a right of way over the lots now owned by the Lindseys. Very clearly he had no intention of abandoning that right of way. He was evidently mistaken as to where it was located; but his grantees, the Sixes, were likewise mistaken, as were also their grantees, the McGhees. Clark's use on the wrong location of the right of way reserved by him did not establish an intention on his part to abandon his right of way on the right location. He could not have intended to abandon his easement on the south of the Lindsey lots when he did not know that that was where his easement was.

The residence built by the Sixes, and now occupied by the Lindseys, encroaches by about two feet on the 10-foot alley when located on the south side, and the Lindsey property on that side within the 10-foot space is terraced and planted with shrubbery and a tree. The Lindseys argue that the Clarks are estopped from claiming a right of way on that side because Clark knew where the Sixes were building the house. The only testimony about that is from Six, who said that Clark was away at work when the house was being built but came and went every day to and from his home on the adjoining property, saw where the house was located and made no objection; but Six also said that Clark had nothing to do with locating the house. There is no evidence that Clark knew, any more than Six knew, that the house was encroaching on the right of way. Clark did not think the right of way was on that side. Even if he had known it was there, he would not likely have known that Six was building on it. The location of the house was not influenced by anything Clark did or said. Clark knew nothing about the matter that Six did not know.

"It is essential to the application of the principles of equitable estoppel, or estoppel *in pais,* that the party claiming to have been influenced by the conduct or declarations of another to his injury, was not only ignorant of the true state of facts, but had no convenient and available means of acquiring such information, and where the facts are known to both parties, and both had the same means of ascertaining- the truth, there can be no estoppel." *Lindsay* v. *James,* 188 Va. 646, 659, 51 S. E. (2d) 326, 332. The Lindseys had both actual and constructive knowledge of the situation. The driveway was there on the north side when they bought the property and Lindsey testified he could see where ears had been using it. They negligently failed to have their title examined but they are, of course, chargeable with the information contained in the recorded deeds.

The suit therefore developed this situation: The Clarks were entitled to a 10-foot right of way along the south side of the Lindsey property. That right of way was partially blocked by the Lindsey house with its terraces and shrubbery. To require their removal would be very expensive to. the Lindseys and damaging to their property.- The Clarks were willing to let their right of way continue to be located on the north side.

The court was well warranted in resolving the matter by applying the maxim "He who seeks equity must do equity." That means that "he who seeks the aid of an equity court subjects himself to the imposition of such term® as the settled principles -of equity require, and that whatever be the nature of the controversy between the parties, and whatever be the nature of the remedy demanded, the court will not confer its equitable relief on the party seeking its interposition and aid, unless he has acknowledged and conceded, or will admit and provide for, all the equitable rights, claims, and demands justly belonging to the adversary party, and growing out of, or necessarily involved in, the subject matter of the controversy." 30 C. J. S., Equity, § 91, p. 461.

A court of equity may in a case in which the principles and rules of equity demand it, condition its granting of the relief sought by the complainant upon the enforcement of a claim or equity held by the defendant which the latter could not enforce in any other way.

The decree of the trial court provided: "The Court will not require the expensive removal of the obstruction, so long as the right-of-way along the north side of the property is made available. However, it is ordered that the defendants desist from the use of the right-of-way for any purpose other than the use of the rear one-third portion of Lots 33 and 34, and only for the right of passage over and across the said-right-of-way to and from the property in the rear." And, further, "Should the complainants make an election under this order, a further order will be entered fiving the rights of the respective parties."

The decree appealed from is affirmed and the cause is remanded for further decree as indicated.

Affirmed and remanded.

9.3.2
Discussion Note #3. Termination of easement by misuse

As discussed above, one way in which an easement could terminate is by misuse of the easement. Note, however, that general misuse alone may not be sufficient to extinguish an easement. A court may issue an injunction to prevent a misuse but not eliminate the easement. For a case where the court did not agree with the owner of the servient estate that the misuse warranted termination of the easement, see *McCann v. R.W. Dunteman Co.*, 609 N.E.2d 1076 (Ill. App. Ct. 1993).

9.4
Licenses

As mentioned above, a license is generally revocable. The general rule is that a licensor can withdraw permission at will. There are three exceptions to this general rule. First, the licensee must have a reasonable time to depart with any belongings.

Second, a license coupled with an interest is irrevocable during the term of the interest. Third, when a licensee expended funds on reasonable reliance on the licensor's representation regarding the duration of the license, revocation at will may be prohibited under the estoppel theory. This third exception is sometimes referred to as the estoppel exception, which, in effect, turns a license into an easement created by estoppel.

9.4.1

Millbrook Hunt, Inc. v. Smith
670 N.Y.S.2d 907 (N.Y. 1998)

New York Supreme Court, Appellate Division

—In an action, *inter alia,* for a judgment declaring that the plaintiff has an easement over the defendant's property and to permanently enjoin the defendant from interfering with the plaintiffs use of that easement, the defendant appeals from (1) an order of the Supreme Court, Dutchess County (Hillery, J.), dated March 26, 1996, which denied his motion for summary judgment dismissing the complaint, and granted the plaintiffs cross motion to dismiss his affirmative defenses and all counterclaims, and (2) an interlocutory judgment of the same court, entered August 20, 1996, which, upon the order dated March 26, 1996, declared that the plaintiff maintains an easement over the defendant's property, and dismissed the defendant's second affirmative defense and all counterclaims.

Ordered that the order and the interlocutory judgment are affirmed, without costs or disbursements.

The plaintiff, Millbrook Hunt, Inc. (hereinafter the Hunt), is an organization dedicated to the preservation and perpetuation of traditional fox hunting. The defendant Edgar O. Smith is the owner of a 285-acre parcel of land situated in the Town of Stanford, Dutchess County, which is subject to an agreement captioned "Lease and Easement Agreement" (hereinafter the Agreement), and which permits the Hunt to use the land for the purpose of fox hunting. The Agreement was entered into by the Hunt and Smith's predecessor in title in 1987, and was for a term of 75 years "unless terminated sooner pursuant to the terms of the Lease or pursuant to law". In 1995 Smith, who objected to hunting and who had undertaken measures to transform his property into a wildlife habitat and nature preserve, ejected members of the Hunt from his property while they were performing routine maintenance of their fox-hunting trails.

The Hunt thereafter commenced this action seeking, *inter alia,* a judgment declaring that it has an easement over Smith's property, and to permanently enjoin Smith from interfering with its use of that easement. Smith moved for summary judgment dismissing the complaint on the ground that at most the Agreement conferred a revocable license to the Hunt, which he had terminated. The Hunt cross-moved to dismiss the affirmative defenses and the counterclaims contained in Smith's answer. The Supreme Court denied Smith's motion and granted the Hunt's cross motion, and an interlocutory judgment was entered August 20, 1996.

To determine the true character of an interest, a court must examine the nature of the right rather than the name given to it by the parties. The mere labeling of an interest as an easement does not necessarily make it an easement; it may be a license. Easements and licenses in real property are distinct in principle, though it is sometimes difficult to distinguish them. An easement implies an interest in land ordinarily created by a grant, and is permanent in nature. A license does not imply an interest in land, but is a mere personal privilege to commit some act or series of acts on the land of another without possessing any estate therein.

Here, paragraph 1 of the Agreement indicates that the Hunt leased a particular one-quarter acre parcel of land for a period of 75 years. In addition, pursuant to paragraph 6 of the Agreement, the Hunt clearly reserved an absolute right to fox hunt on the remaining parcel of land. This right was for the benefit of the Hunt and attached to it without reference to use on any particular lands. Contrary to Smith's contentions, the fact that paragraph 10 of the Agreement reserves to the grantor the "absolute right to develop his land" and the right to redirect the Hunt's trails, does not render the grant a revocable license. Although the agreement provides that the grantor may "relocate" the Hunt's improvements, or redirect their trails "in order to make such improvements to the Land", the grantor does not have the right to completely exclude the Hunt from the property. Furthermore, an essential feature of the type of easement involved herein, which distinguishes it from a license, is that the interest in the land is for some definite period. Here, the agreement specifically provides that the Hunt's right to use the parcel was for a definite period of 75 years.

It is clear that the parties sufficiently expressed their intent to reserve to the Hunt a permanent right to fox hunt on the parcel. Thus, the Hunt has an easement in the disputed area rather than a revocable license. Smith had both actual and constructive notice of this easement prior to the date that he bought the land and is estopped from denying its existence.

We have examined Smith's remaining contentions and find them to be without merit.

9.4.2

MH New Investments, LLC v. Department of Transportation
76 So. 3d 1071 (Fla. Dist. Ct. 2011)

Florida District Court of Appeal

GRIFFIN, J.

L-N-W Pizza ["L-N-W"] appeals the trial court's summary final judgment dismissing L-N-W's business damages claim in an eminent domain proceeding brought by the Florida Department of Transportation ["DOT"] to take land for a drainage easement.

MH New Investments, LLC, owned property which was the subject of DOT's action, but L-N-W had a long term lease and had, for many years, operated a pizza restaurant and delivery business there. The area to be taken was a portion of the parking lot.

DOT sought dismissal of the business damages claim on the ground that L-N-W did not have an interest in the real property at issue, only a license to use the real property. DOT attached a portion of the lease agreement, which provides in pertinent part:

SECTION 1. *PREMISES*. The Lessor does hereby lease and demise unto the Lessee, and the Lessee does hereby rent and take as tenant under the Lessor, the following described premises (the "Premises"):

> The address of said unit being 6310 West Colonial Drive, Orlando FL.

> It shall be conclusively presumed, for all purposes under this Lease, that the Premises contain a total of one thousand seven hundred (1,700) square feet.

SECTION 2. *LICENSE. Lessor does hereby grant to Lessee a nonexclusive license for the use and enjoyment of those certain areas appurtenant to the Premises, consisting of all walkways and approaches to the Premises and the parking area adjacent thereto. The license granted hereby shall exist only during the term of this Lease, and shall terminate simultaneously with any termination of the Lease.*

LNW arg.

(Emphasis supplied). L-N-W contends that, in spite of the denomination of its interest in the common areas and parking lot as a "license," it is, in fact, a nonexclusive easement to utilize the common areas, including parking and approaches, during the term of the lease. L-N-W pointed out that it was obliged to pay a fee for maintenance of the common areas.

The trial court concluded that L-N-W's right to use and enjoy the common areas, driveway and parking lot, was only a license. The trial court reasoned that because the term "license" was used, only a license was intended. Because a license will not support a business damages claim under section 73.071(3)(b), Florida Statutes, the trial court dismissed the claim. We reverse.

In order to be compensated under section 73.071(3)(b) for business damages resulting from a partial eminent domain taking, the party to be compensated must have an interest in the real property taken. Since a license to use real property is a privilege to use, not an interest in real property, business damages may not be predicated upon a license to use real property. *See Brevard County v. Blasky,* 875 So.2d 6, 12 (Fla. 5th DCA 2004) (a license "is a personal privilege, and generally may be revoked at the pleasure of the grantor"); *Devlin v. The Phoenix, Inc.,* 471 So.2d 93, 95

(Fla. 5th DCA 1985) ("[a] license, whether express or implied, is not a right but is a personal privilege, not assignable without express permission"). The terminology used is not dispositive, however. Courts look to what a thing is, not what it is called. By its nature, a license is permissive and readily revocable at the option of the owner. Here, L-N-W had an express and enforceable right to use the areas at issue for the term of the lease. This is sufficient to support a claim for business damages in eminent domain.

REVERSED.

10
Chapter 10 · Real Covenants and Equitable Servitudes

Covenants involve private restrictions to land, *i.e.,* restrictions that private persons make regarding their properties. In Chapter 12, we discuss certain governmental restrictions to land, such as zoning restrictions. A covenant is not an estate in land, but is an interest in land.

You are probably already very familiar with covenants, which are widely used. Virtually every housing subdivision, shopping center, homeowners' association, and condominium association use covenants as part of their legal framework.

A covenant is a promise made by one party to another. The party burdened by the covenant is referred to as the **covenantor.** The party benefited by the covenant is referred to as the **covenantee.**

Initially, the promise's enforceability turns on contract principles, studied in a Contracts course. In the property course, we turn to covenants that not only bind the parties that enter into the promise, but also **run with the land**. A covenant that runs with the land could bind successors in interest to land even though such successors were not parties to the original promise. In this chapter, we discuss how such promises could run with the land **at law** or **in equity**. A covenant that runs with land at law is referred to as a **real covenant**. A covenant that runs with the land in equity is referred to as an **equitable servitude**, or sometimes as a reciprocal negative easement.

Although courts of law and equity have generally merged, whether a covenant runs at law or in equity could still make difference as to the types of remedies available upon a breach of the promise. A breach of a real covenant could result in money damages. A breach of an equitable servitude could give rise to equitable remedies, such as an injunction.

10.1

Elements

covenant

Traditionally, for a covenant to be deemed a real covenant and thus run with the land at law, the covenant must meet five elements. First, the covenant must be **enforceable**. To be an enforceable covenant, the covenant must not be unreasonable as a matter of public policy, must not be so vague that a court could not discern the meaning of the covenant, and must comply with the Statute of Frauds. Second, the original covenanting parties must have had the **intent** that the covenant run with the land. This intent element is examined by reviewing the terms used in the covenant. For example, words such as "forever" or "successors and assigns" could indicate intent to run with the land. Third, the covenant must "**touch and concern**" the land by affecting the land in some way. For this touch and concern element, the covenant must touch the land and not be merely personal. It helps to analyze the covenant to determine if the existence of the covenant could increase the use, utility, or value of the land benefited by the covenant. Fourth, a successor purchaser of the burdened land must have had **notice** of the covenant. Fifth, the covenant must meet the element of **privity**. To meet this element there must be both horizontal and vertical privity. Horizontal privity is privity of estate between the original covenanting parties. Vertical is privity between such parties and their respective successors.

equitible servitude

The elements for an equitable servitude are similar to the elements for a real covenant but are slightly easier to meet. For a covenant to be enforceable as an equitable servitude, the covenant must meet only four elements. First, the covenant must be **enforceable**. As in a real covenant, the covenant must not be unreasonable as a matter of public policy and must not be so vague that a court could not discern the meaning of the covenant. As to the third prong of the first element, however, an equitable servitude is slightly more flexible and could be met by evidence of a common scheme from a common grantor. Second, the original covenanting parties must have had the **intent** that the covenant run with the land. Third, the covenant must "**touch and concern**" the land by affecting the land in some way. Fourth, a successor purchaser of the burdened land must have had **notice** of the covenant. Notice that privity is not required for an equitable servitude.

Runyon v. Paley
416 S.E.2d 177 (N.C. 1992)

Supreme Court of North Carolina

MEYER, Justice.

This case involves a suit to enjoin defendants from constructing condominium units on their property adjacent to the Pamlico Sound on Ocracoke Island. Plaintiffs maintain that defendants' property is subject to restrictive covenants that prohibit the construction of condominiums. The sole question presented for our review is whether plaintiffs are entitled to enforce the restrictive covenants.

On 17 May 1937, Ruth Bragg Gaskins acquired a four-acre tract of land located in the Village of Ocracoke bounded on the west by the Pamlico Sound and on the east by Silver Lake. By various deeds, Mrs. Gaskins conveyed out several lots, which were later developed for residential use.

One and one-half acres of the sound-front property, part of which is at issue here, were conveyed by Mrs. Gaskins and her husband to plaintiffs Runyon on 1 May 1954. On 6 January 1960, the Runyons reconveyed the one and one-half acre tract, together with a second tract consisting of one-eighth of an acre, to Mrs. Gaskins. By separate deeds dated 8 January 1960, Mrs. Gaskins, then widowed, conveyed to the Runyons a lake-front lot and a fifteen-foot-wide strip of land that runs to the shore of Pamlico Sound from the roadway separating the lake-front and sound-front lots. This fifteen-foot strip was part of the one and one-half acre parcel that the Runyons had reconveyed to Mrs. Gaskins.

The next day, 9 January 1960, Mrs. Gaskins conveyed the remainder of the one and one-half acre parcel to Doward H. Brugh and his wife, Jacquelyn O. Brugh. Included in the deed of conveyance from Mrs. Gaskins to the Brughs was the following:

> But this land is being conveyed subject to certain restrictions as to the use thereof, running with said land by whomsoever owned, until removed as herein set out; said restrictions, which are expressly assented to by [the Brughs], in accepting this deed, are as follows:

422

(1) Said lot shall be used for residential purposes and not for business, manufacturing, commercial or apartment house purposes; provided, however, this restriction shall not apply to churches or to the office of a professional man which is located in his residence, and

(2) Not more than two residences and such outbuildings as are appurtenant thereto, shall be erected or allowed to remain on said lot. This restriction shall be in full force and effect until such time as adjacent or nearby properties are turned to commercial use, in which case the restrictions herein set out will no longer apply. The word "nearby" shall, for all intents and purposes, be construed to mean within 450 feet thereof.

To HAVE AND TO HOLD the aforesaid tract or parcel of land and all privileges and appurtenances thereunto belonging or in anywise thereunto appertaining, unto them, the [Brughs], as tenants by the entirety, their heirs and assigns, to their only use and behoof in fee simple absolute forever, [b]ut subject always to the restrictions as to use as hereinabove set out.

Prior to the conveyance of this land to the Brughs, Mrs. Gaskins had constructed a residential dwelling in which she lived on lakefront property across the road from the property conveyed to the Brughs. Mrs. Gaskins retained this land and continued to live on this property until her death in August 1961. Plaintiff Williams, Mrs. Gaskins' daughter, has since acquired the property retained by Mrs. Gaskins.

By mesne conveyances, defendant Warren D. Paley acquired the property conveyed by Mrs. Gaskins to the Brughs. Thereafter, defendant Warren Paley and his wife, defendant Claire Paley, entered into a partnership with defendant Midgett Realty and began constructing condominium units on the property.

Plaintiffs brought this suit, seeking to enjoin defendants from using the property in a manner that is inconsistent with the restrictive covenants included in the deed from Mrs. Gaskins to the Brughs. In their complaint, plaintiffs alleged that the restrictive covenants were placed on the property "for the benefit of [Mrs. Gaskins'] property and neighboring property owners, specifically including and intending to benefit the *plaintiff arg.*

Runyons." Plaintiffs further alleged that the "restrictive covenants have not been removed and are enforceable by plaintiffs."

PP

Defendants moved to dismiss the lawsuit, and plaintiffs thereafter moved for summary judgment. Following a hearing on both motions, the trial court granted defendants' motion to dismiss for failure to state a claim upon which relief could be granted and, pursuant to Rule 54(b), rendered a final judgment after having determined that there was no just reason for delay in any appeal of the matter. The Court of Appeals affirmed the trial court, concluding that the restrictive covenants were personal to Mrs. Gaskins and became unenforceable at her death. Judge Greene dissented in part, concluding that the dismissal of plaintiff Williams' claim was erroneous.

***

Having considered the evidence presented to the trial court, we conclude that plaintiff Williams presented sufficient evidence to show that the covenants at issue here are real covenants enforceable by her as an owner of property retained by Mrs. Gaskins', the covenantee. Accordingly, we reverse that part of the Court of Appeals' decision that affirmed the trial court's dismissal of plaintiff Williams' claim. However, we agree with the Court of Appeals that the covenants are not enforceable by the Runyons, and we therefore affirm that part of the Court of Appeals' decision that concerns the dismissal of the Runyons' claim.

It is well established that an owner of land in fee has a right to sell his land subject to any restrictions he may see fit to impose, provided that the restrictions are not contrary to public policy. *Sheets v. Dillon,* 221 N.C. 426, 431, 20 S.E.2d 344, 347 (1942). Such restrictions are often included as covenants in the deed conveying the property and may be classified as either personal covenants or real covenants that are said to run with the land. *See* 5 Richard R. Powell, *Powell on Real Property* ¶ 673 (1991) [hereinafter *Powell on Real Property*]. The significant distinction between these types of covenants is that a personal covenant creates a personal obligation or right enforceable at law only between the original covenanting parties, whereas a real covenant creates a servitude upon the land subject to the covenant ("the servient estate") for the benefit of another parcel of land ("the dominant estate"), *Cummings* *v. Dosam, Inc.,*273 N.C. 28, 32, 159 S.E.2d 513, 517 (1968). As such, a real covenant may be enforced at law or in equity by the owner of the dominant estate against the owner of the servient estate, whether the owners are the original covenanting parties or successors in interest.

I. Real Covenants at Law

A restrictive covenant is a real covenant that runs with the land of the dominant and servient estates only if (1) the subject of the covenant touches and concerns the land, (2) there is privity of estate between the party enforcing the covenant and the party against whom the covenant is being enforced, and (3) the original covenanting parties intended the benefits and the burdens of the covenant to run with the land.

A. Touch and Concern

As noted by several courts and commentators, the touch and concern requirement is not capable of being reduced to an absolute test or precise definition. Focusing on the nature of the burdens and benefits created by a covenant, the court must exercise its best judgment to determine whether the covenant is related to the covenanting parties' ownership interests in their land.

For a covenant to touch and concern the land, it is not necessary that the covenant have a physical effect on the land. It is sufficient that the covenant have some economic impact on the parties' ownership rights by, for example, enhancing the value of the dominant estate and decreasing the value of the servient estate. It is essential, however, that the covenant in some way affect the legal rights of the covenanting parties as landowners. Where the burdens and benefits created by the covenant are of such a nature that they may exist independently from the parties' ownership interests in land, the covenant does not touch and concern the land and will not run with the land. *See Choisser v. Eyman,* 22 Ariz. App. 587, 529 P.2d 741 (1974) (covenant capable of enforcement regardless of status as owner of interest in land is personal in nature); *Flying Diamond Oil Corp.,* 776 P.2d at 623 (Utah) ("[T]o touch and concern the land, a covenant must bear upon the use and enjoyment of the land and be of the kind that the owner of an estate or interest in land may make because of his ownership right.").

Although not alone determinative of the issue, the nature of the restrictive covenants at issue in this case (building or use restrictions) is strong evidence that the covenants touch and concern the dominant and servient estates. As recognized by some courts, a restriction limiting the use of land clearly touches and concerns the estate burdened with the covenant because it restricts the owner's use and enjoyment of the property and thus affects the value of the property. A use restriction does not, however, always touch and concern the dominant estate. *See Stegall v. Housing Authority*, 278 N.C. 95, 178 S.E.2d 824 (1971) (holding that covenant did not meet the touch and concern requirement where the record failed to disclose the location of the grantor's property "in the area" or the distance from the grantor's property to the restricted property). To meet the requirement that the covenant touch and concern the dominant estate, it must be shown that the covenant somehow affects the dominant estate by, for example, increasing the value of the dominant estate.

In the case at bar, plaintiffs have shown that the covenants sought to be enforced touch and concern not only the servient estate owned by defendants, but also the properties owned by plaintiffs. The properties owned by defendants, plaintiff Williams, and plaintiffs Runyon comprise only a portion of what was at one time a four-acre tract bounded on one side by the Pamlico Sound and on the other by Silver Lake. If able to enforce the covenants against defendants, plaintiffs would be able to restrict the use of defendants' property to uses that accord with the restrictive covenants. Considering the close proximity of the lands involved here and the relatively secluded nature of the area where the properties are located, we conclude that the right to restrict the use of defendants' property would affect plaintiffs' ownership interests in the property owned by them, and therefore the covenants touch and concern their lands.

B. Privity of Estate

In order to enforce a restrictive covenant as one running with the land at law, the party seeking to enforce the covenant must also show that he is in privity of estate with the party against whom he seeks to enforce the covenant. Although the origin of privity of estate is not certain, the privity requirement has been described as a substitute for privity of contract, which exists between the original covenanting parties and which is ordinarily required to enforce a contractual promise. Thus, where the covenant is sought to be enforced by someone not a party to the covenant or against someone not a party to the covenant, the party seeking to enforce the covenant must show that he has a sufficient legal relationship with the party against whom enforcement is sought to be entitled to enforce the covenant.

For the enforcement at law of a covenant running with the land, most states require two types of privity: (1) privity of estate between the covenantor and covenantee at the time the covenant was created ("horizontal privity"), and (2) privity of estate between the covenanting parties and their successors in interest ("vertical privity"). William B. Stoebuck, *Running Covenants: An Analytical Primer,* 52 Wash. L. Rev. 861, 867 (1977) [hereinafter Stoebuck, 52 Wash. L. Rev. 861]. The majority of jurisdictions have held that horizontal privity exists when the original covenanting parties make their covenant in connection with the conveyance of an estate in land from one of the parties to the other. 7 *Thompson on Real Property* § 3155, at 85, and cases cited therein. A few courts, on the other hand, have dispensed with the showing of horizontal privity altogether, requiring only a showing of vertical privity. *See, e.g., Nicholson v. 300 Broadway Realty Corp.,* 7 N.Y.2d 240, 164 N.E.2d 832, 196 N.Y.S.2d 945 (1959) (vertical privity sufficient); *but see Eagle Enters. v. Gross,* 39 N.Y.2d 505, 349 N.E.2d 816, 384 N.Y.S.2d 717 (1976) (referring to vertical privity as meeting horizontal privity requirement).

Vertical privity, which is ordinarily required to enforce a real covenant at law, requires a showing of succession in interest between the original covenanting parties and the current owners of the dominant and servient estates. As one scholar has noted:

> The most obvious implication of this principle [of vertical privity] is that the burden of a real covenant may be enforced against remote parties only when they have succeeded to the covenantor's *estate* in land. Such parties stand in privity of estate with the covenantor. Likewise, the benefit may be enforced by remote parties only when they have succeeded to the covenantee's *estate.* They are in privity of estate with the covenantee.

Stoebuck, 52 Wash. L. Rev. 861, 876 (emphasis added).

We adhere to the rule that a party seeking to enforce a covenant as one running with the land at law must show the presence of both horizontal and vertical privity. In order to show horizontal privity, it is only necessary that a party seeking to enforce the covenant show that there was some "connection of interest" between the original covenanting parties, such as, here, the conveyance of an estate in land.

horizonta

In the case *sub judice,* plaintiffs have shown the existence of horizontal privity. The record shows that the covenants at issue in this case were created in connection with the transfer of an estate in fee of property then owned by Mrs. Gaskins. By accepting the deed of conveyance, defendants' predecessors in title, the Brughs, covenanted to use the property for the purposes specified in the deed and thereby granted to Mrs. Gaskins a servitude in their property.

To review the sufficiency of vertical privity in this case, it is necessary to examine three distinct relationships: (1) the relationship between defendants and the Brughs as the covenantors; (2) the relationship between plaintiff Williams and the covenantee, Mrs. Gaskins; and (3) the relationship between plaintiffs Runyon and Mrs. Gaskins. The evidence before us shows that the Brughs conveyed all of their interest in the restricted property and that by mesne conveyances defendant Warren Paley succeeded to a fee simple estate in the property. Thus, he is in privity of estate with the covenantors. Any legal interests held by the other defendants were acquired by them from defendant Warren Paley. As successors to the interest held by defendant Warren Paley, they too are in privity of estate with the covenantors. Plaintiff Williams has also established a privity of estate between herself and the covenantee. Following the death of Mrs. Gaskins, the property retained by Mrs. Gaskins was conveyed by her heirs to her daughter, Eleanor Gaskins. Thereafter, Eleanor Gaskins conveyed to plaintiff Williams a fee simple absolute in that property. The mere fact that defendants and plaintiff Williams did not acquire the property directly from the original covenanting parties is of no moment. Regardless of the number of conveyances that transpired, defendants and plaintiff Williams have succeeded to the estates then held by the covenantor and covenantee, and thus they are in vertical privity with their successors in interest. Such would be true even if the parties had succeeded to only a part of the land burdened and benefitted by the covenants. Plaintiffs Runyon have not, however, made a sufficient showing of vertical privity. The Runyons have not succeeded in any interest in land held by Mrs. Gaskins at the time the covenant was created. The only interest in land held by the Runyons was acquired by them prior to the creation of the covenant. Therefore, they have not shown vertical privity of estate between themselves and the covenantee with respect to the property at issue in this case. Because the Runyons were not parties to the covenant and are not in privity with the original parties, they may not enforce the covenant as a real covenant running with the land at law. *runyons*

C. Intent of the Parties

def. args. Defendants argue that plaintiff Williams is precluded from enforcing the restrictive covenants because the covenanting parties who created the restrictions intended that the restrictions be enforceable only by Mrs. Gaskins, the original covenantee. According to defendants, such a conclusion is necessitated where, as here, the instrument creating the covenants does not expressly state that persons other than the covenantee may enforce the covenants. We disagree.

Defendants correctly note that our law does not favor restrictions on the use of real property. It is generally stated that "[restrictions in a deed will be regarded as for the personal benefit of the grantor unless a contrary intention appears, and the burden of showing that they constitute covenants running with the land is upon the party claiming the benefit of the restriction." *Stegall*, 278 N.C. at 101, 178 S.E.2d at 828. This, however, does not mean that we will always regard a restriction as personal to the covenantee unless the restriction expressly states that persons other than the covenantee may enforce the covenant. *See, e.g., Reed v. Elmore*, 246 N.C. 221, 98 S.E.2d 360 (1957) (concluding that covenant was intended to benefit land despite the absence of an express statement to that effect).

"Whether restrictions imposed upon land . . . create a personal obligation or impose a servitude upon the land enforceable by subsequent purchasers [of the covenantee's property] is determined by the intention of the parties at the time the deed containing the restriction was delivered." *Stegall*, 278 N.C. at 100, 178 S.E.2d at 828; *Reed*, 246 N.C. at 224, 98 S.E.2d at 362. The question of the parties' intention is one that the court must decide by applying our well-established principles of contract construction.

***

Ordinarily, the parties' intent must be ascertained from the deed or other instrument creating the restriction. *Stegall*, 278 N.C. at 100, 178 S.E.2d at 828. However, when the language used in the instrument is ambiguous, the court, in determining the parties' intention, must look to the language of the instrument, the nature of the restriction, the situation of the parties, and the circumstances surrounding their transaction.

We conclude that the language of the deed creating the restrictions at issue here is ambiguous with regard to the intended enforcement of the restrictions. The deed from Mrs. Gaskins to the Brughs provided that the property conveyed was being made "subject to certain restrictions as to the use thereof, running with said land by whomsoever owned, until removed [due to a change of conditions in the surrounding properties] as herein set out." As noted by the dissent in the Court of Appeals, this provision unequivocally expresses the parties' intention that the burden of the restrictions runs with the land conveyed by the deed. *Runyon v. Paley*, 103 N.C. App. 208, 215, 405 S.E.2d 216, 220 (1991) (Greene, J., concurring in part and dissenting in part). In the habendum clause of the deed, the parties also included language providing that the estate granted shall be *"subject always* to the restrictions as to use as hereinabove set out." (Emphasis added.) We conclude that the language of the deed creating the restrictions is such that it can reasonably be interpreted to establish an intent on the part of the covenanting parties not only to bind successors to the covenantor's interest, but also to benefit the property retained by the covenantee.

Having determined that the instrument creating the restrictions at issue here is ambiguous as to the parties' intention that the benefit of the covenants runs with the land, we must determine whether plaintiff Williams has produced sufficient evidence to show that the covenanting parties intended that the covenants be enforceable by the covenantee's successors in interest. Defendants argue that plaintiff Williams has not met her burden because (1) the covenants do not expressly state that the benefit of the covenant was to run with any land retained by the covenantee; and (2) plaintiff Williams has not shown that the property was conveyed as part of a general plan of subdivision, development, and sales subject to uniform restrictions. While evidence of the foregoing would clearly establish the parties' intent to benefit the covenantee's successors, such evidence is not the only evidence that may be used to prove the parties' intent.

We find strong evidence in the record of this case to suggest that the covenanting parties intended the restrictive covenants to be real covenants, the benefit of which attached to the land retained by Mrs. Gaskins, the covenantee. The covenants at issue here are building and use restrictions that restrict the use of the burdened property to "two residences and such outbuildings as are appurtenant thereto" to be used for "residential purposes." The covenants expressly prohibit the use of the property for "business, manufacturing, commercial or apartment house purposes." The only exception provided by the covenants is that the latter restriction "shall not apply to churches or to the office of a professional man which is located in his residence." As noted by some courts, restrictions limiting the use of property to residential purposes have a significant impact on the value of neighboring land, and thus the very nature of such a restriction suggests that the parties intended that the restriction benefit land rather than the covenantee personally. *See, e.g., Bauby v. Krasow,* 107 Conn. 109, 115, 139 A. 508, 510 (1927) (concluding that only reasonable inference to be drawn from use restriction "is that its sole purpose was to protect the [covenantee's] homestead"). We need not decide whether the nature of a building or use restriction, in and of itself, is sufficient evidence of the parties' intent that the benefit run with the land, however.

In this case, the evidence also shows that the property now owned by defendants was once part of a larger, relatively secluded tract bounded by Silver Lake and the Pamlico Sound. Prior to conveying the property now owned by defendants, Mrs. Gaskins had erected on a portion of the tract a single-family residence in which she lived. At some point, her property was subdivided into several lots. Mrs. Gaskins conveyed several of these lots, on which residences were thereafter erected. Although none of these deeds of conveyance contained restrictions limiting the use of the property to residential purposes, it is reasonable to assume that Mrs. Gaskins, by later restricting the use of defendants' property, intended to preserve the residential character and value of the relatively secluded area. This evidence is further supported by the fact that Mrs. Gaskins retained land across the road from the property now owned by defendants and continued to reside in her dwelling located on the retained land. We believe that this evidence of the parties' situation and of the circumstances surrounding their transaction strongly supports a finding that the covenanting parties intended that the restrictive covenants inure to the benefit of Mrs. Gaskins' land and not merely to Mrs. Gaskins personally.

Moreover, we conclude that the language of the deed creating the restrictive covenants supports a finding that the parties intended the benefit of the covenants to attach to the real property retained by Mrs. Gaskins. The pertinent language of the deed provides that the property was conveyed subject to certain use restrictions "running with said land by whomsoever owned, until removed," and that the property is "subject always to the restrictions." As the Connecticut Appellate Court concluded after analyzing similar language in *Grady v. Schmitz,* 16 Conn. App. 292, 547 A.2d 563, *cert. denied,* 209 Conn. 822, 551 A.2d 755 (1988), we believe that this language suggests a broad, rather than a limited, scope of enforcement. That the deed expressly stated that the covenants were to run with the land and continue indefinitely, unless and until the surrounding property is "turned to commercial use," indicates that the parties intended the restrictive covenants to be enforceable by Mrs. Gaskins as the owner of the land retained by her or by her successors in interest to the retained land.

Having reviewed the language of the deed creating the restrictive covenants, the nature of the covenants, and the evidence concerning the covenanting parties' situation and the circumstances surrounding their transaction, we conclude that plaintiff Williams presented ample evidence establishing that the parties intended that the restrictive covenants be enforceable by the owner of the property retained by Mrs. Gaskins and now owned by plaintiff Williams. Defendants did not offer any contrary evidence of the parties' intent but relied solely upon the theory that plaintiff Williams could not enforce the restrictions because the covenants did not expressly state the parties' intent and because plaintiff Williams had failed to show that the covenants were created as part of a common scheme of development. Based upon the uncontradicted evidence presented by plaintiff Williams, the trial court erred in concluding that plaintiff Williams, the successor in interest to the property retained by Mrs. Gaskins, was not entitled to enforce the restrictive covenants against defendants.

II. Equitable Servitudes

With regard to plaintiffs Runyon, we must go further because, in certain circumstances, a party unable to enforce a restrictive covenant as a real covenant running with the land may nevertheless be able to enforce the covenant as an equitable servitude. Although damages for breach of a restrictive covenant are available only when the covenant is shown to run with the land at law, "*performance* of a covenant will be decreed in favor of persons claiming under the parties to the agreement or by virtue of their relationship thereto, notwithstanding the technical character and form of the covenant." 20 Am. Jur. 2d *Covenants, Conditions, and Restrictions* § 26, at 596 (1965) (emphasis added). To enforce a restriction in equity, it is immaterial that . . . privity of estate is absent. . . .

In this case, plaintiffs seek injunctive relief, which is available for the breach of an equitable servitude. Therefore, we now examine the question of whether plaintiffs Runyon, although unable to enforce the covenants as covenants running with the land, may nevertheless enforce the covenants against defendants on the theory of equitable servitudes.

"Even though a promise is unenforceable as a covenant at law because of failure to meet one of the requirements, the promise may be enforced as an equitable servitude against the promisor or a subsequent taker who acquired the land with notice of the restrictions on it." *Traficante v. Pope,* 115 N.H. 356, 359, 341 A.2d 782, 784 (1975). In order to enforce a restrictive covenant on the theory of equitable servitude, it must be shown (1) that the covenant touches and concerns the land, and (2) that the original covenanting parties intended the covenant to bind the person against whom enforcement is sought and to benefit the person seeking to enforce the covenant.

A. Touch and Concern

***

Plaintiffs Runyon have shown that the covenants at issue here meet the legal requirement that the covenants touch and concern defendants' property as well as the property owned by the Runyons. Because a covenant that touches and concerns the land at law will also touch and concern the land in equity, we need not further examine this requirement.

B. Intent of the Parties

A party who seeks to enforce a covenant as an equitable servitude against one who was not an original party to the covenant must show that the original covenanting parties intended that the covenant bind the party against whom enforcement is sought. To meet this requirement, the party seeking to enforce the covenant must show that the covenanting parties intended that the burden run to successors in interest of the covenantor's land.

***

Applying these principles as well as the rules of construction used to determine the parties' intent that a covenant run with the land, which likewise apply here, we conclude that plaintiffs Runyon have failed to show that the original covenanting parties intended that they be permitted to enforce the covenants either in a personal capacity or as owners of any land they now own. The Runyons were not parties to the covenants, and neither they nor their property are mentioned, either explicitly or implicitly, as intended beneficiaries in the deed creating the covenants or in any other instrument in the public records pertaining to defendants' property. Although they own property closely situated to defendants', in an area which was primarily residential at the time the restrictive covenants were created, they did not acquire their property as part of a plan or scheme to develop the area as residential property. In fact, they acquired their property free of any restrictions as to the use of their property. Finally, the Runyons purchased their property prior to the creation of the restrictive covenants at issue here, and thus they cannot be said to be successors in interest to any property retained by the covenantee that was intended to be benefitted by the covenants.

***

III. Notice

It is well settled in our state that a restrictive covenant is not enforceable, either at law or in equity, against a subsequent purchaser of property burdened by the covenant unless notice of the covenant is contained in an instrument in his chain of title. . . .

***

In this case, a proper search of the public records pertaining to defendants' property would have revealed not only the existence of the restrictive covenants, but also that prior to the conveyance the property was part of a larger tract owned by Mrs. Gaskins. Upon conveying the property to defendants' predecessors, Mrs. Gaskins did not part with all of her property but retained adjacent or nearby property that would be benefitted by the restrictive covenants. From this evidence, it reasonably may be inferred that the restrictive covenants were intended to benefit the property retained by Mrs. Gaskins. Therefore, plaintiff Williams, Mrs. Gaskins' successor in title, has shown that the public records provided sufficient notice to defendants to enable her to enforce the restrictive covenants against them.

The Runyons have not made a sufficient showing so as to charge defendants with notice of the existence of any restriction that may have inured or was intended to inure to their benefit. While the records in defendants' chain of title unambiguously provide notice of the restrictive covenants, they do not in any way suggest any right of enforcement in favor of the Runyons, either personally or as owners of any land. The day before the restrictive covenant was created, the Runyons did acquire from Mrs. Gaskins a fifteen-foot strip of land adjacent to the restricted property. Even assuming *arguendo* that recordation of this conveyance would have provided some notice of Mrs. Gaskins' intent to benefit the Runyons, a question about which we express no opinion, this conveyance is nonetheless of no avail to the Runyons because it was not recorded by them until some fifteen to sixteen years after the Brughs recorded their deed of conveyance from Mrs. Gaskins. Thus, the deed from Mrs. Gaskins to the Runyons provided no notice to defendants that the Runyons claimed any interest in adjacent land that may have been benefitted by the restrictive covenants.

For the reasons stated herein, we conclude that the restrictive covenants contained in the deed from Mrs. Gaskins to defendants' predecessors are not personal covenants that became unenforceable at Mrs. Gaskins' death but are real covenants appurtenant to the property retained by Mrs. Gaskins at the time of the conveyance to defendants' predecessors in interest. As a successor in interest to the property retained by Mrs. Gaskins, plaintiff Williams is therefore entitled to seek enforcement of the restrictive covenants against defendants. We therefore reverse that part of the Court of Appeals' decision that affirmed the trial court's dismissal of plaintiff Williams' claim and remand this case to that court for further remand to the Superior Court, Hyde County, for further proceedings not inconsistent with this opinion.

We further conclude that the Runyons have not proffered sufficient evidence to show that they have standing to enforce the restrictive covenants, either personally or as owners of any land intended to be benefitted by the restrictions. We therefore affirm that part of the Court of Appeals' decision that affirmed the trial court's dismissal of the Runyons' claim.

Affirmed in part, reversed in part, and remanded.

10.1.2

Sanborn v. McLean
206 N.W. 496 (Mich. 1925)

Michigan Supreme Court

WIEST, J.

Defendant Christina McLean owns the west 35 feet of lot 86 of Green Lawn subdivision, at the northeast corner of Collingwood avenue and Second boulevard, in the city of Detroit, upon which there is a dwelling house, occupied by herself and her husband, defendant John A. McLean. The house fronts Collingwood avenue. At the rear of the lot is an alley. Mrs. McLean derived title from her husband, and, in the course of the opinion, we will speak of both as defendants. Mr. and Mrs. McLean started to erect a gasoline filling station at the rear end of their lot, and they and their contractor, William S. Weir, were enjoined by decree from doing so and bring the issues before us by appeal. Mr. Weir will not be further mentioned in the opinion.

Collingwood avenue is a high grade residence street between Woodward avenue and Hamilton boulevard, with single, double, and apartment houses, and plaintiffs, who are owners of land adjoining and in the vicinity of defendants' land, and who trace title, as do defendants, to the proprietors of the subdivision, claim that the proposed gasoline station will be a nuisance per se, is in violation of the general plan fixed for use of all [497] lots on the street for residence purposes only, as evidenced by restrictions upon 53 of the 91 lots fronting on Collingwood avenue, and that defendants' lot is subject to a reciprocal negative easement barring a use so detrimental to the enjoyment and value of its neighbors. Defendants insist that no restrictions appear in their chain of title and they purchased without notice of any reciprocal negative easement, and deny that a gasoline station is a nuisance per se. We find no occasion to pass upon the question of nuisance, as the case can be decided under the rule of reciprocal negative easement.

This subdivision was planned strictly for residence purposes, except lots fronting Woodward avenue and Hamilton boulevard. The 91 lots on Collingwood avenue were platted in 1891, designed for and each one sold solely for residence purposes, and residences have been erected upon all of the lots. Is defendants' lot subject to a reciprocal negative easement? If the owner of two or more lots, so situated as to bear the relation, sells one with restrictions of benefit to the land retained, the servitude becomes mutual, and, during the period of restraint, the owner of the lot or lots retained can do nothing forbidden to the owner of the lot sold. For want of a better descriptive term this is styled a reciprocal negative easement. It runs with the land sold by virtue of express fastening and abides with the land retained until loosened by expiration of its period of service or by events working its destruction. It is not personal to owners, but operative upon use of the land by any owner having actual or constructive notice thereof. It is an easement passing its benefits and carrying its obligations to all purchasers of land, subject to its affirmative or negative mandates. It originates for mutual benefit and exists with vigor sufficient to work its ends. It must start with a common owner. Reciprocal negative easements are never retroactive; the very nature of their origin forbids. They arise, if at all, out of a benefit accorded land retained, by restrictions upon neighboring land sold by a common owner. Such a scheme of restriction must start with a common owner; it cannot arise and fasten upon one lot by reason of other lot owners conforming to a general plan. If a reciprocal negative easement attached to defendants' lot, it was fastened thereto while in the hands of the common owner of it and neighboring lots by way of sale of other lots with restrictions beneficial at that time to it. This leads to inquiry as to what lots, if any, were sold with restrictions by the common owner before the sale of defendants' lot. While the proofs cover another avenue, we need consider sales only on Collingwood.

December 28, 1892, Robert J. and Joseph R. McLaughlin, who were then evidently owners of the lots on Collingwood avenue, deeded lots 37 to 41 and 58 to 62, inclusive, with the following restrictions:

> 'No residence shall be erected upon said premises which shall cost less than $2,500, and nothing but residences shall be erected upon said premises. Said residences shall front on Helene (now Collingwood) avenue and be placed no nearer than 20 feet from the front street line.'

July 24, 1893, the McLaughlins conveyed lots 17 to 21 and 78 to 82, both inclusive, and lot 98 with the same restrictions. Such restrictions were imposed for the benefit of the lands held by the grantors to carry out the scheme of a residential district, and a restrictive negative easement attached to the lots retained, and title to lot 86 was then in the McLaughlins. Defendants' title, through mesne conveyances, runs back to a deed by the McLaughlins dated September 7, 1893, without restrictions mentioned therein. Subsequent deeds to other lots were executed by the McLaughlins, some with restrictions and some without. Previous to September 7, 1893, a reciprocal negative easement had attached to lot 86 by acts of the owners, as before mentioned, and such easement is still attached and may now be enforced by plaintiffs, provided defendants, at the time of their purchase, had knowledge, actual or constructive, thereof. The plaintiffs run back with their title, as do defendants, to a common owner. This common owner, as before stated, by restrictions upon lots

438

sold, had burdened all the lots retained with reciprocal restrictions. Defendants' lot and plaintiff Sanborn's lot, next thereto, were held by such common owner, burdened with a reciprocal negative easement, and, when later sold to separate parties, remained burdened therewith, and right to demand observance thereof passed to each purchaser with notice of the easement. The restrictions were upon defendants' lot while it was in the hands of the common owners, and abstract of title to defendants' lot showed the common owners, and the record showed deeds of lots in the plat restricted to perfect and carry out the general plan and resulting in a reciprocal negative easement upon defendants' lot and all lots within its scope, and defendants and their predecessors in title were bound by constructive notice under our recording acts. The original plan was repeatedly declared in subsequent sales of lots by restrictions in the deeds, and, while some lots sold were not so restricted, the purchasers thereof, in every instance, observed the general plan and purpose of the restrictions in building residences. For upward of 30 years the united efforts of all persons interested have carried out the common purpose of making and keeping all the lots strictly for residences, and defendants are the first to depart therefrom.

When Mr. McLean purchased on contract in 1910 or 1911, there was a partly [498] built dwelling house on lot 86, which he completed and now occupies. He had an abstract of title which he examined and claims he was told by the grantor that the lot was unrestricted. Considering the character of use made of all the lots open to a view of Mr. McLean when he purchased, we think, he was put thereby to inquiry, beyond asking his grantor, whether there were restrictions. He had an abstract showing the subdivision and that lot 86 had 97 companions. He could not avoid noticing the strictly uniform residence character given the lots by the expensive dwellings thereon, and the least inquiry would have quickly developed the fact that lot 86 was subjected to a reciprocal negative easement, and he could finish his house, and, like the others, enjoy the benefits of the easement. We do not say Mr. McLean should have asked his neighbors about restrictions, but we do say that with the notice he had from a view of the premises on the street, clearly indicating the residences were built and the lots occupied in strict accordance with a general plan, he was put to inquiry, and, had he inquired, he would have found of record the reason for such general conformation, and the benefits thereof serving the owners of lot 86 and the obligations running with such service and available to adjacent lot owners to prevent a departure from the general plan by an owner of lot 86.

While no case appears to be on all fours with the one at bar, the principles we have stated, and the conclusions announced, are supported by Allen v. City of Detroit, 167 Mich. 464, 133 N. W. 317;McQuade v. Wilcox, 215 Mich. 302, 183 N. W. 771;French v. White Star Refining Co., 229 Mich. 474, 201 N. W. 444;Silberman v. Uhrlaub, 116 App. Div. 869, 102 N. Y. S. 299;Boyden v. Roberts, 131 Wis. 659, 111 N. W. 701;Howland v. Andrus, 80 N. J. Eq. 276, 83 A. 982.

We notice the decree in the circuit directed that the work done on the building be torn down. If the portion of the building constructed can be utilized for any purpose within the restrictions, it need not be destroyed.

With this modification, the decree in the circuit is affirmed, with costs to plaintiffs.

10.1.3

Tulk v. Moxhay
2 Phillips 774, 41 E.R. 1143 (Ch. D. 1848)

Court of Chancery

A covenant between vendor and purchaser, on the sale of land, that the purchaser and his assigns shall use or abstain from using the land in a particular way, will be enforced in equity against all subsequent purchasers with notice, independently of the question whether it be one which runs with the land so as to be binding upon subsequent purchasers at law.

In the year 1808 the Plaintiff, being then the owner in fee of the vacant piece of ground in Leicester Square, as well as of several of the houses forming the Square, sold the piece of ground by the description of "Leicester Square garden or pleasure ground, with the equestrian statue then standing in the centre thereof, and the iron railing and stone work round the same," to one Elms in fee: and the deed of conveyance contained a covenant by Elms, for himself, his heirs, and assigns, with the Plaintiff, his heirs, executors, and administrators, "that Elms, his heirs, and assigns should, and would from time to time, and at all times thereafter at his and their own costs and charges, keep and maintain the said piece of ground and square garden, and the iron railing round the same in its then form, and in sufficient and proper repair as a square garden and pleasure ground, in an open state, uncovered with any buildings, in neat and ornamental order; and that it should be lawful for the inhabitants of Leicester Square, tenants of the Plaintiff, on payment of a reasonable rent for the same, to have keys at their own expense and the privilege of admission therewith at any time or times into the said square garden and pleasure ground."

The piece of land so conveyed passed by divers mesne conveyances into the hands of the Defendant, whose purchase deed contained no similar covenant with his vendor: but he admitted that he had purchased with notice of the covenant in the deed of 1808.

The Defendant having manifested an intention to alter the character of the square garden, and asserted a right, if he thought fit, to build upon it, the Plaintiff, who still remained owner of several houses in the square, filed this bill for an injunction; and an injunction was granted by the Master of the Rolls to restrain the Defendant from converting or using the piece of ground and square garden, and the iron railing round the same, to or for any other purpose than as a square garden and pleasure ground in an open state, and uncovered with buildings.

On a motion, now made, to discharge that order, Mr. R. Palmer, for the Defendant, contended that the covenant did not run with the land, so as to be binding at law upon a purchaser from the covenantor, and . . . he referred to the present Lord Chancellor's order, on appeal, in *Mann* v. *Stephens* (15 Sim. 379), . . . from which it was to be inferred that his Lordship thought that the right of the Plaintiff to relief in equity depended upon, and was commensurate with, his right of action upon the covenant at law.

The Lord Chancellor [Cottenham], (without calling upon the other side). That this Court has jurisdiction to enforce a contract between the owner of land and his neighbour purchasing a part of it, that the latter shall either use or abstain from using the land purchased in a particular way, is what I never knew disputed. Here there is no question about the contract: the owner of certain houses in the square sells the land adjoining, with a covenant from the purchaser not to use it for any other purpose than as a square garden. And it is now contended, not that the vendee could violate that contract, but that he might sell the piece of land, and that the purchaser from him may violate it without this Court having any power to interfere. If that were so, it would be impossible for an owner of land to sell part of it without incurring the risk of rendering what he retains worthless. It is said that, the covenant being one which does not run with the land, this Court cannot enforce it; but the question is, not whether the covenant runs with the land, but whether a party shall be permitted to use the land in a manner inconsistent with the contract entered into by his vendor, and with notice of which he purchased. Of course, the price would be affected by the covenant, and nothing could be more inequitable than that the original purchaser should be able to sell the property the next day for a greater price, in consideration of the assignee being allowed to escape from the liability which he had himself undertaken.

That the question does not depend upon whether the covenant runs with the land is evident from this, that if there was a mere agreement and no covenant, this Court would enforce it against a party purchasing with notice of it; for if an equity is attached to the property by the owner, no one purchasing with notice of that equity can stand in a different situation from the party from whom he purchased. . . .

With respect to the observations of Lord Brougham in *Keppell* v. *Bailey* , he never could have meant to lay down that this Court would not enforce an equity attached to land by the owner, unless under such circumstances as would maintain an action at law. If that be the result of his observations, I can only say that I cannot coincide with it.

I think the cases cited before the Vice-Chancellor and this decision of the Master of the Rolls perfectly right, and, therefore, that this motion must be refused, with costs.

10.2
Interpretation of Covenants

Courts are often called upon to interpret the terms of restrictive covenants. For example, would short-term rentals violate the terms of a covenant that restricts property to single-family homes? Compare *Santa Monica Beach Property Owners Ass'n v.*

Acord, excerpted below, with *Hensley v. Keith A. Gadd & JHT Props., LLC,* excerpted below.

10.2.1

Santa Monica Beach Property Owners Ass'n v. Acord
219 So. 3d 111 (Fla. Dist. App. 2017)

Florida District Court of Appeal

WETHERELL, J.

The Santa Monica Beach Property Owners Association and the members of its board of directors (collectively "the Association") appeal the order dismissing the declaratory judgment action in which they alleged that the use of Appellees' properties as short-term vacation rentals violates the covenants restricting the properties' use to residential purposes only and prohibiting their use for business purposes. We affirm.

Factual and Procedural Background

Appellees own two properties in the Santa Monica Beach subdivision in Bay County. The properties are subject to restrictive covenants which provide in pertinent part:

> *Said land shall be used only for residential purposes*, and not more than one detached single family dwelling house and the usual outhouses thereof, such as garage, servants' house and the like, shall be allowed to occupy any residential lot as platted at any one time; *nor shall any building on said land be used* as a hospital, tenement house, sanitarium, charitable institution, or *for business* or manufacturing *purposes* nor as a dance hall or other place of public assemblage.

(emphasis added).

In December 2015, the Association sent letters to Appellees stating that "it has been observed that the primary use of your property during 2015 seems to have become VACATION RENTAL; advertised on VRBO[1]." The letters asserted that this use violated the restrictive covenants and requested that Appellees discontinue the "vacation rental business" on their properties by March 2016. The record does not reflect whether Appellees responded to these letters.

Thereafter, in July 2016, the Association filed a complaint for declaratory judgment alleging that Appellees' use of their properties violates the restrictive covenants quoted above. Specifically, the complaint alleged that Appellees' properties were being offered and advertised for rent on the internet as transient public lodging establishments; that Appellees were required to collect and remit state sales tax and local bed tax on the rentals; and that the Acords had obtained a license to operate their property as a transient public lodging establishment under the name "Acord Rental."

Appellees filed a motion to dismiss the complaint for failure to state a cause of action because the uses alleged in the complaint do not violate the restrictive covenants. Specifically, Appellees argued that the short-term vacation rentals were residential uses—and not business uses—because the renters were using the properties for residential purposes: "Critically, the [Association] ha[s] not alleged that the properties are being rented for any purpose other than *residential* use by *residential* tenants. ... [T]he fact that this use is residential in character, and not a commercial or 'business' use, is conclusively established by the fact that [the Association] repeatedly refer[s] to Florida's statute concerning 'public *lodging*,' lodging being an inherently residential use of a dwelling" (emphasis in original).

The trial court agreed and dismissed the complaint. The court reasoned that "[t]he critical inquiry is not the duration of the tenancy, ,but the character of the actual use of the property by those residing thereon." Additionally, the court explained that because the proper focus is on "the actual use which is undertaken on the property," the nature of the properties' use is not transformed from residential - to business simply - because the properties., may be subject to a regulatory scheme that requires licensure and Appellees may earn income from the rentals, Finally, the court noted that because the restrictive covenants are silent on the issue of short-term rentals, any ambiguity as to whether that use is permitted must be resolved in favor of Appellees' free and unencumbered use of their properties.

This appeal follows.

Analysis

Our review of the dismissal order is de novo.

The specific issue in this appeal—whether short-term vacation rentals violate restrictive covenants requiring property to be used only for residential purposes and prohibiting its use for business purposes—appears to be a matter of first impression in Florida. However, courts in a number of other states have considered the issue and those courts have almost uniformly held that short-term vacation rentals do not violate restrictive covenants nearly identical to those at issue in this case.

These decisions explain that in determining whether short-term vacation rentals are residential uses of the property, the critical issue is whether the renters are using the property for ordinary living purposes such as sleeping and eating, not the duration of the rental. See, e.g., Wilkinson, 327 P.3d at 620 ("If a vacation renter uses a home 'for the purposes of eating, sleeping, and other residential purposes,' this use is residential, not commercial, no matter how short the rental duration."; Slaby, 100 So.3d at 579 (explaining that the cabin at issue is "used for 'residential purposes' anytime it is used as a place of abode, even if the persons occupying the cabin are residing there temporarily during a vacation"). The decisions further explain that the nature of the property's use is not transformed from residential to business simply because the owner earns income from the rentals. See, e.g., Lowden, 909 A.2d at 267 ("The owners' receipt of rental income in no way detracts from the use of the properties as residences by the tenants."); Slaby, 100 So.3d at 580 ("[N]either [the] financial benefit nor the advertisement of the property or the remittance of a lodging tax transforms the nature of the use of the property from residential to commercial."); Mason Family Trust, 207 P.3d at 1178 ("While [the owner's] renting of the property as a dwelling on a short-term basis may have constituted an economic endeavor on [his] part, to construe that activity as one forbidden by the language of the deed restrictions [prohibiting use for business or Commercial purposes] is unreasonable and strained. Strictly and reasonably construed, the deed restrictions do not forbid short-term rentals for dwelling purposes."). We agree with the analysis in these decisions.

Here, the Association did not—and apparently could not—allege that Appellees' properties were being used by the renters for any nonresidential purpose. Accordingly, consistent with, decisions cited above, we hold that the use of Appellees' properties as short-term vacation rentals is not prohibited by the applicable restrictive covenants. *holding*

This holding is not inconsistent with Robins v. Walter, 670 So.2d 971 (Fla. 1st DCA 1995). The issue in that case was whether the operation of a bed and breakfast inn violated a restrictive covenant prohibiting the use of the property for business or commercial purposes. The court held that the inn was prohibited because it was essentially a small motel. Notably, the inn at issue in Robins had a number of indicia of a business, such a manager to "control the guests," signs located on the property advertising it as a "Bed and Breakfast Inn," and five bedrooms each with a separate entrance to the outside of the structure. Here, the complaint does not allege that Appellees' properties are being operated like the bed and breakfast in Robins or that they have any other indicia of business use.

Nor is this holding inconsistent with Bennett v. Walton County, 174 So.3d 386 (Fla. 1st DCA 2015), That case involved a land development code, not a restrictive covenant, and the issue in the case was whether the code's prohibition on non-residential uses was sufficiently clear to preclude the owners' use of their property as a venue for weddings and other events. The court rejected the property owners' challenge to the code, explaining that although "people throw parties in their homes in residential neighborhoods all the time," id. the frequency and intensity of the activities on the property demonstrated that the owners "have essentially introduced a wedding venue business into their [residential] neighborhood," id. at 389. Here, the complaint contains no allegations regarding the frequency of Appellees' vacation rentals, but even if the properties are rented to different persons every night, there is no allegation that the renters are using the properties for anything other than ordinary living purposes.

Finally, even if the restrictive covenants were susceptible to an interpretation that would preclude short-term vacation rentals, the omission of an *explicit* prohibition on that use in the covenants is fatal to the position advocated by the Association in this case because "[t]o impute such a restriction would cut against the principle that such restraints 'are not favored and are to be strictly construed in favor of the free and unrestricted use of real property.'" Leamer v. White, 156 So.3d 567, 572 (Fla. 1st DCA 2015); see also Moss v. Inverness Highlands Civic Ass'n, 521 So.2d 359 (Fla. 5th DCA 1988) ("Restrictive covenants are to be strictly construed in favor of the landowner and the free use of his property."). Indeed, the need for explicit language in the covenants is particularly important where the use in question is common and predictable, as is the case with short-term rentals of houses near the beach to vacationers.

Conclusion

For the reasons stated above, we affirm the dismissal of the Association's declaratory judgment action.

AFFIRMED.

1. VRBO—which is short for "Vacation Rentals by Owner"—is a website on which owners can advertise their houses and other properties for rent. VRBO bills itself as "the world leader in vacation rentals with over 1 million listings in 190 countries." See Frequently Asked Questions, Who is VRBO?, https:// www.vrbo.com/lyp? (last visited April 11, 2017). [This is footnote 2 of the opinion.]

10.2.2

Hensley v. Keith A. Gadd & JHT Props., LLC
560 S.W.3d 516 (Ky. 2018)

Supreme Court of Kentucky

OPINION OF THE COURT BY JUSTICE VANMETER

Restrictive covenants governing the use of real property are enforceable according to their terms. The issue we must determine in this case is whether the Garrard Circuit Court erred enforcing Deed of Restrictions for Woodlawn Estates Subdivision Section II, by granting judgment in favor of Don Hensley against Keith A. Gadd and JHT Properties, LLC on the basis that Gadd was renting private residences in the Subdivision as short-term vacation rentals in contravention of restrictions on commercial use of property. We hold that the trial court did not err, and we therefore reverse and vacate so much of the Court of Appeals' Opinion as reversed the trial court's judgment. We, however, affirm the Court of Appeals insofar as it affirmed the trial court's dismissal of Gadd's counterclaim for harassment.

I. Factual and Procedural Background.

In the early 1990s, Hensley and his wife, Marsha, developed the Subdivision as a lakeside development on Lake Herrington. The Hensleys reside in the Subdivision and own several properties there. As a part of the development, they executed and filed Deed of Restrictions Lots 1-15 Woodlawn Estates Subdivision Section II. For purposes of our review, the significant provisions of the Deed of Restrictions are

> 1. Lots 2 thru 15 shall be known and described as single family residential lots and shall be used only for residential purposes. Structures erected thereon shall be designed for and occupied by one family; no more than one residential structure shall be erected on each lot.

> 2. Lot 1 shall be known and described as commercial lot and may be used only for single family, multi-family or commercial purposes. Commercial use shall be limited to food stores, marinas, offices, hotels, restaurants and similar retail of [sic] professional businesses; no wholesale, industrial or manufacturing activities shall be permitted.

> 13. No trade, business, or profession of any kind shall be carried out upon any residential lot nor shall anything be done thereon which may become an annoyance or a nuisance to the neighborhood[.]

> 14. No sign for advertising or for any other purpose shall be displayed any place on any residential lot or on any residential structure on any lot except one sign for advertising the sale or rental thereof[.]

Keith Gadd owns Lot 3 in the Subdivision, and JHT owned Lot 2. No question exists but that both lots were covered by the Deed of Restrictions.

As found by the trial court, Gadd advertised the properties for short-term recreational residential use, placing ads on LexingtonRentalHomes.com using the phrase "vacation rental per night". The ads listed a nightly rental of $375 for Lot 2, and $300 for Lot 3. Ads on Homeaway.com advertised for nightly and weekly renters, with conditions of a 10% tax rate and a cleaning fee of $125.

In October 2013, Hensley filed a complaint against Gadd alleging violations of the restrictions and that Gadd's renters had created an "annoyance and or nuisance" to other owners in the neighborhood. Gadd answered and filed a counterclaim for harassment.

***

In addition to the matters set forth above, the trial court noted the complaints of other residents concerning Gadd's renters: occasional excessive noise, vehicles parked on the street, possible overuse of septic tank causing offensive odors and possible conduct damaging the Subdivision's golf course property. The trial court noted the communications between Hensley and the other deponents concerning complaints about noise, traffic, septic tanks, and potential damage that short-term rentals could have on the deponents' property values. The trial court did not make a finding that Gadd's renters and their activities constituted "an annoyance or a nuisance to the neighborhood" within the meaning of Restriction 13.

The trial court summarized Hensley's testimony, as follows:

> [Hensley's] intention when imposing the restrictions was to limit rentals to single families for longer terms. He acknowledged that the specific term was not stated in the restrictions but indicated that he felt like a six month rental or a year rental would be a reasonable length of time.... He acknowledged that "single family" could include members of an extended family, as well as guest of that family.... [W]hen asked about whether a monthly rental would be okay, he acknowledged the ambiguity in the restrictions but insisted that he did not intend for rentals to be made only on a daily basis.... He described the overnight rentals as giving the properties a "motel atmosphere" inconsistent with the neighborhood.

The trial court summarized the factual statements in Gadd's affidavit that he personally used the Lots approximately three months each year and denied any business use. He stated that various governmental agencies have investigated the neighbors' complaints and found no violations.

The trial court then examined the restrictions and recent case law from the Court of Appeals in which similar restrictions and factual situations were present. The court concluded that Gadd's use of the property, specifically short-term rentals, constituted a business in violation of Restriction 13, and that Hensley had not waived enforcement of the restrictions. The trial court entered judgment in favor of Hensley, enjoined Gadd from further violation of the applicable restrictions, awarded Hensley costs, denied Hensley's request for punitive damages, and dismissed Gadd's harassment counterclaim.

Gadd appealed, as a matter of right, to the Court of Appeals. That court determined that the restrictions were ambiguous in that they permitted rentals, but stated no time limit on those rentals, construed the restrictions against Hensley as the grantor, and noted other residents operated business from their homes (as supporting the imprecision of the restrictions). Ultimately, the Court of Appeals concluded that, in case of doubtful meaning, restrictions should be construed in favor of the free use of property. As to Gadd's counterclaim of harassment, the court concluded that he had not proven harassment. The court therefore reversed the trial court's judgment enjoining Gadd's short-term rentals of the property, but affirmed dismissal of Gadd's counterclaim. Hensley moved this Court for discretionary review, and Gadd similarly requested discretionary review, both of which we granted.

II. Standard of Review.

***

Interpretation or construction of restrictive covenants is a question of law subject to *de novo* review on appeal.

III. Analysis.

A. Restrictive Covenants.

The issues in this case revolve around a proper interpretation of the Deed of Restrictions. Kentucky decisions have recognized that "each case involving restrictions on the use of property, whether it be by reciprocal negative easements contained in conveyances or by a zoning ordinance, must be decided on its merits—on the particular terms of the instrument and the facts of the case." *Robertson v. W. Baptist Hosp.,* 267 S.W.2d 395, 397 (Ky. 1954). As both the trial court and Court of Appeals correctly noted, restrictive covenants are to be construed according to their plain language. "One primary rule of construction relating to all instruments is that every part of the instrument will be given meaning and effect when possible." *McFarland v. Hanley,* 258 S.W.2d 3, 5 (Ky. 1953).

> [A]s a fundamental and supreme rule of construction of contracts, the intention of the parties governs. That intention in respect to a restrictive covenant is to be gathered from the entire context of the instruments. Often the surrounding circumstances and the object which the covenant was designed to accomplish, which may be revealed in part by a general scheme or plan of development, are important considerations where the meaning is doubtful.

Parrish v. Newbury, 279 S.W.2d 229, 233 (Ky. 1955) (citations omitted).

***

"We must seek the intention of the grantor from the language used, considered in light of such factors as the general scheme of the subdivision. We may not substitute what the grantor may have intended to say for the plain import of what he said." *Mascolino v. Noland & Cowden Enters., Inc.,* 391 S.W.2d 710, 712 (Ky. 1965) (citation omitted). A similar rule applies when interpreting ambiguous restrictions, *i.e.,* the intention of the parties governs, with consideration given to the general scheme or plan of development. *Triple Crown,* 279 S.W.3d at 140. That said, courts are not to remake contracts for parties and create ambiguity where none exists. *O.P. Link Handle Co. v. Wright,* 429 S.W.2d 842, 847 (Ky. 1968). In *O.P. Link,* we admonished against giving a writing meaning which is not to be found in the instrument itself under the guise of interpretation based on direct evidence of intention. *Id.* (citing 4 Williston on Contracts, § 610A (3d ed.1961)). Parties are bound by the clear meaning of the language used, the same as any other contract.

These restrictions are unambiguous. In this case, Hensley created a single-family residential subdivision for Lots 2-15. On those lots, the use is limited to residential purposes, and the principal structure is to be a single-family residence. Further, "no trade, business, or profession of any kind [is] permitted to be carried out[,]" although rentals are permitted.[1] These restrictions are clear from Restrictions 1, 13 and 14. The Court of Appeals, however, ignored Restriction 2, which contains the lone exception to the residential use within the subdivision, in that on Lot 1 many uses are permitted: single-family, multi-family or commercial. That restriction further defines the meaning of commercial: "Commercial use shall be limited to food stores, marinas, offices, *hotels*, restaurants and similar retail [or] professional businesses; no wholesale, industrial or manufacturing activities shall be permitted." (emphasis added).

The uses upon Lot 1 are countless: single-family, multi-family or commercial. The meaning of a "multi-family" undoubtedly includes a duplex, triplex, fourplex, an apartment building, and a multi-unit condominium. *See, e.g., Macy v. Wormald,* 329 S.W.2d 212, 213 (Ky. 1959) (holding that a four-unit apartment house, as a multiple family dwelling, violated restriction limiting subdivision to "only one residence ... upon each lot[ ]"). Commercial is defined to include a number of uses, including "hotel." The plain meaning of "hotel" is "an establishment that provides lodging and usually meals, entertainment, and various personal services for the public." Merriam-Webster Dictionary, https://www.merriam-webster.com/dictionary/hotel (last visited October 5, 2018). Kentucky case law supports a definition of "hotel" as place of lodging for the public. In *Clemons v. Meadows,* our predecessor court long ago recognized that

> Hotels are established and maintained for the purpose of serving the public. The opening of a hotel is an invitation to the public to become its guests. Hotels are not conducted for the social enjoyment of the owners, but for the convenience of the public, that is, those whose business or pleasure may render it necessary that they shall ask and receive food and shelter at a place of public entertainment for compensation. A hotel is a quasi public institution. Those who desire to conduct a hotel must first obtain a license from the commonwealth allowing them to do so. Laws have been enacted

for the purpose of protecting the proprietors of hotels because of the public character of the business.

123 Ky. 178, 182-83, 94 S.W. 13, 14 (1906).

Kentucky statutes similarly define "hotel." *See* KRS 219.011(3) (defining "hotel" as "every building or structure kept, used, maintained, advertised, or held out to the public as a place where sleeping accommodations are furnished to the public, and includes motels, tourist homes, and similar establishments, but excludes boarding houses and rooming houses[ ]"); KRS 243.055(1)(a) (defining "hotel" as "any hotel, motel, inn, or other establishment which offers overnight accommodations to the public for hire[ ]"); KRS 306.010(1) (defining "hotel" as "any hotel or inn, and includes an apartment hotel wherein furnished or unfurnished apartments are rented for fixed periods of time and the proprietor, if required, supplies food to the occupants[ ]").

By contrast, the uses upon Lots 2-15 are more limited: residential use, and only one single-family residence per lot. In *Robertson* , the court noted that "[t]he word 'family' is an elastic term and is applied in many ways." 267 S.W.2d at 396. The question in this case does not turn on whether the structure on Gadd's lot is a single-family structure. The restrictions are very clear that Lots 2-15 are to have a single-family residence, as opposed to a multifamily structure or a commercial structure, *e.g.,* hotel. Interpreting a very similar restriction in *Macy,* our predecessor court noted that "[t]he noun 'residence' itself is singular, and the definitions in Webster's New International Dictionary all indicate that a residence is a **dwelling place or abode of a single person or family unit.** This likewise is the commonly understood meaning." 329 S.W.2d at 213 (emphasis added).

As recognized by the trial court, the meaning of the terms "residential" and "reside" are important in deciding this case, as to whether Gadd's use or that of his renters constitutes residential use. The common meaning of the word "reside" is "to dwell permanently or continuously: [to] occupy a place as one's legal domicile." Merriam-Webster Dictionary, https://www.merriamwebster.com/dictionary/reside (last visited October 9, 2018). Similarly, and as noted by the trial court, Black's Law Dictionary defines "residence" as "personal presence at some place of abode with no present intention of definite and early removal and with purpose to remain for undetermined period, not infrequently, but not necessarily combined with design to stay permanently." *Residence,* Black's Law Dictionary (5th ed. 1979).

In analyzing the restrictions and the facts of this case, we agree with the trial court and with Hensley that one-night, two-night, weekend, weekly inhabitants cannot be considered "residents" within the commonly understood meaning of that word, or the use by such persons as constituting "residential." Gadd's use of the property meets the very statutory definition of hotel: a "building or structure kept, used, maintained, advertised, or held out to the public as a place where sleeping accommodations are furnished to the public." KRS 219.011(3). Interpreting every provision of the Deed of Restrictions, as we are required to do, leads to the inescapable conclusion that Gadd is operating a hotel on his property, when such use is permitted only on Lot 1. Gadd registered his operation as a hotel with the Commonwealth of Kentucky and collects tax on the rentals.[2]

We note further support in this interpretation in Restriction No. 10 which prohibits "camping or similar itinerant residency ... upon any lot." Anyone staying in a house in the subdivision is not *camping out,* as one might with a sleeping bag in a tent or under the stars, but "camp" also has a meaning synonymous with temporary residence: "a place usually away from urban areas where tents or simple buildings (such as cabins) are erected for shelter or for **temporary residence** (as for laborers, prisoners, or **vacationers**)." Merriam-Webster Dictionary, https://www.merriam-webster.com/dictionary/camp (last visited October 9, 2018) (emphasis added). "Itinerant" similarly connotes a temporary stay: "traveling from place to place." Merriam-Webster Dictionary, https://www.merriam-webster.com/dictionary/itinerant (last visited October 9, 2018). In *Union Nat'l Bank v. Brown,* 101 Ky. 354, 360, 41 S.W. 273, 274 (1897), the court colorfully defined "itinerant" as "here to-day and there to-morrow." The trial court correctly underscored the importance of these provisions in that transient, "short-term renters are not as motivated to be considerate of the neighbors or the surrounding property. The restriction, therefore, bears a rational relation to the developer's and the permanent residents' desire to maintain a quiet, well-maintained subdivision with sustained property values."

COA conclusions

The Court of Appeals' significant conclusions were that 1) the restrictions permitted ① rental but placed no time limitation on that rental; 2) the restrictions emphasize the ② purpose of the occupation of the property, *i.e.,* "the actual use and activities on the property," and noted that Gadd used it for his living purposes, "sleeping, eating, and other residential purposes," a portion of the time and rented it to others for their living purposes at other times; and 3) Gadd, in fact, did not conduct any business ③ activities on the property since the offering and rental was conducted via the internet and from Gadd's Lexington office. We address each of these considerations in turn.

issue

holding

The fact that the restrictions permit rentals does not render the restrictions ambiguous insofar as this case is concerned. The issue before us is whether Gadd's renting on a short-term, transient basis is permitted under the restrictions. The clear answer is "no." We have no difficulty concluding that short-term rentals are prohibited because Gadd's advertising of such rentals renders his properly the equivalent of a hotel, which is not a permitted use on his lot. Residential rentals are permitted. While we might be tempted to opine that a "residential rental" is one month or more, that issue is not before us.

The Court of Appeals' and Gadd's emphasis on residential uses-eating, sleeping, reading a book, watching TV-misses the point of the restrictions. Such activities could also occur on Lot 1, under the designation of multifamily or commercial, i.e., hotel, since a person occupying an individual unit in a multifamily structure or hotel could do all those things. As an aside, a person could also do those activities while camping. But no one could possibly conclude that a multifamily or commercial/hotel use is permitted on Lots 2-15. The limitation of those items to Lot 1 excludes those items from Lots 2-15, even though the possible activities thereon are virtually identical.

Finally, we reject the Court of Appeals' and Gadd's interpretation that Restriction No. 13- "[n]o trade, business, or profession of any kind shall be carried out **upon** any residential lot[ ]"- was not violated since no commercial activity occurred there based on the reasoning that all advertising and financial transactions were conducted through the internet or telephone at Gadd's Lexington office. The short-term, transient occupancy of the lot was the business activity carried out upon the lot. The assertion otherwise is akin to a claim that the operation of a Webster County mine occurs in Jefferson County because all the paperwork and financial activity occurs at the Louisville home office of a mining company.

***

B. Waiver of Deed Restrictions.

Gadd argues that Hensley waived enforcement of the restriction on commercial use since testimony showed that some owners had rented their properties and used them "as the actual situs of ongoing business." Specifically, Gadd claims that "Thorup operates his engineering consulting business from his property[,]" and "Burton operates a masonry business from his home." The trial court rejected this contention since "[t]he only proof offered was that any other violations of the restrictions were in-home uses which had no impact on the character of the neighborhood."

A waiver of restrictive covenants occurs when " '[a] change in the character of the neighborhood which was intended to be created by restrictions ... generally ... prevent[s] their enforcement in equity, where it is no longer possible to accomplish the purpose intended by such covenant.' " *Logan v. Logan*, 409 S.W.2d 531, 534 (Ky. 1966) (quoting *Bagby v. Stewart's Ex'r*, 265 S.W.2d 75, 77 (Ky. 1954)); *see also Colliver v. Stonewall Equestrian Estates Ass'n, Inc.*, 139 S.W.3d 521, 525 (Ky. App. 2003) (noting that "[a]rbitrary enforcement of covenants does not necessarily render covenants unenforceable[;]" only arbitrary enforcement that results "in a fundamental change in the character of a neighborhood" will render the covenants unenforceable).

We agree with the trial court that the only proof of other business activity concerned in-home uses that did not impact the character of the neighborhood as a residential subdivision. For example, no proof was adduced that Thorup's clients or employees descended on the neighborhood at 9:00 a.m., coming and going throughout the course of the work day, and causing traffic congestion on the neighborhood streets. Nor was Burton operating a brickyard on his property, with commercial vehicles picking up or dropping off brick, sand or mortar. Similarly, Gadd's complaint about other owners' renting of their properties fails. As we have noted, the restrictions in this case permit residential rentals. The trial court correctly held that Hensley had not waived enforcement of the restrictions.

***

IV. Conclusion.

In conclusion, the Restrictions in this case limited commercial uses, such as a hotel, to Lot 1, and required Lots 2-15 to be used for single-family residential purposes. Because Gadd used Lot 3 as the functional equivalent of a hotel, *i.e.,* a structure advertised or held out to the public as a place where sleeping accommodations are furnished to the public on a short-term transient basis, designated it as a hotel on forms provided to the Commonwealth, and correspondingly paid taxes to the Commonwealth on those rentals, his use of the property violated the Deed of Restrictions. We reverse the decision of the Court of Appeals insofar as it reversed the Garrard Circuit Court judgment prohibiting Gadd's short-term rentals of the property. . . . We remand this case to the Garrard Circuit Court for the issuance of injunctive relief in compliance with CR 65.02.

Wright, J., concurs in result only by separate opinion in which Keller, J., joins.

While I concur with the majority's result in this case, I write separately to explain my reasoning. This case and future cases obviously turn on the specific language of any restrictions. In the present case, the restrictions specify that a hotel may only be placed on Lot 1. Therefore, the majority's analysis as to what constitutes a hotel resolves the issue. However, without the provision restricting hotels to Lot 1, the restrictions would have been impermissibly vague, and therefore ambiguous. Ambiguous restrictions are construed against the grantor and in favor of free use of property. *McFarland v. Hanley*, 258 S.W.2d 3, 5 (Ky. 1953). Since I agree that the restrictions in the present case clearly limit commercial use to Lot 1 and define commercial as including hotels, these restrictions are not ambiguous, and that issue is not before us. I therefore concur with the result of the majority opinion.

1. As discussed, infra, short-term transient rentals of the type made by Gadd are not permitted under the Deed of Restrictions. Longer term residential rentals are permitted. Whether residential rentals may be for one month, six months or more,

as testified by Hensley, is not necessary for us to decide. [Editorial Note: This is footnote 7 of the opinion.]

2. In June 2010, Gadd filed an Application for Permit/License to Operate a Hotel with the Cabinet for Health Services, Department for Public Health. The word "Hotel" was handwritten on a preprinted form. To the trial court, Gadd claimed that he only did so because "there was no category for 'vacation rental' and not because [Gadd] actually considered the properties to be [a] hotel or actually operated [ ]88 Hunter Drive as a hotel." Defendants' Reply in Support of Renewed Cross-Motion for Summary Judgment..., November 4, 2015. Gadd's definition of a "vacation rental" is not stated, but if it is a "building or structure kept, used, maintained, advertised, or held out to the public as a place where sleeping accommodations are furnished to the public[,]" that likewise would seem to be a "hotel." [Editorial Note: This is footnote 12 of the opinion.]

10.3
Termination of Covenants

There are various ways in which a covenant could terminate. A covenant could terminate pursuant to *language of specific duration* in the covenant. For example, in *Runyon v. Paley*, excerpted above, the covenant provided that it was to terminate at "such time as adjacent or nearby properties are turned to commercial use." A covenant could also terminate by *abandonment* or *estoppel*. A covenant could terminate if the burdened property is conveyed to a *bona fide purchaser without notice* of the covenant. A covenant could terminate *by prescription*. A covenant also could terminate if the property is *condemned* by the government. A covenant could terminate if *released* by the benefited party. A covenant could terminate by *merger* of the benefited and burdened properties. Finally, a covenant could terminate under the *doctrine of changed conditions*.

10.3.1
Western Land Co. v. Truskolaski
495 P.2d 624 (Nev. 1972)

Supreme Court of Nevada

Batjer, J.:

The respondents, homeowners in the Southland Heights Subdivision in southwest Reno, Nevada, brought an action in the district court to enjoin the appellant from constructing a shopping center on a 3.5-acre parcel of land located within the subdivision at the northeast corner of Plumas and West Plumb Lane. In 1941 the appellant subdivided this 40-acre development, and at that time it subjected the lots to certain restrictive covenants which specifically restricted the entire 40 acres of the subdivision to single family dwellings and further prohibited any stores, butcher shops, grocery or mercantile business of any kind.[1] The district court held these restrictive covenants to be enforceable, and enjoined the appellant from constructing a supermarket or using the 3.5 acres in any manner other than that permitted by the covenants. The appellant contends that the district court erred in enforcing these covenants because the subdivision had so radically changed in recent years as to nullify their purpose. We agree with the holding of the district court that the restrictive covenants remain of substantial value to the homeowners in the subdivision, and that the changes that have occurred since 1941 are not so great as to make it inequitable or oppressive to restrict the property to single-family residential use.

In 1941 the Southland Heights subdivision was outside of the Reno city limits. The property surrounding the subdivision was primarily used for residential and agricultural purposes, with very little commercial development of any type in the immediate area. At that time Plumb Lane extended only as far east as Arlington Avenue.

By the time the respondents sought equitable relief in an effort to enforce the restrictive covenants, the area had markedly changed. In 1941 the city of Reno had a population of slightly more than 20,000; that figure had jumped to approximately 95,100 by 1969. One of the significant changes, as the appellant aptly illustrates, is the increase in traffic in the surrounding area. Plumb Lane had been extended to Virginia Street, and in 1961 the city of Reno condemned 1.04 acres of land on the edge of the subdivision to allow for the widening of Plumb Lane into a four-lane arterial boulevard. A city planner, testifying for the appellant, stated that Plumb Lane was designed to be and now is the major east-west artery through the southern portion of the city. A person who owns property across Plumas from the subdivision testified that the corner of Plumb Lane and Plumas is "terribly noisy from 5:00 p.m. until midnight." One of the findings of the trial court was that traffic on Plumb Lane had greatly increased in recent years.

Another significant change that had occurred since 1941 was the increase in commercial development in the vicinity of the subdivision. On the east side of Lakeside Drive, across from the subdivision property, is a restaurant and the Lakeside Plaza Shopping Center. A supermarket, hardware store, drug store, flower shop, beauty shop and a dress shop are located in this shopping center. Still further east of the subdivision, on Virginia Street, is the Continental Lodge, and across Virginia Street is the Park Lane Shopping Center.

Even though traffic has increased and commercial development has occurred in the vicinity of the subdivision, the owners of land within Southland Heights testified to the desirability of the subdivision for residential purposes. The traffic density within the subdivision is low, resulting in a safe environment for the children who live and play in the area. Homes in Southland Heights are well cared for and attractively landscaped.

The trial court found that substantial changes in traffic patterns and commercial activity had occurred since 1941 in the vicinity of the subdivision. Although it was shown that commercial activity outside of the subdivision had increased considerably since 1941, the appellant failed to show that the area in question is now unsuitable for residential purposes.

Even though nearby avenues may become heavily traveled thoroughfares, restrictive covenants are still enforceable if the single-family residential character of the neighborhood has not been adversely affected, and the purpose of the restrictions has not been thwarted. Although commercialization has increased in the vicinity of the subdivision, such activity has not rendered the restrictive covenants unenforceable because they are still of real and substantial value to those homeowners living within the subdivision. West Alameda Heights H. Ass'n. v. Board of Co. Com'm., 458 P.2d 253 (Colo. 1969); Burden v. Lobdell, supra; Hogue v. Dreeszen, 73 N.W.2d 159 (Neb. 1955).

The appellant asks this court to reverse the judgment of the district court and declare as a matter of law that the objects and purposes for which the restrictive covenants were originally imposed have been thwarted, and that it is now inequitable to enforce such restrictions against the entity that originally created them. This we will not do. The record will not permit us to find as a matter of law that there has been such a change in the subdivision or for that matter in the area to relieve the appellant's property of the burden placed upon it by the covenants. There is sufficient evidence to sustain the findings of the trial court that the objects and purposes of the restrictions have not been thwarted, and that they remain of substantial value to the homeowners in the subdivision.

The case of Hirsch v. Hancock, 343 P.2d 959 (Cal.App. 1959) as well as the other authorities relied upon by the appellant [Key v. McCabe, 356 P.2d 169 (Cal. 1960); Strong v. Hancock, 258 P. 60 (Cal. 1927); Downs v. Kroeger, 254 P. 1101 (Cal. 1927)] are inapposite for in those cases the trial court found many changes within as well as outside the subdivision and concluded from the evidence that the properties were entirely unsuitable and undesirable for residential use and that they had no suitable economic use except for business or commercial purposes, and the appellate courts in reviewing those cases held that the evidence supported the findings and sustained the judgments of the trial courts.

On the other hand, in the case of West Alameda Heights H. Ass'n. v. Board of Co. Com'm., supra, upon facts similar to those found in this case, the trial court decided that the changed conditions in the neighborhood were such as to render the restrictive covenants void and unenforceable. The appellate court reversed and held that the trial court misconceived and misapplied the rule as to change of conditions and said, 458 P.2d at 256: "As long as the original purpose of the covenants can still be accomplished and substantial benefit will inure to the restricted area by their enforcement, the covenants stand even though the subject property has a greater value if used for other purposes." See also Rombauer v. Compton Heights Christian Church, 40 S.W.2d 545 (Mo. 1931).

There is substantial evidence in the record to support the trial court's findings of fact and conclusions of law that the covenants were of real and substantial value to the residents of the subdivision. Here the appellant has not carried its burden of showing that the subdivision is not now suitable for residential purposes because of changed conditions.

In another attempt to show that the restrictive covenants have outlived their usefulness, the appellant points to actions of the Reno city council. On August 1, 1968, the council adopted a Resolution of Intent to reclassify this 3.5-acre parcel from R-1 [residential] to C-1(b) [commercial]. The council never did change the zoning, but the appellant contends that since the council did indicate its willingness to rezone, it was of the opinion that the property was more suitable for commercial than residential use. This argument of the appellant is not persuasive. A zoning ordinance cannot override privately-placed restrictions, and a trial court cannot be compelled to invalidate restrictive covenants merely because of a zoning change.

Another of the appellant's arguments regarding changed conditions involves the value of the property for residential as compared to commercial purposes. A professional planning consultant, testifying for the appellant, stated that the land in question is no longer suitable for use as a single-family residential area. From this testimony the appellant concludes that the highest and best use for the land is non-residential. Even if this property is more valuable for commercial than residential purposes, this fact does not entitle the appellant to be relieved of the restrictions it created, since substantial benefit inures to the restricted area by their enforcement.

In addition to the alleged changed circumstances, the appellant contends that the restrictive covenants are no longer enforceable because they have been abandoned or waived due to violations by homeowners in the area. Paragraph 3 of the restrictive agreement provides that no residential structure shall be placed on a lot comprising less than 6,000 square feet. Both lot 24 and lot 25 of block E contain less than 6,000 square feet and each has a house located on it. This could hardly be deemed a violation of the restrictions imposed by the appellant inasmuch as it was the appellant that subdivided the land and caused these lots to be smaller than 6,000 feet. Paragraph 7 of the agreement provides that a committee shall approve any structure which is moved onto the subdivision, or if there is no committee, that the structure shall conform to and be in harmony with existing structures. The appellant did show that two houses were moved on to lots within the subdivision, but the appellant failed to show whether a committee existed and if so approved or disapproved, or whether the houses failed to conform or were out of harmony with the existing structures. Finally, in an effort to prove abandonment and waiver, the appellant showed that one house within the subdivision was used as a painting contractor's office for several years in the late 1940's, and that more recently the same house had been used as a nursery for a baby sitting business. However, the same witnesses testified that at the time of the hearing this house was being used as a single-family residence.

Even if the alleged occurrences and irregularities could be construed to be violations of the restrictive covenants they were too distant and sporadic to constitute general consent by the property owners in the subdivision and they were not sufficient to constitute an abandonment or waiver. In order for community violations to constitute an abandonment, they must be so general as to frustrate the original purpose of the agreement.

Affirmed.

1. The agreement as to building restrictions for the Southland Heights Subdivision, signed and filed for record by the Western Land Co., Ltd., provides in pertinent part as follows:

"WHEREAS, the said Western Land Co. Ltd. desires to subject said lots to the conditions and restrictions hereinafter set forth for the benefit of said lots and of the present and subsequent owners thereof.

"NOW, THEREFORE, the Western Land Co. Ltd., for the benefits and considerations herein set forth accrued and accruing to it, does covenant and agree that said lots, pieces, and parcels of land shall be held or conveyed subject to the following conditions and restrictions, to-wit:

"1. No structures shall be erected, altered, placed or permitted to remain on any of said lots or parcels of ground other than one single family dwelling. ...

"4. No store, butcher shop, grocery or mercantile business of any kind shall be maintained, carried on, or conducted upon any of said lots or parcels. . . .

"10. These covenants are to run with the land and shall be binding upon all the parties and all persons claiming under them until January 1st, 1966, at which time said covenants shall be automatically extended for successive periods of ten years unless by a vote of the majority of the then owners of the lots it is agreed to change the said covenants in whole or in part; . . . and whether or not it be so expressed in the deeds or other conveyances of said lots, the same shall be absolutely subject to the covenants, conditions, and restrictions which run with and are appurtenant to said lots or every part thereof as herein expressed as fully as if expressly contained in proper and obligatory covenants and conditions in each and every deed, contract, and conveyance of or concerning any part of the said land or the improvements to be made thereon."

10.4
Discussion: Notes, Questions, and Problems

10.4.1
Discussion Problem #1. Fred's farm problem

Fred, a farmer, sold the north 50 acres of his 100 acre tract of farm land to Alvin. Fred only agreed to sell the land to Alvin after Alvin agreed that the land would always be used strictly for farming. At the same time that Alvin purchased the 50 acres from Fred and obtained the properly executed deed to the land in fee simple absolute, Alvin properly executed and signed a document stating that Alvin "and his successors and assigns would always use the land purchased from Fred for agricultural purposes." Both the deed to the land and the document with the restriction were immediately duly recorded. Three years later, Alvin sold his land to Bob in fee simple absolute. Alvin did not tell Bob about the promise he had made to Fred. The deed conveying the land from Alvin to Bob does not contain any restrictive language. Bob wants to use his new land for a gas station and starts

464

building a gas station on the property. Fred wants to sue Bob for damages and wants to prevent Bob from continuing the building of the gas station. Bob argues that he never signed any contract restricting his use of the land and that, if Fred is upset, he should sue Alvin. Which elements would Fred need to show if he wants to obtain monetary damages from Bob? Explain whether the elements would be met under these facts. Also explain whether Fred would be able to obtain an injunction.

11

Chapter 11 · Condominiums and Cooperatives

In this chapter, we introduce **_condominiums_** and **_cooperatives_**. Condominiums and cooperatives are often thought of as very similar and they do, in fact, share numerous characteristics. It is important, however, to understand where they differ from a property law standpoint. Most importantly, a condominium owner has an estate in land in the owner's unit and an undivided interest in the common areas of the complex as tenants in common. By contrast, a cooperative member has an equity interest in the organization, generally a corporation, that, in turn, owns the real property. A cooperative member has (1) a personal property interest (stock ownership) in the corporation that owns the real property and (2) a **_proprietary lease_** which entitles the person to occupy a particular unit in the building. These proprietary leases are often referred to as occupancy agreements.

This real property versus personal property distinction between condominium owners and cooperative members can have certain consequences. For example, while both condominiums and cooperatives are typically subject to numerous restrictive covenants, including restrictions on their use, there could be a difference in terms of restrictions on resale. Because condominiums involve real property and the law favors free alienability of real property, restrictive covenants limiting the resale of condominium units are disfavored. With cooperatives, which involve restrictions on sale of stock – personal property, courts are more lenient in upholding restrictions on resales. The real versus personal property distinction between condominiums and cooperatives can also have an impact when analyzing other issues.

11.1

Jeffrey-Moise v. Williamsburg Towne Houses Cooperative, Inc.
2021 WL 650475 (Mich. Ct. App. 2021)

Court of Appeals of Michigan

Gadola, J.

Defendant appeals on leave granted the order of the trial court denying its motion for summary disposition under MCR 2.116(C)(8) and (10) of plaintiff's claims of negligence and premises liability. We reverse and remand for entry of judgment in favor of defendant.

I. FACTS

This appeal arises from plaintiff's slip and fall on January 8, 2018. The facts underlying plaintiff's claim are essentially undisputed. On that day, plaintiff was a member and resident of defendant, Williamsburg Towne Houses Cooperative, Inc., a corporation operating a housing cooperative in St. Clair Shores, Michigan.

The housing cooperative is governed by its governing documents, being its Articles of Incorporation, Bylaws, and Occupancy Agreements. Each resident member of the cooperative purchases a membership in the cooperative, and thereby enjoys the right exclusively to occupy a housing unit, as well as to use the common areas of the cooperative's premises. In addition, each member has the right to participate in the operation and management of the cooperative.

Plaintiff's Occupancy Agreement with defendant provided that plaintiff had the right to occupy a specific unit under the terms of the agreement for three years, renewable for successive three-year periods. The Occupancy Agreement further provided that defendant had the right to terminate plaintiff's membership upon notice to plaintiff four months before the expiration of the Occupancy Agreement. As a member of the cooperative, plaintiff could sell her membership interest or leave her membership interest to an heir through a will or trust only with the consent of the cooperative corporation. Similarly, plaintiff could sublet her individual unit only with the consent of the cooperative.

The Occupancy Agreement also required plaintiff to pay monthly fees to the cooperative for maintenance and administration of the cooperative. In addition, similar to a traditional landlord-tenant relationship, the cooperative could evict plaintiff if she breached the Occupancy Agreement. The Occupancy Agreement provides:

> The Member expressly agrees that there exists under this occupancy agreement a landlord-tenant relationship and that in the event of a breach or threatened breach by the Member of any covenant or provision of this agreement, there shall be available to [defendant] such legal remedy or remedies as are available to a landlord for the breach or threatened breach under the law by a tenant of any provision of a lease or rental agreement.

On January 8, 2018, at 10:00 p.m., plaintiff cleared snow from her personal walkway in the back of her townhome, then walked around the building on the community walkway toward the front of her townhome where she planned to clear snow from her front porch. While on the community walkway, plaintiff slipped and fell, severely injuring her ankle. Plaintiff testified that she fell on black ice that she described as being "the color of the sidewalk." She testified that before she fell she did not notice any ice on the walkway, and the walkway appeared only wet, but that after she fell she noticed what appeared to be patches of ice "all the way down" the walkway. She further testified that there was no snow on the walkway where she slipped and fell, but there was "lots of snow" on the grass.

Plaintiff's neighbor, Jennifer Jaber, stated that at approximately 10:00 p.m. on January 8, 2018, she saw plaintiff lying on the walkway. Jaber observed that in the area where plaintiff fell a patch of black ice spanned approximately 4 square feet. Jaber testified that the ice was not noticeable and looked like wet concrete. Jaber did not notice any salt on the walkway where plaintiff fell. Defendant's snow removal maintenance records for January 8, 2018, indicate that defendant's maintenance employees removed snow from streets and walkways within the housing cooperative between 7:30 a.m. and 2:30 p.m. that day, applying deicer to the walkways "where needed" during that period.

Plaintiff initiated this action, alleging in Count I of her complaint that defendant was liable under a theory of premises liability. Plaintiff asserted that as a tenant she was an invitee upon defendant's premises, that the icy condition of the sidewalk on which she slipped was not open and obvious, and that defendant had failed to keep the sidewalk fit for its intended use contrary to MCL 554.139. In Count II of her complaint, plaintiff alleged that defendant was liable under a theory of ordinary negligence, having breached its duty to use reasonable care and caution for her health, safety, and well-being, and to warn of dangerous conditions.

Defendant moved for summary disposition of plaintiff's complaint under MCR 2.116(C)(8) and (10). Defendant contended that plaintiff's claim of premises liability failed because plaintiff, as a co-owner of the cooperative, was not on the land of another when she was injured. Defendant further contended that plaintiff's claims failed because the ice on which plaintiff slipped was open and obvious, and that plaintiff had not alleged a valid common law negligence claim.

After a hearing, the trial court denied defendant's motion. The trial court concluded that MCL 554.139 applied because plaintiff did not have possession and control over the cooperative's common walkway, and plaintiff's occupancy agreement established essentially a landlord-tenant relationship between the parties. The trial court further determined that a genuine issue of material fact existed regarding whether the condition upon which plaintiff fell was open and obvious. This Court thereafter granted defendant's application for leave to appeal.

II. ANALYSIS

Defendant contends that the trial court erred by denying its motion for summary disposition under MCR 2.116(C)(8) and (10). We agree.

A. STANDARD OF REVIEW

This Court reviews de novo a trial court's decision to grant or deny summary disposition. A motion for summary disposition under MCR 2.116(C)(8) tests the legal sufficiency of the complaint; we accept all well-pleaded factual allegations as true and construe them in a light most favorable to the nonmovant. . . .

***

B. NEGLIGENCE

***

. . . Because plaintiff's claim sounds in premises liability, defendant was entitled to summary disposition of plaintiff's claim of ordinary negligence.

C. PREMISES LIABILITY

Defendant contends that the trial court also erred when it denied defendant's motion for summary disposition of plaintiff's premises liability claim. Defendant argues that plaintiff can assert premises liability only if she was injured while on the land of another, and that because she was a member of the defendant housing cooperative, she was a co-owner of the cooperative and therefore was not on the land of another when she fell.

. . . In a premises liability action, as in any negligence action, the plaintiff must establish the elements of negligence, being (1) the defendant owed the plaintiff a duty, (2) the defendant breached that duty, (3) the breach proximately caused the plaintiff's injuries, and (4) the plaintiff suffered damages. *Goodwin v. Northwest Michigan Fair Ass'n*, 325 Mich. App. 129, 157, 923 N.W.2d 894 (2018).

***

1.   POSSESSION OF THE LAND

Plaintiff's complaint alleges that she was an invitee upon defendant's land when she fell. Defendant argues that to be deemed either an invitee or a licensee for purposes of premises liability plaintiff must have been on the land of another when she fell. Defendant argues that plaintiff, as a member of the housing cooperative, was a co-owner of the cooperative's premises and therefore was not on the land of another when she fell. In support of this argument, defendant relies upon *Francescutti v. Fox Chase Condominium Ass'n*, 312 Mich. App. 640, 643, 886 N.W.2d 891 (2015). In *Francescutti*, the plaintiff, a condominium co-owner, slipped and fell on an icy sidewalk while walking his dog in a common area of the condominium complex. The plaintiff filed a premises liability action against the defendant condominium association alleging that he was an invitee with respect to common areas of the complex. The condominium association argued that the plaintiff was a licensee. This Court rejected both arguments, stating as follows:

> But neither the parties nor the trial court provide any authority for the proposition that the status of an owner of a condominium unit is either an invitee or a licensee with respect to the common areas of the development. Nor were we able to find any such authority. But this question can easily be resolved by looking at the definitions of those terms. "A 'licensee' is a person who is privileged to enter *the land of another* by virtue of the possessor's consent," while "[a]n 'invitee' is 'a person who enters upon *the land of another* upon an invitation ...'"
>
> The key to the resolution of this case is the phrase in both definitions, "the land of another." Plaintiff did not enter on "the land of another." Plaintiff is, by his own admission, a co-owner of the common areas of the development. Plaintiff's brief acknowledges that the condominium owners are co-owners as tenants in common of the common areas of the development. And because plaintiff is neither a licensee nor an invitee, there was no duty owed to plaintiff by defendant under premises liability.

In this case, plaintiff slipped and fell while in a common area of defendant housing cooperative of which she was a member. A housing cooperative "is a form of real estate ownership in which those who occupy the premises do not own them." 3 Cameron, Michigan Real Property Law, § 26.28, p. 1509. Cooperative housing can take various forms; a common form is corporate, with the corporation owning the fee to the real estate and individual cooperative members holding shares of stock in the corporation and receiving leases from the corporation to individual apartments. The cooperative association retains exclusive control over the common areas of the cooperative, however, and only the cooperative association has authority to maintain the common areas. As a result, a member of a cooperative corporation has a hybrid relationship with the cooperative in which the member is a shareholder of the corporation that owns the real property, but is at the same time is a tenant of the corporation. Stated another way:

> "Cooperative ownership" is a form of ownership in which each owner of stock in a cooperative apartment building or housing corporation receives a proprietary lease on a specific apartment and is obliged to pay a rental which represents the proportionate share of operating expenses and debt service on the underlying mortgage, which is paid by the corporation. The cooperative apartment lease and the lessee's shares in the corporation that owns the apartment building are inseparable, and any transfer of one without the other is futile, and therefore ineffective. A cooperative housing association, comprised of the members who attain their membership by virtue of their purchase of stock in the association, creates a hybrid form of property ownership. The ownership of a cooperative membership, combined with the right to occupy a unit in the cooperative project, is a form of property ownership, even though cooperative owners do not directly hold the title to their properties; this form of home ownership is unlikely to have the economic value of fee simple ownership or a conventional long-term leasehold interest, but it has value and constitutes a right of property beyond mere possession. [15B Am. Jur. 2d, Condominiums and Cooperative Apartments § 56 (2020), (citations omitted).]

Similar to membership in a cooperative, ownership of a condominium unit entitles an owner to the exclusive possession of a unit and an undivided interest as tenants in common with other unit owners of the common areas of the condominium. The basic difference between condominium and cooperative housing is that the individual purchasing a condominium takes title to the condominium unit while the individual purchasing a membership in a cooperative owns stock in a cooperative corporation and receives a lease for a specific unit for which the individual pays a regular amount to the corporation as a proportionate share of the operating expenses of the cooperative. In Michigan, condominiums are governed by the Condominium Act, which provides that a condominium unit is the "portion of the condominium project designed and intended for separate ownership and use, as described in the master deed, ..." MCL 559.104(3), in which the purchaser is a co-owner who enjoys "an exclusive right to his condominium unit and has such rights to share with other co-owners the common elements of the condominium project as are designated by the master deed." MCL 559.163.

In this case, the parties do not dispute that plaintiff purchased a membership in the cooperative, which entitled her to lease living space from defendant, and to enjoy the use of all community property and facilities of the cooperative. Unlike the plaintiff in *Francescutti*, there is little support for the conclusion that plaintiff owned the land on which she fell. Plaintiff's purchase of a membership in the cooperative entitled her to occupy her townhome and entitled her to use the common areas of the cooperative, as long as she paid the required monthly fees and complied with the rules of the cooperative. Plaintiff was thus in a business relationship with the cooperative in which she purchased certain rights of occupancy from the cooperative by buying a membership in the cooperative.

Plaintiff's membership in the cooperative did not give her independent authority over the common areas of the cooperative typically enjoyed by an owner. In fact, the Occupancy Agreement precluded plaintiff, as a member, from making alterations to the common areas of the premises, including the sidewalks. By contrast, defendant retained control over the maintenance of the common areas of the cooperative, including authority over the removal of snow and ice in those areas. Defendant thus retained sufficient control and dominion over the common areas that it may be said that defendant was in possession of the common areas of the cooperative in contrast to plaintiff's membership right to use those areas. Because defendant was in possession of the cooperative's common areas, we conclude that plaintiff was on land that was in the possession of another when she fell.

2. OPEN AND OBVIOUS

Defendant contends that even if plaintiff were deemed to be an invitee upon the land of another when she fell, the ice upon which she slipped was an open and obvious condition, and defendant's duty did not extend to the removal of open and obvious dangers. We agree.

***

3.   MCL 554.139

*de ×
arg*

Defendant also contends that the trial court erred by denying its motion for summary disposition on the basis that defendant breached its duty to keep the walkway fit for the use intended as required under MCL 554.139(1)(a). We agree.

***

In *Francescutti*, this Court determined that MCL 554.139 did not apply where the plaintiff was the owner of a condominium unit in the defendant condominium development because the statute imposes a duty only upon a lessor of land. *Francescutti*, 312 Mich. App. at 642, 886 N.W.2d 891. This Court reasoned that although the plaintiff in that case had the right to use of the common areas of the condominium, the defendant had not leased the common areas to the plaintiff. In this case, although defendant is a cooperative and not a condominium, nonetheless the relationship between plaintiff and defendant is not strictly that of lessor of land and tenant. As a member of defendant cooperative, plaintiff has a hybrid ownership interest in which she leases her housing unit; however, plaintiff also is a member of the cooperative and the cooperative's corporation owns the real property of the cooperative including the common areas. As in *Francescutti*, it cannot be said that defendant in this case leased the common areas of the cooperative to plaintiff, nor that plaintiff acquired the use of the common areas by her lease of her unit in the cooperative; rather, plaintiff acquired the use of the common areas by her purchase of a membership in the cooperative.

Moreover, even if MCL 554.139(1)(a) were applicable to defendant in this case, plaintiff did not create a genuine issue of fact regarding whether the sidewalk was in a condition that rendered it unfit for its intended use. . . .

Reversed and remanded for entry of judgment in favor of defendant. We do not retain jurisdiction.

Griffin v. Sherwood Village, Co-op "C", Inc.
13 N.Y.S.3d 522 (N.Y. App. Div. 2015)

New York Supreme Court, Appellate Division

In an action to recover damages for breach of fiduciary duty, the plaintiff appeals from an order of the Supreme Court, Queens County (Butler, J.), dated May 30, 2013, which granted the defendant's motion for summary judgment dismissing the complaint.

Ordered that the order is affirmed, with costs.

The plaintiff, a shareholder-tenant of the defendant, Sherwood Village, Co-op "C", Inc. (hereinafter the cooperative), commenced this action to recover damages for breach of fiduciary duty. The plaintiff alleged that the cooperative breached its fiduciary duty by denying an application which would have permitted him to resell his shares in the cooperative to a particular prospective buyer. The cooperative moved for summary judgment dismissing the complaint, and the Supreme Court granted the motion.

"In the context of cooperative dwellings, the business judgment rule provides that a court should defer to a cooperative board's determination '[s]o long as the board acts for the purposes of the cooperative, within the scope of its authority and in good faith' " (40 W. 67th St. v Pullman, 100 NY2d 147, 153 [2003], quoting Matter of Levandusky v One Fifth Ave. Apt. Corp., 75 NY2d 530, 538 [1990]. " '[D]ecision making tainted by discriminatory considerations is not protected by the business judgment rule' " (Cohen v Kings Point Tenant Corp., 126 AD3d at 845, quoting Fletcher v Dakota, Inc., 99 AD3d 43, 48 [2012]; see 40 W. 67th St. v Pullman, 100 NY2d at 157).

Here, the cooperative demonstrated its prima facie entitlement to judgment as a matter of law dismissing the complaint by establishing that its denial of the resale application was protected by the business judgment rule. In particular, the cooperative demonstrated that its denial of the resale application was authorized, and done in good faith and in furtherance of the legitimate interests of the cooperative, in light of significant debt the prospective buyer held relating to a separate property. The evidence the plaintiff submitted in opposition to this showing was insufficient to raise a triable issue of fact as to whether the resale application was actually denied for a discriminatory reason, or any other reason not protected by the business judgment rule. Accordingly, the cooperative's motion was properly granted.

In light of our determination, we need not reach the parties' remaining contentions. Skelos, J.P., Balkin, Chambers and Miller, JJ., concur.

Made in United States
Orlando, FL
19 December 2021